SEX TYPING
AND SOCIAL ROLES

A RESEARCH REPORT

This is a volume of

Quantitative Studies in Social Relations

Consulting Editor: Peter H. Rossi, University of Massachusetts, Amherst, Massachusetts

SEX TYPING
AND SOCIAL ROLES
A RESEARCH REPORT

BEVERLY DUNCAN
OTIS DUDLEY DUNCAN

Department of Sociology
University of Arizona
Tucson, Arizona

WITH THE COLLABORATION OF
JAMES A. McRAE, JR.

Department of Sociology
University of Arizona
Tucson, Arizona

ACADEMIC PRESS   New York   San Francisco   London
A Subsidiary of Harcourt Brace Jovanovich, Publishers

ACADEMIC PRESS, INC.
111 Fifth Avenue, New York, New York 10003

United Kingdom Edition published by
ACADEMIC PRESS, INC. (LONDON) LTD.
24/28 Oval Road, London NW1 7DX

Library of Congress Cataloging in Publication Data

Duncan, Beverly
    Sex typing and social roles: A research report.

    (Quantitative studies in social relations series)
    Bibliography.
    1. Women––United States––Social conditions.
2. Women––Employment––United States. 3. Sex role.
I. Duncan, Otis Dudley, joint author. II. McRae, Jr.
James Andrew, Date. joint author. III. Title.
HQ1420.D85   301.41'2'0973   78–13209
ISBN 0–12–223850–8

CONTENTS

LIST OF FIGURES
AND TABLES

FIGURES

TABLES

ACKNOWLEDGMENTS

This research was supported by the Russell Sage Foundation and is an extension of the earlier project (Duncan, Schuman, and Duncan, 1973) likewise supported by the Foundation. We are grateful to Elizabeth Martin and to all the other participants in the 1971 Detroit Area Study whose efforts produced a substantial part of the data analyzed herein (see pp. 125–26 of *Social Change in a Metropolitan Community*); to Howard Schuman for providing tabulations from the 1976 Detroit Area Study as well as for his contribution to the 1971 survey and for facilitating our access to the DAS archives; to James A. McRae, Jr., Bruce C. Rognlie, Thomas E. Sawyer, and Douglas M. Sloane for assistance in computation and data analysis; to Sandra J. Goers for preparing the charts; to Melvin Kohn for unpublished data from his 1964 study and for comments about our use of his results from that study.

Grateful acknowledgment is made for permission to reproduce Mary Gauerke's ALUMNAE cartoons. By permission The Register and Tribune Syndicate, Inc. Pp. 60, 302.

Grateful acknowledgment is made for permission to quote from the following:

Husbands and Wives, by Robert O. Blood, Jr., and Donald M. Wolfe. Copyright © 1960 by The Free Press, A Corporation. Quoted by permission of R. O. Blood and D. M. Wolfe and Macmillan Publishing Co., Inc. Pp. 195–196, 204.

"Aspiration, Satisfaction, and Fulfillment," by Angus Campbell, "Change in the American Electorate," by Philip E. Converse, and "Alienation and Engagement," by Melvin Seeman, in *The Human Meaning of Social Change*, edited by Angus Campbell and Philip E. Converse. Copyright © 1972 by Russell Sage Foundation, New York. Quoted by permission of A. Campbell and Basic Books, Inc. Pp. 104–105, 108, 111, 114.

The Development of Political Attitudes in Children, by Robert D. Hess and Judith V. Torney. Copyright © 1967 by Robert D. Hess and Judith V. Torney. Quoted by permission of R. D. Hess and J. V. Torney. Pp. 140–142.

"Images of Women," by Elizabeth Janeway, from *Arts in Society*, Volume VII, Number 1, "Women and the Arts." Copyright © 1974 by University of Wisconsin Regents. As reprinted in *Between Myth and Morning*, by Elizabeth Janeway. Copyright © 1974 by Elizabeth Janeway. Quoted by permission of E. Janeway and E. L. Karmarck, Editor, *Arts in Society*. P. 93.

"Parents and Children: Sex-Role Development," by Michael Lewis, from *School Review*, Volume 80, published by the University of Chicago Press. Copyright © 1972 by the University of Chicago. Quoted by permission of M. Lewis and the University of Chicago Press. Pp. 244, 258.

"How Fathers Can Teach Their Children Sexual Equality," by Dr. Benjamin Spock, from *Redbook Magazine* 144. Copyright © 1975 by John D. Houston, II, Trustee. Quoted by permission of Robert Lescher Literary Agency. P. 280.

Sexual Identity: Sex Roles and Social Change, by Betty Yorburg. Copyright © 1974 by John Wiley & Sons, Inc. Quoted by permission of B. Yorburg and John Wiley & Sons, Inc. Pp. 208, 261.

1

The Setting and the Survey

In a criticism of the literature of Women's Liberation, published in the spring of 1971, a British journalist remarked, "It is a commonplace observation of anyone who has studied political and social movements that they tend to come into being when the cause has already been won [Fairlie, 1971, p. 29]." In that same spring, we participated in a sociological survey, the purpose of which was to measure social changes occurring in a metropolitan community over the preceding two decades (Duncan, Schuman, and Duncan, 1973; Fischer, 1972). Among the other participants in the study were some two dozen graduate students, one-third of them women. Some of the women were especially insistent that we include changes in sex roles among the topics to be investigated most intensively. To the extent possible, the study was designed to do this.

The major limiting factor arose from the basic strategy of the study itself. In order to detect change, we needed baseline measures from a survey or surveys taken in years preceding 1971. The available baseline surveys were those conducted annually by the Detroit Area Study in metropolitan Detroit, beginning in 1952. None of them dealt with the whole range of issues suggested by the concept, sex roles. One was, however, concerned with parenthood and childrearing; it was directed to a sample of mothers. Another focused on marriage and the relations between spouses; the respondents were a sample of wives. The remaining surveys on which we drew involved interviews with adults of both sexes, although none had the study of men's or women's roles as a primary research goal. Yet the information obtained on a variety of subjects sheds light on a number of similarities and differences between the experiences, behavior, and attitudes of women and men.

We are not really in a position to support or take issue with Mr. Fairlie's contention that the cause of Women's Liberation had already been won. What we can do is employ the apparatus of modern survey analysis to investigate selected questions that *bear upon* the general issue of how the social positions of the sexes had been changing at the time he was writing. Our theme is social change in the 1960s, the period spanned by the baseline studies of 1953–1959 and the replication in 1971. But, for reasons that need not be discussed here, we do not have data from surveys done in the 1960s. So it is a before-and-after assessment that we offer, not a running narrative of that eventful decade.

During the 1960s the status of women was elevated from a private concern to a public-policy issue. First in a chain of events was the establishment of the Presidential Commission on the Status of Women, in December of 1961 (Freeman, 1973, p. 794; Hole and Levine, 1971, p. 24 and Chronology). Enactment of the 1964 Civil Rights Act, Title VII of which banned discrimination in employment on the basis of sex, followed. That "sex" was added as a prohibited basis for discrimination through an amendment offered by an opponent of the Act (Hole and Levine, 1971, p. 30) is worth pondering. But, sponsorship aside, enforcement of Title VII—or laxness therein—kept the issue in the public eye for the rest of the decade. As the decade closed, the report of the 1969 Presidential Task Force on Women's Rights and Responsibilities was being released to the public while the Congress deliberated the Equal Rights Amendment, a response to pressure from organized women.

An Equal Rights Amendment, a call for absolute equality of women and men under the law, had been advocated as early as 1923 by some leaders of the successful fight for women's suffrage. Other leaders of this movement, however, endorsed the principle of a special status for women under the law and saw protective legislation as part of a package of hard-won social reforms. From the outset, there was tension between women who saw protective legislation as an impediment to their occupational success and those who saw it as essential for the well-being of "working women," a group thought of as young, husbandless, in need of protection from ruthless factory owners. (See Chafe, 1972, Chap. 5, for a history of equal rights issues from 1920 to 1940.) As late as 1940 this image of working women had some basis in reality. By 1960 it failed miserably as a description—half the working women were wives who had passed their 25th birthday (U.S. Bureau of the Census, 1964, Table 196). Wartime efforts to increase the female labor supply not only had succeeded in the short run, but had permanently altered the relation between women's work status and their family status. Absolute equality of men and women under the law may have a different meaning for workers than for wives.

Results of polls suggest that the shift in attitudes toward working wives was a postwar, rather than wartime phenomenon, although we cannot pin down the timing of change precisely. A question asked in Gallup polls in 1937, 1945, and 1969 (Erskine, 1971) was, "Do you approve of a married woman earning money in business or industry if she has a husband capable of supporting her [p. 283]?" In 1937 10% of the respondents said *depends* or *don't know*, 18% said *yes* (approve), and 72% said *no*. In 1945 20% said *depends* or *don't know* and, again, 18% said *yes*. Perhaps the increasing uncertainty, if that is the proper interpretation of *depends* or *don't know*, was a harbinger of change. Unfortunately our next reading occurs after a lapse of 24 years; by 1969, 5% said *depends* or *don't know*, whereas 55% said *yes*. But we have no way of determining when approval of working wives became the majority view. Chafe (1972) probably is correct that,

> If the nation—including women—had been asked in 1939 whether it desired, or would tolerate such a far-reaching change, the answer would undoubtedly have been an overwhelming no. But events bypassed public opinion, and made the change an accomplished fact. The war, in short, was a catalyst which broke up old modes of behavior and helped to forge new ones [p. 247].

We would like to trace the tempo of change in attitudes toward the proper roles of women more precisely, both out of curiosity and a desire to see where our baseline and replication readings fall in the sequence. The best series that we have been able to assemble is answers to questions about the acceptability of "a woman for president," asked of national samples at fairly closely spaced intervals from 1937 to 1975, and tabulated by sex of respondent. The data are displayed in Figure 1-1. In 1937 fewer persons were prepared to vote for a woman for president than in any subsequent year, and the question wording itself suggests that the idea is a bit out of the ordinary: Would you vote for a woman for President if she qualified in every other respect? This curious use of the word "other" disappeared from the question in subsequent years.

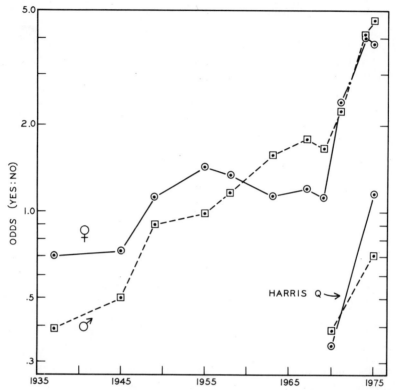

FIGURE 1-1. "A Woman for President?" National data for Gallup Poll question, 1937–1975, and Harris Survey question, 1970–1975, by sex of respondent.

A general rising trend in willingness to vote for a woman is noted, until in 1975 some four-fifths of all respondents said that they would vote for a qualified woman nominated by their party for president.

Comparability among questions is not sufficient to warrant close interpretation of intersurvey changes. At least five variants of the question were used in 1945 and later polls, although all of them stipulated that the woman candidate was nominated by one's own party and that she is qualified, well qualified, or best qualified for the job. There may be a problem as well in comparing the data from the 1970s, collected by the National Opinion Research Center, with those from earlier years, reported by the Gallup Poll. Despite defects in comparability, it seems safe to conclude that the shift in opinion toward the acceptability of a woman for president began to accelerate in the late 1960s. Especially interesting is the difference between the series based on answers of women and that based on answers of men. The results of each survey carried out between 1937 and 1958 show women more willing to vote for a woman for president. In contrast, the surveys of 1963, 1967, and 1969 find men more willing to vote for a woman. And, finally, in the four surveys carried out in the 1970s, the opinions of men and women on this issue are the same. (The apparent sex difference in 1975 is not statistically significant.) Viewed from another perspective, the idea of a woman for president appears to have gained acceptance steadily, though perhaps at varying rates, among men. Among women, however, the idea seemingly failed to gain in popularity from the mid-1950s until the late 1960s.

Also displayed in Figure 1-1 are results for a different question bearing on this issue that was asked in Harris Surveys in 1970 and 1975. Respondents were asked whether they tended to *agree* or *disagree* with the statement, "There won't be a woman President of the U.S. for a long time, and that's probably just as well." We do not know whether respondents who *disagree* reject the view that it will be a long time before a woman is president, or the view that it's "just as well" that it will be a long time, or both. In any event, the ratio of respondents who *disagree* to those who *agree* increased appreciably over the 5-year period, as did the ratio of respondents saying *yes* to those saying *no* when asked if they would vote for a woman for president. That the Harris question produced a substantial sex difference in a year when Gallup's question did not, however, warns us that it is hazardous to generalize from a limited selection of indicators. But since our choice of indicators always is severely limited, we must either accept the risk of stating erroneous conclusions or eschew the statement of conclusions entirely.

If the Gallup–NORC series can be trusted, our 1971 survey catches public opinion on sex roles just at the point of "take off" in acceptance of new social roles for men and women. It may be that the 1960s were a period in which the opinions of men about women's roles "caught up" with the views of women themselves. Our baseline surveys of 1953–1959 would seem to precede any such realignment of public opinion.

DETROIT AND THE UNITED AUTO WORKERS

Our study site is Detroit, a war production center and stronghold of the United Auto Workers (UAW). Between 1940 and 1945, the female work force in Detroit doubled; and three-fourths of the women who had entered the labor force said they wanted to continue work after the war

(Chafe, 1972, pp. 139, 178). When results of the 1940 and 1950 Censuses are compared, the proportion of women aged 18–64 in the labor force is found to have increased from 29 to 33%. More striking is the changed character of the female work force; wives aged 25 or more had grown from 28 to 40% of the total. (Computations based on U.S. Bureau of the Census, 1943, Table 11, and 1952, Tables 68 and 70.) Confronted with a wartime influx of women workers, the UAW established a separate Women's Department in 1944 (Hole and Levine, 1971, p. 105). Although the UAW leadership's view of wartime women workers as temporary (Chafe, 1972, pp. 157, 177) was in part accurate, creation of the Women's Department seems to have had lasting consequences. Hole and Levine (1971) are of the opinion that it has been pressure from the Women's Department that "has often put the union in the vanguard of working women's rights [p. 105]." If Hole and Levine are correct in their assessment of the UAW's positions and policies with respect to women's rights and if the stance of the union leadership influences the views of the rank and file, our respondents who belong to the UAW may express unusually "liberal" attitudes about equality of opportunity for women. A test of this hypothesis would seem to be of interest for its own sake. The outcome, moreover, would tell us whether we might expect a Detroit sample to include unusually large numbers of "liberal" respondents, in view of the composition of Detroit's population by union membership.

Among the 1881 respondents in our 1971 survey are 222 members of the UAW and 287 members of other labor unions. The ratio of UAW members to persons who said they did not belong to a labor union is .17 (222/1344) and the ratio of members of other unions to the nonunion population is .21. (Excluded are the 28 respondents who failed to report on union membership.) Make no mistake about it—this is a very high level of union, specifically UAW, affiliation. The 1970 Census counted 122.7 million persons aged 21 and over; estimates of membership in that year are 1.5 million for the "automobile workers" and 19.2 million for all other unions headquartered in the United States (U.S. Bureau of the Census, 1975, Tables 35, 605, 606). Thus, nationally the ratio of UAW members to nonunion persons was .015, and the ratio of other-union members to nonunion persons was .19.

Our question that bears most directly on the rights of women as workers is, "Are there some kinds of work that you feel women should not have?" This question is answered *yes* more often by UAW members than by either other-union members or nonunion persons; that is, constraints on women's work are endorsed more often by the UAW members. The odds on *yes* (or the ratio of the number of persons saying *yes* to the number saying *no*) are 4.2 for both men and women of the UAW, in contrast to 2.8 for men and 1.6 for women who belong to another union and 2.5 and 1.5 for the nonunion men and women. To ensure that the UAW effect is not really an employment-status or occupation effect, we can restrict our comparisons to those respondents who were, at the time of the 1971 survey, employed as clerical workers, craftsmen or kindred workers, or operatives. This group of workers includes 163 members of the UAW, 151 members of other unions, and 220 persons who do not belong to a labor union. The contrast between UAW members and other workers in similar occupations is as sharp as for the population at large. The odds on *yes* stand at 4.2 for UAW men, 6.5 for UAW women, 2.7 for other-union men, 1.4 for other-union women, 2.4 for nonunion men, and 1.2 for nonunion women.

At this point we digress to introduce the methods that will frequently be used in this study to analyze a set of data like those just described. The problem is viewed as a multiway contingency table analysis. Statistical methods for attacking this problem have recently become available (e.g., Bishop, Fienberg, and Holland, 1975; Goodman, 1970, 1972b; Plackett, 1974). Among the first applications in sociology were two preliminary reports from our project (Duncan, 1975a; Duncan and Evers, 1975).

In the problem at hand, we have a dichotomous response variable (*yes* or *no* on the question of whether there are kinds of work women should not have) by the dichotomous factor of sex and the trichotomous classification of union status (UAW, other-union, nonunion). In the light of work reported in Chapter 3, moreover, we find it advisable further to cross-classify by the factor of color (black versus white), so that the data are in the form of a $2 \times 2 \times 3 \times 2$ contingency table. Since there is a single response variable that may be related to any or all of the three factors, or some combination of them, our problem is somewhat like the usual regression problem. That is, we want to ascertain which of the factors significantly affects response. To this end, we consider various "models" for the data, each including a different set of effects. Models are evaluated by "fitting" them to the data in an iterative calculation that makes use of specified one-way, two-way, or three-way marginal totals of the four-way table. The fewer such totals are needed to secure a satisfactory fit, roughly speaking, the "simpler" the model is and the more desirable strictly on grounds of parsimony. On the other hand, when, by complicating the model (including an additional effect in it), we secure a significant improvement in fit, this is evidence of an effect in the data that cannot be disregarded as a mere accident of sampling fluctuation.

Assessment of goodness of fit is carried out with the likelihood-ratio chi-square statistic (X^2), the interpretation of which is essentially the same as the more familiar goodness-of-fit chi-square statistic of Karl Pearson. The models considered are hierarchical. This means that we compare one model that includes a set of effects with another model including all of these effects and at least one more. The comparison, in taking account of the degrees of freedom used in fitting the additional effect(s), allows us to evaluate whether the improvement in fit is too great to be easily attributed to sampling error. As a matter of practice in this research, we have regarded a chi-square value with $p < .05$ as "significant" and one with $p > .1$ as "not significant." In the intermediate case, $.05 < p < .1$, we sometimes term the result "marginally significant" or "almost significant" or something of the sort and venture an interpretation if it seems useful to do so; but we also feel free to ignore a cliffhanger of this kind if we have difficulty making sense of it.

Our general attitude toward the use of "models" and tests of significance conforms with the remarks of Cox (1970), who suggests that models be regarded as "provisional working bases for the analysis rather than rigid specifications to be accepted uncritically [p. 94]." Thus, we shall always be concerned both with the substantive reasonableness of a model and with whether it adequately fits the data. Our heavy, though not wholly mechanical, reliance on significance tests could be justified by Cox's further observation, "With smaller amounts of data, formal tests of significance become relatively more important, primarily because the possibility of apparently appreciable, but nevertheless spurious departures from the model becomes more important [p. 95]." Given the large number of factors that may affect any of our response variables, and hence the large number of cells in a cross-classification including any substantial proportion of these factors, we are always working with "smaller amounts of data," as, indeed, most sociologists do.

Without showing the chi-square values pertaining to the several models we examined in the problem at hand, we can summarize the outcome of the comparisons as follows: Response, color, and sex are involved in a significant three-way interaction; that is, the effect of sex on response is different for blacks and whites; or, equivalently, the color effect depends on sex. In addition, we find a significant effect of the union-membership trichotomy that does not depend on sex or color. That is, we can fit the data adequately ($X^2 = 8.0$, $df = 7$, $p > .25$) on the supposition that sex and color effects on response are the same for UAW members, other-union members, and nonunion persons. The apparent variation in the direction and magnitude of sex effects in the observed odds cited earlier is, therefore, regarded as a happenstance of sampling variation. We find, moreover, upon partitioning the union-membership variable—considering in turn the contrast of each category with the other two, according to the routine described in Duncan (1975b)—that only the contrast of UAW with the other two categories is significant. For our illustrative problem, we lose no information if we replace the trichotomous union-membership variable, as originally defined, by the dichotomy, UAW versus non-UAW. It is important to note that this is a conclusion reached in the course of the statistical analysis, not a decision imposed a priori on that analysis in accordance with some rule of thumb for dichotomizing polytomous variables.

Having selected the model that provides a satisfactory fit to the data (in that residual variation is readily attributable to sampling error), that includes the particular effects found significant upon testing, and that represents the data in as parsimonious a fashion as possible, given the other two criteria, our final step is to estimate the numerical magnitudes of the effects on response. To this end, we make use of the *expected* frequencies under the model we have accepted. From them we calculate the odds on *yes* for each combination of the factors affecting response; the results follow:

	Black men	Black women	White men	White women
UAW	8.12	1.89	3.66	2.51
Other-union	4.70	1.10	2.12	1.45
Nonunion	4.70	1.10	2.12	1.45

From these fitted or expected odds (as they will usually be termed) we can further calculate odds ratios that compactly summarize the effects. Being a UAW member rather than a member of another union or a nonunion person raises the odds on *yes* by a factor of 1.7, whether we are considering black men (8.12/4.70), black women (1.89/1.10), white men (3.66/2.12), or white women (2.51/1.45). The sex effect among blacks may be calculated from either the UAW response as 8.12/1.89 = 4.3 or from the other-union or nonunion responses as 4.70/1.10 = 4.3. That is, among blacks the odds on *yes* are over four times as great for men as for women. Making the corresponding calculation for whites we obtain 3.66/2.51 = 2.12/1.45 = 1.5, so that the sex effect is much smaller among whites.

No doubt the foregoing exposition falls between two stools. For the reader already acquainted with these methods, it is unnecessarily protracted and elementary. But for those who may not have encountered them before, it is hardly an adequate introduction. Rather than prolong the discussion of methods for their benefit, we provide an Appendix at the end of the volume which offers a somewhat more detailed though far from comprehensive description of the statistical techniques found useful in this research. In that Appendix, among other things, we justify the use of the odds and odds ratios as descriptive statistics, taking the place of the percentages and percentage differences that are conventional in reports on survey data.

Returning to the substance of our problem, we have established that belonging to the UAW elevates the odds on a *yes* response to the question, "Are there some kinds of work you feel women should not have?" (We would tend to discount any argument that the group under study is occupationally too heterogeneous to discern a UAW effect as such. In another problem, occupation—clerical versus crafts–operative —was considered along with color, sex, and union status as a factor that might influence response; no statistically reliable occupation effect was detected.) The finding is, of course, evidence against the hypothesis that UAW members hold unusually "liberal" views. UAW members, in fact, less often endorse the liberal view than do the other-union members and nonunion persons. We cannot say why this is so, but we can gain a little insight into the meaning of a *yes* response since those respondents who said *yes* were asked, "Why do you feel this way?"

Our coders assigned each answer to the question, "Why do you feel this way?" into one of several predesignated code categories. One such category was that some work is too hard for women physically. The odds on *too hard*, relative to all other reasons combined, stand at 6.7 for women with manual jobs, 1.3 for women with clerical jobs. The occupation effect on response is unambiguously significant ($X^2 = 8.05$, $df = 1, p < .005$). The number of female manual workers who give any reason other than *too hard* is so small that any analysis by union status of reasons for objection is impossible. We take this finding to mean that response is influenced not only by ideological factors, but also by situational factors. White men in the UAW, for example, more often say some work is *too hard* for women physically, *injures* a woman's *health*, or *degrades* a woman than do their non-UAW counterparts. Moreover, it is union status—UAW versus other—and not occupation—clerical versus manual—that influences response. This is only one of a number of instances in which a seeming confounding of ideological and situational factors will plague us in interpreting answers to questions that bear on sex typing. (We suspect on the basis of these results that in 1971 there remained a good deal of sentiment in favor of protective legislation among the UAW rank and file even though a resolution supporting the Equal Rights Amendment had been adopted at the UAW 1970 national convention [Hole and Levine, 1971, p. 106].)

Another reading on UAW members' opinions about woman's role is afforded by a question that asks whether four specific household chores should be done on a regular basis by a boy, a girl, or both. (Response patterns for these items are treated extensively in Chapter 12.) The referent is a hypothetical 13 year old, rather than an adult; but this question may be less contaminated by situational factors related to the respondent's work setting than the question of women's work. Two of the household chores are stereotypically female, namely, Dust and make Beds. Relevant responses are *both* and *girl,* and the relation of response to the respondent's sex, color, occupation (clerical versus manual), and union status is examined in a multiway contingency analysis. Response is influenced by sex of respondent and, marginally so, by union membership. The union-status effect is the same for male and for female respondents, and, in this instance, the significant contrast is between nonunion persons and members of a labor union, UAW or other. Belonging to a union decreases the odds on *both,* relative to *girl,* by a factor of .69 for Dust and a factor of .66 for Beds. The other two tasks are stereotypically male: shovel Walks and wash Car. Responses to these items are *both* and *boy,* and a parallel analysis is carried out. The results for Walks are similar to those just reported. Response is influenced by sex and by union membership. Belonging to a labor union reduces the odds on *both,* relative to *boy,* by a factor of .63. The evidence again is against the hypothesis that UAW members hold unusually "liberal" views with respect to the work appropriate for women or to be shared by men and women. Our results for Car, however, do not lend themselves to succinct summary nor such a clear-cut interpretation.

For Car, we find a significant five-way interaction: response by sex by color by occupation (clerical versus manual) by union status, with the significant contrast for the last variable between other-union members and the combination of UAW members and nonunion persons. A model incorporating only this five-way interaction (along with the association among characteristics, other than response, of the respondents) provides an adequate fit to the observed data ($X^2 = 9.82$, $df = 6$, $.25 > p > .1$) and a significant improvement over a model incorporating only the four four-way interactions involving response (difference in $X^2 = 9.28$, $df = 2$, $p < .01$). We will not often have occasion to display a five-way interaction like the one in Table 1-1. Such interactions do not turn up very often. When they do, it is well to remember that even though formally significant they can represent nothing more than acci-

TABLE 1-1
Fitted Odds on Both Girl and Boy (to Boy) Should Wash Car, by Sex, Color, Occupation, and Union Status of Respondent, 1971

Color and sex of respondent	Nonunion		UAW		Other union	
	Clerical	Manual	Clerical	Manual	Clerical	Manual
Black men	.31	.65	.62	1.3	—[b]	.30
Black women	1.8	.56	—[a]	1.1	6.0	4.0
White men	3.4	2.7	1.9	1.5	.29	2.85
White women	4.3	6.4	2.4	3.6	2.8	.67

Note: Model incorporates five-way interaction, response by sex by color by occupation by nonunion–UAW versus other-union, and three-way interaction, response by color by nonunion versus UAW.

[a] No black women in clerical occupations belonging to UAW in sample.

[b] Odds cannot be defined; two respondents say *both*, none says *boy*.

dents of sampling. Sampling variability mimics high-order interaction. Even if the interaction is real and not an artifact of sampling error, the estimates of the several different effects are themselves subject to a large factor of uncertainty. Without attempting an interpretation of the five-way interaction, we note the marginally significant three-way interaction, response by color by union status, which is evident in Table 1-1 in the comparison between UAW members and nonunion persons. Leaving aside comparisons with other-union members, for whom the fitted odds are identical with the observed odds (the implication of the five-way interaction), black UAW members more often say *both* than do black nonunion persons whereas white UAW members less often say *both* than do white nonunion persons. The ratio of the fitted odds, UAW:Nonunion, stands at 2.0 for blacks, in contrast to a ratio of .57 for whites. We cannot help but wonder whether washing the Car carries a special meaning for workers whose job it is to make cars. Thus, even the hypothetical question may not escape contamination by a situational factor.

Our impression is that the overrepresentation of UAW members in the Detroit population poses no special problem in interpreting our findings about public opinion on most social issues. The answers of UAW members have been compared with those of other-union members and nonunion persons for selected additional questions. Restricting the study population to workers in clerical, craft and kindred, or operative occupations and analyzing the effects on response of sex, color, occupation, and union status in the multiway contingency framework described earlier, we find no UAW effect on answers to questions about Why most women work (Chapter 2), Prospects for another depression, Live for today, and Whom to count on (Chapter 4), Required ownership of a flag (Chapter 5), or The younger generation—think or obey (Chapter 10). Freedom of speech (Table 5-3) is the only question examined for which membership in the UAW influences response, net of the effects of sex, color, occupation, and membership in any labor union.

Respondents were asked whether the right of free speech includes speeches Criticizing what the President does, Against religion, In favor of Fascism or dictatorship, and In favor of Communism. No effect specific to the UAW is detected on the last two items—Fascism and Communism. However, a three-way interaction of response by sex by UAW versus other-union–nonunion status is present in the pattern of answers to the President item. The odds on *yes*, relative to *no*, are elevated by a factor of 1.1 for UAW men, but depressed by a factor of .18 for UAW women. A three-way interaction of response by occupation by UAW versus other-union–nonunion status is present in the pattern of answers to the Religion item. The odds on *yes*, relative to *no*, are elevated by a factor of 1.1 for UAW manual workers, but depressed by a factor of .29 for UAW clerical workers. We venture no substantive interpretation of the narrow limits placed on freedom of speech by UAW women or clerical workers, as the case may be, and do not rule out the possibility that the finding is only a fluke. In any event, it is only a minor qualification to the assertion that UAW members do not hold distinctive views on social issues.

WOMEN AS RESPONDENTS AND INTERVIEWERS

The last section of the questionnaire used in the 1971 replication asked the interviewer to record her or his observations about the interview situation and the respondent. In addition to recording general observations, the interviewer answered some questions about the interviewer–respondent interaction.

A total of 828 men were interviewed, as were 1053 women. In Table 1-2, we show how the interviewers rated these men and women with respect to the respondent's understanding of the questions, solicitation of the interviewer's opinions, need for reassurance about answers, and desire to please, as well as how the interviewer liked conducting an interview with this person. A quick scanning of the table is enough to see that although the interviewers liked interviewing men and women

TABLE 1-2
Interviewer's Rating of the Respondent Interviewed, by Sex of Respondent, 1971

Question, and response options available		Percentage distribution		Ratio of women to men
		Men	Women	
1. Respondent's general understanding of questions:	Excellent	36	30	1.03
	Good	46	48	1.31
	Fair	14	19	1.74
	Poor	4	4	1.32
	Total	100	100	
2. Did R[espondent] ask *your* opinions on questions?	Never	72	63	1.11
	Rarely	15	20	1.71
	Occasionally	12	14	1.52
	Often	1	3	2.75
	Total	100	100	
3. Did R[espondent] seem to want reassurance that his answers were adequate or correct or "good ones"?	Never	71	58	1.03
	Rarely	18	21	1.50
	Occasionally	9	16	2.09
	Often	2	5	3.67
	Total	100	100	
4. How much did R[espondent] seem to want to please you? (Offer food; especially friendly; solicitous; etc.)	Not at all	42	36	1.08
	Somewhat	42	46	1.40
	Definitely	13	14	1.44
	Great deal	3	4	1.36
	Total	100	100	
5. How much did you personally like the interview?	A great deal	40	39	1.24
	Somewhat	46	45	1.25
	Slightly	10	12	1.45
	Disliked	4	4	1.31
	Total	100	100	

Note: A total of 828 men and 1053 women were interviewed. Number of respondents (or interviews) not rated ranges from 5 on Q3 to 17 on Q4 for men and from 11 on Q1 to 24 on Q4 for women.

equally well, the interviewers rated men and women differently in their roles as respondents. With respect to understanding of the questions, for example, women respondents are less often rated *excellent*, more often rated *fair*. Women are overrepresented among the respondents who solicit the interviewer's own opinions, seek reassurance about their answers, and want to please the interviewer.

The interviewers number 63. Forty were professional interviewers associated with the University of Michigan's Survey Research Center; together they completed some 1500 interviews. All but one of the professional interviewers were women—an example of occupational sex typing. The other interviewers were 9 women and 14 men who were graduate students at the University of Michigan and participating in the Detroit Area Study seminar in 1971. The graduate-student women completed 189 interviews, the men 165. The distribution of respondents by kind of interviewer is set forth systematically in Table 1-3.

Since we have no third party observing the respondent–interviewer interaction, we are somewhat uncertain as to the correct interpretation of the differences in ratings assigned to men and women respondents. Perhaps women more often cannot understand the questions; or possibly their response style leads interviewers to believe, mistakenly, that the women have understood less well. We are prepared to assume that respondent's education can serve as the report of a third party in this

TABLE 1-3
Information about Interviewers, 1971

Item	Women		Men	
	Student	Professional	Student	Professional
Number of interviewers	9	39	14	1
Distribution of interviewers by number of completed interviews				
5	0	2	0	0
9–13	0	0	12	0
14–18	6	3	2	0
22–40	3	15	0	1
42–75	0	19	0	0
Total number of interviews completed	189	1502	165	25
Number of respondents rated by interviewer	188	1493	165	25
Female respondents	96	840	95	14
Male respondents	92	653	70	11

instance, that is, an objective measure of the respondent's understanding. We then can see whether respondents of the same educational attainment are rated differently depending upon their sex.

When we study the cross-classification of respondents by education (0–8 school years completed, 9–11, 12, 13–15, 16 or more) and rating on understanding (*excellent, good, fair, poor*) treating one characteristic as an ordered classification, we find that its influence on the other characteristic is captured by a linear model. This holds for our relevant subgroups, that is, all women respondents, women interviewed by professionals, and so forth. On this justification, we assign the scores of 4 to an *excellent* rating, 3 to *good*, 2 to *fair*, and 1 to *poor* and then calculate a mean score for respondents in each sex-education group. The mean scores, displayed in Figure 1-2, show the substantial influence of education on rating. More interesting, however, is the fact that the mean score is lower for women respondents than for men respondents at each

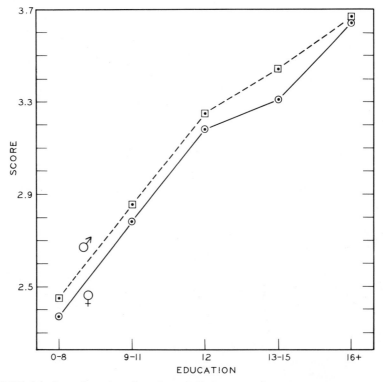

FIGURE 1-2. **Interviewer's rating of respondent's general understanding of questions** (*excellent* = 4, . . ., *poor* = 1), **by sex and education of respondent, 1971.**

educational level. A multiway contingency analysis of the cross-classification, education by rating by sex of respondent, indicates that there are indeed significant additive effects of education and sex of respondent on rating. Being female elevates the odds on a *good* to *excellent* rating by a factor of 1.2, the odds on a *fair* to *excellent* rating by a factor of 1.6, and the odds on a *poor* to *excellent* rating by a factor of 1.3. Moreover, the sex-of-respondent effect on rating is not contingent on the interviewer's status. The tendency for women's ratings to be lower than those for men of like education seems to hold among respondents interviewed by seasoned professionals as well as among those interviewed by neophytes, male or female.

We also can look at the sex-of-respondent difference in rating with respect to general understanding of questions from the standpoint of the individual interviewer. The mean of the scored ratings assigned to women interviewed by a particular interviewer can be compared with the corresponding mean for men interviewed by that person. For 43 of the 63 interviewers, the mean score for male respondents is higher than the mean score for female respondents. Although the greater interviewing experience of the professionals may give them an advantage over the student interviewers in judging the respondent's understanding, 28 of the 40 professionals and 15 of the 23 students are found to have assigned higher ratings to their male respondents. Thus, it is reassuring that the sex-of-respondent effect on rating is not an outcome of the idiosyncratic rating pattern of a few interviewers.

Further confirmation of the sex-of-respondent effect on rating of understanding comes from the General Social Surveys conducted by the National Opinion Research Center in 1972, 1973, and 1976. Interviewers were asked to rate the respondent's "understanding of the questions" as *good, fair,* or *poor.* Being a female respondent elevates the odds of a *fair* to *good* rating by a factor of 1.2, the odds of a *poor* to *good* rating by a factor of 1.4. (The sex effect is not contingent on marital status, color, or survey year.)

At one point in the DAS interview the respondent was asked whether he or she *strongly agreed, agreed, disagreed,* or *strongly disagreed* with the statement, "Sometimes politics and government seem so complicated that a person like me can't really understand what's going on." As we report subsequently (Table 4-4), women more often *agree,* or *strongly agree,* with this statement than do men. On the possibility that this self-perceived inability to understand extends to issues other than politics and government, we have studied the relation between the respondent's answer to this question and the interviewer's rating of this respondent's general understanding of the questions. (How one's self-conception of ability to understand is formed and how it is manifest in the interview situation are issues we do not address.)

The relation between respondent's answer to the Politics and Government Complicated question and the interviewer's rating of respondent's understanding is measured via regression techniques. Interviewer's rating is treated as the dependent variable, with scores of 4, 3, 2, and 1 assigned to the response categories *excellent, good, fair,* and *poor,* respectively. The display in Figure 1-3 represents the regression of rating score on answer, sex of respondent, and respondent's marital status. It is not our contention that marital status as such influences rating, but we have distinguished currently married respondents from others to provide a rough control on age and life style factors that might influence the interviewer's assessment of the respondent. On the basis of our regression analyses, we conclude that no three-way interaction involving sex of respondent is present. That is, neither the relation of rating to answer nor the relation of rating to marital status is different for women than for men. The effect of answer, *strongly agree, . . . , strongly disagree,* on rating is monotonic though not exactly linear; persons who *strongly agree* that "a person like me can't really understand" receive the lowest ratings from interviewers. A sex effect as well as a marital-status effect on rating is shown in Figure 1-3 although the former is only marginally significant ($p = .08$). The mean rating score for

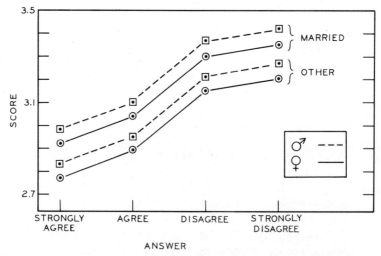

FIGURE 1-3. Interviewer's rating of respondent's general understanding of questions (*excellent* = 4, . . ., *poor* = 1), estimated from regression of rating on respondent's marital status, sex, and answer to "Sometimes politics and government seem so complicated that a person like me can't really understand what's going on," 1971.

men can be seen to exceed that for women by .065 points when persons in the same answer and marital-status group are compared. (The sex effect net of answer only is represented by a partial regression coefficient of .088, $p = .02$, and the gross sex effect by a regression coefficient of .133, $p < .001$.)

Respondents who lack confidence in their ability to understand, as manifest in agreement that "a person like me can't really understand," more often solicit the interviewer's opinions, more often seek reassurance about their answers, have a greater desire to please the interviewer; and the interviewers less often say that they liked interviewing these persons a great deal. The relation between interviewer's rating with respect to any one of these items and the respondent's answer to the Politics and Government Complicated question is the same for male respondents as for female respondents, however; and the sex effect on rating net of answer is substantially the same as the gross effect of sex. (We reach these conclusions via multiway contingency analyses.) Although these findings may help in validating the interviewer's assessment of the interview situation, they fail to illuminate the basis of the sex difference in rating.

An additional item of information about the interview situation suggests a possible basis for the sex difference in rating. At the end of the interview, the interviewer recorded the persons over 10 years of age, if any, who had been present during the interview in addition to self and respondent. The interviewer then answered the questions, "Did this affect the interview in any important way? How and what questions?" The interviewer's answer later was assigned one of four codes: *yes—changed R's answers to some questions, yes—disrupted interview but R's answers not affected, yes—some indication R's answers affected, but ambiguous, no—no effect.* We have identified the wives and husbands whose spouses were present during at least part of the interview and classified them as *yes—changed answers, yes—other,* or *no—no effect.* For some 150 wives and 350 husbands, then, we can measure the influence of spouse's presence on the interview situation. (That interviews with husbands more often are conducted in the presence of the wife than vice versa would seem to follow from the commonplace observation that wives more often are found at home during the day than are husbands.)

The results are quite straightforward. There is, indeed, an association between sex of respondent and the influence of spouse's presence on the interview situation ($X^2 = 16.99$, $df = 2$). No information is lost by dichotomizing the interviewers' answers into *yes—some effect* versus *no—no effect* ($X^2 = 16.87$, $df = 1$). The odds on *yes* are .29 for husbands in contrast to .685 for wives, a Wife:Husband odds ratio of 2.4. When the respondent's answer to the Politics and Government Complicated question also is entered into the analysis, the Wife:Husband odds ratio is unchanged (2.4) even though the odds on *yes* are 1.9 times as great for persons who *agree* that "a person like me can't really understand" as for persons who *disagree*. We cannot say whether nonrespondent husbands are more assertive than nonrespondent wives in an interview situation quite apart from the encouragement received from the respondent spouse, or whether wives more often behave toward the present spouse as they do toward the interviewer—asking his opinions, wanting reassurance, and wanting to please him. We suspect the women are more practiced in deference.

That this is not confined to Detroit-area wives seems to follow from findings based on the General Social Surveys in which interviewers were asked to characterize the respondent's "attitude toward the interview" as *friendly and interested, cooperative but not particularly interested, impatient and restless,* or *hostile.* The Wife:Husband ratio of odds *cooperative* to *friendly and interested* stand at .71, and the corresponding ratio of odds *impatient/hostile* to *friendly and interested* stand at .59. (Among unmarried respondents, women are more often seen as *impatient/hostile;* but the difference may trace to age and its correlates.) Thus, despite their relatively poor comprehension of the questions, wives are more often thought to be friendly and interested in the interview. Do these women feign concern or confusion or both?

Here, as at several other places in the study, we have used data from the General Social Survey, issued by the National Opinion Research Center, to supplement our analyses of the Detroit materials. The GSS data are somewhat more timely and may gain in interest from the fact of their national coverage. While not many of the specific questions asked in DAS are repeated in GSS, we have found quite a few questions with thematic similarities. Limiting our purview to these, we have hardly exhausted the possibilities for studies of sex differences afforded by the GSS and commend such studies to interested investigators.

AN OVERVIEW

Each of the 11 chapters that follow is a more or less self-contained report on a set of analyses related to some facet of our theme, sex typing and social roles. There is no attempt to integrate the disparate findings or to develop a conceptual framework for the study of sex roles. This is a weakness of the work, but in our judgment, not a serious weakness. Explanations of the positions of women and men in the social structure and prescriptions for change now seem to outnumber careful descriptions of those positions and the respects, if any, in which they have changed since the 1950s. Our objective is simply to contribute some reliable observations on the sexual differentiation of social roles in a contemporary community.

Meeting this limited objective has proved difficult. Typically we have several items ostensibly related to the same role. For such a subset of items, one might expect response patterns that are consistent, in the sense that social differentials in response and changes in response to one item parallel those to another item. But often this is not the case. An instance in point is the set of four items related to the sex typing of children's tasks around the home. (See Table 12-5 and Figure 12-1 for a summary of differences among items in the social factors influencing response and the tempo of change in response.) As a consequence, we seldom are able to offer an unequivocal conclusion about the degree to which a social role is sex typed and the degree to which sex typing of the role has changed since the 1950s. In other words, our findings are messy.

What can be said about how women and men define the work roles of women and men, girls and boys? There is, in general, consensus between the sexes about why women work and what is important in a man's job; there also is a good deal of stability in response patterns over time. Possibly we have learned only that norms about work have wide penetration and questions about work roles evoke stereotyped answers. We think that this is not the case, however. Our guess would be that men and nonworking women perceive fairly accurately the motives of the working women they know and that wives understand quite clearly what is important to their husbands on the job. One kind of evidence is the difference between social groups in motives imputed to working women (which runs counter to the idea of a stereotypical working woman) and the absence of such a difference between men and women in the same social group. The well-educated, for example, more often mention work as a means of maintaining one's self-respect; but women and men of similar educational attainment do not differ in their propensity to mention self-respect as a work motive of women (Figure 2-4). Another kind of evidence involves comparisons of "self-reports" with answers given by others. An example par excellence is the shift of High Income from fourth to first place in importance as a job value for black husbands; there is a corresponding shift in the answers of black wives about the importance of different values in their husbands' jobs. No such shift appears in the responses of either white husbands or white wives (Figure 2-6).

When we turn to the questions of whether one approves of married women working in the absence of economic pressure, whether there are some kinds of work women should not have, and whether certain tasks around the home should be done by both girls and boys, we find that women less often would constrain women's work or allocate children's tasks on a sexual basis than would men. (See Figures 3-1, 3-7, and 12-6.) The difference in opinion between women and men typically reappears within each social group, although the groups often differ among themselves. Or, put another way, the effects of sex and such social characteristics as marital status, religion, and education on response usually are additive. Hence, the cleavage in opinion between men and women cuts through the entire structure of the population. Most items register a shift toward disapproval of sex as a criterion of work or task assignment, albeit at differing rates. From the standpoint of social change, it is of considerable interest that differences in opinion between the sexes sometimes are unchanged even during periods when public opinion is shifting rapidly. (See, for example, Figure 12-5. But, for a counterexample, see Figure 1-1.)

Although the issue usually is posed hypothetically, the answers often reflect or are contaminated by the situation and experience of the person answering the question. We present a few excerpts from answers to the question about kinds of work women should not have in which the person answering makes explicit reference to her or his own circumstances. But most of our evidence is indirect: variations in response among social groups that seem to match differences in their positions in the social structure. Married persons more often than unmarried persons mention getting out of the home or keeping busy (but not money, self-respect, the work itself, or independence) as a reason "most women" work; home owners more often than renters say that both boys and girls should shovel the walks (but not wash the car, make beds, or dust furniture). Indeed, one of the few instances in which we detect differential change may say more about the implications of affirmative action programs than about a redefinition of women's work role. Persons who objected to women having some kinds of work were asked why they felt that way. A feeling that women might take jobs from men declined in popularity less among whites than among blacks and less among high-school graduates than among persons of lesser education or those with at least some college training (Tables 3-4 and 3-5).

Possibly this circumstantial component of the answers to questions about work roles obscures differential change in ideology between the sexes or among social groups. We also are aware of the difficulty of detecting differential change with small samples or, stated differently, that the only differential changes we are likely to identify are the large ones. Moreover, we typically have only two observation points, separated in time by a dozen or more years; hence, we often may miss differential changes that occurred as a "new view" diffused through the social structure. Whatever the reason—and we do not rule out the possibility that opinion actually does shift at the same pace throughout the population structure—differences in the tempo of change between men and women or among social groups can seldom be documented.

Age grading in response patterns to the work-role questions sometimes is evident (Figures 2-1, 3-1, 3-3, and 12-4, for example). In some contexts the language used to describe this variation suggests an interpretation in terms of the effects of aging or advancing in the life cycle. In other contexts we think we see patterns most easily described as cohort effects. Sometimes it seems plausible that both may be present, perhaps in combination with other interactions of response with time. In any event, we have *not* systematically tested alternative formulations of the age dynamics or combinations of age, period, and cohort effects that might generate the variation, since our main objective is simply to ascertain whether differences between women and men are found in all age strata or only in some. We find some tantalizing cases in which the pattern of age grading seems to be contingent on sex or survey year (such as the findings displayed in Figures 3-4, 12-4, or 12-7). If these tentative formulations provoke interest on the part of other analysts, we will be well satisfied.

We also have compared the answers of women and men to questions about their perceptions of and participation in the social order. Some, though by no means all, of these questions evoke different answers from women and men. When the sex difference in response does occur, it sometimes depends on the survey year. We would guess that other social analysts will encounter some surprises, just as we did, about which questions elicit a sex difference in response or differential change by sex in response and which questions fail to do so.

In very broad outline, the findings come as no surprise. Women are more pessimistic, more politically uninformed and apathetic, more pious; wives are overrepresented relative to husbands among the members of the PTA, Card/Social Clubs, and Church Groups and among persons who very frequently get together with kin. But the details are less predictable. The answers of women to several questions in the domain of anomia (not all such questions, we emphasize) show a more rapid erosion of confidence and trust. (See findings in Tables 4-2 and 4-3, for example.) The ability of women to name their Congressman correctly relative to that of men is *not* improved when the congressional district is represented by a woman. Women would set narrower limits on free speech, even when the question is prefaced by a reference to a Constitutional guarantee (Figure 5-2), yet they are overrepresented among the persons who maintain that they would pay a parking fine irrespective of the expectation of being caught if they defaulted (Table 5-5). Either the mother–daughter decrease in religiosity has been greater than the father–son decrease (Figure 6-4) or, on another line of argument consistent with the data, sons no longer feel so constrained to describe their mothers as devout.

It makes for better reading as well as smoother writing to focus on the broad sweep. But we think that it would be a mistake to do so, for the specific findings are what trip us up on too hasty explanations. Occasionally, we take explicit note of findings that seem at variance with generalizations proposed by other observers of the social scene or with our own conjectures. Wives, for example, no longer are overrepresented relative to husbands among workers who frequently get together with their co-workers (Figure 7-4); and the explanation might be thought to lie in an increased share of working wives who have young children and little free time. But that explanation becomes suspect when we also find a lessening overrepresentation of wives, nonworking as well as working, among persons who frequently get together with kin. We have not, however, made it a practice to search the literature for assertions counter to the findings and then report our results as negative evidence.

Our other analyses touch on the roles of men and women as spouses and parents. Here we encounter two very "active" items: the Morality of Divorce and whether the Younger Generation should be taught to think for themselves or do what is right. Opinions about both issues are age graded, and on one interpretation, there is evidence of differential change by cohort. Striking differences in the pace of change in opinion about the Morality of Divorce are found among religious groups (Figure 9-1), and the positions of blacks and whites on the Younger Generation issue literally reverse between surveys (Figure 10-1). Educational attainment influences response to the Younger Generation question in both surveys and response to the Morality of Divorce question in only one of the surveys. Yet there is *no* difference between women and men in their answers to these questions about matters so central to the family.

Men and women, mothers and fathers, also seem to be in substantial agreement about the goals of childrearing or the qualities they would like to inculcate in their children (Figure 10-3); but it is on the matter of sex role, "acting like a boy or girl should," that their views begin to diverge (Figure 10-5). Fathers (we do not know about mothers), moreover, think that in early childhood it is more important that boys act like boys than that girls act like girls; but the importance they attach to sex role decreases with age for boys while holding steady for girls (Figure 10-4). The national data on which we rely here also suggest that the salience of sex-role socialization to parents may be decreasing. (See Table 10-6.)

That boys learn the man role and girls the woman role can be documented, inasmuch as adolescent boys and girls differ in their answers to work-role and political questions just as men differ from women. Our data and findings do not disclose how this learning occurs. Childrearing techniques for boys and girls are much the same according to the reports of mothers, although mothers rely somewhat more heavily on psychic rewards for good behavior and physical punishments for wrong behavior of the boys (Tables 10-1 and 10-2). Evidence of intergenerational transmission of sexual stereotyping is tenuous and not wholly consistent (Table 11-1). It is true, however—to cite a single example—that mothers whose husbands play some part in washing the dishes are less likely than mothers who do the dishes alone to sex type the children's tasks (Table 11-2). We must add that the division of labor between spouses has undergone only minor modification and that not all changes have been in the direction of less sexual stereotyping (Figure 8-1).

Although the original aim of this research was to provide measurements of social change, as it turns out much of our evidence serves to document the essential stability of patterns over periods of 12–18 years. Such documentation is worth having in view of the ease with which one can fabricate accounts of the "Dark Ages" or the "Good Old Days" to take the place of historical data.

This overview may offer some flavor of the style and substance of the reports that follow.

2

Work Motives and the Female Role

Answers to a question about the motives imputed to working women offer some insight into popular views on the issue of whether gainful work is an appropriate part of the female role. The baseline reading was made in 1956, long enough after the close of World War II to minimize mentions of contributions to the war effort (though the 1956 coding scheme included a category for such answers). At the same time, the baseline reading is early enough to minimize answers cast in the rhetoric of the Women's Liberation movement.

Information about work motives comes from the question, "Why do you think most women work?" The respondent's answer was recorded by the interviewer, and up to two reasons for working were subsequently coded. The data set that we are using here is the 1956 and 1971 responses as coded in 1971 by the same individuals into the categories developed for the 1956 study. (See Duncan and Evers, 1975, for details of the coding operation.)

What the responses imply with respect to definitions of the female role seldom is clear-cut and often is hopelessly ambiguous. Since the response patterns are open to differing interpretations, the changes over time and the social differentials in response are set forth in considerable detail.

POPULARITY OF THE MOTIVES

Our first concern is to establish whether the motives changed in their relative popularity between 1956 and 1971 and whether men and women differ with respect to the motives they attribute to "most working women."

The most frequently mentioned reason for women working is *money,* that is, an unambiguous economic motive. The odds are eight to one that the respondent will mention *money* in answering the question, "Why do you think most women work?" Moreover, a consensus with respect to the primacy of an economic motive holds between survey years, between men and women, and among social strata defined by marital status, color, employment status, religious preference, subjective class identification, or educational attainment.

Were it possible to code reliably the connotation of each *money* mention, change over time and differentiation among social strata might be detected. The coding scheme developed in 1956 did distinguish "have to earn a living, have to work, for the money" from "want extra things, luxuries" and "to supplement family income, to help out husbands." (An answer might be assigned two of these codes.) The code *have to work* was assigned to 40% of the responses in both 1956 and 1971. The code *want extras* was assigned less often to the 1971 responses, 15 as compared with 23%; and the code *help out* was assigned more often to the 1971 responses, 50 as compared with 40%. The shift suggests that the question evokes an image of a married woman working because of economic pressure more often now than in the past. The word suggests is used advisedly, however; for code selection is fraught with difficulty.

Which code best captures the meaning of "most women work for extra money it takes to live on nowadays," or "no good men, so they work to support their children—what else are they going to do," or "takes more money than man alone can make to maintain way of living"? Coders almost certainly will agree that *money* is the reason for working, but they will not necessarily agree as to which *money* code(s)—*have to work, want extras,* or *help out*—should be assigned to the response. Answers of the 797 respondents in 1956 were recoded in 1971 using the 1956 coding scheme. When the original 1956 code and the 1971 recode for first reason mentioned are compared, the agreement is 93% for *money* versus some other reason. For the 562 answers assigned a *money* code, however, the agreement is 82% as to whether the appropriate code is *have to work, want extras,* or *help out.* Moreover, the greater the discretion of the coder—the more that must be read into the answer to determine the appropriate code—the greater is the risk that the frequency of currently popular views will be amplified. *Help out* was perceived by the 1971 coders to be mentioned more often in the 1971 answers than in the 1956 answers; *help out* also was perceived by the 1971 coders to be mentioned more often in the 1956 answers than it had been perceived by the 1956 coders when they assigned codes to the 1956 answers (30% versus 24%).

We can say with confidence only that the economic reasons so often cited by women entering the work force (e.g., Rosenfeld and Perrella, 1965) are recognized through all sectors of the population. But attribution of an economic motive to "most working women" cannot be taken as evidence that gainful work is viewed as an integral part of the female role. A query about why men work might elicit frequent mentions of money, but seldom, if ever, would the context imply that the money helps out or is for extras.

Five less frequently mentioned reasons for women working may be more informative about the distinctive meaning of gainful work for a woman. The response categorized as *get out of home* conveys dissatisfaction with the homemaker role as the motive for work—bored at home, don't like housework, don't like married life, to get out of the home. The *keep busy* response—to fill idle time, to keep occupied—is more neutral with respect to the push from the home, but neutral also with respect to the attraction of gainful work as such. More positive with respect to the meaning of work are the answers categorized as *self-respect,* that women work to feel useful and important, or *work itself,* a career, interest in the work, enjoyment of the work. The fifth reason, *independence,* would seem to connote more than a purely economic motive although financial independence may be implicit in most answers to which the code is assigned.

The word "fulfillment" does not appear in the 1956 coding scheme although in 1971 it was a catchword in discussions of women and work. In our early work on coding consistency, we found that 1971 coders, both graduate students and professionals at the Survey Research Center, unhesitatingly assigned the *self-respect* code to answers in which the word appeared. When asked subsequently about the code selection, they seemed confident that the appropriate choice had been made. (The 1971 coders assigned the *self-respect* code to 24 of the 1956 answers; the 1956 coders assigned the *self-respect* code to only 13 of these answers. It is our impression that the word "fulfillment" seldom, if ever, appeared in the 1956 answers.)

The only reason mentioned more often in 1971 than in 1956 is *get out of home,* a seeming rejection of the traditional homemaker role; and its

popularity increased among both men and women. The ratio of odds
1971 : 1956 is estimated to be 1.3 for both male and female respondents.
Moreover, this is the only reason mentioned more often by women than
by men; the odds on *get out of home* for female respondents stand in the
ratio of 1.6 to the corresponding odds for male respondents in each
year.

In contrast, a marginally significant decrease is observed with respect
to the odds on *independence;* the odds ratio 1971 : 1956 is estimated to be
.73 for both male and female respondents. In each survey, *independence*
is mentioned less often by women than by men, with the odds ratio
Female : Male estimated as .66.

The odds on mention for *keep busy, work itself,* and *self-respect* differ
neither by year nor by sex of respondent. (See Table 2-2 for odds on
each reason by survey year and sex of respondent.) We are persuaded
that the coders were sensitive to the then current theme of fulfillment
through gainful work. The absence of change in the frequency of mention for these reasons and the low frequency of mention in 1971 might
suggest that the ideology of the women's movement had not diffused
widely. Perhaps the message of the movement had been found wanting
by many persons who heard it; perhaps only that part of the message
that said being a wife and mother is not enough had penetrated.

In sum, economic motives are seen as paramount. But they also are
unchanging. Dissatisfaction with a full-time homemaker role gained
popularity among both women and men as the imputed motive of
"most working women" over the 15-year period. Possibly losing
ground was independence, which may or may not mean more than
"one's own money" to the person who mentions it. In both 1956 and
1971, the rejection of homemaking was more salient to women, the
matter of independence less so. Shifts in opinion occurred at the same
rate for men as for women. A redefinition of woman's role is implied in
the shifting response pattern; but the emphasis is on shortcomings of a
traditional role, not positive features of an alternative role. Gratification
to be derived from homemaking was more often being devalued, yet
there was no concomitant increase in mentions of the intrinsic rewards
of gainful work.

MULTIVARIATE ANALYSIS

That more widespread mention of dissatisfaction with the homemaker role is accompanied by a decrease in mentions of a desire for
independence might be an artifact: Provision was made for coding two,

and only two, reasons. By treating each reason mentioned independently, rather than as one of a pair of possible reasons, we may be
obscuring significant features of the response pattern or attaching substantive meaning to artifacts. We have, therefore, reestimated the effects of year and sex (and estimated the effect of color) on mentions of
money, get out of home, independence, and any *"other"* reason(s) taking
into account the number of reasons mentioned by the respondent and
the associations among the four reasons.

Respondents are classified into ten categories defined by a single
reason or a pair of possible reasons in Table 2-1. The modal category is
money only, the answer of some 55% of the respondents in each year.
Most other respondents did offer (at least) two reasons, one of which
usually was *money.* Although the distributions for the sex–color subgroups in each survey resemble one another in these respects, differences in the frequency of single-reason responses and the popularity of
particular reasons seem sufficiently large to warrant systematic study.

In the lower panel of Table 2-1 we show the response distributions
expected on the basis of a model fitted by the method described by
Duncan (1975b). In addition to the year–sex–color marginal frequencies, the model fits five substantively interesting effects or associations:

1. An association between mentions of *money* and of *independence.*
2. An association between mentions of *get out of home* and of some
   "other" reason.
3. Effects of color on mentions of *get out of home, independence,* and
   "other" reason(s).
4. Effects of sex on mentions of *get out of home* and *independence.*
5. Effects of survey year on mentions of *get out of home* and *independence.*

While this list may seem like a long one, the preferred model (which
provides an acceptable fit and includes all significant effects) actually
omits a great many logically possible relationships. It is noteworthy that
number of reasons (one versus two) is not related to any specific reason
nor to any of the three factors, color, sex, or year. Of the six possible
pairwise associations among reasons, only two are significant; and we
find no higher order interactions among the responses. Finally, effects
of color, sex, and year are separate rather than joint; that is, there are no
three-way or four-way interactions involving a response and a pair or
triple of factors.

We comment briefly on the substance of the relationships listed in the
preceding paragraph.

TABLE 2-1

Percentage Distribution of Respondents by Reasons They Say Most Women Work, by Color and Sex, 1956 and 1971: Observed and Expected on Basis of Model

Reasons women work	All respondents		1956				1971			
			Male		Female		Male		Female	
	1956	1971	Black	White	Black	White	Black	White	Black	White
All respondents	100	100	100	100	100	100	100	100	100	100
Money only	56	55	51	59	59	53	59	56	68	50
Money and										
Independence	5	4	15	5	11	2	14	2	7	2
Get out of home	11	15	5	8	3	16	6	14	8	19
Other reason	17	16	17	19	11	17	9	18	9	17
Independence only	1	1	5	<1	6	1	5	1	3	<1
Independence and										
Get out of home	<1	<1	0	1	0	<1	0	<1	<1	<1
Other reason	1	<1	2	0	3	1	1	1	0	<1
Get out of home only	3	4	2	2	3	3	1	3	1	5
Get out of home and										
Other reason	2	1	0	2	0	3	0	2	1	2
Other reason(s)	4	4	5	4	4	4	5	4	3	3

Expected distributions[a]

All respondents	100	100	100	100	100	100	100	100
Money only	58	57	62	54	62	55	63	51
Money and								
Independence	16	4	12	2	12	3	8	2
Get out of home	3	10	5	15	5	13	8	20
Other reason	11	18	12	17	12	18	12	16
Independence only	6	2	4	1	5	1	3	1
Independence and								
Get out of home	<1	<1	<1	<1	<1	<1	<1	<1
Other reason	1	1	1	<1	1	<1	1	<1
Get out of home only	1	2	1	4	1	3	2	5
Get out of home and								
Other reason	<1	1	<1	2	<1	2	1	2
Other reason(s)	3	4	3	4	3	4	3	4

[a] See text for list of relations and effects incorporated in model. $X^2 = 49.85$, $df = 59$.

1. If a respondent mentions *independence*, the odds on *money* are lowered by a factor of .63. This association is consistent with our suspicion that specifically financial independence is implicit in most answers categorized as *independence*.
2. If a respondent mentions *get out of home*, the odds on *"other"* reason are elevated by a factor of 1.6. That is, the respondent who begins by answering in noneconomic terms—rather than with the typical response, *money*—seemingly elaborates by referring to other noneconomic motives.
3. The only factor with significant effects on *"other"* is color. We estimate the odds ratio White:Black as 1.7 for *"other."* It happens that 1.7 is the average of the color effects for the three *"other"* reasons selected for detailed analysis (Table 2-3).

3, 4, 5. Color, sex, and year effects on *get out of home* and *independence* as estimated from the model (M) and as estimated from analyses wherein each reason is analyzed separately (S) are shown below:

	Get out of home		Independence	
Odds ratio	(M)	(S)	(M)	(S)
1971:1956	1.4	1.3	.68	.73
Female:Male	1.6	1.6	.66	.65
White:Black	3.3	3.1	.25	.22

Change in—that is, year effects on—mentions of *get out of home* and *independence* accompanied by lack of change in *money* and *"other"* is, it appears, a datum to be explained, not an artifact generated by constraints of the coding procedure. Moreover, distinctive effects of sex and color on each kind of reason are confirmed in the multivariate analysis. The similarity of results from the two analytical procedures is probably attributable to a certain "looseness" in the structure of the answers, which was noted earlier. Apart from the empirical interest in this finding, it tends to justify the procedure of looking at the reasons one at a time; and we shall henceforth employ this more convenient procedure at the risk of some errors in estimating effects of other social characteristics.

EFFECTS OF SOCIAL CHARACTERISTICS

Response differentials by year and social stratum are shown in full detail in Table 2-2 although many differences may represent nothing more than chance fluctuations. Those effects of social characteristics on response that cannot readily be attributed to chance are distinguished in Table 2-3. A quick scanning of the significant effects on response discloses a distinctive profile of social influences on mentions of each work motive. The substantial effects of marital status and religious preference on mentions of *get out of home*, for example, are absent on mentions of *self-respect* that are, in contrast, strongly influenced by employment status and education. Equally important, however, is the finding that the effects of year and sex on response are similar within each social stratum, save for three exceptions.

1. Although 1971 respondents do not differ from 1956 respondents in the frequency with which they mention *keep busy*, the frequency of mention did decline between 1956 and 1971 for each cohort, or group of persons born during the same years. Because each successively younger cohort mentioned *keep busy* more often, the replacement of old by young cohorts in the population resulted in no net change between years.

2. The sex effect on mentions of *get out of home* is unusually pronounced for the cohort born in 1907–1921, whose members were between the ages of 35 and 49 at the time of the 1956 survey and 50–64 in 1971. Women in the cohort attribute this motive to "most working women" more often than do same-sex persons in other cohorts; men in the cohort do not.

3. A religious differential in the year effect on *get out of home* is detected. This motive gained popularity more rapidly among Catholics than within the rest of the population between 1956 and 1971.

All effects of social characteristics reported in Table 2-3 are net of the effects of survey year and sex of respondent, if any, that have been allowed for in each analysis. The question addressed is: Do respondents who differ in marital status, or in religious preference, or with respect to some other social characteristic, differ also in their propensity to mention a given reason why women work?

Cohort

The youngest, or most recently born, cohort identified in Table 2-2 is made up of persons aged 21–34 in 1971, persons too young to have been surveyed in 1956. They also are persons whose attitudes about working women were being formed at a time when the majority held that wives could work for noneconomic reasons and the rhetoric of the women's movement was available. Nonetheless, their responses do not differ from those given in 1956 by members of the earlier cohort then aged

TABLE 2-2

Odds on Mention of Given Reason Why Most Women Work, by Characteristic of Respondent, 1956 and 1971

Respondent characteristic	Reason most women work										Percentage of respondents	
	Get out of home[a]		Keep busy		Self respect		Work itself		Independence			
	1956	1971	1956	1971	1956	1971	1956	1971	1956	1971	1956	1971
All respondents	.19	.25	.075	.067	.032	.039	.052	.067	.084	.061	100	100
Sex												
Female	.25	.29	.080	.060	.032	.043	.045	.063	.071	.048	54	56
Male	.12	.20	.070	.077	.031	.034	.061	.071	.099	.077	46	44
Cohort												
Aged 21–34 in 1971	—	.25	—	.092	—	.044	—	.079	—	.090	—	33
Aged 35–49 in 1971	.18	.26	.11	.055	.038	.055	.060	.055	.10	.040	38	31
Aged 50–64 in 1971	.25	.23	.073	.065	.027	.021	.048	.067	.069	.052	34	24
Aged 65+ in 1971	.14	.24	.033	.033	.028	.019	.047	.068	.083	.053	28	12
Color and marital status												
White, married	.22	.32	.073	.084	.031	.049	.058	.071	.046	.028	67	59
White, unmarried	.22	.24	.070	.050	.034	.038	.052	.079	.089	.056	16	19
Black, married	.082	.11	.11	.049	.029	.017	.029	.059	.27	.15	13	13
Black, unmarried	0.0	.069	.034	.024	.034	.0059	.034	.024	.25	.20	4	9

Employment and marital
status (females only)

Employed, married	.19	.26	.067	.083	.032	.078	.021	.078	.055	.013	12	13
Employed, unmarried	.26	.16	.054	.062	.054	.049	.073	.037	.093	.076	8	9
Other, married	.30	.39	.10	.069	.032	.035	.052	.067	.072	.037	29	24
Other, unmarried	.14	.24	.025	.010	0.0	.016	.025	.059	.079	.095	5	10
Religion												
Catholic	.16	.30	.079	.082	.036	.037	.044	.060	.063	.040	37	38
Protestant	.21	.23	.076	.053	.025	.035	.056	.068	.10	.069	57	51
Other	.069	.16	.069	.079	.033	.079	.033	.058	.069	.079	4	6
No preference	.23	.20	0.0	.087	.14	.047	.14	.11	.067	.11	2	6
Class identification												
Upper	.36	.14	.12	.079	0.0	0.0	.056	.051	0.0	.14	2	2
Middle	.17	.28	.092	.089	.050	.070	.067	.084	.067	.050	35	46
Working	.19	.24	.068	.046	.024	.015	.045	.051	.099	.063	61	48
Lower	.14	.16	0.0	.052	0.0	.012	0.0	.066	.14	.12	1	4
Education												
0–7 years	.11	.21	.076	.014	.021	0.0	.065	.098	.088	.13	13	8
8 years	.19	.24	.024	.040	.016	0.0	.068	.083	.086	.074	16	7
9–11 years	.22	.26	.056	.051	.025	.012	.056	.040	.095	.059	26	22
12 years	.19	.30	.11	.085	.027	.026	.037	.062	.091	.060	29	34
13–15 years	.26	.22	.079	.070	.046	.066	.030	.062	.046	.052	9	17
16+ years	.12	.18	.098	.10	.12	.15	.077	.11	.057	.028	7	12

a This item, but no other, shows a significant change 1956–71 in the total population. See Table 2-3 for indication of significant effects and interactions of respondent characteristics with each item.

TABLE 2-3
Ratio of Fitted Odds on Mention of Given Reason Why Most Women Work, for Respondents with Specified Characteristics, 1956 and 1971

	Reason most women work				
Characteristic	Get out of home	Keep busy	Self-respect	Work itself	Inde-pendence
Year and sex					
1971:1956	1.3	1.0	1.0	1.0	.73[a]
Female:Male	1.6	1.0	1.0	1.0	.66
Cohort					
(See Figure 2-1)	Effect	Effect	Effect	None	None
Intracohort					
change, 1956–1971	1.3	.67	1.0	1.0	.55
Color and					
marital status					
White:Black	3.1	1.0	2.5	1.7	.22
Married:Unmarried	1.5	1.7	1.0	1.0	.56
Employment and					
marital status					
(females only)					
Employed:Other					
Married	.71	.97	2.1	1.0	1.0
Unmarried	.71	4.7	2.1	1.0	1.0
Married:Unmarried					
Employed	1.5	1.3	1.0	1.0	.44
Other	1.5	6.3	1.0	1.0	.44
Religion					
Catholic:Other					
1956	.77	1.0	1.0	1.0	.59
1971	1.4	1.0	1.0	1.0	.59
Class identification					
Upper, middle:					
Working, lower	1.0	1.7	3.5	1.0	.71
Education					
(See Figure 2-4)	None	Direct	Direct	U-shape	Inverse

Note: Effect of each social characteristic is net of effects of year and sex, if any. Estimates of year and sex effects net of a social characteristic are similar to gross effects shown in first panel here, except for year–religion interaction (Figure 2-3).
[a] Significantly different from 1.0 at the .1 level although not at the .05 level.

21–34. In fact, only with respect to mentions of *keep busy* and *independence* do the members of the youngest cohort differ from members of this earlier cohort in 1971. The odds ratio Age 21–34, 1971:Age 35–49, 1971 stands at 1.7 for *keep busy* and 2.3 for *independence*. (Working with more highly disaggregated age data, we find that in both survey years respondents still in their twenties mention *keep busy* and *independence* more frequently than do older respondents; they less often mention *money*.)

The older 1971 respondents belong to cohorts whose members were surveyed in 1956 and for which estimates of both intracohort changes and intercohort differences can be made. In the former case, we ask whether persons born at a given time answered the question differently in 1971 than they had in 1956. In the latter case, we ask whether persons born at one time answer the question differently than do persons born at another time. An intracohort change, resembling the year effect, is established for *independence*. In other words, *independence* lost popularity at the same rate among the groups of persons born at different times. An intracohort change, again similar in magnitude to the year effect, is found for *get out of home*. But, as shown in the upper panel of Figure 2-1, intercohort differences that are contingent on the sex of the respondent also are present in the response pattern. Being a member of the cohort aged 50–64 in 1971 elevates the odds on *get out of home* for women, lowers the odds for men. *Keep busy* was as popular a response for 1971 respondents as for 1956 respondents. The cohort analysis reveals, however, that the odds on *keep busy* decreased for each cohort over the 15-year period. This intracohort change was "cancelled out" by the replacement of old cohorts who seldom mentioned *keep busy* by new cohorts who more often mentioned this reason. Finally, there is the intercohort difference for *self-respect* that is mentioned more often by the cohort aged 35–49 in 1971. Working with more highly disaggregated data, we cannot establish an effect of birth year on *self-respect*, however; and we venture no further comment on what may be only a fluke.

Insofar as the effect of birth year on response can be captured in a linear model, we can describe the cohort effect more succinctly by regressing the logarithm of the odds on birth year. In these analyses, respondents are classified into 5-year birth cohorts; the possibility that the cohort effect is contingent on sex or year is checked routinely. The results can be reconciled fairly readily with the findings just reported, as should be the case.

We reported earlier that young persons less often mention *money* and more often mention *keep busy* and *independence* than do older persons. A statistically reliable linear cohort effect is detected for each of these reasons. As date of birth becomes 5 years later, the logarithm of the odds decreases by .050 for *money*, increases by .093 for *keep busy* (net of year effect), and increases by .053 for *independence* (net of the sex and year effects). We also reported that *keep busy* and *independence* lost popularity among members of each cohort between 1956 and 1971. The intracohort change (year effect in the regression models) is estimated as

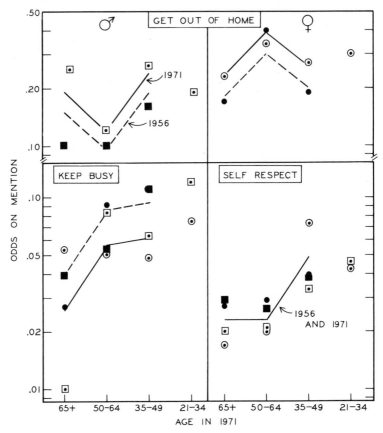

FIGURE 2-1. Cohort effects on response to "Why do you think most women work?" observed and fitted, by sex, 1956 and 1971.

a decrease of .443 in the logarithm of the odds on *keep busy* and a decrease of .516 in the logarithm of the odds on *independence*. These are equivalent to odds ratios of .64 and .60 and are similar in magnitude to the intracohort changes reported in Table 2-3. We find no evidence that the cohort effect is contingent on sex or year. The results reported in this paragraph were obtained by the technique of minimum logit chi-square regression (Ashton, 1972; Berkson, 1953). This technique is especially convenient when at least one of the independent variables is a scaled quantity (here, date of birth) and the dependent variable is a dichotomy. The goodness of fit of the model is measured by the logit chi-square statistic, Y^2, which is evaluated in the light of its degrees of freedom by referring to the chi-square distribution. The models considered here fit acceptably well; we find $Y^2 = 41.70$, $df = 38$ for *money*; $Y^2 = 37.96$, $df = 37$ for *keep busy*; and $Y^2 = 32.53$, $df = 36$ for *independence*.

The initial cohort analysis showed that *get out of home* gained popularity among both men and women in each cohort between 1956 and 1971 and that the cohort effect was contingent on sex. Membership in the cohort born 1907–1921 (age 50–64 in 1971) elevated the odds for women, lowered the odds for men. In Figure 2-2 we display the observed odds for each 5-year birth cohort by sex and year; also shown are odds calculated from regression models that fit the observations for the overlapping cohorts. For men (lower panel), the birth-year effect on response is estimated to be nil. There is, however, an intracohort change that is constant over cohorts, such that the 1971:1956 ratio of

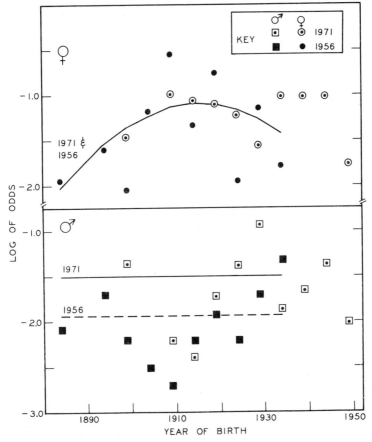

FIGURE 2-2. Cohort effects on *get out of home* as reason most women work, observed and estimated from logit regression, by sex, 1956 and 1971.

odds on *get out of home* stands at 1.6. (For the model incorporating a year effect only, $Y^2 = 20.16$, $df = 15$.) Although all observations for men in the cohorts born 1902–1916 lie below the appropriate regression line, the fit of the model is not significantly improved by allowing for a curvilinear cohort effect. For women (upper panel), the birth-year effect is curvilinear, the odds peaking for women born 1912–1916. We are unable to establish a year effect, that is, intracohort change, or a year–cohort interaction. (For the model incorporating the code for birth year and the square thereof only, $Y^2 = 15.49$, $df = 14$; this cohort effect falls just short of our usual level of significance, with $Y^2 = 5.89$, $df = 2$.) In sum, we can be sure of little more than that propensity to mention *get out of home* is at a maximum for women born in 1910 or shortly thereafter.

Attempts to structure the unambiguously significant variation by age or cohort in *get out of home* have been many and quite unsuccessful. Age groups differ, but the pattern does not lend itself to a plausible life-cycle interpretation. If we are prepared to assume that women are projecting their own feelings about full-time homemaking to "most women," we may have an instance of true cohort differences. This conclusion is reached by comparison of Figures 2-2 and 8-10, the latter of which shows that interest in the "chance to have children" bottomed out for women born around 1910 and then rose to a high for women born in the early 1930s. Perhaps we have here real changes in women's "taste" for homemaking and childbearing.

Marital Status and Color

Respondents are classified as either married at the survey date or unmarried (never married, separated, divorced, widowed) and also as either black or white (not black). The odds on being currently married are lower in 1971 than in 1956 for respondents in each sex–color group, but the decline is unusually pronounced among black women, for whom the 1971 odds on married is below unity. Simultaneous consideration of color and marital status precludes mistaking an effect of marital status for that of color or overlooking an effect of marital status that exists only among members of one color group.

The effects found to be present in the data set can be described rather succinctly. Both color and marital status influence *get out of home*, which is mentioned more often by whites and by married persons, and *independence*, which is mentioned less often by whites and by married persons. Only color influences *self-respect* and *work itself*, each of which is mentioned more often by whites. And only marital status influences *keep busy*, which is mentioned more often by the married. That no interaction effects need be posited to account satisfactorily for the observed response patterns merits emphasis. The effect of marital status does not differ by survey year, sex of respondent, or color of respondent; nor does the effect of color differ by year, sex, or marital status.

Employment and Marital Status of the Woman

The effects of employment and marital status are examined simultaneously, and the analysis is restricted to female respondents. Although the employment status of male respondents is known, the nonworking males are relatively few in number and concentrated in the older age groups. Wife's employment status—perhaps a suitable counterpart to the employment status of the married woman herself—is known only for the married men surveyed in 1971.

A sense of feeling useful and important, *self-respect,* is mentioned more often by the women currently working than by the nonworking women. The workers and married nonworkers mention the need to *keep busy* more often than do the unmarried nonworkers. But the working women less often mention *get out of home* as a work motive.

If working women tend to attribute their own motives to "most women," these findings bear on the accuracy with which the motivation of workers is perceived by nonworkers. On this line of argument, nonworking women underestimate the sense of fulfillment brought by work and overestimate its importance as an escape mechanism.

The Influence of Religion

An effect of religious preference on frequency of mention is detected for only two reasons, *get out of home* and *independence.* The significant contrast is between respondents who express a preference for the Catholic faith and all other respondents. Catholics less often mention *independence,* an effect that might be attributed in part to doctrinal support for the traditional homemaker role. It also is among Catholics, however, that a substantial increase in mentions of *get out of home* occurs between 1956 and 1971. The graphic display in Figure 2-3 makes clear the lesser frequency with which Catholics mentioned *get out of home* in 1956 and the differential change that reversed their position relative to other respondents in 1971.

Class Identification

The vast majority of survey respondents chose to identify with either the middle class or the working class. The responses of the few persons

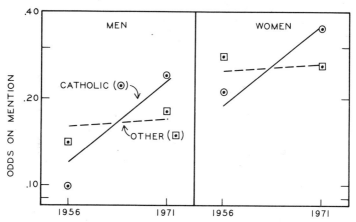

FIGURE 2-3. **Effect of religion on** *get out of home* **as reason most women work, observed and fitted, by sex, 1956 and 1971.**

identifying with the upper class cannot be shown to differ from those of middle-class respondents; neither do the answers of the few respondents identifying with the lower class differ from those of working-class respondents. The odds on *keep busy* and *self-respect* are elevated for respondents identifying with the upper or middle class, and the odds on *independence* are lowered for these classes. Insofar as subjective class identification parallels objective socioeconomic status, the relations of response with class are consistent with the relations of response with education.

Educational Attainment

The influence of educational attainment on mentions of *keep busy* and *self-respect* is unambiguous: Better educated respondents have the greater propensity to mention each reason. The strong, direct, and linear relations are displayed in Figure 2-4. Given these relations, one might anticipate a rise in the odds on *keep busy* and *self-respect* between 1956 and 1971; for the educational attainment of the 1971 respondents is substantially greater than that of the 1956 respondents (Table 2-2). No such increase occurred, and its absence implies that offsetting forces were operating over the 15-year period. But a caution is in order.

Change generated by an education effect, the increasing educational attainment of successively younger cohorts, and the replacement of old by new cohorts in the population come about slowly. A model that fits our observations adequately and allows for both (*a*) the effect of educa-

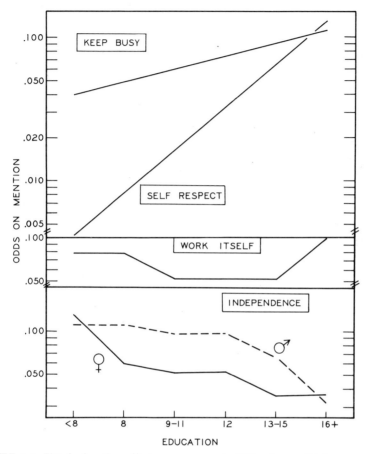

FIGURE 2-4. Fitted education effects on response to "Why do you think most women work?" by sex, 1956 and 1971.

tion on mentions of *self-respect* and (*b*) the education by year by sex relation yields an estimate of .012 as the increase in odds on *self-respect* between 1956 and 1971. The estimated increase is very modest, even though it exceeds the nonsignificant recorded increase of .007. The urgency of identifying the offsetting forces recedes.

The odds on *work itself* are higher for respondents with no more than an elementary-school education and for college graduates than for persons with nine to 15 years schooling. Coincidentally perhaps, a similar U-shape pattern has been observed in answers to queries about job satisfaction. The percentage of "satisfied" workers was lowest among persons with 9–12 years of schooling in two of six surveys and among persons with 13–15 years schooling in three of the remaining four surveys (Quinn, Staines, and McCullough, 1974, Appendix B).

Mentions of *independence* vary inversely with educational attainment for both men and women although the form of relation may be contingent on the respondent's sex (test for three-way interaction yields $X^2 = 3.67, df = 1, p = .06$). For men, the odds on *independence* decrease slowly with increasing education through high-school graduation and then fall sharply. In contrast, the odds fall sharply with completion of elementary school and again with college attendance for women. From an alternative perspective, the sex difference in response becomes negligible at the extremes of the education distribution. We can offer no plausible explanation of the sex-linked pattern.

REJECTION OF HOMEMAKING

The only motive gaining popularity between surveys is *get out of home*; indeed, this is the only instance of unequivocal change. Moreover, only for this motive do we detect differential change; its popularity grew faster among Catholics than among other persons. Women mention *get out of home* more often than do men, and differences by cohort are contingent on sex of respondent. *Get out of home* is mentioned more often by whites than by blacks, by married persons than by the unmarried; but neither class identification nor education influences its popularity. Finally, working women less often attribute this motive to "most working women" than do women not themselves at work. The distinctive configuration of effects seems sufficient justification for investigating further the correlates of this response.

The Religious Differential

Let us take another look at the effect of religious preference on propensity to mention *get out of home*. Our finding is that Catholics less often mentioned this reason in 1956, but did so more often in 1971. Black respondents seldom expressed a preference for a Catholic denomination (about 5% in each year, or a total of 34 respondents) so that, in effect, we are contrasting white Catholics with the black and the white non-Catholics; and we reported earlier (Table 2-3) that the odds for whites were three times the odds for blacks. Possibly the year-by-religion interaction can be illuminated by introducing color into the analysis. We treat each category in the threefold color–religion classification—(non-Catholic) black, white Catholic, non-Catholic white—as a formal variable.

Shown in the upper panel of Table 2-4 are the odds on *get out of home* for 24 subgroups of respondents defined by combination of survey year, sex of respondent, marital status, and the threefold color–religion classification. The corresponding odds expected on the basis of our preferred model are shown in the lower panel of the table. The previous estimates of sex and marital-status effects are essentially unchanged: being a woman elevates the odds by a factor of 1.7, and being married elevates the odds by a factor of 1.5. Effects of religion and color also are incorporated in the preferred model. The odds ratio non-Catholic white to (non-Catholic) black stands at 3.3 in each year. A more rapid increase in mentions of *get out of home* on the part of white Catholics, however, heightens their difference from blacks between 1956 and 1971 (odds ratio White Catholic:Black of 2.1 in 1956 and 3.2 in 1971) and leads to convergence with non-Catholic whites (odds ratio White Catholic:Non-Catholic White of .64 in 1956 and .99 in 1971).

Our initial finding of a reversal in the positions of Catholics and all other persons between 1956 and 1971 can be redescribed as a persistent color effect coupled with convergence between Catholics and other persons in the white population. Moreover, the year–Catholic interaction is only marginally significant in a statistical sense (difference in X^2 between model with year–Catholic interaction and model with additive year and Catholic effects = 3.23, $df = 1$; difference in X^2 between model with additive year and Catholic effects and model with year effect only = 1.35, $df = 1$). Indeed, we must question not only the presence of a year–Catholic interaction, but the presence of a Catholic effect on response.

Before settling on a final description of the religious differential, we estimate the Catholic effect in models that incorporate not only the effects of year, sex, marital status, and color, but also the effect of female work status or cohort membership. In these models, we find an effect of female work status and a sex-specific effect of cohort membership; but our interest here is in the effects of color and Catholicism. The conclusion is unchanged. The odds on *get out of home* for non-Catholic whites are some three times the corresponding odds for (non-Catholic) blacks in 1956 and 1971. The odds on *get out of home* for white Catholics are some two-thirds the corresponding odds for non-Catholic whites in 1956; but the odds ratio is approximately unity in 1971. These effects are the same for working women, women not at work, and men. They also are the same for members of each birth cohort. The statistical reliability of the year–Catholic interaction, or of a Catholic effect, is in serious question, however. (For the analyses including female work status: difference in X^2 between model with year–Catholic interaction and model with additive year and Catholic effects = 2.99, $df = 1$; difference

TABLE 2-4

Odds on Mention of Get Out of Home as Reason Why Most Women Work, by Color and Religion, Sex, and Marital Status, 1956 and 1971: Observed and Expected on Basis of Model

Color and religious preference	1956				1971			
	Male		Female		Male		Female	
	Married	Unmarried	Married	Unmarried	Married	Unmarried	Married	Unmarried
Black	.082[a]	0.0[a]	.083[a]	0.0[a]	.080	.049[a]	.15	.077
White								
Catholic	.11	.062[a]	.24	.15[a]	.24	.17[a]	.39	.33
Other	.15	.21[a]	.37	.39[a]	.27	.16[a]	.40	.24
			Expected[b]					
Black	.062	.043	.10	.072	.074	.051	.13	.087
White								
Catholic	.13	.088	.22	.15	.24	.16	.41	.28
Other	.20	.14	.34	.24	.24	.17	.41	.29

Odds ratios implicit in the model

1956 and 1971	
Female : Male	1.7
Married : Unmarried	1.5
Other white : Black	3.3

	1956	1971
White Catholic : Black	2.1	3.2
White Catholic : Other white	.64	.99

	1971 : 1956
Black	1.2
Other white	1.2
White Catholic	1.9

[a] Subgroup includes fewer than 100 respondents.

[b] Model incorporates effects shown above and demographic constraints (year by sex by marital status by color–religion group associations); $X^2 = 11.46$, $df = 17$, $p > .75$. Alternative model with year and Catholic effects, but no year–Catholic interaction, $X^2 = 14.69$, $df = 18$; model with year effect, but no Catholic effect, $X^2 = 16.04$, $df = 19$.

in X^2 between model with additive year and Catholic effects and model with year effect only = 1.45, df = 1. For the analyses including birth cohort: difference in X^2 between model with year–Catholic interaction and model with additive year and Catholic effects = 2.41, df = 1; difference in X^2 between model with additive year and Catholic effects and model with year effect only = 1.78, df = 1.)

In sum, we have a strong and persistent color effect on response; being white elevates the odds on *get out of home* by a factor of three. White Catholics may have mentioned *get out of home* less frequently than did non-Catholic whites in 1956; if so, by 1971 the religious differential had disappeared.

Sex and Work Status

We reported earlier that women more often mention *get out of home* than do men. Among the women, both married and unmarried, we found that women not themselves working more often attribute this motive to "most working women" than do women who work. Here we introduce color as an additional factor influencing response, take into account the marital status of male and female respondents, and treat as a formal variable each category in the threefold classification—male, employed female, and other female.

The odds on *get out of home* for men, working women, and women not at work in each color and marital-status group are displayed in the upper panel of Table 2-5 for 1956 and 1971. The main features of the response pattern are captured by a model that incorporates the effects on response of color, marital status, and survey year, respectively, along with the effect of being a man, a working woman, or a woman not at work. The employed women more often mention *get out of home* than do the men, with the odds ratio standing at 1.3; not working elevates the odds by a factor of 1.5 among the women. The net effects of color, marital status, and survey year are similar in magnitude to the effects reported earlier (bottom panel of Table 2-5).

The group of respondents who most often mention *get out of home* as the work motive of "most working women" are married white women not themselves gainfully employed. It is easy to imagine that they are using the question to vent their dissatisfaction with their roles as homemakers and that talk of Women's Liberation has intensified their restlessness. The former speculation may be accurate. The second speculation, however, is tenable only if we assume somewhat complicated chain effects; for there is no evidence of differential change by subgroup. Full-time homemakers became more restless; working

TABLE 2-5
Odds on Mention of Get Out of Home as Reason Why Most Women Work, by Sex and Work Status, Color, and Marital Status, 1956 and 1971: Observed and Expected on Basis of Model

Sex and work status	1956				1971			
	Black		White		Black		White	
	Married	Unmarried	Married	Unmarried	Married	Unmarried	Married	Unmarried
Male	.082[a]	0.0[a]	.14	.14[a]	.080	.050[a]	.26	.16
Female								
Employed	0.0[a]	0.0[a]	.21[a]	.31[a]	.15[a]	.068[a]	.27	.25
Other	.11[a]	0.0[a]	.36	.19[a]	.16[a]	.091[a]	.47	.34
			Expected[b]					
Male	.054	.040	.17	.12	.078	.058	.24	.18
Female								
Employed	.072	.054	.22	.16	.10	.077	.32	.24
Other	.11	.079	.33	.24	.15	.11	.47	.35

Odds ratios implicit in the model

	1956 and 1971		1956 and 1971		1971:1956
Married:Unmarried	1.3	Employed female:Male	1.3	Any	1.4
White:Black	3.1	Other female:Employed female	1.5		

[a] Subgroup includes fewer than 100 respondents.
[b] Model incorporates effects shown above and demographic constraints. $X^2 = 13.38$, $df = 18$, $p \cong .75$.

women who did in fact take a job to relieve their boredom with home-making became more numerous; other women and men became aware of the greater numbers of women working for this reason. Possibly so. But our data are not sufficient to build a convincing link between talk of Women's Liberation and the greater propensity of all subgroups to mention *get out of home*.

We can seemingly discount the possibility that the curious sex–cohort interaction effect observed (Figure 2-1) is an outcome of additive effects of color, marital status, and work status on response. Recall that membership in the cohort aged 50–64 in 1971 elevates the odds on *get out of home* for women, but not for men. Systematic analysis is constrained by the fact that respondents with certain combinations of characteristics are few and married working women aged 65 or more are nil. We did, however, classify respondents who had reached their majority by 1956 into 36 subgroups defined by year, color, cohort, and the threefold classification of sex and work status. Implicit in the preferred model, which offers a satisfactory fit to the observations ($X^2 = 27.34, df = 27, p \cong .5$), are odds ratios Working Women:Men of .80 for the youngest cohort, 2.3 for the cohort aged 50–64 in 1971, and .69 for the oldest cohort; not working elevates the odds by a factor of 1.9 among the women in each cohort. Another analysis in which color was controlled by excluding blacks and marital status was introduced as another explanatory factor yielded substantially the same results.

Somewhat disquieting is the fact that we cannot establish any effect of work status on response in 1971 for the respondents too young to have been surveyed in 1956. Effects of sex, color, and marital status on *get out of home* reappear when analysis is restricted to persons aged 21–35 in 1971 (odds ratios Female:Male 1.9, White:Black 2.6, and Married:Unmarried 1.7). We cannot improve upon the fit of the model incorporating only these effects ($X^2 = 7.43, df = 8, p \cong .5$) by allowing for a work-status effect among women or an interaction of work status with marital status or color. Do full-time homemakers forget why "most women" work only as they age? Or have we another instance of a persisting intercohort difference? There is no way to tell until results of a mid-1980s replication are in hand.

Educational Attainment

We reported earlier (Table 2-3) that *get out of home* was the only reason unaffected by education. We know, however, that in the population at large the net effect of education is to increase the employment rate for women (e.g., Sweet, 1970, Table 3); and we have established that working women less often mention *get out of home* than do women not at work. Thus, it seems prudent to reassess the education effect controlling for sex and work status.

The effects on response of color and marital status are controlled by restricting analysis to married white respondents. Survey year, the threefold classification by sex and work status, and education enter the analysis as variables that may influence response. Our preferred model ($Y^2 = 27.65$, $df = 29$, $p \cong .5$) incorporates a year effect (odds ratio 1971:1956 1.5) and a female work status effect (odds ratio Nonworking Women:Working Women 1.7) similar in magnitude to those reported earlier. We find also an education effect that is contingent on the sex of the respondent (difference in Y^2 between model with sex-education interaction and model with additive sex and education effects = 7.91, $df = 1$; difference in Y^2 between model with additive sex and education effects and model with sex effect only = 1.54, $df = 1$). More schooling elevates the odds on *get out of home* for women and depresses the odds for men.

The graphic display of the estimated odds on *get out of home* in relation to education, sex, and work status in Figure 2-5 is more informative than verbal description of the relation. Among women, the odds ratio College Graduate:Elementary-school Dropout stands at 1.4. In contrast, the corresponding odds ratio among men stands at .38. These sex-linked education effects coupled with the effects of being a man, a working woman, or a woman not at work describe a pattern of differentials whereby working women least often mention *get out of home* among the poorly educated, but men least often mention *get out of home* among the well educated. The scatter of points representing the observed odds around the lines representing relations implicit in the model make clear the fact that the model is an abstraction, but nonetheless a potentially illuminating abstraction.

We continue to entertain the notion that working women may project their personal work motives to "most working women." The dissatisfactions with the homemaker role categorized here as *get out of home* were not separately recorded in a 1964 survey in which women who had taken jobs during 1963 were asked their reasons for going to work. Indeed, women might be loath to verbalize their dissatisfactions as a personal work motive. But it is the case that as educational attainment increased, women more often said they went to work because they were "offered a job" or for reasons other than money and personal satisfaction. Their reports are not, then, inconsistent with our finding of a positive effect of education on mentions of *get out of home* for working women. (See Table 2-6.)

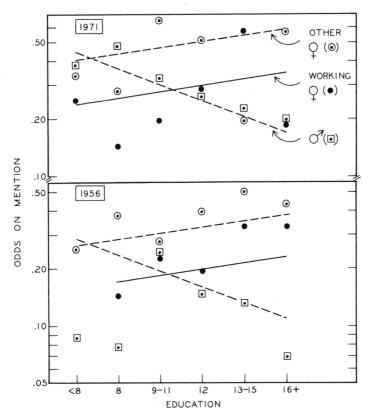

FIGURE 2-5. Education effects on *get out of home* as reason most women work, observed and estimated from logit regression, for white married persons by sex and work status, 1956 and 1971.

In a purely speculative vein, one could assert that the phrase "most working women" means self, if I were to work, and friends who do work for the other female respondents. Thus, the education effect parallels that observed for working women themselves although the women not at work consistently overestimate the importance of escape from the home. For the male respondents, however, reference to personal motives is meaningless; and the image of "most working women" is itself a function of education. If the less educated men view homemaking as the only appropriate female role, gainful work must be seen as rejection of that role. If the better educated men view homemaking as only one of several appropriate female roles, the motivation of the working woman becomes less clear-cut.

TABLE 2-6

Percentage Distribution of Women Aged 18–64 Who Took a Job in 1963 by Most Important Reason for Going to Work, National Sample, 1964

Most important reason	Total	Currently married by education (years)				Never married	All other
		Total	<12	12	13+		
All reasons	100	100	100	100	100	100	100
Money	62	65	69	62	52	51	62
Financial necessity[a]	47	48	52	46	36	38	54
Earn extra money	15	17	17	16	16	13	8
Offered job	8	10	9	11	15	3	4
Personal satisfaction[b]	16	19	18	19	22	13	7
Other reason	14	6	4	8	11	33[c]	27[d]
Percentage distribution of women by status	100	64	27	24	13	22	14

Source: Rosenfeld and Perrella, 1965, Tables 1 and A.

  [a] Includes "husband lost job."

  [b] Includes such reasons as: just decided to work; have something to do; gain satisfaction; and interested in particular line of work. Treated as single category in original source.

  [c] Most respondents (30%) reported "finished school or training."

  [d] Most respondents (17%) reported "husband died or respondent was divorced."

VALUES RELATING TO WORK ROLES OF MEN

An effort to measure adherence to the "Protestant Ethic" in the 1958 survey (Lenski, 1963, p. 89) provides an opportunity to ascertain whether there is consensus between the sexes in regard to the values a *man* should strive to realize in his pursuit of an occupation. To quote the question wording verbatim:

Would you please look at this card and tell me which thing on this list you would most prefer in a job (would want most for your husband's job)?

[A] High income
[B] No danger of being fired
[C] Working hours are short, lots of free time
[D] Chances for advancement
[E] The work is important and gives a feeling of accomplishment

Which comes next? Which is third most important? Which is fourth most important [in 1958: Which is least important]?

Unmarried women were asked the same question as the men. Hence, to insure that all respondents are referring to the *male* occupational role, our analysis is limited to married men and women.

The mean of the ranks received by each work value is shown in Figure 2-6 where respondents are classified by color, sex, and year. The husbands and wives are independent samples from the same population of married couples; there is no matching of responses at the level of the individual couple. We have not carried out tests of the significance of the several differences in mean rank that seem to warrant discussion. However, study of the cross-classification of first and second rankings by color, sex, and year suffices to demonstrate that there are significant differences in the sex effects as between blacks and whites as well as significant differential changes by both color and sex. We shall, therefore, feel free to comment on the more salient differences in Figure 2-6.

Perhaps it is best to note at the outset, though, that there is broad agreement between the sexes within each color category as to the overall ranking of job values. Indeed, among whites, apart from the virtual tie between *D* and *A* for husbands in 1971, there is complete agreement on the ranking *E–D–A–B–C* in both years. (This happens to be exactly the rank order of the values suggested by Lenski as running from the Protestant Ethic to its opposite.) The consensus between black men and

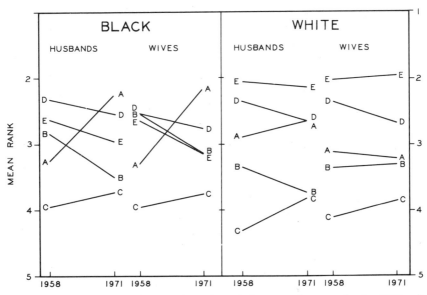

FIGURE 2-6. Mean ranks of work values of married persons, by sex and color, 1958 and 1971: [A] High income; [B] No danger of being fired; [C] Working hours are short; [D] Chances for advancement; [E] The work is important.

women is marred by the disagreement over where to put value *B*, job security. That disagreement aside, they concur as to the remainder of the value structure as well as the striking change in it during the period 1958–1971.

The major sex differences appear to be these. Black wives, as just noted, rank job security for their husbands (*B*) higher than black husbands do, while the men put perhaps just a slightly greater emphasis on chances for advancement (*D*). Among whites, the wives, particularly in 1971, stress high income (*A*) less strongly than the husbands; in the later year, like black wives, they value the husband's job security (*B*) somewhat more highly than the husbands do. Whereas the black wives and husbands show the same changes, at least as far as direction of change is concerned, there is disagreement between white wives and husbands as to the direction of change for three of the values (*A, B,* and *E*). Hence, the locations, on the scale of mean ranks, assigned the five values by husbands and wives are not as closely similar in 1971 as they were in 1958. The aggregate consensus between white men and women seems to have been breaking down during this period, although there is not much evidence that this was occurring in the black population, where the most noteworthy change was the major shift in value *A*, high income, from fourth to first place for both husbands and wives.

Figure 2-7 sheds further light on the differential changes by sex in the white population. It shows the linear relationships of the mean rankings of the five job values to respondent's educational attainment. We note, first, that job values do respond strongly to education. Within each sex, the more highly educated respondents show greater consensus on the rankings than do the less well educated respondents, as is evident from the greater dispersion of the means on the right side of each graph than on its left. Irrespective of sex and year, with increasing education there is rapidly increasing emphasis on importance of the work (*E*) and just the opposite shift for job security (*B*). In 1958, there was a clear rise in stress on chances for advancement (*D*) with increasing education; this was barely in evidence in 1971. For men in both years, increasing education produced a very mild drop in the uniformly low endorsement of short working hours (*C*); but for women the slope of the regression was in the opposite direction albeit, again, very modest.

But the most striking difference between the sexes is the one that occurs only in 1971 with regard to high income (*A*). The mean rank assigned to this value drops sharply as education increases for wives. For the husbands, on the contrary, the regression is in the opposite direction in 1971, while the slope is essentially nil for both sexes in

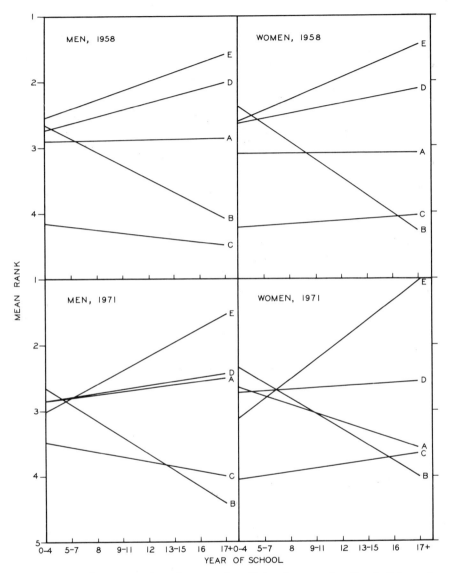

FIGURE 2-7. Linear regression of mean ranks of job values on educational attainment, for white married men and women, 1958 and 1971: [A] High income; [B] No danger of being fired; [C] Working hours are short; [D] Chances for advancement; [E] The work is important.

1958. Between 1958 and 1971, therefore, well-educated wives, unlike the less well-educated ones, came to put less emphasis on high income as a desirable feature of their husbands' jobs. The change gave rise to a salient discrepancy in the way well-educated husbands and wives look at the relative importance of high income—a discrepancy that was not observable among less well-educated married men and women in 1971 or at any educational level in 1958. Perhaps by 1971 the college-educated wife took for granted her own contribution to the family income, whether actual (in the case of the working wife) or potential (in the case of the wife who is confident that she can work if her income is needed), and thus was not so concerned that her husband's job by itself be capable of responding to the couple's economic aspirations. If so, it appears that the husbands were not quite so ready to take the wife's economic contribution for granted. But that, too, could change in time.

THE ALUMNAE

"Like they say, we women are too fragile to take on
a job like that."

Reprinted by permission of *The Register and Tribune Syndicate*, copyright 1975.

3

Constraints on Women's Work

A substantial majority of 1971 Detroit-area respondents answered in the affirmative when asked, "Are there some kinds of work you feel women should not have?" Respondents who objected to women having some kinds of work then were asked, "What are they?" and "Why do you feel this way?" Only a tiny minority offered a comment, such as "well, actually women should not work at all" or "she should be staying home with the kids," which signifies blanket disapproval of women working. We begin our report on constraints on women's work with these observations to highlight the difference between approval of women "working" and approval of women "having any kind of work."

A time series gauging public opinion on this topic over the past 40 years almost certainly would register a loosening of constraints on women's work or growing approval of gainful work on the part of women. It also is probable that approval always would be found more widespread among women than among men. The level of public acceptance of the rights of women as workers, however, would depend heavily on the form of the question. Our confidence in these assertions comes primarily from comparisons of answers to the question, "Do you approve or disapprove of a married woman earning money in business or industry if she has a husband capable of supporting her?" asked in Gallup polls (1937, 1938, 1945, 1969) and the General Social Surveys conducted by the National Opinion Research Center (1972, 1974, 1975), and the DAS question, "Are there some kinds of work you feel women should not have?" (asked in 1956 and 1971).

APPROVE OF WORKING,
BUT OBJECT TO SOME WORK

At the end of World War II, as in the late 1930s, about one-fifth of the public approved of a married woman working in the absence of economic pressure; but, as noted in Chapter 1, one-fifth of the respondents in the 1945 survey as compared with one-tenth of the respondents in the 1937 survey avoided a direct answer. By 1969 a slim majority of the public approved (55%), and uncertainty had become negligible (5%). The trend toward approval continued in the 1970s, perhaps even gained momentum, with the percentages approving rising from 65 in 1972 to 69 in 1974 to 71 in 1975 (omitting respondents not coded as either approve or disapprove).

A loosening of constraints on women's work also is observed among Detroit-area residents between 1956 and 1971. In the earlier year, 20% of the respondents felt that there were no kinds of work that women should not have; 33% shared this view in 1971. Blanket disapproval, on the other hand, had diminished (.5% of the 1971 answers versus 1.4% of the 1956 answers to the question "What are they [kinds of work women should not have]?" were assigned the code *women should not work*).

In both the national and the Detroit-area samples, women more often gave answers signifying support for the rights of women as workers. Distributions of response by sex were published for only one of the early national surveys, 1938. We calculate the Female: Male ratio of odds on *approve* relative to *disapprove* of a married woman working in the absence of economic pressure as 1.4. That same odds ratio holds for the 1970s data sets. For the DAS data sets, we estimate the Female: Male ratio of odds on *no*, there are no kinds of work women should not have, relative to *yes* to be 1.8 in both 1956 and 1971. These findings lead us to think that an appreciable sex effect on response persists, even as approval becomes more widespread. This view is supported by the findings of Entwisle and Greenberger (1972) who studied the responses of boys and girls attending ninth grade in 1968 to three questions about women's role, two of which related to women's work. They report, "There is a marked difference in opinion between boys and girls about women's role, with boys consistently holding more conservative opinions. . . . Both sexes are decidedly on the negative side for Question 1 (women holding men's jobs), with boys about one scale point lower than girls. . . . On the third question (whether women should work) most of the girls are mildly positive, boys are consistently negative, and almost two points separate them [on a scale taking the values 1 to 9] [p. 654]." Is more rapid "liberation" among boys probable?

The findings of Entwisle and Greenberger also bear upon our third general point, that the level of public acceptance of women's work depends heavily upon the question form. Question 1 asked the boys and girls to select between the statements, "Women should do many things including being leaders in politics, the professions and business (the same work as men)." and "Women should center their lives in the home and family and their jobs should be in such fields as teaching, nursing, and secretarial service (different work from men)." Question 3 asked them to select between the statements, "It is not a good idea for women to work. They should devote themselves to their home and family." and "It is a good idea for women to work. They don't have to devote themselves only to their homes and family." Question 3 elicits far more "liberal" responses than does Question 1. Among youths as among adults, approval of women working is apparently often qualified by objection to women having some kinds of work.

We suspect that deletion of the phrase "if she has a husband capable of supporting her" in the Gallup–GSS question would increase the proportion of respondents approving, and striking the adjective "married" might have the same effect. That variants in wording have an impact on response patterns is not in doubt. In October 1945 the Gallup poll, for example, asked not only, "Do you approve of a married woman earning money in business or industry if she has a husband capable of supporting her?" but also, "If there is a limited number of jobs, do you approve or disapprove of a married woman holding a job in business or industry when her husband is able to support her?" The qualification "a limited number of jobs" results in shifts from both the *approve* category (18 to 10%) and the *depends/don't know* category (20 to 4%) into the *disapprove* category (62 to 86%). (See Erskine, 1971, pp. 283–284.)

From the form of the DAS questions, we know something of the grounds of objection. As reported later, the grounds of objection are diverse—threats to the job security of men, characteristics of particular jobs, immutable qualities of women. We do not know why the persons who do not object to women having any kind of work feel as they do, but we cannot presume that they are of one mind on the matter. Indeed, some volunteered comments of nonobjectors (persons who said *no* when asked, "Are there some kinds of work you feel women should not have?") serve as a reminder that the transition from approving to objecting is far from clear-cut.

1. NONOBJECTOR. No kind. If there's something they want to do, they should do it—if they're qualified. Same work, same pay. They should do the same work and get the same pay. But they shouldn't ask for special privileges.
2. NONOBJECTOR. Not if they want it. I may not want certain kinds, but if some want it, they should have it.
3. NONOBJECTOR. If they can train and qualify, they should be able to get the same jobs as men.
4. NONOBJECTOR. I don't really know. No, it depends on her ability. If she can do the job, then she should.
5. NONOBJECTOR. I have never given it a thought. I suppose if they're tough jobs and they're tough—strong enough to take them—I don't see anything wrong.

And, in contrast, a comment of an objector (person who said *yes* when asked, "Are there some kinds of work you feel women should not have?").

6. OBJECTOR. It's the way I relate to a woman. They should be feminine. I can't think of any job that a woman couldn't do if trained, but I wouldn't want to see her doing the ones I mentioned [digging ditches, manual labor, working in sewers, collecting garbage].

At least some respondents framed their answers in terms of personal experiences. One respondent, for example, objected to women having "jobs requiring a lot of physical strength" and explained her feeling by saying, "I did it, and I know." Another objected to women having "factory work" and said, "It's too hard on them. It's a man's job. I worked in a factory before and let me tell you." Or, "Handling steel, quarter paneling, hoods for cars. Women have to do that at [automobile manufacturer]. It's too heavy for them." and "Jobs endangering health of women. I work at [automobile parts manufacturer]. There are many jobs women can handle, but I don't like endangering health. I've talked to them about this." Insofar as the mix of jobs in Detroit is atypical, answers to the questions about constraints on women's work should not be generalized without qualification.

With these cautions about the form of the DAS questions and how respondents seem to have interpreted them, we proceed to examine differences among social strata in the frequency of objection and the grounds for objection.

SOCIAL CORRELATES OF OBJECTING

The 1971 odds on *object* (that is, *yes*, there are some kinds of work women should not have) stand at two to one, appreciable in magnitude even though significantly lower than the 1956 odds of four. The year effect, 1971 : 1956 ratio of (fitted) odds on *object*, is .52; and there is no evidence of differential change by sex. There is, however, a substantial sex effect, with the Female : Male ratio of (fitted) odds on *object* equal to .56. The observed odds by year and sex appear in Table 3-1, and the statistically reliable differences in response are summarized in Table 3-2.

The absence of any well-defined set of differences among cohorts in response has received comment previously (Duncan and Evers, 1975, pp. 154–155). A variety of analyses make clear that neither intercohort variation nor age grading is pronounced in the response pattern although the odds on *object* tend to fall for successively younger cohorts, perhaps more noticeably so in 1971 than in 1956. When the log of the odds on *object* is regressed on year, sex, and cohort, a model that incorporates cohort is found to provide a significantly better fit to the response pattern than does a model allowing only for the effects of year and sex (difference in $Y^2 = 9.39$, $df = 1$); the results are reported graphically in the panel of Figure 3-1 identified as Model *A*. An alternative Model *B* wherein the cohort effect differs by survey year may provide a still more faithful representation of the response pattern (difference in Y^2 between Models *A* and *B* = 3.10, $df = 1$); the results again are reported graphically in Figure 3-1.

The sex effect on response in both Models *A* and *B* is similar in magnitude to that reported earlier, a Female : Male odds ratio of .56. Under Model *A*, we estimate that the odds on *object* in 1971 is just .61 the odds on *object* in 1956 for each cohort. Model *B*, however, implies that opinion shifted more rapidly between 1956 and 1971 for the younger cohorts for those born earlier; the 1971 : 1956 ratio of odds, for example, changes from .50 for the cohort aged 35–39 in 1971 to .67 for the cohort aged 60–64 in 1971. Whichever model one prefers, it is clear that most of the change in opinion in the general population came about via intracohort shifts in opinion, not via the replacement of old by new cohorts. It also is clear that the cleavage between men and women on this issue is more noteworthy than any cohort chasm; the ratio of odds on *object*, Age 21–24 : Age 65+, in 1971 is no greater than the Female : Male odds ratio.

There is a pronounced difference between blacks and whites with respect to response. The odds on *object* for whites stand in the ratio of

TABLE 3-1

Odds on Object to Women Having Some Kinds of Work, by Characteristic of Respondent, 1956 and 1971

Respondent characteristic	Odds on *object*	
	1956	1971
All respondents	4.0	2.0
Sex		
Female	3.0	1.6
Male	5.6	2.9
Cohort		
Aged 21–34 in 1971	—	1.7
Aged 35–49 in 1971	3.9	1.9
Aged 50–64 in 1971	3.7	2.6
Aged 65+ in 1971	4.5	2.6
Color and marital status		
White, married	3.7	1.8
White, unmarried	3.6	2.0
Black, married	5.7	3.7
Black, unmarried	6.8	2.2
Employment and marital status (females only)		
Employed, married	3.6	1.5
Employed, unmarried	3.2	1.3
Other, married	2.8	1.5
Other, unmarried	3.1	2.3
Religion		
Catholic	4.1	1.8
Protestant	4.3	2.4
Other	1.4	1.7
No preference	3.0	1.7
Class identification		
Upper	5.3	2.8
Middle	3.0	1.9
Working	4.4	2.3
Lower	8.0	1.6
Education		
0–7 years	4.0	2.9
8 years	4.9	2.3
9–11 years	4.7	2.5
12 years	3.7	2.1
13–15 years	3.2	1.7
16+ years	2.3	1.5

Note: See Table 3-2 for indication of significant effects and interactions of respondent characteristics with item.

TABLE 3-2
Ratio of Fitted Odds on Object to Women Having Some Kinds of Work, for Respondents with Specified Characteristics, 1956 and 1971

Characteristic	Effect
Year and sex	
1971 : 1956	.52
Female : Male	.56
Cohort	
(See Figure 3-1)	
Color and marital status	
White : Black	.62
Married : Unmarried	1.0
Religion	
Catholic : Protestant	
1956 and 1971	.82
Other : Protestant	
1956	.37
1971	.70
Color and religion for white respondents	
White Catholic : Black	
1956 and 1971	.62
White Protestant : White Catholic[a]	
Male	.86
Female	1.2
Other white : White Catholic	
1956	.32
1971	.74
Class identification	
Middle : All other	.78
Education	
(See Figure 3-2)	

Note: Effect of each social characteristic is net of effects of year and sex. Estimates of net effects of sex and year are similar to gross effects shown in first panel above, except for sex- and year-religion interactions (F : M .68 for WP, .47 any other; 71 : 56 1.1 for White other, .48 any other).

[a] Difference in X^2 between models with and without sex-religion interaction = 4.05, $df = 1$; difference between models with additive sex and religion effects and sex effect only = .56, $df = 1$.

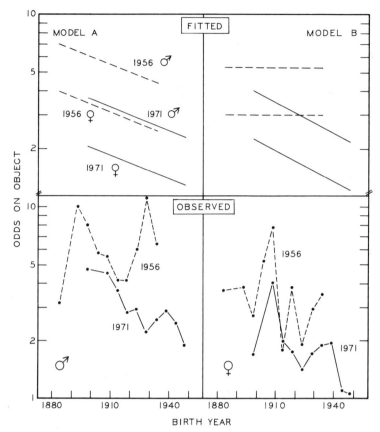

FIGURE 3-1. Cohort effects on response to "Are there some kinds of work you feel women should not have?" observed and estimated from logit regression, by sex, 1956 and 1971.

.62 to the corresponding odds for blacks, and the color effect is estimated to be invariant by survey year and by sex and marital status of the respondent. This substantial color effect and the underrepresentation of whites among Protestants "explains" the religious difference whereby Catholics *object* less often than do Protestants.

A conceptually interesting, but statistically tenuous interaction effect whereby white Protestant men *object* somewhat less often and white Protestant women *object* somewhat more often than do their Catholic counterparts is reported in Table 3-2; but the foregoing statement of no difference between white Catholics and white Protestants cannot be rejected. We can do no more than suggest that the difference between men and women in their views about appropriate constraints on women's work may be especially pronounced among Catholics. The tension between a home-centered role for women and a role that incorporates gainful work might be more salient to them.

There remains a small minority of white respondents who do not state a preference for either a Catholic or a Protestant denomination. The odds on *object* were lower for these persons than for white Catholics and Protestants in both 1956 and 1971 although the difference became less pronounced between surveys.

In sum, there is a very substantial influence of color on response, with whites less often voicing objection. The difference between white Catholics and white Protestants, if any, is modest and sex-linked. The opinions of the small, but growing minority of whites who are neither Catholics nor Protestants have become less distinct.

We find that the odds on *object* are lower for respondents who identify with the middle class and for respondents who are well educated; these effects are summarized in Table 3-2 and Figure 3-2. In magnitude,

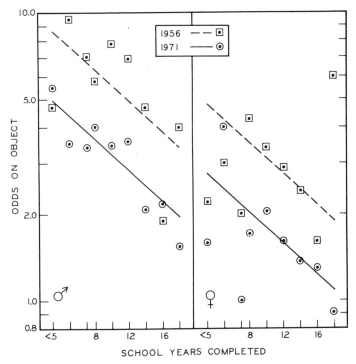

FIGURE 3-2. Education effects on response to "Are there some kinds of work you feel women should not have?" observed and estimated from logit regression, by sex, 1956 and 1971.

however, the class and education effects do not match the effects of sex and color. The odds on *object* for persons with 7 years of schooling stand in the ratio of .57 to the corresponding odds for college graduates, for example. This difference in opinion between groups who differ by 9 years in schooling is no greater than the difference between women and men or between whites and blacks.

Finally, we call attention to the absence of a work-status effect on the responses of women. The odds on *object* do not differ appreciably among groups of women defined by current employment status and marital status (Table 3-1), and no statistically reliable effect of work status, net of marital status, is detected. One might expect that working women would have encountered, and resented, constraints on their work that would lower the odds on *object* for working women relative to the corresponding odds for nonworking women. But, on the other hand, in recounting their own experiences, some working women made clear their support for protective legislation. And the price of protection is constraint, as feminists recognized many years ago.

GROUNDS OF OBJECTION

About four-fifths of the respondents in each survey mentioned either factory jobs or physically hard jobs as a kind of work women should not have, and some analyses of these responses have been reported previously (Duncan and Evers, 1975). Here we have chosen to confine attention to the answers given to the question, "Why do you feel this way?"

The full answer of each respondent was assigned to one, and only one, of the six codes developed for the 1956 study. Our data sets are the 1956 and 1971 responses coded in 1971 using the 1956 coding scheme. The code categories can be described briefly.

1. *Too hard,* or too heavy, or too dangerous.
2. *Injures health.*
3. *Not women's work,* which includes answers distinguishing men's jobs from women's jobs (e.g., factory work is a "man's job— woman should be more like secretary, doctor, or something besides factory work") as well as blanket disapprovals of women working.
4. *Takes men's jobs* (e.g., women should not have factory jobs because "they take a man out of a job").
5. *Degrading,* or coarsening, cheapening, or leading to a loss of dignity (e.g., "Like an article I saw in the news yesterday about a lady brick layer. I don't think that's proper, jobs like that. A woman should remember she's feminine.").

6. *Not as capable,* or not as skilled, or not as stable (e.g., "Women have emotional problem; they are weak. They see problems in a more drastic way. Don't feel it out first. Not as cool as a man.").

Of somewhat special interest from the standpoint of gainful work and the female role is the kind of objection categorized as *takes men's jobs* which seems to assume a limited supply of jobs and a male prerogative thereto. Recall that in 1945 including the phrase "a limited number of jobs" in the question format resulted in a substantial shift toward disapproval of women working.

The distributions of answers by the basis for objection are shown in Table 3-3 for men and women in 1956 and 1971. Beliefs that some work is *too hard* for women and that women are *not as capable* became relatively more popular grounds for objection between 1956 and 1971. Shifts toward these grounds of objection proceeded at the same rate for women as for men over the 15-year period. Their increasing popularity, or greater endurance as bases of objection, possibly traces to some element of biological fact. A response categorized as *too hard* was, "Men have more muscles, and they are bigger." A response categorized as *not as capable* was, "Emotionally women are different. It's been proven that at some times of the month women are more emotional—a physical thing." Alternatively, of course, the shifts in popularity may simply mirror a redefinition of the socially acceptable grounds for constraining women's work. A marginally significant differential change by sex is detected for *degrading;* its popularity fell among both men and women, but perhaps did so more rapidly among women. *Injures health, not women's work,* and *takes men's jobs* slipped in popularity at the same pace among women and men.

In both years, objections based on the feeling that some work is *too hard* were more common in the answers of men than in the answers of women. In contrast, a feeling that women's work *takes men's jobs* was voiced more often by women in each year. Are her fears that "her" man would lose out in competition with women greater than his fears? The *degrading* nature of some kinds of work may have been of more concern to women than to men in 1956; if so, the sex difference in response had disappeared by 1971.

Color

We reported earlier that the odds on *object* were substantially lower for whites than for blacks. Insofar as opinions about constraining women's work are molded by the work experiences of the respondent and her or his intimates, there is reason to suspect differences between

TABLE 3-3
Percentage Distribution of Respondents by Grounds of Objection to Women Having Some Kinds of Work, by Sex, 1956 and 1971: Observed and Expected on the Basis of Alternative Models

Grounds	Observed				Expected, Model A				Expected, Model B			
	1956		1971		1956		1971		1956		1971	
	Male	Female	Male	Female	Male	Female	Male	Female	Male	Female	Male	Female
All	100	100	100	100	100	100	100	100	100	100	100	100
Too hard	43	31	59	52	42	33	59	51	43	32	58	51
Injures health	6	5	3	4	6	6	3	4	6	5	3	4
Not women's work	18	17	13	15	17	18	13	15	18	17	13	14
Takes men's jobs	12	20	6	8	13	19	5	9	13	19	5	9
Degrading	11	19	9	10	15	15	9	10	11	19	9	10
Not as capable	10	8	11	12	8	8	11	12	8	8	11	12

Odds ratios, observed or implicit in model

Grounds	Observed				Model A		Model B			
	71:56		F:M		71:56	F:M	71:56		F:M	
	M	F	56	71	M and F	56 and 71	M	F	56	71
Too hard	1.2	1.1	.92	.81	1.0	.75	1.0	1.0	.80	.80
Injures health	.48	.45	1.1	1.0	.41	1.0	.41	.41	1.0	1.0
Not women's work	.62	.56	1.2	1.1	.53	1.0	.53	.53	1.0	1.0
Takes men's jobs	.43	.27	2.0	1.3	.30	1.4	.29	.29	1.5	1.5
Degrading	.71	.35	2.1	1.0	.43	1.0	.59	.33	1.8	1.0
Not as capable	—	—	—	—	—	—	—	—	—	—

Note: For Model A, $X^2 = 7.83$, $df = 9$. For Model B, $X^2 = 2.23$, $df = 7$. Model B incorporates sex–year interaction for *degrades*, Model A year effect only for *degrades*. Both models incorporate all responses and demographic constraints, year effects for *injures health*, *not women's work*, and *takes men's jobs*, and sex effects for *too hard* and *takes men's jobs*.

whites and blacks in the grounds of objection as well. Cursory inspection of the relative frequency with which respondents in each year–sex–color group mention each ground of objection shown in Table 3-4 tends to confirm this suspicion.

The earlier description of shifts in the popularity of the several grounds of objection between 1956 and 1971 holds for both whites and blacks, although the loss in popularity for *takes men's jobs* was detectably greater among blacks. The sex effect is different within the white population than within the black population, however, for *too hard* and *degrading*. Both *too hard* and *degrading* are relatively more popular among black women than among black men. In contrast, among whites, *too hard* is relatively less popular among women; and *degrading* does not differ in popularity by sex of respondent.

The color effects as such are reported in the bottom panel of Table 3-4. They do not lend themselves to succinct summary since the preferred model incorporates the year–color interaction for *takes men's jobs* and sex–color interactions for *too hard* and *degrading*. *Takes men's jobs* is a relatively more popular ground for objection among whites in each year, but the color effect is heightened in 1971. *Too hard* and *degrading* are more popular among white men than among black men; but they are less popular among white women than among black women. *Not as capable* has greater popularity within the white population; *injures health* has less popularity among whites.

It does not seem too farfetched to argue that the answers of blacks and whites reflect their distinctive labor-market experiences. Relative to the other grounds of objection, for example, *injures health* is of greater concern to the blacks. Black women more often voice concern that the work may be *too hard* physically or *degrading* than do white women. In the 15 years separating the surveys, a fear about *takes men's jobs* became a near exclusive white objection; and the threat of displacement by a woman may realistically be greater for the white man.

Marital Status

A further indication that the objections voiced are, at least in part, situational is a greater concern with *takes men's jobs* on the part of the married. Controlling the effect of color on response by restricting analysis to white respondents, we assess the effect of marital status, sex, and year on the six grounds of objection. The sex and year effects on response are similar in magnitude to those shown for whites in Table 3-4 and are not recapitulated here.

The effect of marital status on response is clear-cut. Only the relative

TABLE 3-4

Percentage Distribution of Respondents by Grounds of Objection to Women Having Some Kinds of Work, by Sex and Color, 1956 and 1971: Observed and Expected on Basis of Model

	1956				1971			
	Male		Female		Male		Female	
Grounds	Black	White	Black	White	Black	White	Black	White
All	100	100	100	100	100	100	100	100
Too hard	41	43	55	26	66	56	63	48
Injures health	11	5	6	5	5	3	8	2
Not women's work	28	16	15	18	15	12	13	15
Takes men's jobs	9	13	4	23	1	7	1	11
Degrading	4	13	19	19	6	10	12	9
Not as capable	7	10	2	9	7	12	4	14
				Expected				
All	100	100	100	100	100	100	100	100
Too hard	46	41	46	30	64	57	66	46
Injures health	12	4	9	5	7	2	5	3
Not women's work	23	17	16	18	17	12	12	15
Takes men's jobs	7	15	6	22	1	7	1	11
Degrading	7	15	19	16	4	9	12	11
Not as capable	5	9	3	9	7	12	5	14

Effects incorporated in model

	Significant effects			Ratio of odds			
				1971:1956		Female:Male	
	Year	Color	Sex	Black	White	Black	White
Too hard	0		x	1.0	1.0	1.4	.67
Injures health	x	x	0	.40	.40	1.0	1.0
Not women's work	x	0	0	.53	.53	1.0	1.0
Takes men's jobs		x	x	.074	.34	1.4	1.4
Degrading	x		x	.43	.43	3.6	1.0
Not as capable	0	x	0	—	—	—	—

	White:Black			
	56M	56F	71M	71F
Too hard	1.3	.59	1.3	.59
Injures health	.50	.50	.50	.50
Not women's work	—	—	—	—
Takes men's jobs	3.1	3.1	14	14
Degrading	2.8	.78	2.8	.78
Not as capable	2.5	2.5	2.5	2.5

Note: Model incorporates all responses and demographic constraints, as well as the significant effects identified above. $X^2 = 18.05$, $df = 20$, $p \cong .5$.

popularity of *takes men's jobs* is influenced by marital status, and the ratio of odds, Married:Unmarried, stands at 1.8 for both men and women in each survey year. The significance of the marital-status effect is not in doubt in a statistical sense (difference in X^2 between models with and without the effect = 7.63, df = 1); there is no support, however, for the intuitively appealing interaction whereby being married would elevate the odds more for women than for men. Apparently fear of the "main earner's" displacement is shared by wife and husband.

Education

When respondents are classified as persons with less than 12 years of schooling, high-school graduates, or persons with some college training, the effects of education on response are found to be several. These effects are identified in Table 3-5, which also shows the relative popularity of each ground of objection for each sex–year group by educational attainment.

The year effects on response for persons in each education group are similar to those described earlier for all respondents, aside from a differential change by education level in the popularity of *takes men's jobs*. At the time of the baseline survey, *takes men's jobs* was a less popular ground for objection among persons who were high-school graduates or had attended college than among persons who had not completed high school. The odds on *takes men's jobs* decreased during the intersurvey period for each education group, but the decline was substantially less rapid for the high-school graduates, that is, persons who had completed exactly 12 years of schooling. By 1971 the popularity of *takes men's jobs* was at a maximum among the high-school graduates. Since a diploma has, in the past, made possible entry into kinds of work where physical strength offers no competitive advantage, equal opportunity policies may have intensified competition between the sexes for jobs requiring a diploma. And since completion of high school, though not advanced training, is as frequent among women as among men, competition may be especially fierce for high-school graduates.

With the possible exception of *degrading,* the sex effects on response resemble those described for all respondents. When we do detect a sex effect on *degrading,* it is in the direction of greater popularity among women. But the effect, though perhaps present in 1956 for all respondents, could not be established in 1971 and, though present for blacks in both 1956 and 1971, could not be established for whites. We estimate this effect as a Female:Male odds ratio of 1.2 for persons in each education group in both 1956 and 1971. The popularity of *degrading* is clearly greater among high-school graduates and persons with some

TABLE 3-5

Percentage Distribution of Respondents by Grounds of Objection to Women Having Some Kinds of Work, by Sex and Education, 1956 and 1971: Observed and Expected on Basis of Model

	1956						1971					
	Male			Female			Male			Female		
Grounds	<12	12	13+	<12	12	13+	<12	12	13+	<12	12	13+
All	100	100	100	100	100	100	100	100	100	100	100	100
Too hard	40	46	49	32	27	37	63	55	58	53	49	55
Injures health	8	2	4	5	4	9	4	4	2	4	4	3
Not women's work	18	20	16	18	19	9	13	13	12	17	16	9
Takes men's jobs	16	5	10	24	15	14	5	8	6	9	11	2
Degrading	10	17	8	16	25	14	8	11	8	7	11	14
Not as capable	8	11	12	4	10	17	8	10	14	10	10	17
						Expected						
All	100	100	100	100	100	100	100	100	100	100	100	100
Too hard	43	42	41	34	34	33	62	57	57	54	48	50
Injures health	6	6	5	6	6	5	4	3	3	4	3	4
Not women's work	18	18	18	18	18	18	14	13	13	15	14	14
Takes men's jobs	16	8	10	24	12	15	5	7	3	8	11	5
Degrading	11	18	14	14	22	18	7	10	8	9	13	11
Not as capable	6	8	11	6	8	12	9	10	16	10	11	17

Effects incorporated in model
Ratio of odds

	Significant effects			1971:1956			Female:Male 1971
	Year	Educ.	Sex	<12	12	13+	
Too hard	0	0	x	—	—	—	.79
Injures health	x	0	0	.43	.43	.43	1.0
Not women's work	x	0	0	.53	.53	.53	1.0
Takes men's jobs		} x	x	.23	.65	.22	1.5
Degrading	x	x	x	.41	.41	.41	1.2
Not as capable	0	x	0	1.0	1.0	1.0	—

	1956		1971	
	12:<12	13+:<12	12:<12	13+:<12
Too hard	—	—	—	—
Injures health	1.0	1.0	1.0	1.0
Not women's work	1.0	1.0	1.0	1.0
Takes men's jobs	.52	.63	1.5	.62
Degrading	1.6	1.4	1.6	1.4
Not as capable	1.3	1.9	1.3	1.9

Note: Model incorporates all responses and demographic constraints, as well as the significant effects identified above. $X^2 = 39.04$, $df = 40$, $p \cong .5$.

college training than among persons who did not complete high school.

The relative popularity of *not as capable* also is influenced by educational attainment. Its popularity is greater among high-school graduates than among persons who did not complete high school and greater still among persons with some college training. We surmise that concern on this score gains popularity with increasing education because the question more often evokes an image of a job where physical strength is not an issue. One respondent, for example, felt women should not have "administrative" work—"can't see them as vice presidents or in top management positions"—because "The ones I've known haven't the capabilities to manage other people. They may have certain professional or technical skills but can't manage people."

Work Status

Working neither elevated nor depressed the odds on *object* for a woman, and we find that her work status has an effect on only one of the six possible grounds of objection. This analysis is restricted to female respondents and considers the effects of work status, marital status, and year on the grounds of objection.

Not women's work is a relatively less popular basis for objection among the working women. The odds for workers stand in the ratio of .59 to the odds for women not at work, and the work-status effect is not contingent on marital status. The model incorporating only this effect and an effect of marital status on *takes men's jobs* fits the observations adequately ($X^2 = 31.09$, $df = 29$, $.50 > p > .25$), and the work-status effect is unambiguously significant (difference in $X^2 = 7.27$, $df = 1$). Recall that answers that implied that women really should not engage in gainful work at all were coded *not women's work*. Thus, our single reliable difference in response between working women and nonworking women may reflect little more than the respondent's reluctance to condemn her own behavior.

A marital-status effect on *takes men's jobs* among white respondents was reported earlier. We find this effect present for both working women and women not at work. The odds, *takes men's jobs:not as capable,* for the married stand in a ratio of 2.2 to the odds for the unmarried. On this issue, wives identify with the interests of their husbands, not their sisters, it would seem.

Age/Cohort

We have left until last an assessment of differences in the grounds of objection by age (or birth year). If the sixfold classification of grounds of objection is crossed with a detailed age classification for subgroups of respondents defined by sex and survey year, the cell frequencies become thin. At the same time, the number of "variables," that is, categories within the classifications, becomes unwieldy. We have, therefore, carried out several analyses, trading off collapsed classifications of the grounds of objection against collapsed classifications by age. We are reasonably confident that two age (or birth year) effects, contingent on sex, are present, involving the responses *takes men's jobs* and *too hard*; possibly two age effects, contingent on survey year, are present as well.

A first analysis retains the six separate bases of objection and uses a threefold age classification, to wit, 21–34, 35–49, and 50 or more. The initial model incorporates the established year and sex effects on response (Model *B*, Table 3-3), the association among responses, and the demographic constraints (now age by sex by year). We then test for the presence of an age effect, either similar for each subgroup or contingent on year or sex, on each of the six grounds of objection taken one at a time. An age effect, contingent on sex of respondent, is detected for *takes men's jobs* and *too hard*. An age effect, contingent on survey year, is detected for *not women's work* and *injures health*. No age effect on mentions of *degrading* or *not as capable* is detected. A parallel analysis using a threefold cohort classification for the respondents who had reached their majority by 1956 yields the same results.

Given the presence of both age–sex and age–year interaction effects on the response pattern, a second analysis focuses on age differentials in response within subgroups of respondents defined by sex and survey year. Age is treated as a tenfold classification, 21–24, …, 65 or more, and crossed with the sixfold grounds classification. The analysis makes use of the fact that the age classification is ordered and asks whether the age–grounds association, if any, can be captured by a model which assumes that response changes linearly with age. Results for the 1971 data sets are clear-cut. The popularity of *takes men's jobs* relative to other grounds tends to increase linearly with age for females, and the popularity of *too hard* relative to other grounds tends to increase linearly with age for males. The 1956 data sets are less tractable. A model assuming only the presence of linear age effects on response fails to fit the data set for females ($X^2 = 73.9$, $df = 40$) and provides a rather poor fit to the data set for males ($X^2 = 53.2$). Further study reveals a linear effect of age on mentions of *too hard* relative to mentions of *not capable* and *degrade* for males, but also a nonlinear age effect on mentions of *not women's work*. Nonlinear age effects on *injures health, takes men's jobs,* and *too hard* appear to be present in the data set for females. The results tend to confirm the age–sex interaction effect on mentions of *takes men's jobs* and *too hard;* and it is presumably the presence of nonlinear age effects on *injures health* and *not women's work* in the 1956 data sets, and their absence in 1971, that was detected earlier as an age–year interaction. The effects detected are displayed in Figure 3-3.

Unfortunately, there is no convenient way to combine the estimates of effects derived from the foregoing analyses of the four data sets. Since sex of respondent has no effect on the popularity of *not capable* or *degrade* relative to other grounds in 1971 (Table 3-3), we might feel

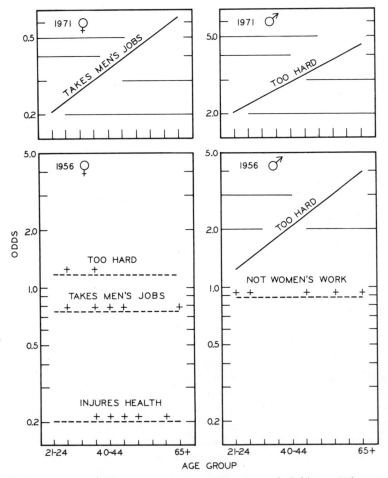

FIGURE 3-3. Fitted age effects on response to "Why do you feel this way?" by persons who object to women having some kinds of work, by sex, 1956 and 1971 (the dashed line locates the odds for all age groups combined; the "+" marks identify age groups with higher odds).

justified in comparing the estimated odds on *takes men's jobs* for females
of a given age in 1971 (Figure 3-3) with the odds on *takes men's jobs* for
males of all ages (our estimate for males at each age given the absence of
an age effect). The estimated Female : Male odds ratio, then, would be
.70 for persons aged 21–24 (.205/.292) as compared with 2.2 for persons
aged 65 or more (.637/.292). The implication, of course, would be that
takes men's jobs is a relatively less popular basis of objection among
young women than among young men, but a more popular basis of
objection among older women than among older men. Following the
same procedure, the Female : Male odds ratio for *too hard* would stand at
1.2 for persons aged 21–24 as compared with .52 for persons aged 65 or
more. A way in which to juxtapose other results is not clear, however.

A third analysis is an attempt to estimate the age–sex interaction
effects on the popularity of *too hard* and *takes men's jobs,* respectively,
relative to other grounds of objection. Our logic is that if age–sex
interaction effects are present, then the sex ratio of respondents in an
age group will differ depending upon whether the respondent answered *too hard, takes men's jobs,* or some other ground of objection. We
then regress the log of the sex ratio (female/male) on age group (scored
0, …, 9), year, answered *too hard,* answered *takes men's jobs* (each scored
0, 1), and another age-group variable with which we hope to capture
the nonlinearity in the 1956 data set for females (scored 1 if 25–29 or
45–49, otherwise 0), and interaction terms formed as products of these
variables. The interaction terms that prove statistically significant are
three: answered *too hard* by age group; answered *takes men's jobs* by age
group; and answered *takes men's jobs* by the additional age-group variable. The results are altogether consistent with the earlier findings, and
we seem to have succeeded in capturing the main features of the four
data sets ($Y^2 = 43.65$, $df = 51$). The aim of the analysis was to obtain an
estimate of the sex effect on response for persons of different ages, and
the results are displayed in Figure 3-4. *Too hard* is no more popular as a
basis for objection among men than among women during early adult-
hood, but it is nearly twice as popular among men as among women at
the oldest ages (odds ratios, Female : Male, 1.1 for persons age 21–24 and
.52 for persons age 65 or more). In contrast, *takes men's jobs* is more
popular among young men than among young women, but less popular
among old men than among old women (odds ratios, Female : Male, .62
for persons age 21–24 and 2.2 for persons age 65 or more). Moreover,
women in their late twenties and late forties seem to mention *takes
men's jobs* with unusually high frequency relative to their male age-
mates. Whether this elevation merits interpretation as a life-cycle phenomenon or whether it is only a fluke of the particular data set is moot.

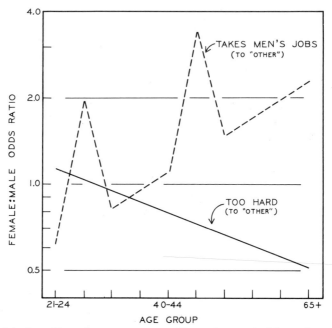

FIGURE 3-4. Sex effects, by age, on responding *takes men's jobs* and *too hard*, for persons who object to women having some kinds of work, estimated from logit regression of sex ratio on response and age, 1956 and 1971.

Summary

Two of the six grounds of objection—*too hard* and *not as capable*—gained in relative popularity between 1956 and 1971. In both years, the popularity of *too hard* was greater among white men and black women than among other persons; and among men, its popularity gained with advances in age. *Not as capable* was more popular among white persons and among the college-educated.

Injures health, not women's work, and *degrading* each slipped in popularity between surveys. In both years, however, *injures health* was mentioned more often by black persons; *not women's work* was mentioned more often by women not at work than by working women; and *degrading* was mentioned more often by white men and black women and by persons with at least a high-school education.

Takes men's jobs underwent a substantial drop in overall popularity. It also was highly differentiated among social strata in popularity. *Takes men's jobs* was relatively more popular among women and among whites. Its loss in popularity was detectably less among whites than among blacks. It is mentioned relatively more often by the married than by the unmarried. Older women mention *takes men's jobs* more often than do younger women, and the response may be especially common among women at the onset and end of their family building. In 1956 its popularity was greater among persons without a high-school education; in 1971 its popularity peaked among persons with exactly a high-school education.

Why does *takes men's jobs* evidence a denser set of relations with social characteristics than does any other ground of objection? Possibly it is because women now have been declared to have a rightful place in the labor market—even though some government policies still implicitly assume a male "breadwinner." The response maintains or gains popularity, in a relative sense, among the subgroups who perceive their interests most threatened by shifting official posture.

THE DECISION TO WORK

For married respondents in 1971, we can explore the relation between attitudes toward women's work in the abstract, the roles of wife and husband, respectively, in deciding whether the wife works, and the actual work status of the wife. All information is provided by one spouse, either husband or wife. (The women's work and decision-making questions appeared in different baseline surveys.) Attitude toward women's work is indexed by the combination of responses *yes* to the question "Do you feel women have special problems in working?" and *no* to the question "Are there some kinds of work that you feel women should not have?" versus any other pair of answers. We assume that respondents who say "women do have special problems, but no line of work should be closed to them" are *equal opportunity* advocates. The decision-making question takes the form, "Who usually makes the final decision about whether or not your wife should go to work or quit work?" for male respondents, ". . . about whether or not you go to work or quit work?" for female respondents. The response options are five: Husband always, Husband more than wife, Husband and wife exactly the same, Wife more than husband, Wife always. Here the responses are grouped as *husband* (always), *shared,* or *wife* (always). Wives are classified as *currently employed* versus other status on the basis of their own reports (female respondents) or the reports of their husbands about them (male respondents).

In a first problem, we treat *equal opportunity* and *currently employed* as dependent variables; sex of respondent and style of decision making are seen as characteristics that may influence the respective dependent variables as well as their association with one another. Aside from demographic constraints, only three effects need be incorporated in a model that describes the data set adequately ($X^2 = 8.33$, $df = 15$). First, the odds on *equal opportunity* are higher for wives than for husbands, with the Wife:Husband odds ratio standing at 1.8. Second, the odds on *equal opportunity* are elevated by a factor of 1.6 if the respondent reports that the decision is made by the *wife* or *shared*. Third, the odds on *currently employed* are elevated by a factor of 4.4 if the respondent reports that the decision is made by the *wife* or *shared*. (Formal partitioning shows that only the contrast *husband* versus *wife* or *shared* is needed to describe these associations.) The possibilities of an association between *equal opportunity* and *currently employed* and of three-way interactions involving sex of respondent or style of decision making were explored systematically. No such relations can be established. The most interesting finding to emerge from the analysis is the impact of decision-making style on wife's work status. Evidently, a report that the husband makes the decision about whether the wife works is tantamount to the husband saying no and the wife accepting it. It is not hard to imagine how this equivalence comes into being. If he says no and she takes a job or if he says yes and she refuses, the ultimate decision was not his. Instances in which he says yes and she sees her work as coerced probably become redefined as a shared decision or are resolved by leaving the population of currently married persons.

In a second problem, the impact of the decision-making style, *husband* versus *shared* or *wife*, along with the educational attainment of each spouse (under 12 years, 12, 13 or more), and the sex of the respondent on *equal opportunity* was evaluated. Of somewhat special interest would be a finding of an interaction of sex with respect to the effect of spouse's education, which would bear on the question of whether the husband's or the wife's education is more influential in shaping the opinions of the other marriage partner. We cannot establish such an interaction, however; nor can we show that the influence of own education on *equal opportunity* differs from that of spouse's education. (Results are based on a logit regression analysis.) The statistically significant effects on *equal opportunity* can, then, be summarized by the following set of odds ratios: Wife:Husband, 1.8; *wife* or *shared*:*husband* 1.45; and for education, 12:Under 12, 1.25, and 13 or more:Under 12, 1.6.

ATTITUDES ASSOCIATED WITH OBJECTING

All respondents in the 1956 and 1971 surveys were asked their opinions on several issues unrelated to women's work. In an earlier report on the 1971 replication (Duncan *et al.*, 1973), four questions common to the 1956 and 1971 surveys (nos. 1–4 in Table 3-6) were classified in the domain of morale, that is, optimism or pessimism about the state of society and prospects for the future. Another five questions (nos. 5–9) tapped the political orientations of the respondent. We see nothing in the question wordings that might lead some respondents to think about women's work, and only one question includes a phrase that might be linked to sex roles (no. 2, "to bring children into the world").

Although the morale and political-orientation questions seem independent of the women's work question in content, respondents who *object* to women having some kinds of work differ from other respondents in their answers to a majority of these "unrelated" questions. Moreover, it is always the pessimistic or conservative position that is endorsed most often by persons who *object*. By way of illustration, for the statement "These days a person doesn't really know who he can count on," the pessimistic response is *agree*. The odds on *agree* for persons who *object* are 1.5 times the odds on *agree* for persons who do not object. Odds ratios measuring the association between *object* and endorsement of what we take to be the pessimistic or conservative position are shown in Table 3-6 for each of the nine morale and political-orientation questions (items 1–9).

The finding of no association between *object* and response to one morale question (item 4) and one political-orientation question (8) is somewhat troubling, for it is not obvious in what respect they differ from the other questions. Somewhat easier to understand is the finding that the association between *object* and endorsing an interventionist policy in foreign affairs (9) changed between 1956 and 1971. Although the locale of the hypothetical Communist take-over is Latin America, the question of whether to send arms or troops must be contaminated with feelings about Vietnam in 1971; and the "conservative" position may well have been transformed from nonintervention to intervention by that experience. On the basis of the consistency of association over questions and between years, one might venture an argument that pessimism, conservatism, objecting—resisting change—"go together," despite a bit of negative evidence.

The relation between objecting to women having some kinds of work and response to a morale or political-orientation question is less simple than the consistency of association over questions and between years might suggest. Substantial year and sex effects on *object* have been amply documented. The odds on *object* fall between 1956 and 1971 and the odds on *object* are lower for women than for men. The odds on a pessimistic answer to a morale question, in contrast, rise between 1956

TABLE 3-6
Associations between Objecting to Women Having Some Kinds of Work and Other Attitudes, and Year and Sex Effects on Each Attitude: Expected on Basis of Models

Attitude (item and odds computed)	Yes, ob-ject:No	1971: 1956	Female: Male
Are there some kinds of work you feel women should not have? (*yes*:*no*)	—	.52[a]	.56[a]
1. These days a person doesn't really know who he can count on. (*agree*: *disagree*)	1.5	M 1.1 / F 1.6	56 1.0 / 71 1.5
2. It's hardly fair to bring children into the world the way things look for the future. (*agree*:*disagree*)	1.2[b]	3.9	1.4
3. Nowadays a person has to live pretty much for today and let tomorrow take care of itself. (*agree*:*disagree*)	1.2	1.9	1.4
4. Most people don't really care what happens to the next fellow. (*agree*: *disagree*)	1.0	M 1.7 / F 2.5	56 .71 / 71 1.0
5. In order to keep America great, which of these four statements do you think is best?			
A. We should rarely, if ever, make changes in the way our country is run. (A:D)	2.3	.43	1.0
B. We should be very cautious of making changes in the way our country is run. (B:D)	1.5	.47	1.0
C. We should feel free to make changes in the way our country is run. (C:D)	1.2	.45	1.0
D. We must constantly make changes in the way our country is run.	—	—	—
6. If a new and appropriate national anthem were written, would you object to substituting it for the Star Spangled Banner? (*yes*:*no*)	1.2	.41	1.0
7. Which of these two kinds of men would make the best official for a town or city government?			
A. A man who is as much like the average person in the town as possible, so that he can understand and help the common man. (A:B)	1.2[b]	.80	1.6

TABLE 3-6 (*continued*)

	Odds ratio		
Attitude (item and odds computed)	Yes, object: No	1971: 1956	Female: Male
B. A man who is superior to the average man in order to make wise decisions for the town.	—	—	—
8. Which of these two statements do you agree with more?			
A. The Founding Fathers had so much wisdom that our Constitution handles most modern problems very well. (A:B)	1.0	.60	1.0
B. While the Founding Fathers were very wise, the Constitution they wrote needs frequent changes to bring it up to date.	—	—	—
9. If a revolution takes place in a country in South America and it looks as though the communist side might win, what action should we take?			
A. Do not interfere.	—	—	—
B. Send arms to the side fighting the Communists. (B:A)	56 .59 71 1.3	Yes .46 No .20	 1.0
C. Send U.S. troops in to fight the Communist group. (C:A)	56 .84 71 1.5	Yes .43 No .25	 1.0
10. Which statement do you agree with more?			
A. The younger generation should be taught by their elders to do what is right. (A:B)	1.5	1.0	1.0
B. The younger generation should be taught to think for themselves even though they may do something their elders disapprove of.	—	—	—

[a] Effect of year net of sex and of sex net of year. For other items, year effect is net of sex and response to women's work item and sex effect is net of year and response to women's work item. Effects of sex and year on women's work item are similar in magnitude when response to other item is allowed for except item 9: odds ratio 1971:1956 of .32 for A, .72 for B, and .55 for C.

[b] Significantly different from 1.0 at the .1 level although not at the .05 level.

and 1971; and typically it is the female respondents who are more pessimistic. Although endorsement of a conservative position in the political sphere is less common in 1971 than in 1956, the opinions of women do not differ from those of men on most issues. Year and sex effects on response to each question are reported in Table 3-6, and the combination of effects observed for *object* is found for no other item.

A skeptic might recall the finding that whites *object* less often than do blacks, suspect that pessimistic or conservative attitudes are less widespread among whites, and conclude that the associations between attitudes for all respondents mean only that "white" attitudes differ from "black" attitudes.

The relation between *object* to women having some kinds of work and *agree* that "These days a person doesn't really know who he can count on," is reexamined in a model that allows for the effects of year, sex, and color, and for white respondents, whether the respondent is Catholic. The effects of year and the social characteristics on *object* and *agree*, as well as the effect of response to one question on response to the other question, included in the preferred model are displayed in Figure 3-5. The model provides a succinct, and adequate, description of the observations ($X^2 = 25.28$, $df = 24$, $p \cong .5$).

Objecting elevates the odds on *agree* by a factor of 1.4 for each

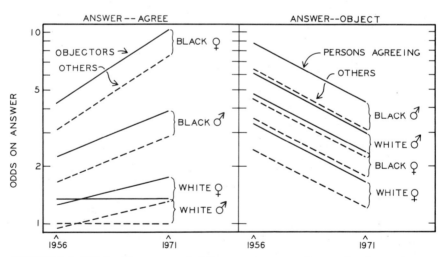

FIGURE 3-5. Fitted odds on a pessimistic answer to a morale question (*agree*, item 1, Table 3-6) and *object* to women having some kinds of work: effects of year, sex, color and religion, and response to the other question.

subgroup of respondents in each survey year, or conversely, agreeing elevates the odds on *object* by a constant factor of 1.4. Thus, the association between attitudes within each subgroup is nearly as strong as for all respondents taken as a single group (odds ratio of 1.5).

For *object* the cleavage in opinion is more pronounced by sex than by color (odds ratios, Female : Male .54 and White : Black .69). The tempo of change in opinion is similar from one subgroup to another (odds ratio, 1971 : 1956 .50).

For *agree* the cleavage in opinion is less pronounced by sex than by color, and differential rates of change in opinion heighten the differences among sex–color subgroups between surveys. The odds on *agree* for white men were the same in 1971 as in 1956. The views of white women were similar to those of white men in 1956 (odds ratio, White Female : White Male .95), but pessimism spread among the women between 1956 and 1971 (odds ratio, 1971 : 1956 1.4). Black men were more pessimistic than whites in 1956 (odds ratio, Black Male : White Male 1.7), and the odds on *agree* increased more rapidly for the black men than for whites (odds ratio, 1971 : 1956 1.8). Most pessimistic at the time of the 1956 survey were black women (odds ratio, Black Female : White Male 3.1), and the increase in pessimism over the next 15 years was greatest for this group (odds ratio, 2.4).

The results suffice to counter an argument that the overall association is an outcome of distinctive attitudes held by blacks and whites, respectively. On the other hand, the attitudes are dissimilar in their relations to time and social characteristics. This renders suspect the notion of a common causal structure for the two items.

The final attitude question outside the domain of women's work to appear in both the 1956 and 1971 surveys asks the respondent whether the Younger Generation should be taught to *do right* or *think for themselves*. One might imagine some link between a respondent's view on the exercise of authority toward the young and the degree to which women's work should be constrained. At least such a linkage seems to have been made in a Supreme Court ruling of 1908 upholding protective legislation for women (*Muller v. Oregon*, cited by Hole and Levine, 1971): "As minors, though not to the same extent, she has been looked upon in the courts as needing especial care that her rights may be preserved [pp. 32–33]." An answer of *do right* elevates the odds on *object* by a factor of 1.5 (see item 10, Table 3-6). We study this association further in a model incorporating the effects, if any, of year, sex, and color and religion and display the results from the preferred model (X^2 = 22.66, df = 23, p ≅ .5) in Figure 3-6.

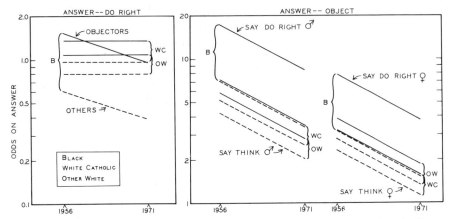

FIGURE 3-6. Fitted odds on the younger generation should be taught to *do right* (item 10, Table 3-6) and *object* to women having some kinds of work: effects of year, sex, color and religion, and response to the other question.

An answer of *do right* elevates the odds on *object* by a factor of 2.5 for black respondents and a factor of 1.4 for white respondents. Although in this instance the association is tighter for one subgroup, the direction of association is similar over all subgroups.

The effects on *object* are familiar. The 1971:1956 odds ratio is constant over subgroups (.48). Women less often *object* than do men, although the sex effect is less pronounced for non-Catholic whites than for blacks or Catholics (Female:Male odds ratios of .66 for non-Catholic whites, .44 for others). (Recall the tenuous evidence presented in Table 3-2 for a sex–religion interaction.) The graphic display offers another perspective on the sex–religion interaction. Among men, objections are voiced less often by non-Catholic whites than by Catholics; but the reverse holds for women.

The configuration of significant effects on *do right* is quite different. The odds on *do right* change between 1956 and 1971 only among blacks (odds ratio, 1971:1956 .64). Sex of respondent does not influence response. In both 1956 and 1971 non-Catholic whites said *do right* less often than did white Catholics (odds ratio, Non-Catholic White:White Catholic .82). The position of blacks relative to the other groups is best conveyed by the graphic display.

Again the outcome is a finding that the association holds among subgroups, but a negative verdict on the hypothesis that the two items have a common causal structure. Our general conclusion, then, is that changes and demographic variations in popular concepts of women's work roles are not merely part and parcel of more general ideological trends and differences.

CHANGE IN THE 1970s

At the outset we reported that the climate of opinion toward women working had become more favorable and ventured the guess that the rate of change was accelerating. We called attention to changes in response to the question, "Do you approve or disapprove of a married woman earning money in business or industry if she has a husband capable of supporting her?" The percentage approving rose from 58% in 1969 (Gallup poll) to 65% in 1972, 69% in 1974, and 71% in 1975 (General Social Surveys). We were especially interested in the possibility of differential change by cohort and sex during the 1970s; and it also seemed important to take into account the labor-force status of respondents.

Figure 3-7 presents in graphic form the results of a regression analysis. We allow the logarithm of the odds, *approve : disapprove*, to vary linearly with cohort and with year. (Constraining both these trends to be linear loses some information, but allows us to focus quite precisely on the differential changes of interest.) The figure shows regressions for women. The same chart will apply for men, if the scale is shifted by .3. That is, the odds on *approve* for women are $e^{.3} = 1.35$ times as high as the corresponding odds for men, irrespective of year, cohort, or labor-force status. There is, then, no differential change by sex.

If we look only at persons in the labor force, however, there is quite a striking differential change by cohort. Cohorts at the upper end of the conventional age range for labor-force participation hardly changed in their attitude toward women's work between 1972 and 1975. But the recent cohorts showed substantial increases in approval over a mere three-year period. The general trend toward greater approval of women working is, therefore, disproportionately due to changes on the part of the younger cohorts, men and women, themselves engaged in gainful economic activity. Among persons not in the labor force, there is also a rising trend of approval with more recent date of birth; but here we do not detect any change between 1972 and 1975 in the magnitude of cohort differences.

Continuation of the trend toward greater approval of women working seems assured for the pattern of intracohort change amplifies the shift that would inevitably follow from the replacement of old by new

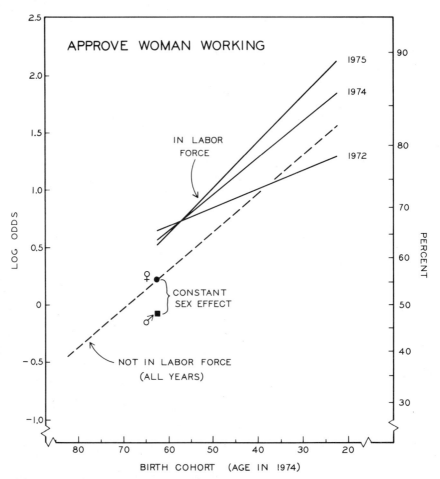

FIGURE 3-7. Fitted odds on approving of a married woman earning money, by sex, labor-force status, and birth cohort, for national samples in 1972, 1974, and 1975.

cohorts. The growth of approval between 1972 and 1975 is the more remarkable given the state of the economy. The Index of Consumer Sentiment plummeted between Spring 1972 and Spring 1974 (see Figure 4-1), and the unemployment rate was in a sustained upswing from Spring 1974 through Spring 1975. Had the public not accepted gainful work as a proper part of woman's role, we should have witnessed an erosion of approval in the face of "a limited number of jobs."

4
The Collective Sadness

Much that has been written to explain the positions of women in the social order and their feelings about these positions does not persuade us intellectually or touch us emotionally. The words of Elizabeth Janeway (1975) do, however, evoke a "so it is" from one of us. She writes,

> [O]ften *his* mind is entangled with the sentiment and principle that appears to be needed by those charged with sustaining and justifying the structure of an imperfect world; the sentiment and principles and prejudices embodied in the mythology of any society. Imprisoned in her image, the feminine mind has sometimes questioned that mythology, turning on it a gaze so bleak, so cynical, if you will, that men who have felt its penetration have drawn back in terror. For this is a view removed from the possibility of action, and therefore from the need to justify that action by setting up pious reasons for its validity.

> We will follow sardonically the course of action, unmoved ourselves by failure or success since we have had no hand in achieving either one and know only that all action ends at last in the grave [p. 168].

For one of us, at least, this is a possible meaning of the mix of diffidence, disengagement, and pessimism that distinguishes the answers of women.

If we believe with Janeway (1975) that *her* "mind has surely seen the world more clearly and realistically than a man can do [p. 168]," we should attend carefully to the feminine vision revealed by the answers. The conclusion could follow from a different premise, of course. One of us prefers slightly the older version of H. L. Mencken (1922): "The mark of that so-called [feminine] intuition is simply a sharp and accurate perception of reality, an habitual immunity to emotional enchantment, a relentless capacity for distinguishing clearly between the appearance and the substance [p. 3]."

WHAT THE FUTURE HOLDS

In responding to "The chances are very good that some day we'll have another depression as bad as the one in the thirties," women were more pessimistic than men in both 1959 and 1971. The odds, *agree:disagree* were .58 and .72, respectively, for men and women in the earlier year and .70 and 1.36 in the later year. Hence, the Female:Male odds ratio was 1.2 in 1959 and 1.9 in 1971. Or, to state the same interaction the other way around, the 1971:1959 odds ratio was 1.2 for men as compared with 1.9 for women. (It is only a coincidence that the two ways of expressing the odds ratios give the same numerical values.) The three-way interaction is not quite significant by our usual standard; a model allowing for separate sex and year effects yields $X^2 = 3.6, df = 1, p = .06$. If we accept the latter model, so as to average out the differential changes, we estimate the Female:Male odds ratio as 1.8 for both years and the 1971:1959 odds ratio as 1.5 for both sexes. That women see the prospect of another major depression as more real is not in doubt, however.

The direction of the year effect in these data is consistent with movements of the Index of Consumer Sentiment of the Institute for Social Research, which was around 93 at the time of the 1959 DAS survey and about 82 when the 1971 interviewing was done (Figure 4-1). The differential change by sex (if it is real) is not so easy to explain by changes in the national economic climate. Either the changes must affect the sexes differently, as would be true of unemployment, or the meaning read into the changes depends upon the sex of the reader, as might be true of common stock prices. Only the former possibility can be checked. Unemployment statistics do suggest that the rate for adult women was slightly higher in 1971 than in 1959, whereas the reverse was true for men. The differences are not large, however. The unemployment rate was higher for women than for men in both years, but we cannot establish that this factor accounts for the sex difference in our data.

A quite different kind of explanation becomes tenable if one can

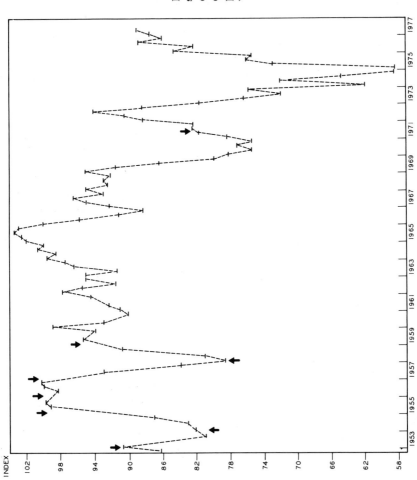

FIGURE 4-1. Index of consumer sentiment, 1952–1977, plotted by quarter in which survey occurred, with arrow denoting approximate timing of DAS surveys.

believe that economists are scientists. Will a major depression come some day? "Some day" may be too far distant for the current behavior of the economy to inform us of the chances for depression. Our estimate of the chances, then, must reflect our faith in economists who say they know how to avert economic disaster. And confidence that science can solve problems is less widespread among women and in 1971.

Respondents were presented with this statement that deals with the indefinite future: "Given enough time and money, almost all of man's important problems can be solved by science." Response alternatives were strongly agree, agree, disagree, and strongly disagree. No sex or year effects were found for the use of the modifier "strongly," so the answers may be dichotomized without loss of relevant information. The *agree*:*disagree* ratio was lower for women than for men in both years and lower in 1971 than in 1959 for both sexes. Although the observed odds suggest that dissent from the proposition developed more rapidly among women, there is insufficient evidence to warrant a conclusion that the changes occurred at different rates for men and women. Hence we estimate the odds ratios as .67 for the sex effect (Female:Male) in both years and .60 for the year effect (1971:1959) for both sexes. Again the evidence is that women are more pessimistic than men about the long-run outlook for the world.

A third question on long-term future prospects is "What would you say are the chances that the United States will be in an atomic war with Russia in the next 25 years?" Here we cannot be quite so unequivocal as to the sex difference in pessimism. It should be noted, first, that women were much more likely to avoid a direct answer to this question; the odds on *don't know* were over four times as great for women as for men, pooling the data for the 2 years in the absence of any significant change in those odds. Among respondents accepting one of the five predesignated answer categories, women were disproportionately represented in the three intermediate categories, while men more often saw *no chance at all* but also were at least as likely as women to consider atomic war *certain*. One way of describing the distributions, shown in Figure 4-2, is to note that the ratio of women to men does not vary significantly over the three intermediate categories. Neither does the ratio of women to men differ as between the two extreme categories. But men use the extremes more while women use the intermediate answers more. This summary may be misleading, however, in view of the small absolute numbers who are *certain* of atomic war, irrespective of sex. Possibly women are both more pessimistic and less inclined to make extreme estimates, but these data do not lend themselves to definitive estimation of the strength of the two somewhat contrary tendencies.

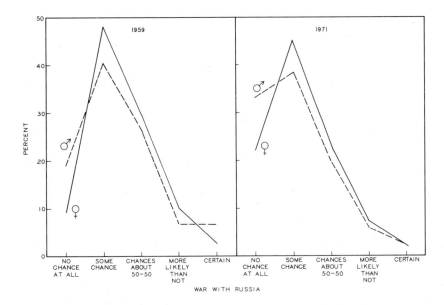

FIGURE 4-2. Frequency distribution of responses to ". . . chances that the United States will be in an atomic war with Russia in the next 25 years," by sex, 1959 and 1971.

Greater pessimism among women on this general topic has not gone unnoted. In the summary of findings of The Gallup Poll, typically no information is provided about differentials in response over population subgroups. In the summary of "September 28, Chances of Another War" in the year 1955, however, a sex difference receives comment. The questions asked were, first, "Now that Russia and other countries have atom and hydrogen bombs, do you think the chances of another war are greater or less?" and, second, "If an all-out atom and hydrogen bomb war should occur between Russia and the United States, do you think all mankind would be destroyed, or not?" The accompanying text says, "Women are considerably more pessimistic than men on both questions. Whereas only 2 men in every 10 (21%) feel that the chance of another war is greater now that others have nuclear weapons, 3 women in 10 (31%) feel that way. By roughly the same proportion, more women than men believe that all mankind might be destroyed in the event of all-out atomic warfare between East and West [Gallup, 1972, p. 1365]."

Included in the General Social Surveys of 1973 and 1976 was the question, "Do you expect the United States to fight in another war within the next ten years?" Women and men answer the question differently. Neither group is sanguine; the observed odds *yes*:*no* stood at 1.37 for men in 1973 and 1.82 in 1976, at 1.64 for women in 1973 and 1.47 in 1976. The sex effect on response, net of any effects of year, color, and marital status, is not pronounced for the contrast *yes : no* (Female : Male odds ratio 1.05), but rather for the *don't know : no* contrast (Female : Male odds ratio 1.9). As was the case among Detroit-area residents, women are less willing to give a direct answer; but whether they can be said to be more pessimistic depends on the meaning attached to *don't know*. The sex–year interaction, suggested by the observed odds, is marginally significant in the statistical sense ($X^2 = 5.02$, $df = 2$). Between 1973 and 1976, the Female : Male ratio of odds *yes : no* decreased from an estimated 1.2 to .795 and the ratio of odds *don't know : no* decreased from an estimated 2.3 to 1.4. If this differential change is to be taken seriously, we should have to say that events of 1973–1976 were less threatening to women than to men. Or perhaps the doubt of women has greater constancy, while the moods of men swing with the times.

Perhaps questions linking the possibility of war to the use of nuclear weapons evoke a particularly strong sex effect. In September 1945 and again one year later, the National Opinion Research Center asked, "In the long run, do you think people everywhere will be better off or worse off because somebody learned how to split the atom?" The answers (reported in Cantril and Strunk, 1951, p. 26) leave little doubt that the scientific breakthrough was no cause for optimism among women.

	Odds relative to *better off*								
	Worse off			No difference			Don't know		
	F	M	F:M	F	M	F:M	F	M	F:M
1945	.44	.33	1.3	.12	.11	1.2	.52	.32	1.6
1946	1.37	.74	1.8	.20	.11	1.8	.77	.33	2.4

A supposedly benign use of nuclear energy currently elicits less favorable response from women than from men. A report of a "recent public opinion survey" in Britain (*Science*, 6 May 1977) indicates that while the "British show a somewhat grudging acceptance of nuclear power," the proportion of men favoring the building of more nuclear plants was 58%, as against 41% of women. United States data from Harris surveys in 1975 and 1976 (Table 4-1, Question [A]) show much the same difference in proportion favoring nuclear expansion. Also noteworthy in the American figures is the much larger fraction of women who did not answer the question as posed and were, under the

TABLE 4-1
Percentage Distributions of Responses to Selected Questions on Nuclear Energy, by Sex, from 1975 and 1976 Harris Surveys of National Samples

Question	1975 Male	1975 Female	1976 Male	1976 Female
[A] In general, do you favor or oppose the building of more nuclear power plants in the United States?				
Favor	73	54	70	52
Oppose	16	21	19	25
Not sure	11	25	11	23
[B] Would you personally favor or oppose having nuclear power as the main source of energy for the electric power you use in your community?				
Favor	66	43	58	41
Oppose	21	27	29	33
Not sure	13	30	13	26
[C] All in all, from what you have heard or read, how safe do you think nuclear power plants that produce electric power are?				
Very safe	38	15	34	16
Somewhat safe	35	42	38	39
Not so safe	10	15	14	17
Dangerous (vol.)	5	5	6	9
Not sure	12	23	8	19

Source: Harris and Associates, 1976.

coding rules of the Harris organization, classified as "not sure." We think that this category includes a mixture of persons who really have not thought about the issue (or are not informed about it, or have little interest in it) and those who wish to express some reservation short of outright opposition. It is interesting that among both men and women *not sure* is more frequent when, as in Question [B], the reference is not to the United States but to the respondent's own community. We doubt that they are less involved in what happens locally.

Taking note of the Harris results and other evidence on the sex difference, Kasperson *et al.* (1976) suggest that one source of it is the safety issue. They observe that women are less favorable toward capital punishment than men, are less prone to violence and more concerned about loss of life. If women make a connection between nuclear weapons and nuclear plants, supposing that the latter too can "explode," they would be disposed to question the use of nuclear energy. It is true that women are more pessimistic about nuclear safety, as may be seen from Question [C] in the Harris data. In particular, the proportion who see nuclear plants as *very safe* is much lower for women, while again the proportion *not sure* is much greater. It is also true that for all respondents there is an association of the assessment of safety with the view on the advisability of building more plants. But as Figure 4-3 indicates, the sex difference on each question is preserved when the two questions are cross-classified. Thus, even if they agree that nuclear plants are *very safe,* women are more likely to oppose building additional plants than are men.

There are other possible explanations of the sex difference. One that we investigated, making use of unpublished tabulations from the 1975 Harris survey, is that women have less confidence in the nation's nuclear engineers. The question reads, "In your judgement, if the U.S. decided it wanted to depend much more on nuclear power for electricity,

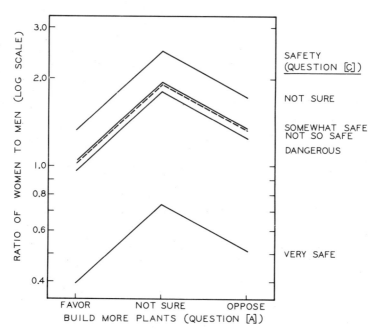

FIGURE 4-3. Sex differences in response to questions on nuclear power and plant safety, for national sample, 1975 (Harris data).

do you think we now have the technical know-how to build enough nuclear plants that could meet our electric power needs, or do you think the technology has not yet been developed?" Ratios of women to men within answer categories are .87 for *have the technical know-how now,* 1.1 for *technology not yet developed,* and 2.0 for *not sure.* There is a sex difference in the anticipated direction; but with the *not sure* respondents omitted, it is only marginally significant ($.05 < p < .1$). Clearly, women's reservations about nuclear expansion must reflect something more than their skepticism about technical feasibility.

In a further analysis, the details of which will not be shown, we analyzed Questions [A] and [C] in relation to education as well as sex, using the 1975 Harris data tape. Among both women and men, the ratio of *oppose* to *favor* building more plants rises with education, but there is a constant sex effect at all education levels; for both sexes, the ratio *not sure : favor* declines as education increases, the decline being somewhat more rapid for men. Especially at the highest education levels, where an explanation in terms of simple ignorance becomes less plausible, women more often are *not sure* on this matter. This is perhaps our best support for the conjecture that *not sure* is as much a way of stating reservations as it is a sign of disinterest. As far as safety (Question [C]) is concerned, the sex difference does not interact with education. Again, the evidence speaks to the inadequacy of a purely cognitive explanation of the divergence of female and male views on matters nuclear. We have encountered an explanation of this divergence that attributes it to the "lioness syndrome," and it is perhaps just as well to leave it at that until such time as all the divers differences noted in this chapter have been reduced to some rational pattern.

Currently women more often endorse a policy of isolation than do men. A question in the 1973 and 1976 General Social Surveys was "Do you think it will be best for the future of this country if we take an active part in world affairs, or if we stay out of world affairs?" The sex effect on response, net of any effects of year, color, and marital status, is captured in the Female:Male ratios of (fitted) odds: 1.7 for *stay out* relative to *active part* and 2.4 for *don't know* relative to *active part.*

We located findings from several earlier surveys that show women more loath to endorse military involvement. A 1936 survey, for example, asked "Would you be willing to fight, or to have a member of your family fight, in case a foreign power tried to seize land in Central or South America?" We calculate the Female:Male ratio of odds as 2.6 for *no : yes* and 2.2 for *don't know : yes* (see Cantril and Strunk, 1951, p. 780). An example from the postwar period is a 1951 survey in which respondents were asked, "Do you think the United States should keep all of her troops over here and defend only North and South America, or do you think we should send more troops to Europe to be ready to help fight communism there?" The ratio of odds, Female:Male, are 1.6 for *keep here:send* and 1.9 for *don't know:send* (see Gallup, 1972, p. 961).

Responses to an October 1939 survey question suggest that more is at stake than the thought of battle casualties. Respondents were asked, "Which of these courses of action comes closest to describing what the United States should do?" Seven alternatives were presented, and we have calculated the ratio of women to men in each response category. The women/men ratio is at a maximum, 2.2, for *don't know* and is in excess of unity, 1.5, for only one other category—*Refuse any aid of any kind to either side, and refuse to sell anything at all to either side*. With women/men ratios near unity were the categories, *Enter the war on the side of England, France, and Poland only if it looks as though they were losing, and in the meantime help that side with food and materials, Do not enter the war, but supply EFP with materials and food, and refuse to ship anything to Germany*, and *Find some way of supporting Germany*. The response categories in which women were underrepresented were *Take no sides, and offer to sell to anyone, but on cash-and-carry basis* (ratio .71), *Enter the war at once, but send only our navy and air force to help EFP* (.33), and *Enter the war at once on the side of EFP, and send an army to Europe* (.30). (See Cantril and Strunk, 1951, p. 969.) It would seem that for some 40 years women have more often endorsed a policy of isolation.

These results of other surveys are of considerable interest, because the 1956 and 1971 DAS surveys included a question about the appropriate stance of the United States in the face of a hypothetical communist takeover in South America. The interviewer said,

> Here is a possible situation. There is no right or wrong answer, but we are interested in knowing how you feel about it.
>
> If a revolution takes place in a country in South America and it looks as though the communist side might win, what action should we take?
>
> 1. Do not interfere.
> 2. Send arms to the side fighting the communists.
> 3. Send U.S. troops in to fight the communist group.

The noninterventionist position gained in popularity between 1956 and 1971, perhaps reflecting disenchantment with intervention in Vietnam. The significant contrast is between *Arms/Troops* and *Do not interfere;* the ratio of odds on *Do not interfere*, 1971:1956, stands at 2.7. But there is no evidence of differential change in opinion by sex, nor does sex influence response in either year. We simply do not know why men and women answer this question in the same way. Indeed they do so whether they belong to the "new" cohorts who entered the survey population between 1956 and 1971 or to the older cohorts.

As if to confirm their pessimism about prospects of depression, their skepticism about the problem-solving ability of science, and uncertainty about war, women more often foresee a bleak future for "children born today." Their response pattern on this item is described later, along with responses to other items drawn from Srole's anomia scale. Perhaps the women are anomic; perhaps they are only describing the future "clearly and realistically," in the phrase of Janeway.

DISENGAGEMENT

We have a number of questions which bear on people's confidence in their fellows. We certainly would not maintain that these questions are interchangeable or get at the same thing, whatever that thing may be. Whenever we encounter differential change by sex in response to one of these questions, however, it is clear that disengagement is proceeding more rapidly among women.

Are "most people" more inclined to help others than look out for themselves, and can they be trusted? In 1959 we would have said that women's belief in the goodness of human nature surpasses that of men; now we are less certain. The full questions and a summary of responses are given in Table 4-2. A third response category, *it depends,* is found to behave like an intermediate category as far as sex differences are concerned and so is omitted for convenience. Confidence that most people are inclined to help others diminished between 1959 and 1971, but did so no more rapidly among women than among men. Women remain more confident on this score. In contrast, the deterioration in trust was much more rapid for women than for men. There is a highly significant three-way interaction; a model allowing for additive year and sex effects yields $X^2 = 9.0$, $df = 1$. Indeed, the direction of the sex difference is reversed. In 1959 women were more trusting than men, in 1971 less so. (We refer to this kind of result, informally, as a "vicious" interaction.)

The first four items in Table 4-3 are drawn from Srole's anomia scale. The fifth was introduced in the 1958 DAS in an attempt to circumvent what was thought to be a tendency for some respondents to give acquiescent responses. The increase in anomia (as measured by these items) in Detroit between the late 1950s and 1971 has been analyzed by Fischer (1974a) who did not, however, analyze the responses by sex. Three items show differential change by sex, and for each, the shift in

TABLE 4-2
Sex Differences in Confidence in Human Nature, 1959 and 1971

Question wording, response, sex	1959	1971	1971:1959
Would you say that most people are more inclined to help others, or are they more inclined to look out for themselves?			
help others:look out for themselves			
Observed odds			
Male	.46	.17	.36
Female	.56	.27	.48
Fitted odds			
Male	.42	.17	.42
Female	.64	.27	.42
Female:Male	1.5	1.5	1.0
In general, do you think that most people can be trusted, or do you feel that a person can't be too careful in his dealings with others?			
most can be trusted:can't be too careful			
Observed odds			
Male	.90	.74	.83
Female	1.29	.53	.41
Female:Male	1.4	.71	.50

the anomic direction was more pronounced for women than for men. In the case of "Most people don't really care what happens to the next fellow," the change eliminated the sex difference observed in the 1950s when women were less anomic than men. For both "These days a person doesn't really know whom he can count on" and "It's hardly fair to bring children into the world the way things look for the future," there was no significant sex difference in the 1950s; but by 1971 women gave the more anomic responses. The other two items ("Nowadays a person has to live pretty much for today and let tomorrow take care of itself" and "Children born today have a wonderful future to look forward to") showed no differential change, but on all occasions elicited more anomic responses from women.

Four of the five items in Table 4-4 are discussed by Converse as indicators of the respondent's "sense of political efficacy." He notes that other writers put somewhat different interpretations on these items, but contends that the general notion underlying them is seen in much the same way. By whatever terms the items are described—as measures of competence, efficacy, or alienation—they have to do with the fact that "people differ markedly in the degree to which they feel

TABLE 4-3
Odds Ratios, Female:Male, Computed from Expected Frequencies under Preferred Model, for Responses to Anomia Items, 1956–1971

Item	1956	1958	1959	1971
1. Nowadays a person has to live pretty much for today and let tomorrow take care of itself.				
agree:disagree	1.3	1.3	1.3	1.3
2. Most people don't really care what happens to the next fellow.				
agree:disagree	.73	.73	—	1.0
3. These days a person doesn't really know whom to count on.				
agree:disagree	1.0	1.0	1.0	1.4
4. It's hardly fair to bring children into the world the way things look for the future.				
agree:disagree	1.0	1.0	1.0	1.5
5. Children born today have a wonderful future to look forward to.				
agree:disagree	—	1.65	—	1.65

confident about participating in politics and getting some meaningful response from 'the system' " (Converse, 1972, p. 325). The first item, not one of the set discussed by Converse, invites the respondent to reject one of the cardinal injunctions of a democratic political system—that everyone must vote. Perhaps because of its normative component, it receives little endorsement; and there are no significant sex differences in either 1954 or 1971. Only one item decisively exhibits a sex effect and differential change by sex; it is number (3). Women agree more often than men with the proposition that "a person like me" cannot really understand what is going on in politics and government. Women are more strongly differentiated from men by their answers in 1971 than in 1954. The remaining items do show sex differences, although in order to detect them we must partition the response categories in just the right manner. In each case the women give a somewhat more alienated response or signify a lowered sense of political efficacy.

Willingness to confess inability to understand what the government

TABLE 4-4

Observed Response Distributions, in Percentages, and Fitted Sex Ratios, for Five Political Efficacy Indicators, 1954 and 1971

Question	Year	Sex	Response SA	A	D	SD	Total	(N)
1. So many other people	1954	M	2.6	7.0	42.2	48.1	100.0	(341)
vote in elections that		F	2.6	6.8	42.6	47.9	100.0	(380)
it doesn't matter much	1971	M	2.2	10.5	56.7	30.5	100.0	(825)
whether I vote or not.		F	2.2	10.0	55.4	32.4	100.0	(1045)
2. People like me don't	1954	M	2.9	17.4	52.4	27.4	100.0	(340)
have any say about what		F	1.9	19.7	53.2	25.3	100.0	(376)
the government does.	1971	M	4.6	28.7	57.0	9.6	100.0	(821)
		F	6.0	31.5	54.6	8.0	100.0	(1041)
3. Sometimes politics and	1954	M	5.3	58.4	29.3	7.0	100.0	(341)
government seem so com-		F	10.3	59.5	23.0	7.1	100.0	(378)
plicated that a person	1971	M	13.2	47.8	33.7	5.4	100.0	(820)
like me can't really		F	16.2	59.2	21.8	2.9	100.0	(1043)
understand what is going								
on.								
4. Voting is the only way	1954	M	11.6	52.5	32.2	3.6	100.0	(335)
that people like me can		F	13.2	52.7	30.0	4.1	100.0	(370)
have any say about how	1971	M	12.7	47.2	34.1	6.0	100.0	(818)
the government runs		F	12.4	49.0	35.3	3.4	100.0	(1041)
things.								
5. I don't think public	1954	M	4.8	23.3	58.3	13.6	100.0	(331)
officials care about		F	8.2	19.8	57.9	14.1	100.0	(368)
what people like me	1971	M	7.4	40.3	48.3	3.9	100.0	(813)
think.		F	8.9	41.9	45.5	3.8	100.0	(1038)
Fitted ratio, F:M								
(1)	1971		1.3	1.3	1.3	1.3	—	—
(2)	1971		1.4	1.4	1.2	1.2	—	—
(3)	1954		1.2	1.2	.92	.92	—	—
	1971		1.6	1.6	.80	.80	—	—
(4)	1971		1.3	1.3	1.3	.85	—	—
(5)	1971		1.7	1.2	1.2	1.2	—	—

is doing may be more characteristic of women on specific issues as well. For example, ''Do you feel that you have a clear idea of what the Vietnam war is all about—that is, what we are fighting for,'' was asked in a 1967 Gallup Poll. Responses are reported as 56% *no* for women (4% expressing no opinion), in contrast to 39% *no* for men (3% no opinion) (Gallup, 1972, pp. 2068–2069).

In sum, by the late 1950s, women were (*a*) more likely than men to think one must live for today and let tomorrow take care of itself, (*b*) more doubtful than men that children being born faced a wonderful future, and more convinced than men that (*c*) they had no say about what government did, (*d*) they could influence government only by voting, and (*e*) public officials did not care what they thought. Between the late 1950s and 1971, their views shifted more rapidly than did those of men toward (*f*) less trust in most people, (*g*) less confidence that people cared what happened to others, (*h*) less certainty about who could be counted on, (*i*) greater conviction that bringing children into the world is hardly fair given the future, and (*j*) stronger belief that politics and government can't be understood.

The General Social Surveys permit a more recent reading on what we might call psychological disengagement for the nation as a whole. Women now have less trust in "most people" than do men. The Female : Male ratio of (fitted) odds *most can be trusted : can't be too careful* is estimated as .86 from data of the 1972, 1973, and 1976 GSS; this sex effect on response, net of any year, color, and marital-status effects, falls just short of our usual level of significance. There is no evidence of differential change by sex between 1972 and 1976, but recall the finding for Detroit-area residents (Table 4-2): In 1959 women were more trusting, in 1971 less so. The same General Social Surveys included a question that resembles our other question on confidence in human nature, to wit, "Would you say that most of the time people try to be helpful, or that they are mostly just looking out for themselves?" Although women remain more confident that "people try to be helpful," their confidence is eroding more rapidly. The ratio of the (fitted) odds, Female : Male, falls from 1.7 in 1972 to 1.3 in 1973 and 1976. A third item in this domain, however, shows women less cynical and registers no differential change by sex. "Do you think most people would try to take advantage of you if they got a chance, or would they try to be fair?" The odds on *be fair* for women are 1.3 times the corresponding odds for men.

Inconsistencies between items in regard to the sex effects reinforce the advisability of cautious interpretation already noted in this chapter. We are working with fragmentary evidence of a syndrome or pattern whose relevant theoretical dimensions we have not yet ventured to formulate. Our objective here is not to defend a thesis but to explore a problem. There is an obvious need for systematic investigation of the feminine image of what the world is like, and the items considered here only hint at some features of it.

QUALITY OF PERSONAL EXPERIENCE

At about the time the 1971 replication was being carried out, Campbell (1972) was writing of his concern with measuring "the quality of personal experience, with the frustrations, satisfactions, disappointments, and fulfillment that people feel as they live their lives in our changing society [p. 442]." We have some information about the satisfactions and disappointments that wives encounter in their marriages and changes therein (reported in Chapter 8), but we lack reports from husbands with which to compare the wives' assessments. We also have some information on how men and women rate the performance of institutions, such as the schools, the local police, the Federal Courts, which we summarize in Chapter 5. The topic of sex differences in the quality of personal experience seems sufficiently important, however, that we have compiled a few supplementary indicators from the General Social Surveys and other opinion polls.

In reporting the results of the 1972 Virginia Slims American Women's Opinion Poll, Louis Harris and Associates observed (n.d.), "In spite of a strong desire to change women's status in society, women feel an even greater sense of satisfaction with their lives than men do [p. 9]." Distributions of men and women by Personal Satisfaction with Own Life Today are published, in which respondents are classified as *very satisfied, somewhat satisfied, only slightly satisfied, not at all satisfied,* or *not sure* (p. 11). This is a case in which women are no more reluctant than men to give a direct answer; 1% of each group is *not sure*. We find that the ratio of women to men among the *very satisfied* is 1.4 times as great as in any other response category, but the remaining categories— all registering a lesser degree of satisfaction with one's Own Life Today—do not differ in the sex ratio among themselves. We have not undertaken any formal analysis of the Harris data, but the published tabulation shows women overrepresented among *very satisfied* respondents in each stratum of education, each stratum of income, each age group, within both the black and white populations, and within both the single and married populations (though not among the divorced/ separated or the widowed).

Campbell (1972) has reminded us that "satisfaction is a subjective experience, and it is better understood in relation to another subjective fact, level of aspiration, than it is to objective reality [p. 446]." Noting that almost half the white poor describe themselves as "very satisfied" with their lodgings, he continued: "No doubt they would be pleased to have something better, but their perception of the discrepancy between their achievement and their aspiration is not strong enough to produce an acute sense of deprivation." We suspect that some spokespersons for women's liberation would argue that women's greater overall satisfaction with their lives bespeaks a need for consciousness raising.

Respondents in the 1973 and 1976 GSS were asked to select the phrase "that shows how much *satisfaction* you get from that area," the "areas" being the five items shown in the stub of Table 4-5. We have scored the alternatives presented to the respondent as 6 for *a very great deal*, 5 for *a great deal*, 4 for *quite a bit*, 3 for *a fair amount*, 2 for *some*, 1 for *a little*, and 0 for *none*. Shown in Table 4-5 is the regression coefficient, net of any effects of year, color, and marital status, associated with the factor sex, where women are scored 1 and men 0. An alternative way of describing the coefficient is to say that its magnitude is the estimated mean score for women minus the estimated mean score for men on the satisfaction scale for respondents surveyed in the same year and of the same color and marital status.

Women are more satisfied than men with their Community [A] and their Friendships [D], but they are less satisfied with their Nonworking Activities [B]. The differences are reliable statistically, but their magnitudes seem too small to sustain an argument that these facets of life

TABLE 4-5
Sex Difference (Women Minus Men) in Mean Satisfaction Score with Respect to Five Items, Estimated from Regression Models Incorporating Effects of Year, Color, and Marital Status, National Samples, 1973 and 1976

| Item | | All persons | | |
		Mean	Standard deviation	Sex difference
[A]	The city or place you live in	4.13	1.53	.125
[B]	Your nonworking activities—hobbies and so on	4.26	1.62	−.124
[C]	Your family life	4.88	1.37	—
	Married persons	—	—	−.037
	Unmarried persons	—	—	.501
[D]	Your friendships	4.77	1.24	.154
[E]	Your health and physical condition	4.41	1.51	—
	Married whites	—	—	−.053
	Unmarried whites	—	—	−.270
	Married blacks	—	—	−.376
	Unmarried blacks	—	—	−.593

offer satisfaction to persons of one sex but not the other. Working with the data in a multiway contingency analysis (seven response categories by year by sex by color by marital status), we detect a differential change in response by sex for Nonworking Activities. The satisfaction ratings, *a great deal, quite a bit,* and *a fair amount,* apparently gained in relative popularity more rapidly among women than among men between 1973 and 1976. The greater concentration of women's responses toward the middle of the distribution does not result in differential change in mean level of satisfaction by sex, however. If the sex-linked change in response pattern is to be taken seriously, it may anticipate growing disenchantment with traditional female hobbies and social activities paralleling the devaluation of the full-time homemaker role (suggested by the findings reported in Chapter 2).

The sex difference with respect to satisfaction with Family Life [C] is contingent on marital status, and it would be somewhat surprising if this were not so since some unmarried persons must be reporting their satisfaction with their relative lack of family life. Wives and husbands (that is, married women and married men) differ little in their satisfaction with Family Life. This congruence is of some interest because we can think of these data as reports of wives and reports of husbands about a particular set of relations which make up Family Life; these relations apparently offer equal satisfaction to each marriage partner. (The Friendships and Nonworking Activities, and to some extent even the Community, with respect to which wives and husbands describe their satisfaction are not, in fact, the same.) Unmarried women clearly are more satisfied with Family Life than are unmarried men. The difference may say little more than that the living arrangements of the unmarried differ by sex. (In any event, the extreme age heterogeneity of the unmarried—the never married and the previously married—must be borne in mind.) The possibility that men value Family Life more highly than do women and, hence, are more disappointed by its absence cannot be dismissed, however. The Roper Organization reported, in connection with the 1974 Virginia Slims American Women's Opinion Poll (n.d.), that: "Men are more likely than women to consider sex, family life, and the avoidance of loneliness as important reasons for marrying [p. 37]."

The last item with respect to which the GSS respondents reported their satisfaction is Health [E]. The sex difference is contingent on color or marital status and perhaps both color and marital status (results reported in Table 4-5 are from a model incorporating sex–color and sex–marital status interactions). Wives and husbands in the white population report about the same level of satisfaction with their Health, but in the other groups defined by color and marital status, women are less satisfied with their Health than are men. The sex difference in satisfaction with Health parallels the sex difference in self-assessed state of health. In 1972, 1973, and 1976 the GSS interviewer asked, "Would you say your own health, in general, is excellent, good, fair, or poor?" The sex effect depends on marital status, and after allowing for any effects of year, color, and marital status on response, we find the Female:Male ratios of (fitted) odds to be those shown here.

| | Odds relative to *excellent* | | |
	Good	*Fair*	*Poor*
Married	1.2	1.4	1.2
Unmarried	1.2	2.1	2.5

Thus, in assessing the state of their own health, wives are only a bit less enthusiastic than husbands. It is among the unmarried that the sex effect is pronounced; the odds on *fair* or *poor* relative to *excellent* for the women, who are on the average older, are double the odds for the men.

Campbell (1972) calls attention to "an increase in the sense of insecurity and apprehension at being abroad in the streets of our cities [p. 448]" and cites the inclusion of a relevant question in the Gallup poll as evidence of the growing salience of "safety needs." There now is a time series extending from 1965 to 1976 for that particular question, "Is there any area right around here—that is, within a mile—where you would be afraid to walk alone at night?" The odds *yes:no* for women and men are displayed in Figure 4-4, along with the Female:Male ratio of the odds on *yes*. There can be no doubt that from the mid-1960s to the present women have been far more fearful, even though the "areas" in question would be common to women and men. In other words, women are simply more apprehensive about what is to be encountered in these "areas." Inspection of the graphic display is sufficient to reach the conclusion that the odds on *yes* have increased for both women and men since the question was first asked in 1965, with a good part of that increase occurring in the intersurvey period 1968–1972. Although we have undertaken no formal tests, the Female:Male ratio of odds on *yes* may have been greater in the early 1970s than in the late 1960s as well. (A change in polling organization occurred, but fortunately that change was not coincident with the change in response. The question was asked by the Gallup Organization through 1972, by National Opinion Research Center as part of the GSS in 1973 and 1976.)

We can report the results of a more systematic analysis of answers to

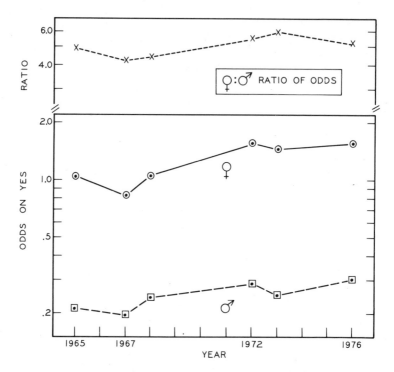

FIGURE 4-4. Trend in and sex effect on response to ". . . afraid to walk alone at night?" for national samples, 1965–1976.

this question in the 1973 and 1976 surveys. There is a very strong sex effect on response: the Female:Male ratio of (fitted) odds on *yes* stands at 5.6, a remarkably high value by comparison with other items studied. The sex effect is not contingent on year or color or marital status. That the sex effect is not contingent on marital status warrants special note, for the married men and married women are roughly matched on socioeconomic status, life style, kind of neighborhood, and various other factors that might be thought to influence the objective threats to be encountered within a mile and the home milieu in which perceptions about the dangers lurking are formed.

We cannot say why women are more fearful, but a few explanations can be ruled out. In the 1973 and 1976 GSS respondents were asked, "During the last year—that is, between March and now—did anyone break into or somehow illegally get into your (apartment/house)?" and "During the last year, did anyone take something directly from you by using force—such as a stickup, mugging, or threat?" The answers of women do not differ from the answers of men. Respondents also were asked, "Have you ever been punched or beaten by another person?" The ratio of (fitted) odds on *yes*, Female:Male, are .19. "Have you ever been threatened with a gun, or shot at?" The ratio of (fitted) odds on *yes*, Female:Male, are .14 for married persons and .24 for unmarried persons. (Effects of year, color, and marital status on response, if any, have been allowed for in these analyses; and the possibility that the sex effect on response is contingent on one of these factors has been checked routinely.) In sum, there is no support for an argument that the women have been victimized more frequently than the men. Do the women perchance feel that police protection is wanting should a threatening situation arise? In the Detroit area, the women are a bit more satisfied with police protection than are the men (see Chapter 5). And recall that women respondents in the GSS were a bit more satisfied with the Community, notwithstanding their greater fear of walking alone at night near their homes. It might be illuminating to see the answers of husbands and wives to the question, "Is there any area right around here—that is, within a mile—where you would be afraid to walk with your (wife/husband) at night?"

We close this brief review of sex differences in the quality of personal experience by returning to "global" indicators of that quality: for married persons, "Taking things all together, how would you describe your marriage? Would you say that your marriage is very happy, pretty happy, or not too happy?"; for everyone, "In general, do you find life exciting, pretty routine, or dull?" and "Taken all together, how would you say things are these days—would you say that you are very happy, pretty happy, or not too happy?"

Wives in the 1973 and 1976 GSS do not rate their marriages as high on the happiness scale as do husbands. The answer categories, *very happy*, *pretty happy*, and *not too happy*, relate linearly to the logarithm of the sex ratio, that is, the ratio of wives to husbands. From the regression model which incorporates the color effect on response, we estimate the sex ratio for *pretty happy* to be 1.2 times the ratio for *very happy* and the sex ratio for *not too happy*, in turn, to be 1.2 times the ratio for *pretty happy*, or 1.44 times the ratio for *very happy*. The respondent presumably is assessing the happiness of a relationship between one's self and another person, so that perception of the pleasure the marriage partner derives from the relationship as well as one's own pleasure presumably enters the rating. Without attempting to guess how respondents arrive at their ratings, however, we can say that the gap between the kind of marriage they would like to have and their own marriage is greater for women than for men.

Despite their greater disappointment with their marriages, wives do not differ from husbands in their assessments of life as *exciting, pretty routine,* or *dull.* And it is pleasant to report that only a tiny minority of husbands and wives find life *dull.* Among the unmarried, in contrast, the Female:Male ratio of (fitted) odds stands at 1.7 for the contrast *routine:exciting* and 2.2 for the contrast *dull:exciting.* We have allowed only for the effects of year, color, and marital status on response in these analyses, so the finding of a sex difference among the unmarried may only be telling us that the zest of life diminishes with age.

Finally, we come to avowed happiness. Women are happier than men. Allowing for any effects of year (1972, 1973, or 1976 GSS), color, or marital status on response, a sex effect is present; and its strength does not depend upon year, color, or marital status. The Female:Male ratio of (fitted) odds stands at .84 for the contrast *pretty happy :very happy* and .78 for the contrast *not too happy :very happy.* Or to cast the finding in another way, the ratio of women to men among the *very happy* is 1.2 times as great as in any other response category; but the remaining categories—each registering a lesser degree of Personal Happiness—do not differ in the sex ratio among themselves. We have come full circle. Just as the women feel a greater sense of satisfaction with their lives, so their avowed happiness is greater.

OBITER DICTUM

Why did one propose to call this chapter The Collective Sadness when women avow they are happier? Fischer (1974b) used the phrase as a synonym for anomy. She reported a shift toward more anomic responses between the late 1950s and 1971 among Detroit-area residents. We find that women ventured more anomic answers, or were shifting more rapidly toward the anomic stance, in several instances.

One of Seeman's (1972) conclusions about the "present state of affairs" in the study of alienation and engagement is that:

> "The emphasis is heavily weighted toward the 'problem' theme: alienation, not engagement, is the focus. The best parallel, perhaps, is found in the psychological literature that dwells on mental disorder without a corollary interest in health. We seem to take it rather much for granted that engagement is easy, natural, and unproblematic, and turn our attention to the 'disengaged.' Yet, we hardly have a clear image, much less understanding of, the authentic or unalienated man, or of how the 'normal' state of coordinated everyday action is achieved [p. 515]."

But who is the "healthier" person—the one who is certain that science can solve all man's important problems and that children born today can look forward to a wonderful future, or the one who has doubts on these scores? Perhaps the women are telling it like it is. Freer from the need to defend the mythology, the women may be able to find greater personal contentment.

5
Civics and Sex

Kirkpatrick introduces her study of *Political Woman* (1974) with the observation,

> Even today, the most important and interesting question about women's political role is why that role is so insignificant. The most important and interesting question about women's political behavior is why so few seek and wield power. Women are numerous enough at the lowest level of politics—in the precincts, at party picnics, getting out the vote, doing the telephoning, collecting the dollars—but remarkably scarce at the upper levels where decisions are made that affect the life of the community, state, nation [p. 3].

We could not expect to find enough high-level political figures among our respondents to estimate the sex differential in high-level political activity. We are, however, in a position to say something about low-level activity since one question asks, "Have you ever helped campaign for a party or candidate during an election—like putting in time or contributing money?"

The odds on an affirmative answer to this question, that is, "have helped," were 2.6 times as great in 1971 as in 1954 for both men and women. The sex effect showed no significant change, with the odds for women .67 as great as those for men. A somewhat different question was asked in 1957: "Have you ever done any sort of political work or activity?" If we assume that this question is comparable to the 1971 question, we may compute the 1971:1957 odds ratio as 2.9 and the Female:Male ratio as .70, with both results pertaining to Wayne County only, since the 1957 survey did not include the two outlying counties. In each case, the model with no sex differential in the change provides a very good fit.

Although the substantial escalation of political activity was at the same rate for the two sexes, thus preserving the initial sex difference, it may not be without some ultimate significance for the political roles of women that involvement at the level captured by our question extends to well over a fourth of all women in 1971. In judging this possibility, it may be useful to take note of the kinds of activity included in the affirmative responses; this information is available for 1971, but not for earlier years. Table 5-1 suggests that there was a good deal of similarity between the sexes with respect to the kinds of campaign activity they engaged in. The discrepancy in regard to the very tiny minority of actual candidates would no doubt be significant with a larger sample.

TABLE 5-1
Percentage Reporting Various Kinds of Campaign Activity, by Sex, 1971

Activity	Percentage of	
	Men	Women
1. Ran for office or is/was an elected official	1.3	0.0
2. Party or precinct official (includes higher level party work, e.g., gave open house for candidate)	10.9	10.9
3. Low-level party or campaign work (passed out literature, canvassed, made phone calls, took around a petition, typed)	65.6	72.3
4. Contributed money	37.3	27.7
5. Attended rallies, listened to speeches		
6. Signed a petition		
7. Minimal activity (talked to friends, put bumper sticker on car)	8.4	9.9
8. Other		
9. Not described		
One activity	76.5	79.2
Two activities	23.5	20.8
Total	100.0	100.0

Note: Based on 311 men and 303 women reporting that they helped campaign during an election; one or two activities coded for each respondent.

Otherwise, we can demonstrate only that contributing money is a significantly less common activity for women; "collecting the dollars" may be their forte. The difference between men and women in proportion reporting as many as two activities is not significant although a difference might appear if the roster of separately recognized kinds of activity was changed. (The analysis takes account of the multiple coding of activities; see Duncan, 1975b, p. 174.) Most activity, whether of women or men, must be characterized as low-level work. But men, who perhaps have greater freedom to offer financial contributions, seem to substitute the giving of money for the giving of personal time and effort to a greater extent than women.

POLITICAL INFORMATION

If one believes that the medium is the message, it is of interest to find out whether women and men get political messages from the same media. Table 5-2 provides observed percentage distributions that describe the sources of political news. The gain for television between 1954 and 1971 is hardly newsworthy. Slightly more so, perhaps, is the finding that the greater usage of this medium by women was as characteristic of the 1971 as the 1954 population. Formal partitioning of the table indicates that there are no significant differential changes, while both year and sex effects may be adequately summarized by referring to just two categories. The odds on *television*, relative to newspapers or

TABLE 5-2
Percentage Distribution of Sources of Political News, by Sex, 1954 and 1971

Source[a]	1954		1971	
	Men	Women	Men	Women
Newspapers	61.9	57.3	45.7	37.7
Radio	12.9	14.6	10.6	9.5
Television	17.0	21.2	36.1	43.7
Newspapers and television	2.0	1.8	1.8	3.5
Other sources and combinations	6.2	5.1	5.8	5.5
Total	100.0	100.0	100.0	100.0
(N)	(341)	(391)	(812)	(1029)

[a] "Of all the ways of getting the news about government officials and bureaus, which would you say you depend on most?"

radio or "other" sources and combinations thereof, are estimated to be 1.4 times as high for women as for men in both years and the odds on the combination, *newspapers and television,* 1.8 times as high. The 1971:1954 odds ratios, for odds defined in the same way, are 2.9 for *television* alone and 2.0 for *newspapers and television.*

Possibly the greater reliance of women on a visual medium for political news is related to their relatively poor performance on a political information "test" that asks the length of term for a United States Senator and Congressman, respectively, the names of the Senators from Michigan, and the name of the Congressman from the respondent's District. We cannot help but wonder if the sex difference in performance would change if the "test" involved identifying one's Senators and Congressman from among a set of photographs.

After being asked the names of the United States Senators from Michigan, each respondent was asked, "Can you tell me how long the term of office is for a United States senator?" We have information for three populations—residents of Wayne County in 1957 and in 1971 and, in 1971 only, residents of the two outlying counties in metropolitan Detroit. The item on length of a senator's term shows significant effects of sex and location (in 1971), but no significant change between 1957 and 1971 (within Wayne County). The odds on a *correct* answer versus an incorrect or "don't know" response computed from the fitted frequencies are .13 for women and .32 for men in Wayne County, 1957 or 1971. Thus, the Female:Male odds ratio is .41. For men and women alike, the odds are raised by a factor of 1.6, comparing suburban counties with Wayne County in 1971.

A similar item concerning the length of a congressman's term was included in the political-information test. The location effect again is present; the odds on a *correct* answer are raised by a factor of 1.5, comparing suburban counties with Wayne County in 1971, for both men and women. There is, however, significant change between 1957 and 1971 (within Wayne County). Although respondents are better informed about the length of a congressman's term than about the length of a senator's term, or their guesses are more often on the mark, the odds on a *correct* answer fell appreciably for both men and women. The odds on a *correct* answer computed from the fitted frequencies, allowing for a marginally significant sex effect as well as the year effect, are .68 and .34 for women in 1957 and 1971, respectively, and .79 and .40 for men. Thus, the 1971:1957 odds ratio stands at .51. There is no evidence of differential change by sex, and the Female:Male odds ratio is estimated as .86 in each year. Here the sex effect does not quite reach significance by our usual criterion, although it is significant at the .08

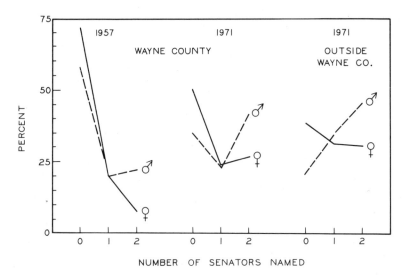

FIGURE 5-1. Frequency distribution of male and female respondents by number of senators correctly named, 1957 and 1971.

level in the data for the 2 years. We can show, moreover, that it is significantly less than the sex differential with respect to senator's term. In sum, the female disadvantage is clearly more pronounced, for reasons unknown to us, on the item dealing with senator's term than on the similar item concerning congressman's term.

Only a minority within each population (Wayne County, 1957 and 1971, and suburban counties, 1971) were able to name both United States Senators from Michigan (Potter and McNamara in 1957, Hart and Griffin in 1971). And, within each population, women are underrepresented among those who do name both correctly and overrepresented among those who can name neither. Figure 5-1 shows the percentage distributions of men and women according to the number of Senators named correctly. A very simple model, which allows the log of the sex ratio to vary linearly with number of Senators named correctly, fits the data beautifully ($Y^2 = 7.0$, $df = 6$). According to this model, the sex ratio (female/male) among those naming one Senator is just .63 as high as among those naming none; and just .63 as high among those naming both Senators as among those naming one. Thus, the mean number of Senators named correctly is higher for men than for women in all three populations, and there is no significant sex difference in regard to the change from 1957 to 1971 in Wayne County (which involved an improvement in knowledge of the Senators' names) nor any sex differential in regard to the difference between Wayne and the two outlying counties in 1971 (which favored the latter).

In both years, there is a strong association between ability to name one Senator and ability to name the other. Thus, in 1957, if Senator Potter was known, Senator McNamara was also quite likely to be known, and vice versa. But we find no sex difference in regard to the strength of this association, even though sex affects the knowledge of each Senator's name. Similarly, in 1971 the association between naming Hart and naming Griffin is invariant with respect to sex.

A further detail that may be of interest is the test for the hypothesis of differential sex appeal on the part of the incumbents. That is, even though women are less likely to know either Senator than men, it could be that the sex difference in name recall is more pronounced for one Senator than the other. We find, however, that there is no such effect in either year. The ratio of the number of persons knowing Potter but not McNamara to the number knowing McNamara but not Potter does not differ reliably by sex in 1957, and the comparable ratio for Hart versus Griffin shows no significant sex effect in 1971. These results, of course, may tell us as much about the personalities and political styles of the particular politicians concerned as about sex differences in political involvement. It is not difficult to imagine that differential sex appeal could come into play under other circumstances. Still, there is no obvious advantage for a candidate in exploiting his or her appeal to one sex, unless this can be done without alienating the other, since the sexes are so nearly balanced in the electorate.

An especially interesting point arises in the analysis of the item on name of Congressman, for we have a natural experiment. In both 1957 and 1971 there was one Congressional District (17) with a female Representative, Martha Griffiths. Are female respondents any more likely to name their representative in Congress when the representative is a woman? Griffiths, moreover, is identified as a "long-time women's rights advocate" (Hole and Levine, 1971, p. 31; see also other references to Griffiths therein).

We must take account of the possibility that Martha Griffiths would be better known to both men and women than the Congressman in some other Districts, or vice versa, for any of several reasons extraneous to our interest here. In Districts with more highly educated populations, the Representative might be better known, other things being equal. Or, a Representative, male or female, might be well or poorly known according to length of tenure in office or other factors, besides sex, affecting visibility. In short, we must take account of normal variation by District in ability to name the Congressman before we can infer any effect of sex matching on that ability. The problem is handled as a three-way contingency table, ability to name Congressman, by sex of respondent, by District. The latter variable is partitioned into the dichotomy, District 17 versus other Districts, when testing for a sex matching effect. That effect would be manifested, then, as a three-way interaction: sex by ability by District 17 versus other. That interaction is utterly insignificant in both 1957 and 1971. The sex effect, however, is clearly significant in 1971 and significant at the .06 level in 1957. In the earlier year the Female:Male ratio of the odds on *naming the Congressman correctly* was .67, while in 1971 it was .68. As it happens, there were wide variations among Districts in both years. In 1957 Martha Griffiths was actually better known than any of the other five Congressmen from Wayne County; the odds ratio for her District to the lowest District was 4.6 (estimated as the same for men and women, in the absence of a significant sex differential). In 1971, four of the nine Congressmen were better known than Griffiths and four were not as well known. The High:Low ratio in that year was 4.2.

In summary:

1. We find no significant temporal or geographic variation in regard to the sex difference in political information.
2. That difference clearly favors men in the instance of the items on names of Senators, length of a Senator's term, and Congressman's name.
3. The sex effect is less clear but in the same direction for length of a Congressman's term.
4. There is no evidence of differential sex appeal of the two Senators in either year.
5. We find no significant effect of sex matching on knowledge of Congressman's name.

Findings on matters 4 and 5, however, may be strongly dependent on the particular political personalities involved, so that we do not suggest that they be generalized.

RESPECT FOR RULES

The items treated under this rubric can be given a variety of interpretations. Moreover, we cannot be sure whether the respondent is more sensitive to the principle embodied or to the particular situation to which the principle is applied in a question format.

A series of questions about freedom of speech was introduced with the statement, "In our country the Constitution guarantees the right of free speech to everyone." The respondent then was asked whether this included the right to make speeches criticizing what the President does, against religion, in favor of Fascism or dictatorship, in favor of Communism. Statements about sex effects as well as about change over time must be qualified with respect to color. The observed odds ratios (Table 5-3) suggest that among both blacks and whites in 1958 women put the narrower limits on freedom of speech, whereas this was no longer true for blacks in 1971 although it remained so for whites. Our 1958 sample of blacks is very small, however, so that the ostensible four-way interaction is not significant. If we consider only the statistically significant differences, we find no change in the sex effect for either blacks or whites. Instead, the standard sequence of tests suggests that for two items (speeches criticizing what the President does, and speeches in favor of Communism) the sex effect is virtually nil among blacks but appreciable among whites. On the matter of differential change by color, the data are less equivocal. For all four items, blacks showed more rapid shifts toward the libertarian (*yes*) response than did whites, for whom an actual decline in the *yes:no* ratio occurred in regard to speeches criticizing what the President does. Whereas blacks were less

TABLE 5-3

Observed and Fitted Odds Ratios (Female:Male) for Sex Effect on Odds on Responding Yes to Free Speech Questions, by Color, 1958 and 1971

Question[a]	1958		1971	
	Black	White	Black	White
Observed ratio				
President	.62	.53	1.3	.67
Religion	.79	.90	1.1	.66
Fascism	.65	1.0	1.2	.74
Communism	.85	.84	1.1	.63
Fitted ratio				
President	1.1	.64	1.1	.64
Religion	.77	.77	.77	.77
Fascism	.84	.84	.84	.84
Communism	1.1	.68	1.1	.68

[a] "In our country the Constitution guarantees the right of free speech to everyone. In your opinion, does this include the right for someone to make speeches criticizing what the President does? . . . against religion? . . . in favor of Fascism or dictatorship? . . . in favor of Communism?"

libertarian than whites on all items in 1958, they were more so on two items in 1971, while the color difference had virtually disappeared on the other two (Figure 5-2).

It is interesting that the decade of the 1960s would have seen an elimination or actual reversal of the color difference on the question of free speech but no change—at least among whites—in the sex difference. It seems plausible that the civil rights movement had a greater or different kind of impact on the political thinking of blacks than the women's rights movement did on the thinking of women, at least in the particular period studied here. In Chapter 10, examining the Younger Generation question, we shall again encounter a differential change with respect to color that one might have expected to see—but does not—with respect to sex.

For what it is worth, we note that a more cautious endorsement of the Bill of Rights may have been characteristic of women for some time.

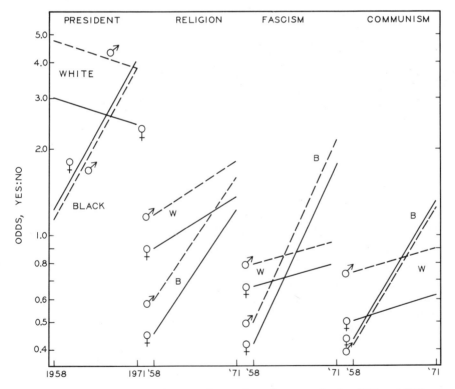

FIGURE 5-2. Response to free speech questions, by sex and color, 1958 and 1971.

Data from a 1937 *Fortune* poll (cited by Cantril and Strunk, 1951, p. 416) yield a Female:Male ratio of .62 for the odds, *yes*:*no*, in response to the question, "Do you think newspapers should be allowed to print anything they choose except libelous material?" Women were more ready to draw the line on freedom of the press specifically in regard to stories about sex, crime, and personal scandal than were men.

National data collected through the General Social Surveys of 1972, 1973, and 1976 confirm the less liberal stance of women with respect to speeches against religion and in favor of Communism, although the question wordings differ in important respects. The preambles, in this instance, make no reference to Constitutional right; and the speaker is explicitly identified as one who espouses a particular ideology. "There are always some people whose ideas are considered bad or dangerous by other people. For instance, somebody who is against all churches and religion. . . . If such a person wanted to make a speech in your community against churches and religion, should he be allowed to speak, or not?" Allowing for any effects of year and color on response, we find that women, and especially unmarried women, less often say "yes" than do men. The Female:Male ratio of odds *yes*:*no* stands at .87 among married persons and .46 among the unmarried. The reluctance of women to give a direct answer also is manifest, with the Female:Male ratio of odds *don't know*:*no* equal to 2.9 for the married and 1.2 for the unmarried. "Now I should like to ask you some questions about a man who admits he is a Communist. Suppose this admitted Communist wanted to make a speech in your community. Should he be allowed to speak, or not?" Note that although the speaker is an admitted Communist, the topic of the speech is unspecified. The results, however, are substantially the same. From a model incorporating any effects of year and color on response, we estimate the Female:Male ratio of odds *yes*:*no* as .87 for the married and .53 for the unmarried; the corresponding ratios of odds *don't know*:*no* are 1.8 and 1.6.

Detroit-area women also give somewhat less liberal (more patriotic) answers on the issue posed by the statement, "Every American family should be required by law to own a flag." Although men and women alike endorsed this proposition much less frequently in 1971 than in 1958, there was a persistent sex difference, reflected in the estimated odds ratio of .73 (Female:Male) in regard to the odds on disagreeing with the statement. The sex effect is estimated net of color, with respect to which there is a differential change of the kind noted earlier for the questions on free speech. The 1971:1958 ratio of the odds, *disagree*:*agree*, is 6.0 for blacks, 2.9 for whites, in a model including this differential change and a separate sex effect common to blacks and whites. (Again, however, we caution that estimates pertaining to blacks in baseline survey years rest on quite small samples.) The question examined here has more than one facet. It is possible that the sex difference relates to the desirability of owning a flag rather than the propriety of making flag ownership a subject of legislation, while the change represents an increasing rejection of an ostensibly authoritarian view of the matter.

Four years after the Supreme Court decision in the case of *Brown v. Board of Education,* white respondents in metropolitan Detroit were asked, "Personally, do you think white students and Negro students should go to the same schools, or to separate schools?" If there was a sex difference in response, it was confined to the greater propensity of women to use the answer *unsure.* No difference between the answers of men and those of women appears when the question is asked again in 1971. Since the evidence of a three-way interaction here is tenuous, with $.05 < p < .1$, and the *unsure* response is used quite infrequently, the safest conclusion seems to be that women and men shared about equally in the pronounced shift in white attitudes recorded between 1958 and 1971. Not only attitudes toward school integration, but also toward neighborhood integration became more favorable among whites during this period. Again, however, the view of women is distinctive only in that the odds, *unsure : no,* were twice as great for women as for men on the neighborhood integration question in both 1958 and 1971. Responses to this pair of questions are summarized in Table 5-4.

Another issue is how one would handle a parking violation ticket. The question is, "If you were driving in another state and got a ticket for parking just a few minutes overtime while getting your lunch, would you bother to pay the fine?" This question was followed by the probe, "Would you pay it even if you were in a big hurry and knew that the police in that town would never bother you if you didn't pay the fine?" addressed to those responding *yes* to the first question. We have two alternative readings on this indicator, therefore, and it is pertinent to note that the effect of the probe is indeed significantly different for men and women. The ratio of *yes* to *no* responses on the probe among those saying *yes* initially is 1.5 times as great for women as for men, using the data for both years in the absence of differential change or, indeed, any year effect at all on that ratio. Hence, men who initially take the conventional position that they would pay the fine are more easily tempted to accept evasion of it than are women, however implausible this may seem to serpents recalling experience with Eve.

In Table 5-5 the two questions are treated jointly, incorporating in the

TABLE 5-4
Attitudes of White Respondents Toward School and Neighborhood Integration, by Sex, 1958 and 1971

Question[a] and response	1958		1971	
	Men	Women	Men	Women
	Observed odds			
Schools				
same : separate	1.8	2.0	5.0	4.3
unsure : separate	.10	.25	.28	.20
Block				
yes : no	1.4	1.3	.45	.39
unsure : no	.10	.17	.036	.070
	Fitted odds			
Schools				
same : separate	1.9	1.9	4.6	4.6
unsure : separate	.11	.24	.26	.21
Block				
yes : no	1.3	1.3	.42	.42
unsure : no	.10	.20	.033	.065

[a] Schools: "Personally, do you think white students and Negro students should go to the same schools, or to separate schools?"
    Block: "Would you be at all disturbed or unhappy if a Negro with the same income and education as you moved into your block?"

model constraints that take account of the impossibility of certain response combinations (e.g., *no* on the first question, *yes* on the second). The preferred model provides for sex effects that do not change between years, and a year effect that consists largely in the lesser frequency of the response *it depends* in 1971. (Since this response was not explicitly offered to respondents but was coded only when volunteered, there is some question as to the comparability of the 2 years in regard to it; perhaps the 1971 interviewers probed more assiduously for a decisive answer.) Women are disproportionately numerous among respondents who steadfastly answer *yes*, that is, those who would pay the fine, irrespective of the expectation of being caught if they defaulted. Men are overrepresented among those who would not pay the fine, even though no assurance that they will not be caught has been given. It is possible, though, that they take that for granted. Whereas answers to the first question could reflect the men's greater experience with such matters, as it affects their estimate of the probability of getting caught,

TABLE 5-5
Fitted Response Distributions, in Percentages, to Parking Fine Question, by Sex, 1958 and 1971

Response		1958		1971		Ratio	
First question	Second question	Men	Women	Men	Women	Women:Men	1971:1958
Yes	Yes	55.6	70.0	59.1	74.4	1.3	1.1
	It depends	6.7	7.5	3.0	3.3	1.1	.45
	No	12.6	9.4	15.5	11.6	.75	1.2
It depends		10.9	7.0	4.9	3.1	.64	.45
No		14.2	6.1	17.5	7.5	.43	1.2
Total		100.0	100.0	100.0	100.0	—	—
(N)		(302)	(337)	(819)	(1039)	—	—

the second question should have put the sexes on the same basis in regard to any assumption about this probability. The results, therefore, speak to the somewhat greater proclivity of women to choose the lawful or conventionally moralistic response.

We have a question about gambling which is posed in moralistic, not legalistic terms. When asked, "How do you feel about gambling? From the moral standpoint, would you say it is Always wrong, Usually wrong, Sometimes wrong, Never wrong?" women are more inclined to take a strict position than are men. A model that lets the logarithm of the ratio of women to men vary linearly with answer category fits the data very well. It implies that in both 1958 and 1971 the ratio of responses *usually wrong* to *always wrong* is only .86 as high for women as for men; the *sometimes : always* ratio is .74 as high; and the *never : always* ratio is .64 as high. The stability of these ratios over time implies that women and men were equally involved in the observed shift toward the more liberal position, that is, a gain for the *never* response at the expense of *always*.

INSTITUTIONAL PERFORMANCE

When women do differ from men in their ratings of social institutions, the women typically are a bit more indulgent, or more accepting of current institutional performance as good enough. Their greater satisfaction or resignation, as the case may be, does not bespeak greater resistance to change, however.

Three questions included in the 1956 survey and repeated in the 1971 survey bear directly on attitudes toward change. One is "Many people find the *Star-Spangled Banner* difficult to sing. If a new and appropriate national anthem were written, would you object to substituting it for the *Star-Spangled Banner*?" We estimate that the ratio of *no* to *yes* answers rose from .32 to .81 over the 15-year period, but we find no difference in response between men and women in either year. Another question asks,

Which of these two statements do you agree with more?

1. The Founding Fathers had so much wisdom that our Constitution handles most modern problems very well.

2. While the Founding Fathers were very wise, the Constitution they wrote needs frequent changes to bring it up to date.

Preference for statement 2, an endorsement of change, increased between 1956 and 1971; but again, in each year, the answers of women resemble those of men. The final, and more cumbersome, question states, "People feel differently about making changes in the way our country is run. Which of these four statements do you feel is best? 1. We should rarely, if ever, make changes in the way our country is run. 2. We should be very cautious of making changes in the way our country is run. 3. We should feel free to make changes in the way our country is run. 4. We must constantly make changes in the way our country is run." Statement 1, which endorses changes only rarely, loses in relative popularity between the surveys; and statement 4, which endorses constant changes, gains in relative popularity. In neither year, however, do the choices of men differ from those of women.

Insofar as women hold a distinctive view of institutional performance, its main features are elicited by a question about the demands and benefits of government vis-à-vis the people. The women's view, in short, is that you get what you give—and it perhaps follows that you have, then, no grounds for complaint. The question takes the form,

> As some people see it, there are different kinds of things the government has to do. The government has to provide help for people. The government also has to make people carry their share of the burdens and make sacrifices. Which one of these statements comes closest to your own opinion about this . . .
>
> 1. The help and services that the public gets from the government is worth what it asks from the public.
> 2. The government asks more from the public than it gives in help and services.
> 3. The public gets more from the government than it gives the government.

We find, through a formal partitioning of the response categories, that we cannot combine any two of these responses without losing significant information about sex effects and patterns of change. The analysis is simplified, however, by the fact that sex and year effects can be separately described; that is, there is no significant differential change by sex for any contrast among the three categories. Both the odds *government asks more : worth what it asks* and *public gets more : worth what it asks* are lower for women than for men—by a factor of .74 for the former and .59 for the latter. Thus, women accept the more neutral position disproportionately often. It is that position, though, which loses ground between 1954 and 1971 for both sexes, as is indicated by a 1971:1954 ratio of 3.1 for the odds *government asks more :worth what it asks* and 2.3 for the odds *public gets more :worth what it asks.*

When the respondents are asked to rate the performance of their local and State officials, the tendency for women to avoid condemnation, or strong praise, becomes apparent. The two questions requested ratings of local community officials and bureaus and State officials and bureaus, respectively, as to whether they were "doing a poor, fair, good, or very good job" as of 1954 and 1971. Both men and women gave markedly fewer *good* or *very good* ratings in 1971 than in 1954; but we cannot detect any differential change by sex. Nor is there a clear relationship of sex to the degree of favorableness toward either of these levels of government. Instead, we find that women are more prone to use the intermediate categories (*fair* and *good*) and less likely to accept the extremes (*poor* and *very good*) than men. This tendency is represented by an odds ratio of 1.3 for the question on local community government and one of 1.5 for the question on State officials and bureaus.

Incidentally, men and women differ in their image of the "best" local official, although the men between whom a choice must be made are described in such a way that we are left uncertain whether his style or his results are at issue. The question asks, "Which one of these two kinds of men would make the best official for a town or city government? 1. A man who is as much like the average person in the town as possible, so that he can understand and help the common man. 2. A man who is superior to the average man in order to make wise decisions for the town." Women more often prefer the man described in statement 1—average, understanding, helpful, and for all we know, making unwise decisions for the town. This average man would clearly have won the local election in both 1956 and 1971 although his margin would be less in the latter year. Estimates of the odds *average :superior*, estimated from a model that incorporates additive year and sex effects, are 2.1 and 1.4 for women and men, respectively, in 1956, 1.7 and 1.1 in 1971.

Employees in the public sector are held in comparatively high esteem by the women. The questions were intended by Janowitz and Wright (1956) to replicate L. D. White's earlier work on prestige of public employment. Let us quote the wording in full: "We'd like to know what people think of government jobs and government workers. If these jobs are about the same in kind of work, pay, and so forth, which has the most prestige? (1) Stenographer in a life insurance company/ . . . in the city tax assessors office. (2) Accountant in a private accounting firm/

. . . in the Detroit Department of Public Works. (3) Night watchman in a bank/ . . . in the city hall. (4) Doctor on staff of private hospital/ . . . in the Detroit Receiving Hospital." For none of these items is there a significant sex effect on frequency of answering "no difference" (an alternative not explicitly offered to the respondent). Nor are there significant sex differences in the changes between 1954 and 1971 (for the most part small and not significant) in the odds on favoring public over private employment. For each of the four occupations, however, the Female:Male ratio for the *public:private* odds exceeds unity in a model allowing for the same sex effect in both years. Specifically, we estimate the odds ratio at 1.45 for stenographer, 1.23 for accountant, 1.19 for night watchman, and 1.38 for doctor; only the ratio for night watchman does not differ significantly from unity. The women, in summary, are more favorably disposed to public employment than men. And, interestingly, the magnitude of the effect is greatest for the occupation (stenographer) that has the greatest proportion of female incumbents. Perhaps the women know whereof they speak.

We can only infer from answers to the foregoing question that women might rate the performance of these units of local government a bit more favorably than would men. We also have, however, a series of ratings of local government services that was obtained by asking, "In general, would you say that you are well satisfied, more or less satisfied, or not at all satisfied with the job the public schools here are doing? . . . with the city garbage collection here? . . . with the protection provided for your neighborhood by the police?" As reported more fully in *Social Change in a Metropolitan Community* (p. 84), all three services were rated less favorably in 1971 than in 1959. We find no significant sex differences in the rate of change in these ratings, however. Indeed, there is no significant sex difference at all in the rating of Public Schools and Garbage Collection in either year. (The analysis explicitly sought for an interaction of sex with marital status in regard to these ratings, but none was found.) In evaluating Police Protection, women are ever so slightly inclined to award higher marks than men: the ratio of *well satisfied* to *not at all satisfied* was 1.1 times as high for women in both 1959 and 1971, while that ratio dropped by a factor of .58 for both sexes between the two years. (Again, no sex by marital status interaction was noted.)

At another point in the interview respondents were presented with a list of organizations and groups, some in the public sector, "that people have different opinions about. After each one, would you tell me if, in your opinion, it is doing a good job, just a fair job, or a poor job." The men and women do not differ in their assessments of High Schools, of Colleges, or of Scientists, who perhaps are identified with educational institutions, just as they did not differ in satisfaction with their local schools. We cannot reassess the tendency of women to avoid strong praise, for "very good" no longer is a response option. But women do shun the *poor* rating for each other institution in the public sector— Most Michigan State Officials, The Federal Courts, and Radio and TV Networks, which are publicly regulated if not in public ownership. Indeed, in the case of The Federal Courts, women avoid the *good* rating as well as the *poor* rating by comparison with men.

Only two institutions outside the public sector were rated. The patterns of response by sex are somewhat different from those described heretofore. Unfortunately, we have no way of knowing whether the public versus private distinction is critical, or whether Most Doctors and The Boy Scouts elicit atypical responses. Women are the more polarized sex insofar as opinions of the Scouts are concerned. They rate the organization as *fair* less often than do the men, more often opting for either a *good* or a *poor* rating. Possibly a youth-serving organization evokes stronger reaction from women, or at least from mothers, although we found no sex difference in ratings of schools. The only differential change detected in the rating of institutional performance relates to doctors. In 1959 women were much more favorable to doctors than were men. In fact, the 1959 evaluation of doctors reveals the strongest cleavage between the sexes recorded in Table 5-6. By 1971

TABLE 5-6
Sex Effects on Ratings of Selected Groups and Organizations, 1959 and 1971

Group or organization[a]	Odds ratio, Female:Male[b]	
	Fair:good	Poor:good
Most Michigan State officials (1971 only)	.81	.65
The Federal Courts	1.3	.68
Radio and TV networks	.86	.74
The Boy Scouts	.68	1.0
Most doctors		
1971	.85	.72
1959	.58	.33

[a] Excludes: Most high schools in this country; Most colleges; Most scientists. No significant sex effects detected for these.

[b] Calculated from model providing acceptable fit to the data. The model involves a linear relationship of log sex ratio to rating (*good, fair, poor*) of radio–TV, doctors, and Michigan officials, but a nonlinear relationship obtains for courts and Boy Scouts. *Don't know* responses are excluded from the analysis.

women were only somewhat more favorable, the Female : Male ratio of the odds *poor* to *good* having risen from .33 to .72.

We can enlarge the list of institutions rated by drawing upon the 1973 and 1976 General Social Surveys. This maneuver enables us to detect some sex effects that may have been missed in the Detroit data because of the small size of the 1959 sample. However, the national and the Detroit data are only roughly comparable. In the General Social Survey, interviewees were asked, "As far as the *people running* these institutions are concerned, would you say you have a great deal of confidence, only some confidence, or hardly any confidence at all in them?" The response categories were repeated on a printed card handed to the respondent. Despite this reminder, women were more prone to answer "don't know" (or, to be more exact, to give an answer that the interviewer coded as "don't know") on most of the questions (see last column, Table 5-7). We have encountered this tendency elsewhere in our study, although it is by no means an invariant tendency. Francis and Busch (1975) found the same sort of thing, analyzing a large number of questions in three national election studies done by the Survey Research Center. It is perhaps significant that their results pertain to surveys with many questions related to politics and public affairs. As we have seen (Chapter 4), women agree more readily than men that "a person like me can't really understand what is going on" in government and politics. For our part, we "don't know" what the women would say if pressed to declare whether it would be worth their time to try to "understand" such things. In any event, we suspect that *don't know* as a distinctively feminine response is subject-matter specific, even though it is very prevalent here. In Table 5-7 we find just one example where the odds on *don't know* are smaller for women. This occurs for Education, and is restricted to married women. We had better believe that wives—the bulk of whom have, have had, or will have children in school—know what they think about that subject.

Table 5-7 gives the impression of greater complexity than the previous analysis, partly because we have introduced the factors of marital status and color as controls. For only two institutions, TV and Congress, is there a sex effect on confidence that does not show significant variation by one of these factors.

Let us examine first those institutions in Table 5-7 that are similar to agencies named in Table 5-6. For Education in the national data, as for Most High Schools and Most Colleges in the Detroit data, there is no significant sex effect. The two studies differ, however, in regard to scientists. Whereas the Detroit data show no sex difference in ratings of Most Scientists, in the national sample women (or, at any rate, married

TABLE 5-7
Sex Effects on Confidence in People Running Various Institutions, National Samples, 1973 and 1976

Institution and population	Odds ratio, Female:Male		
	Only some : great deal	Hardly any : great deal	Don't know : all other
1. Major companies			
1973 Married	1.4	1.9	1.9
Unmarried	1.5	.72	4.0
1976 Married	2.2	1.8	1.9
Unmarried	.85	.94	4.0
2. Organized religion			
1973 Married	1.0	1.0	1.0
Unmarried	.74	.54	15.4
1976 Married	1.06	1.13	1.0
Unmarried	.87	.76	1.0
3. Education			
Married	1.0	1.0	.39
Unmarried	1.0	1.0	3.5
4. Executive branch of the federal government	1.4	1.2	2.0
5. Organized labor			
1973	1.45	1.45	2.0
1976	1.45	.99	2.0
6. Press			
White	1.3	1.0	1.0
Black	.66	1.0	1.0
7. Medicine			
Married	1.0	.67	2.0
Unmarried	1.3	1.1	2.0
8. TV	1.1	.85	1.0
9. U.S. Supreme Court			
White	1.2	.82	2.9
Black	2.2	2.0	1.0
10. Scientific community			
Married	1.2	1.5	1.0
Unmarried	1.04	1.08	3.0
11. Congress	1.3	.84	2.5
12. Military			
White	1.3	.95	2.3
Black	3.1	3.2	2.3

women) have less confidence in the Scientific Community than do men. The national data for white women's confidence in the U.S. Supreme Court give the same pattern as the ratings of Federal Courts by Detroit women; that is, women choose the middle category more frequently than men. In the national data, however, black women definitely do not have as much confidence in the Supreme Court as black men. If we may compare TV in Table 5-7 with Radio and TV Networks in Table 5-6, we must conclude that there is a discrepancy between the two sets of results. In Detroit, women rated the networks more favorably than men, but in the national data the sex comparison is equivocal, since the women chose the middle category with greater relative frequency than either end category. Finally, we note that married women in the national sample have more confidence in Medicine, just as Detroit women rate Most Doctors more favorably than men do. But the national evidence suggests that this tendency does not carry over to the unmarried. (We must bear in mind that the unmarried women have a rather different age distribution from the unmarried men, so that the implications of this contrast are not wholly clear, given that sample sizes preclude a close control on age.)

There are several institutions in Table 5-7 for which the sex effect takes the form of women selecting the middle category disproportionately often. This occurs for Executive Branch of the Federal Government, Organized Labor (but only in 1976), Press (white women only), TV, U.S. Supreme Court (white only), Congress, and Military (white only). Whatever the explanation for this tendency, it means that the sex comparison cannot be reduced to a matter of men or women having greater confidence in the institution than the other sex. In fact, for the institutions mentioned, we cannot actually show that the Female:Male odds ratio for *hardly any:great deal* differs significantly from unity. In that event, it is utterly unclear whether either sex could be said unequivocally to have the greater amount of confidence.

For only two institutions, Organized Religion (unmarried women only) and Scientific Community (married women only or principally), is there a linear relationship of response to sex that renders the sex comparison quite unequivocal. Unmarried women have greater confidence in Organized Religion than do unmarried men, while married women have less confidence in the Scientific Community than do married men.

Of the dozen institutions in Table 5-7, only one shows a change in the sex effect uncomplicated by another factor. Women gained some confidence in Organized Labor, relative to men. In the case of Organized Religion, women lost confidence, relative to men, although this change was really manifested mainly among the unmarried. For Major Companies, we find a four-way interaction that defies simple summary. Whereas there was a relative shift of married women toward the middle category, the opposite shift occurred for unmarried women, relative to unmarried men. Despite the differential changes, married women remained less confident about Major Companies than unmarried women (when each is compared with the corresponding group of men).

Our recital of this congeries of findings has a limited function in the present investigation. We have no hope of explaining, with the information at hand, the various detailed differences and changes that were noted. We do think that the propensity to respond *don't know* is a matter of general though perhaps minor interest, and perhaps the same is true of the tendency to opt for the intermediate category, if that could be replicated with a different set of adjectives and adverbs. On the substance of the confidence ratings, we can only conclude that women are neither more nor less demanding or complaisant than men as a general proposition. Sex differences in confidence in institutions are not just a function of sex but are compounded of the different experiences of and perspectives on the specific institutions that women and men have. There may be some clues to these differences in experience and perspective in the other chapters of this study, but we do not know how to mobilize them for a systematic explanation of the sex variations in confidence ratings. Indeed, we suspect that not enough is known as yet about what causes variation in such ratings, quite apart from the factor of sex, to sustain any protracted exercise in hypothesis formation. We only want to suggest, therefore, that as analysts do try to understand the substantive meaning of this kind of social measurement, they not overlook the insights that may come from paying attention to sex along with other personal characteristics.

While the focus on sex differences comports with the purpose of this study, it is perhaps well to be reminded from time to time that women and men live in the same world. Figure 5-3 may serve as such a reminder. Here we use the dozen institutions as units of observation and note the scatter of relationship between the proportions of *hardly any* and of *great deal* ratings that each of them receives. The 12 points for white married men in 1976 are shown in juxtaposition with the 12 observations for white married women in that year. The general negative correlation is to be expected, in view of the constraint on the three proportions, *hardly any, only some,* and *great deal,* which must add up to unity. Indeed, the third proportion is implied from the location of the point describing the other two, so that the further to the SW of the graph, the greater the proportion of *only some* responses. Every point for women lies further toward the SW on the NE–SW axis than the

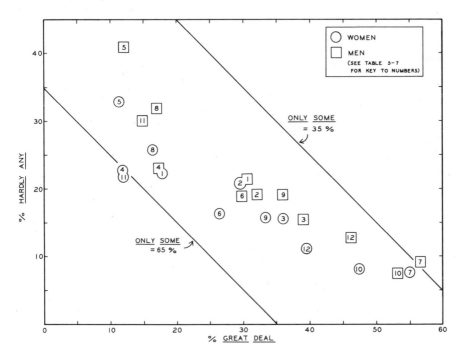

FIGURE 5-3. Scatter diagram, percentage of *hardly any* versus *great deal* of confidence, for 12 institutions in Table 5-7, from ratings of white married persons in 1976, national sample, by sex of respondent.

corresponding point for the men. Thus the tendency for (white, married) women to choose the middle category is quite general, although, as noted earlier, it is not statistically significant for every item. We do not, however, find any general tendency for women to give either of the ratings, *great deal* or *hardly any*, more often than men, once an allowance is made for their preference for the middle category. Exactly half a dozen institutions have a higher ratio, *great deal:hardly any*, for women. The main purpose of the figure, however, is not to reiterate the sex differences, but to call attention to basic similarities. First, the general scatter of points is much the same for the two sexes, notwithstanding a few instances where the points for women and men are widely separated. Whatever their differences in the details of confidence ratings, the two sexes generally agree as to which institutions merit high confidence and which do not. Spearman's rank correlation coefficient over the 12 institutions for the male and female *great deal:hardly any* ratio is .97; for the male and female proportions of *only some* confidence, it is a bit lower but still substantial, .85. All these results are for white married persons in 1976 and would no doubt differ somewhat for the other populations.

ATTITUDES OF BOYS AND GIRLS

The work of Entwisle and Greenberger (1972) cited in Chapter 3 shows that sex differences in attitudes about constraints on women's work are present among adolescents. Just as adult women less often favor constraints, so adolescent girls less often favor constraints. The work of Hess and Torney (1968) on political socialization permits some comparisons between adults and children with respect to the presence and direction of sex differences in political attitudes and behaviors. They report findings from a 1961–1962 survey of 12,000 elementary school children in eight communities.

To begin with, children evidently perceive a sex differentiation of political roles among adults. Hess and Torney confirm earlier findings that fathers are mentioned more often than mothers as "the best place to look for help" in deciding whom to vote for (pp. 98, 199). That such perceptions have a basis in reality is suggested by Ernest's (1976, p. 598) finding that mothers more often help with homework in English at each grade level. Only in grades 2–6, however, do mothers more often help with homework in arithmetic or mathematics; the fathers replace them in grades 7–12. Whether such perceptions are an important factor in the perpetuation of social differentiation by sex is not established by either the cited research or our own data. But their existence tends to justify our later (Chapter 11) attention to intergenerational aspects of sex typing.

Hess and Torney constructed a "Don't know" Index, the number of *don't know* responses given in answering 32 questions, including questions about partisanship, efficacy, and definition of democracy (p. 292). The answer format for some of these questions offered *don't know (no opinion)* as the middle response category in a series of five response options (p. 267). A sex difference with respect to the Index appears for children in grades 4, 5, 6, and 8, though not grade 7; and girls more often say *don't know* each time a sex difference appears (Figure 55, p. 202). In recounting an interview with a 12-year-old girl during a pretest to illustrate lack of subjective involvement with perfunctory participation, the authors observe, "The interview continues, revealing a good deal of information about current hit records, movie actors and Oscar awards, features on the women's page of the local newspaper. The lack of interest in politics is not part of a more general apathy but is specific [p. 20]." Their report on these matters conforms with our impressions about adults. Women have a somewhat greater propensity to say *don't know* and a tendency to avoid the extremes of the response options, but by no means all questions elicit this stereotypically feminine response pattern. Even within the domain of public affairs, women or wives or mothers show no reluctance in expressing their views about the people running the Education establishment or venting strong feelings about the Boy Scouts.

Children rated five stimulus objects—President, Policeman, Supreme Court, Government, and Senator—on several dimensions—such as "would want to help me if I needed it"—using six-point scales (example, p. 268). Most of the "pronounced" sex differences occur for the Policeman, whom girls rate more favorably on "never makes mistakes," "knows a lot," "makes decisions," "is a leader," and "works hard." Equally pronounced sex differences in the same direction appear for the President on the dimensions "makes decisions" and "works hard." The only instance in which boys assign the more favorable rating (statistically reliable, but less pronounced) is the Supreme Court on "never makes mistakes." In interpreting the overall configuration of sex differences in rating (shown in Table 27, p. 207), the authors write, "Girls emphasize the protective quality of personal figures and are attached to them, while boys stress protection by more impersonal and institutionalized structures [p. 205]." One of the few areas of institutional performance with which women express greater satisfaction is local Police Protection, despite their greater fears about personal safety on the streets. Men express more confidence in the Supreme Court than do women within the black population, whereas among whites men more often opt for an extreme category, favorable or unfavorable, rendering the direction of the sex difference equivocal.

When asked "Are all laws fair?" girls in grades 6, 7, and 8 expressed stronger positive feelings than did their male classmates (Figure D.11). When asked which two persons make the best citizens—someone (1) who works hard, (2) everybody likes, (3) who votes and gets others to vote, (4) who helps others, (5) who is interested in the way our country is run, (6) who obeys the laws, (7) who goes to church, or (8) I don't know what *citizen* means—girls in each grade more often select the person (6) who is law abiding (Figure 61, p. 208). (Recall the determination of the Detroit women to pay the parking violation fine.) Hess and Torney link these responses, stating, "Girls define the system as one in which all the laws are just. Reciprocally, they define the citizen's role as obedience to these laws [p. 211]." Is this perhaps the view embedded in

"The help and services that the public gets from the government is worth what it asks from the public," a statement which we found to be endorsed more often by women than by men?

Hess and Torney (1968, p. 213) report that although "adult surveys show that males feel more efficacious," boys and girls do not differ with respect to the Index of Efficacy, a set of five items (appropriately modified for children) from among items previously used by the Survey Research Center (p. 294). Two items are modified versions of our items 2 and 5 in Table 4-4, neither of which showed a pronounced sex difference in response. Indeed, the only "efficacy" item included in the DAS replication to show a strong sex difference in response was item 3, Politics and Government Complicated. They also report no sex differences among the children in "identifying voting as a mark of democracy" and "in selection of voting as a symbol of government [p. 216]" or in "perceiving that the good citizen's duty is to vote [p. 218]." As we reported, women and men do not differ in their endorsement of the importance of voting (item 1, Table 4-4).

As the discussion thus far has suggested, the questions asked the children differ just enough from the questions asked the adults to render systematic comparison impossible. We therefore report the response distribution of children for only one additional question: "Many people would like to be President, a Senator, or a Mayor. Why do you think these people would like to have these jobs? (1) They want to change things that are not good in the government; (2) They want to make a lot of money or be important; (3) They want to keep things as good as they are in the country [p. 87]." A sex difference in response appears among fifth-graders and grows progressively larger. Girls more often select (3) keep things as good as they are (Figure 69, p. 217). Hess and Torney see this response as "consistent" with the girls' "tendency to see government as a protective system [p. 217]." But perhaps it is also the case that girls, like women, foresee a more threatening future which requires effort simply to keep things as good as they are, let alone change them for the better.

6
Religion

It has everywhere been noted that women are much more devoted to religion and more faithful in the performance of conventional, religious, and moral duties.

[C. C. North, 1926, p. 111].

Students of the sociology of religion have little difficulty in mounting criticisms of the most readily available religious indicators on the grounds that these indicators are defective as measures of religiosity. Demerath (1968), for example, observes that "church attendance, like church membership, measures only one facet of religiosity and one that is decidedly 'middle-class' in style [p. 368]." But whatever attending religious services may mean in purely religious terms—and it might be best to allow those who attend the services to decide that for themselves—it clearly is a *social* activity. Moreover, it is a fairly salient one in the time budgets of those who make attendance a regular habit. In an inquiry into sex differences in social roles, therefore, there need be no apology if we put some emphasis on a kind of religious activity that has no *necessary* relation to piety or theologically relevant qualities of the religious life.

RELIGIOUS PARTICIPATION

We commence with an examination of the data on frequency of attendance at religious services. Data by sex are available from five surveys in the 1950s (1954, 1956–1959) as well as the 1971 survey. The wording of the question varies slightly, but in all surveys the end result is to place the respondent in one of five categories with respect to frequency with which she or he "usually attends" services or attended "last year." These are once a week or more, two or three times a month, once a month, a few times a year or less, or never.

The ratio of female to male respondents typically declines as we proceed from the first to the last of these categories; women attend services more frequently than men do. Indeed, if the five response categories are assigned the scores 5, 4, 3, 2, and 1, respectively, we find that in each year the relationship of sex to response is satisfactorily described by a linear regression of the log sex ratio (women:men) on score. For all the years but 1956 (1971 included) the slope is estimated as .193; but for 1956 it is .310. No obvious explanation of this difference is available. The wording used in the 1956 survey is exactly the same as that used in 1954, 1957, and 1959, while 1958 and 1971 shared a slightly different wording (see *Social Change in a Metropolitan Community*, Table 19). Had only the 1956 and 1971 surveys been available, we would have reported a diminution of the sex effect on attendance. In view of the additional evidence, no report on differential change is advisable.

Analyses not reported here suggest that the sex difference depends somewhat on color. Moreover, there is a difference by marital status that may confound the estimate of the sex effect, given the disproportionate number of women among the unmarried. Hence, in a further analysis of attendance, we confine attention to white married persons. The purpose of the analysis is to ascertain whether the sex effect varies by educational attainment. We pool the data for 1954, 1957, 1958, and 1959 (omitting 1956 for the reason mentioned in the preceding paragraph) for comparison with 1971. Attendance is scored 1,..., 5 as described in the preceding paragraph. Education is scored 0, 1,..., 7 for the following intervals of school years completed: 0–4, 5–7, 8, 9–11, 12, 13–15, 16, 17+. With Y = attendance and X = education, we obtain the equations,

$\hat{Y} = .008X + 3.82$, women in the 1950s
$\hat{Y} = .073X + 3.25$, men in the 1950s
$\hat{Y} = .089X + 3.17$, women in 1971
$\hat{Y} = .143X + 2.53$, men in 1971

In both years, the education effect is stronger for men. In both years, the average level of attendance is higher for women than for men at any education level; but the sex difference is greatest at the lower end of the education scale. For both women and men, the education effect is stronger in 1971 than in the 1950s. In effect, this means that the decrease in attendance was most pronounced (irrespective of sex) at the lower end of the education scale. Indeed, for well-educated women there was hardly any decrease, according to the equations just cited. The sex-education interaction here is rather similar to that reported in Chapter 7 (Figure 7-3) with respect to participation in church-connected groups.

National data from the Gallup poll agree broadly with the Detroit results in showing a persistent sex difference in attendance (see Table 6-1). Moreover, while there is a faint suggestion of a diminution of this difference over time, one would have to be bold to reach any firm conclusion about trend.

Data on formal church membership from the 1954, 1959, and 1971 surveys all are consistent with an estimate that the ratio of members to nonmembers is 1.8 times as great for women as for men. There is evidence that the sex difference is larger, at least in the later year, among blacks than among whites. But since the direction of the difference is the same in both groups, we do not elaborate on this interaction here.

TABLE 6-1
Percentage Giving Affirmative Responses to "Did you happen to attend church in the last seven days?" Gallup Poll, 1955–1974

Year	Men	Women	Difference
1974	35	44	9
1970	38	46	8
1969	38	46	8
1968	39	48	9
1967	41	49	8
1966	39	49	10
1965	40	48	8
1964	40	49	9
1963	41	51	10
1958	45	54	9
1957	43	51	8
1955	43	54	11

Source: Gallup, 1972. (Omits years for which sex classification is not given or for which data seem to refer to only one week in the year.) 1974 data from *The Arizona Daily Star,* December 28, 1974. 1966 and 1958 data from *Gallup Opinion Index.*

Excluding persons never attending religious services, the 1958 and 1971 surveys inquired whether the respondent takes part in activities or organizations of her or his church (synagogue, temple) other than attending services. Data for both women and men point to an increase in this kind of activity, with the 1971:1958 ratio being 1.3 for both sexes. The sex effect is the same, sampling errors aside, in the 2 years; being female raises the odds on this activity by a factor of 1.5. Incidentally, the 1958 survey included some details about the activity not covered in 1971. Those data indicate that a substantial part of the church-connected activities pertain to groups or clubs based in the religious organization but not having specifically religious or devotional functions. Again, therefore, it is emphasized that we are here measuring sex-role differentiation with respect to the social aspect of religious participation and not testing specifically for sex differences in the religious experience.

Reports on the practice of saying a prayer before meals were elicited by a question that referred explicitly to the participation of the family in this ritual. The data in Table 6-2 are, therefore, restricted to married respondents, with a cross-classification by the presence of a child (person under age 21) in the household. In principle, the male and female respondents should comprise two independent samples from the same population of married couples. The finding of a significant sex effect is, therefore, anomalous. Irrespective of year or the presence of a child, for women the odds on saying a prayer *quite often* (relative to never doing

TABLE 6-2
Fitted Odds on Saying a Prayer Before Meals, Married Respondents Only, 1958 and 1971, by Sex and Presence of Child

		Odds on response[a]	
Sex	Child present?	*yes, quite often : no*	*yes, on special occasions : no*
Male	Yes	1.34	.92
	No	1.04	.79
Female	Yes	2.10	.99
	No	1.64	.85
Odds ratio			
Female : Male		1.57	1.08
Yes : No		1.28	1.16

[a] Question wording: "In your family, do you ever say a prayer before meals? (If yes) How often is this done—quite often, or just on special occasions?"

so) are about 1.6 times as high as for men. For both men and women the odds on saying a prayer apparently are slightly raised by the presence of a child in the family, although this effect is not formally significant by the usual standard. There is no significant year effect nor any significant interaction among sex, year, and presence of child with respect to response.

There is a loophole in the wording of this question, ". . . do you ever say a prayer. . . ." It is just conceivable that a prayer is said regularly in some families at just those meals where the children are present but the father is away. Neglecting this possibility as well as the chance that we are victims of a sampling fluke, we would have to surmise that the question is in part a projective one—that at least some respondents answer primarily in terms of what they think is expected of them. If so, then women feel under greater constraint than men to acknowledge their participation in a religious ritual. Of course, if observations by an impartial third party were available to establish the facts of the matter, we might find that men underreport the practice of praying before meals, that women overreport, or both. In any case, our results do seem to imply that women at least nominally acknowledge a special responsibility for some kinds of religious observance.

As already noted, participating in a formal activity of some religious group need not be synonymous with being subjectively religious. The possibility of comparing these two facets of religiosity arises from the replication with half the 1971 sample of two questions used in the 1958 survey. One question referred to behavior: "Would you say you attend religious services more often, about the same, or less often than you did 10 or 15 years ago?" The other question called for a self-assessment of subjective involvement in religion: "All things considered, do you think you are more *interested,* about as interested, or less interested in religion than you were 10 or 15 years ago?" It appears to be an advantage of these questions that they ask for assessments of change, inasmuch as a self-assessment of degree of interest on an absolute scale might be difficult for some respondents.

Table 6-3 presents the cross-classification of the two responses for men and women in the 2 years. It is immediately obvious that the questions are not measuring the same thing; only about half of all respondents give the same answer to the two questions. Where there is a discrepancy, moreover, it is strongly in the direction of increasing interest in religion while attendance stays the same or decreases, or interest holding firm while attendance decreases; discrepancies in the opposite direction are comparatively rare. We might summarize this pattern roughly by stating that steadfast or increasing interest in reli-

TABLE 6-3
Percentage Distribution of Change in Interest in Religion by Change in Attendance at
Religious Services in Last 10 or 15 Years, for Men and Women, 1958 and 1971

| | | Change in attendance, by sex | | | | | | | |
| | | Men | | | | Women | | | |
Year	Change in interest	More	Same	Less	Total	More	Same	Less	Total
1958	More	19.7	15.1	11.2	46.0	19.8	14.6	18.1	52.5
	Same	2.6	26.7	17.1	46.4	5.2	21.3	15.8	42.3
	Less	0.3	0.7	6.6	7.6	0.3	0.3	4.6	5.2
	Total	22.6	42.5	34.9	100.0	25.3	36.2	38.5	100.0
					($N = 304$)				($N = 348$)
1971	More	12.1	11.4	9.7	33.2	13.9	10.9	15.4	40.2
	Same	4.4	18.7	14.0	37.1	2.6	14.9	18.3	35.8
	Less	0.7	3.6	25.4	29.7	0.4	2.1	21.5	24.0
	Total	17.2	33.7	49.1	100.0	16.9	27.9	55.2	100.0
					($N = 413$)				($N = 531$)

gion is a necessary but not a sufficient condition for a steady or increased rate of attendance.

The association between the two indicators does not vary significantly by sex, by year, by marital status, or combination thereof. (The result for marital status is obtained from data not shown here; the finding tends to justify disregarding the factor of marital status in further analysis of sex differences.)

Although the association of the two indicators is invariant with respect to sex, the difference between the marginal distributions for interest and for attendance is greater for women than for men. Consequently, the proportion of women giving discrepant answers to the two questions is higher. Aggregating cells on and off the diagonals of the 3 × 3 subtables of Table 6-3, we define a dichotomous variable *consistent* (on the diagonal) versus *inconsistent* (off the diagonal). This variable shows no significant year effect, but the same sex effect in both years: the odds on a *consistent* answer to the two questions are .78 as high for women as for men.

Given that response is inconsistent, in the sense that different response categories are selected for change in interest and change in attendance, is the type of inconsistency a function of sex? Aggregating frequencies above and below the diagonal of each 3 × 3 subtable, we get a ratio of *above* (change in interest minus change in attendance is positive) to *below* (negative) of 12.0 for men in 1958, 8.45 for women in that year, and 4.0 and 8.8 for men and women, respectively, in 1971. This set of four odds is incompatible with the assumption of either a constant sex effect or the same change for men and women; that is, the three-way interaction in the table describing direction of change by sex by year is significant ($X^2 = 5.7$, $df = 1$). The observed odds suggest that there was no change for women in the relative preponderance of positive over negative discrepancies, whereas for men the latter gained at the expense of the former.

We need not seek an explanation of these results in terms of factors other than those affecting the marginal distributions of change in interest and change in attendance by sex and year. This follows from the fact that the data conform to the hypothesis of quasisymmetry. (Chi-square values, each with 1 df, are 1.1 and 0.4 for men and women in 1958, 0.15 and 0.02 in 1971.) That is, the observed frequencies in the cross-classification of interest by attendance are as close as they can be to symmetry around the (upper left to lower right) diagonal, given the dissimilarity of row and column marginals. Thus, no special explanation is required for the relative numbers of women and men reporting a specific kind of inconsistency, such as more interest coupled with less attendance.

Continuing to focus on the diagonals, we raise the question of whether there are sex and/or year differences in the relative frequency of *more, same,* and *less* participation, if only persons who classify themselves consistently on the two indicators are considered. There is indeed a year effect, but no significant sex effect. The fitted ratio of *more* to *same* responses is .81 for men and women in both years; the fitted ratio of *less* to *same* responses is .23 for both sexes in 1958, 1.42 for the two sexes in 1971.

In summary, when attendance and interest in religion change in the same way, the aggregate changes for men and women are the same. But discrepant changes are more frequent for women. If, therefore, we look at the two indicators one at a time, we need not expect to get the same sex effects.

Data on change in attendance, Figure 6-1, include information for 1959 as well as 1958; and the 1971 data are for the full sample, not the half of it considered earlier. Clearly, men and women alike gave reports in 1971 differing from those in the late 1950s, especially in regard to the substantial increase in proportion with *less* attendance at the time of the survey than 10 or 15 years earlier. There are no significant differential changes by sex. On the contrary, the 3 years share a peculiar sex effect: Men respond *same* more frequently than women, at the expense of both *more* and *less* attendance. For each year, a model that fits quite well ($X^2 =$

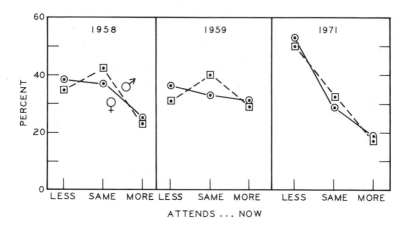

FIGURE 6-1. Percentage distribution of changes in church attendance in last 10 or 15 years, by sex, 1958, 1959, and 1971.

2.0, $df = 6$) provides the estimate that the sex ratio (women:men) is 1.25 times as high among those responding either *more* or *less* as among those reporting no change in either direction. Accepted at face value, this result means that over the course of the life cycle, women are more variable in their religious habits from one period to another, men more steadfast in whatever pattern they have adopted. (We recall, of course, that women do attend services more than men as a general rule.) Temporal variability for women could well reflect increases and decreases in family responsibilities that compete with religion for shares in the woman's time budget.

The sex effect on change in interest takes a different form. Using the marginals (by sex and year) for the changes in interest in Table 6-3, we find that a model allowing the sex ratio to vary linearly with response fits beautifully in both years ($Y^2 = 0.1$, $df = 3$). Despite the pronounced alteration of the response distribution between 1958 and 1971, observable for both women and men, there is no significant differential change by sex. For both years we estimate that the ratio of women to men among those reporting *same* interest is only 0.8 times as great as among those with *more* interest; and, in turn, among those with *less* interest the female:male ratio is but 0.8 as large as among those with *same* interest. The growth in interest with aging (over the 10- to 15-year period specified in the question) could, of course, reflect some kind of cohort effect. We suspect, however, that it is tied in with the general process of changing commitments as the life cycle progresses. The linear effect just described implies that the enhanced subjective involvement in religion with advancing age is even more characteristic of women than of men.

RELIGIOUS BELIEFS

If the indicators available to us may be relied on, the area of religious beliefs was one of fairly rapid change in the decade or so before 1971. There is, of course, no logical necessity for such change to be accompanied by a shift in the pattern of sex differences in regard to belief, although one might think that "fluidity" in one aspect of a situation would be associated with the same feature in another. Be that as it may, we do not find significant differential changes by sex. There were unmistakable sex differences at the beginning of our period (1958 or 1959), and the same differences were in evidence at its end. Of the six items to be examined, five show significant sex differences that may be broadly construed as indicating that women are more pious or at least more conventional in expressing themselves on the subject of religious belief. Although a different subset of five items show significant change over time, there is no item that exhibits a significant three-way interaction, response by sex by year.

Table 6-4 shows response distributions for the standard question on belief in God, to which the vast preponderance of Americans give an affirmative answer. But the magnitude of the majority leaves room for significant variation. The data in this particular table show nontrivial differences by both sex and year; the data can be fitted almost perfectly ($X^2 = 0.01$, $df = 2$) with a model that uses only the three sets of two-way marginals. The sex effect can be reduced to the contrast, *yes* versus (*uncertain* + *no*), with no loss of information. But the year effect is best

TABLE 6-4
Percentage Distribution by Belief in God, by Sex, 1958 and 1971

Do you believe there is a God, or not?	1958		1971	
	Men	Women	Men	Women
Yes	94.7	98.3	90.7	96.7
Uncertain	3.6	1.1	5.4	1.9
No	1.7	0.6	3.9	1.4
	100.0	100.0	100.0	100.0
(N)	(303)	(349)	(826)	(1050)

expressed by regarding *uncertain* as a third category, midway between *yes* and *no*; that is, the logarithm of the ratio of 1971 to 1958 frequencies is linearly related to a scoring of the three response categories with consecutive integers.

As Table 6-4 suggests, men will more often than women volunteer that they are *uncertain* about the existence of God. But even among those who initially answer *yes*, there are quite a few of both sexes who will admit some degree of uncertainty under the more probing inquiry used in the 1959 survey. In 1959, to be sure, a healthy majority of both male and female believers were *very sure* of their beliefs (Figure 6-2, left panel); but by 1971 this majority had dwindled to a mere plurality for men and to a bare majority for women (right panel). Of interest here are the facts that women claim greater certainty than men in both years and there is no significant change in this pattern. Scoring *not sure, not too sure, rather sure,* and *very sure* as 0, 1, 2, 3, respectively, we find that the logarithm of the sex ratio is linearly related to response in both years and the slope of the regression does not shift significantly between years.

Again excluding unbelievers, we look at kind or degree of commitment to belief with the question, "Do you believe that someone who

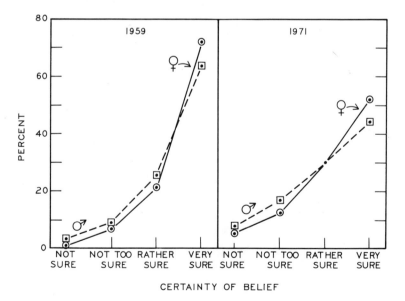

FIGURE 6-2. Percentage distribution by certainty of belief in God, by sex, 1959 and 1971 (excludes unbelievers).

doesn't believe in God can be a good American, or not?" A small minority of both men and women signify that they are unsure of their opinion on this question. But a partitioning of the three response categories in the analysis by sex and year suggests that all significant effects are captured if *unsure* is combined with *cannot*. We then find that the odds on responding *can* (versus *unsure + cannot*) are 1.8 for men and 1.0 for women in 1958, rising to 4.9 and 2.5, respectively, in 1971. The observed odds are very close to the odds obtained from a model allowing for a sex effect and a year effect, but no differential change. The fitted odds on *can* are .54 as great for women as for men in both years; the odds on *can* are increased by a factor of 2.5 between 1958 and 1971 for both sexes.

Table 6-5 presents results for the only item that fails to show an unequivocal sex effect. There is no significant sex difference in the ratio of *yes* to *no* responses to the question, "Do you believe in life after death, or not?" It is true, however, that women put themselves into the *uncertain* category more often than men. To that extent, they are slightly more skeptical of religious doctrine than men; or, perhaps, men are just a little more egoistic than women.

An important caution concerning the results in the preceding paragraph relates to the footnote to Table 6-5. To maintain comparability with the 1958 coding rules, we tabulated the 1971 data excluding persons not believing in God. With these persons restored to the tabulation, the 1971 odds ratio measuring the sex effect on belief in life after death is 1.3; that is, the odds on *belief* are that much higher for women. A somewhat conjectural adjustment of the 1958 data yields exactly the same ratio. These results are much more nearly in conformity with national data than are the figures in Table 6-5. Both the 1973 and the

TABLE 6-5
Belief in Life after Death, by Sex, 1958 and 1971

Do you believe in life after death, or not?	1958		1971	
	Men	Women	Men	Women
Observed odds[a]				
yes : no	5.3	5.3	2.7	3.2
uncertain : no	.82	.98	.58	1.1
Fitted odds[a]				
yes : no	5.1	5.1	3.0	3.0
uncertain : no	.66	1.0	.66	1.0

[a] Excludes respondents who do not believe in God.

1976 General Social Surveys yield ratios of 1.3, while the Gallup Poll's published percentage distributions (Gallup, 1972, pp. 475, 1663) imply ratios of 1.4 in 1944 and 1.6 in 1960. The suggestion from the Detroit data, therefore, is that the sex difference on the life-after-death question is derivative from the sex difference on belief in God. The sex difference in uncertainty does not turn up in the two cited Gallup Polls nor in the 1973 General Social Survey. But in the 1976 GSS we find that the ratio of *don't know* to *no* responses is 1.8 times as high for women as for men, producing a significant sex differential in the change in response to the question.

The one item that shows no significant change is the question, "When you have decisions to make in your everyday life, do you ask yourself what God would want you to do?" The answer categories, *often, sometimes,* and *never* relate linearly to the logarithm of the sex ratio. From the estimated regression we can calculate that the ratio of women to men for *sometimes* is just twice as great as for *never* and, in turn, is twice as great for *often* as for *sometimes*. For women the modal response is *often;* for men it is *sometimes*. (The analysis again excludes respondents who profess not to believe in God.) Make no mistake about it, this is a truly substantial sex difference. We find little in the literature on sex roles or feminism that helps us to understand it or to give an interpretation beyond the obvious one that it is utterly consistent with C. C. North's half-century old observation.

Finally, in analyzing responses to "Do you feel you have the right to question what your church teaches, or not?" we ignore the small number of *unsure* responses. Observed odds, *yes : no,* are 2.8 and 2.2 for men and women, respectively, in 1958, 5.7 and 4.2 in 1971. These are so close to the odds under a model fitting all two-way marginals that it is superfluous to quote the latter. The Female : Male odds ratio computed from the fitted counts is .75 in both years, so that women are seen to be somewhat more timorous in asserting this right in both years, although gaining in temerity along with men between 1958 and 1971.

COMMUNAL INVOLVEMENT

Whereas the several items registering sex differences in religious beliefs told much the same story about sex differences, we find no such consistency across items in analyzing communal involvement. Nor is it possible to offer an unequivocal statement about the effect of sex on prejudice or antipathy toward religious outgroups.

We begin with attitude toward religious endogamy: "As a general rule, do you think it is wiser for (Protestants/Catholics/Jewish people) to marry other (Protestant/Catholic/Jewish people) or not?"—the wording being varied in accordance with the respondent's own stated preference. Although there is a decrease in endorsement of endogamy for all groups between 1958 and 1971, there is no significant sex differential in the change. There is, however, a sex effect on response, albeit one observed only among Protestant and Jewish respondents. For them, the ratio, *wiser : no,* is 1.4 times as high for women as for men and the ratio, *unsure : no,* is 1.2 times as high. (The latter figure need not be taken too seriously, since there were actually no Jewish respondents who were unsure and rather few Protestants or Catholics. Nevertheless, we do not find here, as in several other contexts, that women opt for the intermediate category at the expense of both extremes to a greater extent than men.)

The parallel question relating to informal association within one's religious group reads, "As a general rule, do you think it is wiser for (Protestants/Catholics/Jewish people) to choose other (Protestants/Catholics/Jewish people) as their really close friends, or not?" Again, there is a decline between 1958 and 1971 in endorsement of ingroup choice for all groups, but no sex differential in the change. Nor is there any difference among the religious groups in the magnitude of the sex effect. The latter is in the opposite direction to the one noted for endogamy, since the ratio, *wiser : no,* is only .75 as large for women as for men, and the ratio, *unsure : no,* is only .86 as large (making the calculations from a model that achieves an acceptable fit by letting the logarithm of the sex ratio be related linearly to response, with the response categories, wiser, unsure, and no, scored 0, 1, 2).

We do not find the same sex difference, or, indeed, any significant sex difference when inquiring about actual choices of friends: "Thinking of *your* closest friends, what proportion are (Protestants/Catholics/Jewish)?" Six response categories were offered: all of them, nearly all of them, more than half of them, about half of them, less than half of them, none of them. Whether we treat this item as a polytomous categorical variable or as a linear scale, we find no significant sex effects, interactions of sex with religious group, or differential changes by sex—although there are effects of religious preference and significant changes between 1958 and 1971, as described in *Social Change in a Metropolitan Community* (p. 64).

Catholic respondents were asked, "Do you believe that the Catholic Church is the only true Church established by God Himself, and that other churches were only established by men?" If we disregard the rather small minority who were "unsure" of their opinion, there would appear to be no significant sex effect or differential change by sex. The odds, *yes* : *no,* are 2.2 and 2.8 for men and women, respectively, in 1958, and the corresponding figures are .82 and .81 in 1971, with neither difference significant. In 1971, however (although not in 1958), women were more prone to evade the issue; in 1958 the *unsure* : *no* odds was .28 for both men and women, but in 1971 it was .086 for men, .16 for women, a ratio of almost 2.0. Here we encounter the first of several findings that leave the sex comparison in an ambiguous state. If women really mean *yes* when they answer *unsure,* then (at least in 1971) the "true believer" is somewhat more likely to be female than is the less committed Catholic. But if *unsure* means *no,* just the opposite is true. Splitting the difference is tantamount to ignoring the ambiguous response and reporting no sex difference on the question.

Protestant respondents (for whom, as a heterogeneous collectivity, there can be no single "true church," whatever each may feel about his particular denominational allegiance) were asked a not quite parallel question: "Do you feel that Catholics have been trying to get too much power in this country, or not?" Both women and men volunteer a response that is coded *unsure* rather often, but women do so much more frequently than men; the ratio of *unsure* responses to the aggregate of *yes* and *no* answers is about twice as high for women as for men in both years. Again, the interpretation would have to depend on an unverifiable assumption about the possibly different meaning of *unsure* for women and men. Are the women simply telling us that they are not so interested in an abstraction like "power," or are they more reluctant to reveal their true feelings about Catholics? If we look only at the two definite responses, a curious result turns up. The *yes* : *no* odds are .406 and .521 for men and women in 1958, in contrast to .570 and .314 respectively in 1971. Hence, the direction of the sex effect was reversed; the Female : Male odds ratio was 1.3 in the earlier year, .55 a little more than a decade later. Stating the same result in an alternative form, there was a significant differential change by sex, as registered in the 1971 : 1958 odds ratio, 1.4 for men, .60 for women. Neglecting the equivocal *unsure* answers, then, we should have to conclude that apprehension about the power of Catholics increased for Protestant men while it was decreasing for Protestant women. The two changes virtually cancel out, so that for all Protestants (as reported in *Social Change in a Metropolitan Community,* p. 66) there was no significant change.

Two questions asked of both Protestants and Catholics to ascertain prevalence of anti-Semitic feelings are analyzed in some detail in Tables 6-6 and 6-7. The details are necessary inasmuch as the findings are mixed. The simpler pattern occurs for Fair in Business. There are both

TABLE 6-6

Attitude Toward Jews ("Fair in Business"), for Protestants and Catholics, by Sex, 1958 and 1971

Compared with (Protestants/ Catholics), do you think that the Jewish people as a whole are more fair, as fair, or less fair in their business dealings?		Protestant		Catholic		
		Men	Women	Men	Women	Women:Men
Observed percentage distributions						
1958	More	4.3	1.9	2.9	2.2	—
	As	46.8	53.5	46.1	57.1	—
	Less	48.9	44.6	51.0	40.7	—
		100.0	100.0	100.0	100.0	—
	(N)	(141)	(157)	(102)	(91)	—
1971	More	6.7	3.9	2.9	2.0	—
	As	54.2	61.5	67.3	73.6	—
	Less	39.1	34.6	29.8	24.4	—
		100.0	100.0	100.0	100.0	—
	(N)	(389)	(488)	(272)	(344)	—
Fitted odds						
1958	*more : as*	.082	.043	.067	.035	.52
	less : as	1.07	.815	1.02	.778	.76
1971	*more : as*	.122	.064	.048	.025	.52
	less : as	.731	.556	.440	.334	.76
Fitted odds ratio						
1971 : 1958	*more : as*	1.5	1.5	.72	.72	1.0
	less : as	.68	.68	.43	.43	1.0

sex effects and religious-group effects, as well as a decrease in overtly anti-Semitic responses over time. But there are neither significant differentials in rate of change by sex nor significant differences in the magnitude of the sex effect as between Protestants and Catholics. Again we find that women use the intermediate category more than men; but the result may not have the same explanation here as in the case of the earlier questions, since the *as* response is the modal one for both sexes in 1971 and for women in 1958. Nevertheless, the result is somewhat equivocal, for the *less : as* odds is only three-quarters as large for women as for men, implying that the men are the more anti-Semitic; but the

TABLE 6-7

Attitude Toward Jews ("Too Much Power"), for Protestants and Catholics, by Sex, 1958 and 1971

Do you feel that the Jewish people have been trying to get too much power in the country, or not?		Protestant		Catholic		Women:Men	
		Men	Women	Men	Women	Prot-estant	Cath-olic
Observed percentage distributions							
1958	Yes	28.2	25.9	32.4	19.5	—	—
	Unsure	10.9	27.4	9.0	19.4	—	—
	No	60.9	46.7	58.6	61.1	—	—
		100.0	100.0	100.0	100.0	—	—
	(N)	(156)	(201)	(111)	(113)	—	—
1971	Yes	25.7	20.0	25.9	15.1	—	—
	Unsure	7.1	16.2	6.9	12.3	—	—
	No	67.2	63.8	67.2	72.6	—	—
		100.0	100.0	100.0	100.0	—	—
	(N)	(408)	(556)	(290)	(383)	—	—
Fitted odds							
1958	yes:no	.58	.52	.60	.33	.90	.56
	unsure:no	.17	.46	.17	.29	2.7	1.7
1971	yes:no	.35	.32	.36	.20	.90	.56
	unsure:no	.10	.28	.11	.18	2.7	1.7
Fitted odds ratio							
1971:1958	yes:no	.61	.61	.61	.61	1.0	1.0
	unsure:no	.61	.61	.61	.61	1.0	1.0

more:as odds is also smaller among women, implying that fewer of them are highly favorably disposed toward Jews.

In the case of Too Much Power (Table 6-7), while there is again no differential change by sex or religion, the religious and sex effects are involved in a decided interaction. There really is little or no difference between Protestant and Catholic views on the issue of Too Much Power where men are concerned, but Protestant women are perceptibly more suspicious of Jews on this score than are Catholic women. However, the sex difference itself is ambiguous, since the *yes:no* ratio is greater for men while the *unsure:no* ratio is greater for women. Here again, the high incidence of *unsure,* particularly for women, makes the result intrinsically equivocal. If, for illustrative purposes, we take *unsure* to be an anti-Semitic response, along with *yes,* we find that the ratio of (*yes* + *unsure*) to *no* is .60 for Protestant women in 1958, .46 for Protestant men, .47 for Catholic men, and .38 for Catholic women, demonstrating nicely the irrelevance of religious group for men's responses and its substantial effect for women. The corresponding ratios in 1971 are all just .61 as large, since there are no differential changes, according to the model used in the computations, which includes the significant interactions.

GENERATION GAPS IN RELIGIOSITY

Our most tantalizing data on sex differences in religious orientations were produced by the following question:

When your (father/mother) was about your age, was (he/she) more religious than you are, about as religious, or would you say (he/she) was less religious than you are?

Each respondent was asked about both parents, so that intergenerational comparisons may be defined in four ways: father–son, father–daughter, mother–son, and mother–daughter. Moreover, we may ascertain the relationship between the changes reported with reference to the father and those in which the mother's religiosity is the stipulated baseline. The data structure is somewhat complex, therefore; and the analysis is a bit tortuous. Hence, for sake of clarity, it seems best to record at the outset the frequencies on which the analysis is based. They appear in Table 6-8. We have excluded those respondents who were not able to report on both parents. The table is confined to married respondents, inasmuch as this restriction implicitly controls for some potentially distracting variables not of immediate interest in this context.

To begin the inspection of these data, Figure 6-3 summarizes the marginal distributions for each possible combination of sex of respondent and sex of parent. We find, for example, that about two-thirds of the male respondents in both 1958 and 1971 reported that their mothers were *more religious* than themselves. Only about one-quarter (in 1958) or one-third (in 1971) of female respondents made such a report concerning their fathers. These marginals define the extremes; the marginals for women reporting on their mothers and men on their fathers are intermediate.

Among the noteworthy comparisons emphasized in Figure 6-3 are these.

1. For both women and men, there is a pronounced intergenerational

decline in religiosity when the baseline in religiosity is the same-sex parent. That is, the *more* outweigh the *less* responses for women reporting on their mothers and for men reporting on their fathers. We might note the possibility that such intergenerational changes, even if real, do not unambiguously establish a long-term trend in religiosity. If it were the case that very religious persons had large numbers of offspring and less religious persons had small numbers of offspring, on the average, then there would be an oversampling of highly religious parents in a study collecting data on the parental generation via a random sample of the offspring generation. (To see this most easily, imagine that atheists have no children; in that case, none of our respondents could report that their parents were utterly irreligious.) Whether or not this bias occurs or is important here, it remains true that both men and women tend to see themselves, on the average, as less religious than their fathers and mothers, respectively.

TABLE 6-8

Percentage Distribution by Reported Religiosity of Parents as Compared with Self, for Married Men and Women, 1958 and 1971

Year	Sex of respondent	Mother compared with respondent	Father compared with respondent			
			More religious	About as religious	Less religious	Total
1958	Male	More religious	31.5	27.6	8.8	67.9
		About as religious	4.4	17.1	7.2	28.7
		Less religious	0.6	0.6	2.2	3.4
		Total	36.5	45.3	18.2	100.0
						(N = 181)
	Female	More religious	19.1	16.2	5.9	41.2
		About as religious	3.4	32.8	10.3	46.5
		Less religious	1.5	2.0	8.8	12.3
		Total	24.0	51.0	25.0	100.0
						(N = 204)
1971	Male	More religious	28.1	24.4	11.4	63.9
		About as religious	2.9	18.4	6.1	27.4
		Less religious	0.5	1.0	7.2	8.7
		Total	31.5	43.8	24.7	100.0
						(N = 587)
	Female	More religious	24.7	13.2	12.2	50.1
		About as religious	5.2	19.7	11.7	36.6
		Less religious	1.5	1.5	10.3	13.3
		Total	31.4	34.4	34.2	100.0
						(N = 583)

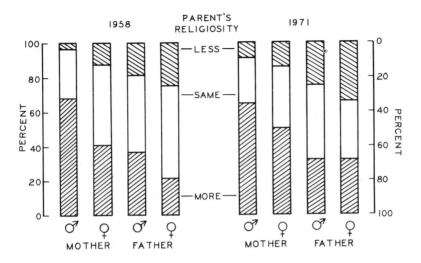

FIGURE 6-3. Percentage distribution of intergenerational changes in religiosity, for married respondents reporting on both parents, by sex of respondent, 1958 and 1971.

2. When the comparison is made with the opposite-sex parent, the result just reported is exaggerated for men but absent for women. That is, men perceive themselves as much less religious than their mothers; but women do not report any systematic difference between themselves and their fathers. The ratio of *more* to *less* is quite large for men reporting on their mothers, but about unity for women reporting on their fathers.

3. Fixing the sex of the respondent, the female parent is clearly seen as more religious than the male parent; both women and men report their mothers as more religious than their fathers, in the sense that the ratio of *more* to *less* reports is greater for mothers than for fathers.

4. Fixing the sex of the parent, female respondents are more religious than male respondents. That is, the ratio of *more* to *less* reports is greater for men than for women, whether they are both reporting on mothers or both reporting on fathers.

5. While the differences so far described obtain in both 1958 and 1971, there are indications of differential change in Figure 6-3. But the figure itself does not tell us quite all we need to know to specify these differentials. Hence the more elaborate analyses reported subsequently.

Despite the interest in the details supplied by these analyses, it is well to keep in mind that female and male respondents clearly agree that the former is the more religious sex and that this sex difference describes

the parental generation as well as the present one. These are constants
in the data from the two surveys.

To bring out one important aspect of the differential changes between
1958 and 1971 we consider in Figure 6-4 only the reports on same-sex
parents. The points and lines describe the ratio of women to men
among respondents answering, respectively, *more, same,* and *less.* In
both years, departures from linearity are easily ascribed to sampling
fluctuations, so that it suffices to discuss the slopes of the lines. The
slope is significantly greater (in absolute value) in 1971 than in 1958.
Indeed, the slope for 1958 cannot be shown to differ significantly from
zero. The regression analysis, therefore, confirms what the eye detects
in the earlier Figure 6-3, where the two middle bars for 1958 look rather
similar while their counterparts for 1971 are quite different. In measuring intergenerational change with same-sex parent as the baseline,
there was no significant sex difference in the earlier year but an unmistakable one in the later year. If we could assume that the parental
generation provided a fixed benchmark, these results would mean that
there was a more rapid decline in religiosity for women than for men
during the period 1958–1971. Unfortunately, we cannot rule out the
possibility that the benchmark itself was shifting.

At this point, one is led to reflect on the nature of the task that the
respondents were asked to perform. They were not required to assess
their own or their parents' religiosity on an absolute scale. In some

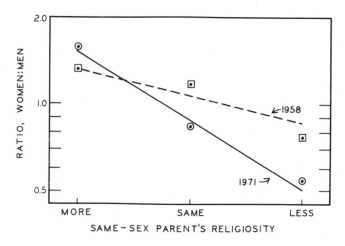

FIGURE 6-4. Parental religiosity by respondent's sex, 1958 and 1971, for married respondents reporting on both parents.

ways, this was probably all to the good, for comparative judgments are often easy to make even though exact locations on a scale would be difficult to estimate. Thus, one might find it easy to report whether one's father was taller, shorter, or about the same height as oneself but difficult to estimate the father's height in inches. Indeed, if the latter were required, one would probably proceed by estimating one's own height and then the father's height by reference thereto. Thus, there is an argument in favor of the kind of question that was used. At the same time, our results would be ever so much easier to report if they derived from a scale of religiosity as such rather than from a scale of intergenerational changes in religiosity. The analyst is almost irresistibly led to interpret the former in terms of postulates about the latter, even if those postulates are left implicit. Perhaps it would be better to make them explicit.

What follows, then, is a conjectural interpretation of the data, designed to be consistent with the data but not to exclude other possible interpretations. We suppose that each respondent actually judges her or his own religiosity on a 3-point scale as high, medium, or low; and each parent's religiosity is then estimated on the same scale. In that event, if the respondent has low religiosity and the parent medium or high, the response to our question will be *more*; but if the respondent is high on the religiosity scale and the parent is medium or low, the response will be *less*; and so on. Since parent and respondent are independently assessed as high, medium, or low, there are nine possibilities for the hypothetical cross-classification of respondent by parent. Actually, we must imagine that both parents and the respondent are placed on this scale, so that there are altogether 27 possibilities for the cross-classification of respondent's religiosity by mother's religiosity by father's religiosity. These 27 possibilities are enumerated in Table 6-9. We assume that after the respondent determines which of these 27 possibilities describes his own family of orientation, he collapses his report into one of the nine possible classifications of intergenerational change in religiosity shown in the note to Table 6-9. Our conjectures, therefore, must take the form of statements as to how the 9 observed frequencies were produced from the 27 hypothetical frequencies.

Table 6-9 offers three formulas (out of the infinity of possible formulas) according to which the observed data *could* have been generated on our postulates. Formula (i) simply distributes the nine observed frequencies among the 27 hypothetical possibilities in proportion to the number of the latter that contribute to each of the former. For example, there are five ways in which a respondent might come to report that both father and mother were *more* religious:

Respondent	Mother	Father
medium	high	high
low	high	high
low	high	medium
low	medium	high
low	medium	medium

If a is the number of *more–more* responses, then the frequency $a/5$ is assigned to each of the above possibilities. It may be noted that the frequency i in the note to Table 6-9 similarly is distributed into five cells of the hypothetical cross-tabulation; frequencies b, d, e, f, and h are evenly distributed each into three cells; and frequencies c and g can be assigned uniquely.

Formula (ii) assumes that there is a strong correlation between the religiosity of father and mother and between that of each and the respondent, such that there are no instances of one of the three persons being high in religiosity while another is low. After 11 cells are assigned zero frequencies on this basis, the remainder are filled on the principle of even division. Formula (iii) is just the negative of Formula (ii), except for the constraint on any formula that frequencies c and g in the observed data each correspond to a single possibility in the hypothetical classification.

Each formula defined in Table 6-9 was used to create a hypothetical set of frequencies for each of the four sets (sex by year) of observed frequencies in Table 6-8. When that was done, summaries of the univariate distributions of religiosity of mothers, fathers, and respondents were used to calculate the ratios in Table 6-10.

We will do well to note only those features of Table 6-10 in regard to which all three formulas give the same sort of results, since none of the formulas can be shown to be preferable to any other. Consistently with our earlier summaries of the observed distributions, we find that in both generations there is a pronounced sex difference in religiosity. Women are, or are perceived to be, or consider themselves to be more religious than men in their own generation. But, curiously, women see themselves as just about as religious as their fathers. Men perceive their mothers as more religious than women do. That this must be a bias in perception or reporting rather than a veridical reflection of a "real" state of affairs follows from the observation that the mothers reported on by male respondents comprise essentially the same population as those reported on by female respondents, unless we are prepared to assume

TABLE 6-9
Formulas for Deriving Frequencies of Hypothetical Religiosity from Observations in Terms of Respondents' Comparisons of Self with Parents

Hypothetical religiosity			Formula[a]		
Respondent	Mother	Father	(i)	(ii)	(iii)
High	High	High	$e/3$	$e/2$	0
		Medium	$f/3$	$f/2$	0
		Low	$f/3$	0	f
	Medium	High	$h/3$	$h/2$	0
		Medium	$i/5$	$i/2$	0
		Low	$i/5$	0	$i/3$
	Low	High	$h/3$	0	h
		Medium	$i/5$	0	$i/3$
		Low	$i/5$	0	$i/3$
Medium	High	High	$a/5$	$a/2$	0
		Medium	$b/3$	$b/2$	0
		Low	c	c	c
	Medium	High	$d/3$	$d/2$	0
		Medium	$e/3$	0	e
		Low	$f/3$	$f/2$	0
	Low	High	g	g	g
		Medium	$h/3$	$h/2$	0
		Low	$i/5$	$i/2$	0
Low	High	High	$a/5$	0	$a/3$
		Medium	$a/5$	0	$a/3$
		Low	$b/3$	0	b
	Medium	High	$a/5$	0	$a/3$
		Medium	$a/5$	$a/2$	0
		Low	$b/3$	$b/2$	0
	Low	High	$d/3$	0	d
		Medium	$d/3$	$d/2$	0
		Low	$e/3$	$e/2$	0

[a] Fractions of the frequencies in the table below:

	Father		
Mother	More	Same	Less
More	a	b	c
Same	d	e	f
Less	g	h	i

TABLE 6-10
Ratio of Derived Frequencies of High to Low Religiosity on Hypothetical Scale, for
Parents and Respondents

Formula	Year	Mothers, reported by		Fathers, reported by		Respondents	
		Men	Women	Men	Women	Women	Men
(i)	1958	5.2	2.2	.73	.69	.67	.24
	1971	4.0	2.7	.62	.66	.61	.35
(ii)	1958	4.0	1.8	.76	.75	.75	.33
	1971	3.3	2.4	.65	.68	.69	.44
(iii)	1958	9.2	3.5	.59	.51	.54	.16
	1971	6.6	3.5	.50	.56	.55	.26 .

that women who have only or predominantly male children somehow
differ in religiosity from those whose children are mostly or entirely
females. According to all three formulas, the sex bias in reporting of
mother's religiosity diminished appreciably between 1958 and 1971.
(Compare the ratios of men and women reporting on mothers in the 2
years.)

Insofar as the reputed religiosity of women is a product of the male
imagination, we have evidence here of a distinct decline in sex typing.
There is, moreover, some slight indication of a convergence of female
and male religiosity in the respondent generation between 1958 and
1971. But the data provided by both men and women continue to insist
that "women are much more devoted. . . ."

7

Social Participation of Husbands and Wives

Mention of the PTA or a bridge club will bring to mind a roomful of persons never to be mistaken for the members of the union local or a veterans' post. The former are stereotypically women's organizations, in contrast to the latter, which are associations of men. The imagery is grounded in reality for the odds on *belong* to the Parent–Teacher Association or a Card/Social Club were twice as great for women as for men. The odds on *belong* to a Labor Union or a Veteran's Organization for men exceeded the corresponding odds for women by an even larger factor. (See Duncan *et al.*, 1973, Table 17, p. 48.)

This information about formal participation was obtained when the interviewer said: "Now here is a list of clubs and organizations that many people belong to. Please look at this list and tell me which of these kinds of organizations you belong to." Whenever the respondent named a kind of organization, the interviewer asked, "Do you usually attend meetings of this group at least once a month, or not?" Thus, respondents can be classified as (*a*) *active*, belongs and attends meetings at least once a month, (*b*) *inactive*, belongs but attends a meeting less than once a month, or (*c*) *not a member* of any club or organization of the given kind. Since organizations differ in the frequency with which meetings are held, *active* does not necessarily connote greater organizational commitment. Moreover, we cannot distinguish persons who belong to two or more organizations of the same kind from those who belong to only one such organization. The list of 14 organizational titles shown to the respondent is reproduced in the stub of Table 7-1, which also presents selected summary measures of participation in each kind of organization.

Measures of informal participation derive from answers to four questions that were introduced with the statement, "We are also interested in how Detroiters spend their spare time. Many people get together every once in a while to visit, or play cards, or do something else."

> How often do you usually get together
> . . . with any of your relatives other than those living at home with you?
> . . . with any of your neighbors?
> . . . outside of work with any people you (or your husband) work with?
> . . . with any other friends who are not neighbors or fellow workers?

Respondents were given a card listing eight possible frequencies, ranging from 1. Every Day to 8. Never, and asked to choose one. We suspect that visiting kin and neighboring often are viewed as activities especially appropriate for women.

Our concern is not patterns of social participation as such, but rather what these patterns may suggest about the separate and shared interests of husbands and wives and the intensity of sex typing at the organizational level or with respect to particular kinds of informal association. Most analyses are restricted to the currently married population, which means that men and women—husbands and wives—are roughly matched with respect to a number of characteristics that might influence participation. In studying sex differences in participation, some control for age and color, family socioeconomic level, tenure and type of neighborhood, and the presence of children and other relatives in the home or locality seems essential. On occasion, the possibility that the sex effect is contingent on membership in a particular social stratum is checked; but we rely primarily on restriction of the study population to the currently married as a means of controlling "other" factors.

WIFE–HUSBAND DIFFERENCES IN FORMAL PARTICIPATION

The odds on *belong* are greater for wives than for husbands when the kind of organization in question is a Parent–Teacher Association or a

TABLE 7-1

Participation in Clubs and Organizations of Different Kinds, Based on Self Reports of Married Respondents, 1959 and 1971

Kind of club or organization	Total[a]	Odds on *belong*				Odds on *active* for members[a]
		Wives		Husbands		
		1959	1971	1959	1971	
Labor Unions	.40	.12	.11	.93	.85	1.0
Church-Connected Groups	.50	.82	.49	.46	.34	3.3
Fraternal Organizations or Lodges	.17	.11	.11	.24	.22	1.0
Veteran's Organizations	.059	.032	0.0	.10	.11	.80
Business or Civic Groups	.074	.032	.049	.083	.13	2.7
Parent-Teacher Associations	.29	.41	.47	.15	.18	1.5
Neighborhood Clubs or Community Centers	.10	.082	.14	.083	.10	2.2
Organizations of People of the Same Nationality	.046	.082	.027	.050	.034	1.8
Sports Teams	.16	.10	.12	.14	.29	19
Professional Groups	.088	.043	.046	.12	.15	1.4
Political Clubs or Organizations	.031	.028	.030	.033	.034	.95
Neighborhood Improvement Associations	.12	.14	.10	.18	.087	.87
Card Clubs; Women's or Men's Social Clubs	.15	.22	.20	.087	.10	11
Charitable and Welfare Organizations	.087	.11	.093	.079	.066	1.1

[a] Calculated from data for all currently married respondents in the 1959 and 1971 surveys.

Church Group. Wives also are more often *active* in Card/Social Clubs. These wife–husband differences seem to represent three bona fide instances of sex typing at the organizational level, for membership criteria as such would not produce such substantial imbalances. Indeed, for every eligible mother, there is a father equally eligible for membership in the PTA. Husbands, in contrast, more often *belong* to Fraternal Organizations, Business/Civic Groups, Professional Groups, and Labor Unions and are more often *active* in Sports Teams. Insofar as membership in Unions or Professional Groups follows from a person's occupation, sex typing at the organizational level may be derivative, that is, a reflection of the occupational segregation between men and women. Fraternal Organizations, Sports Teams, and perhaps Business/Civic Groups, however, can be seen as additional instances of sex typing at

TABLE 7-2

Difference between Wives and Husbands and Change between 1959 and 1971 in Participation, by Kind of Club or Organization, Based on Self-Reports of Married Respondents

			Odds ratio (given status to *nonmember*)			
	Ratio of odds on *belong*		Wife:Husband		1971:1959	
Club or organization	Wife: Husband	1971: 1959	*active member*	*inactive member*	*active member*	*inactive member*
PTA	2.7	1.0	2.7	2.7	1.0	1.0
Card/Social	2.2	1.0	2.4	1.0	1.0	1.0
Church Group	1.6	.65	1.6	1.6	.65	.65
Charitable	1.4[a]	1.0	1.0	1.8[a]	1.0	1.0
N/C Club	1.0	1.5[a]	1.0	1.0	1.5[a]	1.5[a]
Political	1.0	1.0	1.0	1.0	1.0	1.0
NIA	1.0	.57	1.0	1.0	.57	.57
Nationality	1.0	.46	1.0	1.0	.46	.46
Sports Teams	.53	1.7	.52	1.0	1.9	.13
Fraternal	.47	1.0	.64	.32	1.0	1.0
Business/Civic	.38	1.6[a]	.38	.38	1.6[a]	1.6[a]
Professional	.33	1.0	.33	.33	1.0	1.0
Labor Union	.13	1.0	.08	.18	1.0	1.0
Veteran[b]						
1959	.31	—	1.0	.02	—	—
1971	0.0	—	0.0	.02	—	—
Husbands	—	1.1	—	—	1.9	1.0
Wives	—	0.0	—	—	0.0	1.0

[a] Significantly different from 1.0 at the .1 level although not at the .05 level.

[b] No wives reported membership in a Veterans' Organization in 1971.

the organizational level. Veteran's Organizations, the only kind of organization for which a change in the magnitude of the wife–husband difference is detected between 1959 and 1971, is something of a special case in terms of membership criteria; but in both years husbands greatly outnumbered wives among the members (see Table 7-2).

The persistence of sex typing on the organizational level can be documented further by examining data from the 1957 and 1954 surveys. The questions about participation in clubs and organizations asked in 1957 and 1954 differ somewhat in format from the questions asked in 1959 and 1971. Nonetheless, some comparisons with respect to organizational sex typing can be made over the 17-year span, 1954–1971.

In 1957, the interviewer said, "Here is a list of the different kinds of clubs and organizations that are found in greater Detroit. Which of these groups do you belong to?" Kinds of organizations were listed in the same order as in 1959 and 1971 (stub of Table 7-1), and most organizational titles were similar. "Card Clubs; Women's or Men's Social Clubs" was represented only by "Women's Clubs," however; and as a consequence, membership in such groups is reported only for wives. Moreover, the names of specific groups to which the respondent belonged were recorded so that coders could reassign groups by kind of organization if the respondent's understanding was at variance with that of the investigator. In the coding operation, for example, "hobby clubs" were included with Sports Teams. Perhaps equally serious as a source of noncomparability is the fact that whenever the respondent indicated membership, he or she was asked a series of nine questions about the group and its political stance. In addition, all 1957 respondents were living in Wayne County.

In 1954, the interviewer said, "One way in which some people in Detroit spend their time is in clubs and organizations. I would like you to look at this list of kinds of organizations and tell me if you belong to any organizations like labor unions, a church, and so on—. What organizations or clubs do you belong to?" Superficially the procedures resemble those of the 1957 survey. We know that in practice at least the coding operation differed, for an appreciable number of husbands report membership in "Women's Clubs," which is retitled "Women's Club, Social Clubs, or 'Cultural' Group" in the code book.

We find the level of sex typing for Veteran's Organizations unchanged between 1954 and 1957 and between 1957 and 1959. The ratio of odds on *belong* for wives to the corresponding odds for husbands stand at .28 in the 1950s, in contrast to the 0.0 recorded in 1971. The Neighborhood Improvement Association, for which we estimated the Wife:Husband odds ratio as unity for 1959 and 1971, may have evolved from a predominantly male organization. The observed odds ratios progress from .39 in 1954 to .71 in 1957, .80 in 1959, and 1.1 in 1971 ($X^2 =$ 5.95, *df* = 3). For each other kind of organization, the level of sex typing is similar at each observation over the 17-year span. Displayed in Figure 7-1 are the estimates which we take to be most reliable given the data available.

Up to this point, we have not exploited the most interesting feature of the 1959 and 1971 data sets, to wit, that information is available for marriage partners. If the respondent was married, information about the memberships and attendance of her or his spouse also was obtained. In effect, the interviewer started over, saying "Which of these kinds of groups does your (husband/wife) belong to, if any?" and, when

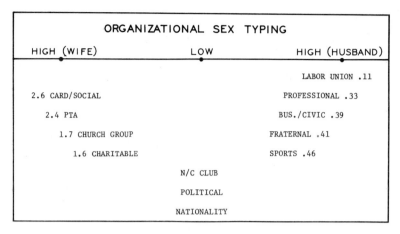

FIGURE 7-1. Kinds of organizations by sex typing of the membership (ratio of odds on *belong* for wives to the corresponding odds for husbands).

appropriate, "Does (he/she) usually attend meetings of this group at least once a month, or not?" In consequence, we have reports on the formal participation of married couples. The wife provided the information for 291 couples in 1959 and 342 couples in 1971; the husband provided the information for 313 couples in 1959 and 338 couples in 1971.

For each couple, the information about one marriage partner comes from a self-report and the information about the other partner comes from a proxy report (that is, the respondent's report about her husband or his wife). If each marriage partner were fully informed about the activities of her or his spouse, the proxy report should match the self-report. We suspect, however, that the proxy reports will show less participation than the self-reports; and we are inclined to interpret the shortfall as a measure of incomplete information. We choose not to entertain the perverse interpretation that the shortfall results from the respondent's exaggeration of her or his own participation in organizations. To lend concreteness, we show in Table 7-3 the mean number of organizational types in which wives and husbands, respectively, hold membership by their own account (self-report) and according to information provided by their spouses (proxy report). For example, the average number of organizational types in which husbands in the 1971 survey said that they held membership was 1.98; but the average number of organizational types in which husbands were said to hold membership by their wives was smaller, 1.62. We take the difference to

TABLE 7-3
Mean Number of Organizational Types in Which Membership Is Held, as Reported by Married Respondents and as Reported by Them for Their Spouses, 1959 and 1971

| Year | Reported by | Mean Number of Types | | Wife–Husband difference |
		Husband	Wife	
1959	Husband	1.93	1.15	.78
	Wife	1.85	1.69	.16
	Self	1.93[a]	1.69[a]	.24
1971	Husband	1.98	1.24	.74
	Wife	1.62	1.57	.05
	Self	1.98[a]	1.57[a]	.41

[a] Based on respondent's report of own memberships.

mean that some wives never knew or failed to recall that their husbands belonged to an organization.

Whatever substantive interpretation is placed on the shortfall, there is a methodological caution. Had only husbands been interviewed, the husband (self-report)–wife (proxy report) difference in extent of formal participation would have been large. The husband (proxy report)–wife (self-report) difference would have been small if only wives had been interviewed. Moreover, since we will show that the severity of the shortfall depends on organizational type and sex of respondent, no simple adjustment for proxy reports would seem promising.

The statistically reliable differences between self-reports and reports of spouses with respect to membership in organizations of specific types, summarized in Table 7-4, are instructive. Proxy effects present in the 1959 data set tend to reappear in the 1971 data set; in only two instances do we detect change between surveys. Furthermore, the organizations for which wives understate the participation of husbands are not those for which husbands understate the participation of wives.

In both years, husbands understate the frequency with which wives belong to Church Groups, Card/Social Clubs, the PTA, and Political Clubs, are active in Sports Teams, and are inactive members of Neighborhood Clubs/Community Centers. Wives, on the other hand, understate the frequency with which husbands belong to Business/ Civic Groups and Veteran's Organizations and are active in Charitable Organizations. On the basis of these findings, we suspect that husbands are least informed about (or interested in, perhaps) their wives' daytime activities in the neighborhood and that wives are least in-

TABLE 7-4
Difference between Self-Reported Participation of Married Respondents and Participation Reported for Them by Their Spouses, by Kind of Club or Organization

Club or organization	Ratio of odds on *belong* Spouse:Self		Odds ratio (given status to *nonmember*) Spouse:Self, for			
			Husbands		Wives	
	Husbands	Wives	*active*	*inactive*	*active*	*inactive*
Political	1.0	.43	1.0	1.0	.43	.43
PTA	1.0	.57	1.0	1.0	.57	.57
Card/Social	1.0	.68	1.0	1.0	.68	.68
Church Group	1.0	.75	1.0	1.0	.75	.75
N/C Club	1.0	1.0	1.0	1.0	1.0	.46
Fraternal						
1959	1.0	.65	1.0	1.0	.24	1.0
1971	1.0	.65	1.0	1.0	1.1	1.0
Sports Teams						
1959	1.0	.55	1.4	1.0	.57	1.0
1971	1.0	.55	.65	1.0	.57	1.0
Labor Union	.80	.68[a]	.80[a]	.80[a]	.68[a]	.68[a]
Professional	.72[a]	1.0	.72[a]	.72[a]	1.0	1.0
Business/Civic	.64	1.0	.64	.64	1.0	1.0
Veteran	.56	1.0	.56	.56	1.0	1.0
Charitable	.40	1.0	.27	1.0	1.0	1.0

Note: All effects shown above are net of year effects, if any.

[a] Significantly different from 1.0 at the .1 level although not at the .05 level.

formed about their husbands' activities that are extensions of job duties.

We doubt that the changes in proxy effects detected between surveys imply either change in communication between marriage partners or a redefinition of shared interests. They number only two. In 1959, but not in 1971, husbands understate the active participation of wives in Fraternal Organizations. Wives overstate the active participation of husbands in Sports Teams in 1959, but understate their participation in 1971. These shifts may tell us little more than that respondents are uncertain about what groups are "fraternal" organizations for women and "organized" sports teams for men.

As to whether husbands and wives differ in intensity of formal participation or frequency with which they join voluntary associations, the available data provide no answer. The question did not elicit a count of organizations in which membership was held, but rather asked how many different kinds of organizations a respondent belonged to. Husbands hold membership in a somewhat greater number of the 14 organizational types recognized, but a different mix of types, say distinguishing card clubs from social clubs or combining unions and professional groups, might well change the direction as well as magnitude of the wife–husband difference.

ASSOCIATION BETWEEN SPOUSES' MEMBERSHIPS

In order to study the influence of husband's membership status on that of his wife, or vice versa, we must work with the self-report of one marriage partner and the proxy report for the spouse. If the association between husband's status and wife's status differs depending upon whether the report about the couple was made by the husband or by the wife, there is no way of determining which account, if either, is veridical.

For each kind of organization, four data sets describing the relation between husband's status and wife's status are available—reports of married men in 1971, married women in 1971, married men in 1959, and married women in 1959. The data are arrayed in a format that shows status of husband (active member, inactive member, or not member) by status of wife. Fortunately, although proxy effects on membership status are common, a statistically reliable difference between the husband–wife association estimated from the reports of married women and the association estimated from the reports of married men is detected only for Neighborhood Improvement Associations. This difference, moreover, traces to disagreement about the activity status of the member spouse among couples with only one member spouse. Thus, the mix of self- and proxy reports can be used with confidence to measure the husband–wife association. Analytically, the major problem is posed by small cell frequencies.

On the basis of these findings, two decisions were made. First, only the statuses of member and nonmember are distinguished. Second, reports of 726 wives who answered questions about own and husband's participation in 1955 are examined along with the 1959 and 1971 data sets. We routinely allow for the effects of year and sex of respondent, if any, on the membership status of husband and wife, respectively. We also routinely check whether the strength of the husband–wife association differs by sex of respondent. Our aim is to obtain an estimate of the strength of the husband–wife association in participation for each kind of organization and test whether the association differs by survey year.

We assume that participation in all organizations save Unions and Professional Groups is a matter of volition for both wives and husbands and that the membership status of one spouse can influence the other's status directly. In some cases, the spouses might belong to the same organizational unit—the "same" PTA, for example. In other cases, belonging to explicitly companion units—Fraternal and Veteran's Organizations and their auxiliaries—or functionally similar units would be more common. Although sex-linked constraints on opportunities to participate may exist, we can at least entertain the possibility that the decision to join on the part of one spouse influences the decision of her or his marriage partner.

A statistically reliable association between husband's status and wife's status is found for Labor Unions and Professional Groups as well as for each other kind of organization. Of most interest in the present context is the fact that the wife–husband association is weaker for Unions and Professional Groups than for any voluntary organization where the influence of spouses, one upon the other, might come into play.

The wife–husband association in membership status is measured by the ratio of odds on *belong* for the person whose spouse is a member to the corresponding odds for the same-sex person whose spouse is not a member. We are unable to establish change over time in the strength of this association for any kind of organization. In a few instances one or more data sets yield an estimate of the association that differs from the estimate based on a majority of data sets; but the differences do not suggest temporal change. (Church Groups, an estimate of 10 from the 1959 reports of husbands versus 24 from the 1971 reports of husbands and the 1955, 1959, and 1971 reports of wives; Labor Unions, 1.6 from the 1959 reports of wives versus 4.4 from the other four data sets; Neighborhood/Community Clubs, 238 from the 1955 reports of wives, 16 from the 1959 reports of wives, versus 72 from the other three data sets). Thus, a single estimate is selected to represent the strength of the wife–husband association for each kind of organization save one. For Charitable/Welfare Organizations, we know of no basis for choosing between the 60 estimated from the reports of wives and the (significantly different) 19 estimated from the reports of husbands.

Two organizational characteristics that might influence the strength of the wife–husband association come to mind. One is the degree of sex typing in membership. There is no arithmetic reason that the wife–

husband association should be high in organizations where husbands and wives are equally represented in the membership. But perhaps the wife's decision to join influences her husband most if the organization in question is not stereotypically a "woman's group," and vice versa. Second, we suspect that the marriage partner's influence is greatest if the organization is one that permits couples to participate in the same organizational unit. Indeed, one marriage partner may decide that "they" will join. Fortunately we have some direct, though meager, evidence on how the kinds of organizations differ in this respect. In 1955 each wife who said that she and her husband belonged to the same kind of organization was asked whether they belonged to the same club or group. From these reports, we can calculate the odds on *same club* relative to *different clubs of the same kind* for each kind of organization except Card/Social Clubs for which no equivalent kind appeared in the organizational list.

Figure 7-2 offers a graphic multiple-regression analysis; shown are the influences of sex typing and same-unit membership, respectively, on the strength of the wife–husband association for each kind of organization. The relation between the wife–husband association (ratio of odds on *belong* for the person whose spouse is a member to the corresponding odds for the same-sex person whose spouse is not a member) and the odds on same club for marriage partners over the 14 kinds of organizations is shown by the configuration of points in Figure 7-2. The point representing Charitable Organizations might be shifted higher or lower along the vertical line depending upon one's preference for wives' reports or husbands' reports as the base for estimating the association, and the point representing Card/Social Clubs might shift to the left or right along the horizontal line were information on joint memberships available. The tendency toward a positive relation is clear, however; the kinds of organizations for which belonging as a couple is common (high odds on *same club*) tend to be those for which the wife–husband association is strong. Level of organizational sex typing is introduced into the graphic display by the use of symbols differentiating the points. Recall that there was no sex effect on membership in Nationality, Political, or Neighborhood/Community Clubs; in contrast, sex typing was pronounced for Veteran and Professional Groups as well as Labor Unions. The kinds of organizations for which sex typing is relatively weak tend to be those for which the wife–husband association is strong, whether comparisons are made with respect to all organizations or only organizations similar in terms of the relative frequency of joint memberships. The organizations for which the wife–husband association is strongest—the Neighborhood Improve-

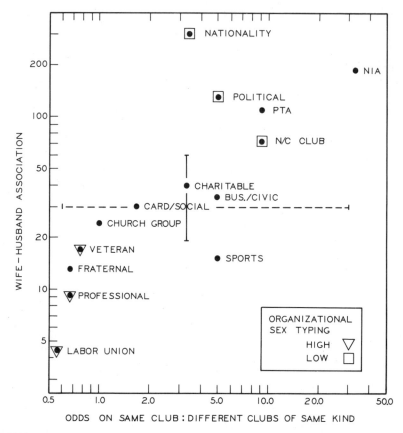

FIGURE 7-2. Wife-husband association in participation, wife-husband participation in same organization, and level of organizational sex typing, by kind of organization.

ment Association, the Parent–Teacher Association, the Neighbor-hood/Community Club, the Political Club, and the Same-Nationality-Group—all evidence relatively frequent involvement of married persons as couples rather than as individuals and/or relatively low sex typing at the organizational level. (As the display suggests, a high frequency of joint memberships and low sex typing are themselves positively associated.)

The data base is too thin to permit systematic exploration of other aspects of the relation between spouses' statuses. For the PTA, Church Groups, and Fraternal Organizations, however, we can report a few additional findings. The wife–husband association in PTA participation is much stronger than the corresponding association for either

Church Groups or Fraternal Organizations when active or inactive members are contrasted with nonmembers; but when active members are contrasted with inactive members, the organizations do not differ with respect to the relevant odds ratios.

Contrast	Church Group	Fraternal	PTA
Active versus Nonmember	29	18	111
Inactive versus Nonmember	24	19	238
Active versus Inactive	28	19	15

Can a marriage partner more easily join on behalf of the couple than induce joint activity? The case of the PTA suggests this might be so.

EDUCATION AND FORMAL PARTICIPATION

Working with the self-reports of husbands and wives about their participation in voluntary associations, we find that the odds on *belong* vary directly with educational attainment for most organizations, are invariant over education levels for a few organizations, and decrease as attainment rises only in the case of the Labor Union. We cannot rule out the possibility that these differentials are produced by an education effect on completeness of reporting, but the results for Labor Unions and Professional Groups suggest that the rank of organizations by direction and strength of the education effect on participation is accurate. For no organization save the Union does advanced schooling lower participation; advanced schooling raises the odds on *belong* more sharply for Professional Groups than for any other voluntary association.

Our interest is not the education effect as such. Instead, we want to know whether the inclusion of respondent's education, as well as survey year, in the model will change our estimate of the husband–wife difference in participation. If the education effect is different for wives than for husbands, our initial findings should be qualified. Measures of the wife–husband difference in participation, net of any effects of education and year, appear in Table 7-5. They can be compared with the corresponding measures in Table 7-2 wherein allowance was made only for the year effect. (The participation of wives in Veteran's Organizations is too slight to sustain analysis.)

The initial description of the wife–husband difference in participation must be qualified only for Church-Connected Groups. Wives have

TABLE 7-5
Difference between Wives and Husbands, Influence of Educational Attainment, and Change between 1959 and 1971 in Participation, by Kind of Club or Organization, Based on Self-Reports of Married Respondents

Club or organization	Ratio of odds on *belong*		
	Wife: Husband	17+ grades: 9–11 grades	1971: 1959
PTA	2.9	2.8	1.0
Card/Social[ab]	2.6	4.6	1.0
Church Group			
9–11 grades	1.8	—	.65
17+ grades	.92	—	.65
Husband	—	1.9	.65
Wife	—	.98	.65
Charitable[a]	1.6	5.0	1.0
N/C Club	1.0	1.0	1.0
Political[a]	1.0	7.4	1.0
NIA	1.0	1.0	.67
Nationality	1.0	1.0	.52
Sports Teams[b]	.60	2.1	1.6
Fraternal	.52	1.7	1.0
Business/Civic[a]	.50	7.2	1.0
Professional	.50	74	1.0
Labor Union			
9–11 grades	.11	—	1.0
17+ grades	.76	—	1.0
Husband	—	.10	1.0
Wife	—	.73	1.0

Note: Estimates of odds calculated from regression of logit thereof on sex and year (each scored 0, 1) and grades completed (number, with addition of variable taking value 1 if grades under 7, 0 otherwise for Union). Too few wives reporting membership to permit analysis for Veteran.

[a] Restricted to respondents with at least 9 grades completed.

[b] Odds on active, rather than belong.

the greater propensity to participate in these groups among the poorly educated, but the difference lessens with advancing educational attainment and disappears among college graduates. Or, viewed differently, there is a positive relation between participation and education for husbands; but the odds on *belong* are invariant over education levels for wives. These features can readily be seen in the graphic display in Figure 7-3. Interpretation of these sex-specific education effects is moot given that the motivations of the members are unknown and the organizations may be, but need not be, social in purpose.

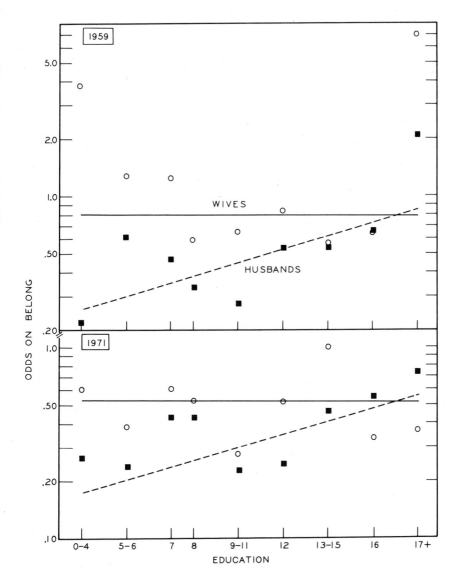

FIGURE 7-3. Education effects on participation in church-connected groups, observed and estimated from logit regression, for married respondents by sex, 1959 and 1971.

A possible check on the plausibility of some explanations of this sex-education interaction involves a comparison between the 1959 and 1971 data sets, on the one hand, and the 1954 and 1957 data sets, on the other. In the earlier surveys, names of specific groups in which membership was held were recorded; and coders were instructed to reclassify the kind of membership held "if appropriate." We do not know the informal understandings that guided the coding operation, but we find this notation in the 1954 codebook, "Church-Connected Group—with mainly religious or church-maintenance function. For example, a bowling team representing a church would not be coded here." The preferred model for the 1954 and 1957 data sets includes additive sex and education effects, but no sex-education interaction ($Y^2 = 29.64$, $df = 33$). The model yields estimates of 1.7 for both the Wife : Husband odds ratio and the odds ratio $17 + : 9-11$ years of schooling. In contrast, the preferred model for the 1959 and 1971 data sets incorporates a sex-education interaction ($Y^2 = 38.80$, $df = 31$; difference in Y^2 between models without and with interaction term $= 4.53$, $df = 1$). Working with all four data sets, we find that a model that allows for a sex-education interaction in 1959–1971, but not in 1954–1957, offers little improvement over a model that incorporates only additive sex and education effects (difference in $Y^2 = 2.84$, $df = 1$). It would seem, then, that the absence of an education effect on participation for wives in 1959 and 1971 is the anomaly. All evidence is consistent as to the education effect for groups with a "religious or church-maintenance function": The effect is positive for both wives and husbands. But we do not know how education influences participation in church-connected groups with social functions. Should it be that this effect is negative for wives, but not for husbands, our findings could be reconciled readily. It does not seem altogether implausible that wives of modest educational attainment might place the heaviest reliance on the church as a center of social life.

BLACK COUPLES AND UNMARRIED PERSONS

In very few instances is the wife–husband difference in formal participation for black couples dissimilar to that for white couples or the sex effect among the unmarried unlike the wife–husband difference. When the sex effect is found to be contingent on color or marital status, the kind of organization usually is one for which membership status is linked with or constrained by job status.

Reports on own memberships and memberships of spouses were made by a black respondent for 190 couples surveyed in 1959 or 1971.

Insofar as possible, we have supplemented these reports with those of the 79 black respondents surveyed in 1954 and the 67 black respondents living in Wayne County who were surveyed in 1957. The number of black husbands and wives reporting is small, but we should be able to say whether an argument that black couples have a distinctive pattern of formal participation is tenable.

Color influences participation most strikingly for Labor Unions and Professional Groups. The Wife:Husband ratio of odds on *belong* to a Labor Union stands at .046 for blacks in contrast to .15 for whites. (The odds on *belong* increased more rapidly among blacks than among whites between surveys, but the sex effect is estimated to be the same in 1971 as in 1959.) For Professional Groups, not only the magnitude, but also the direction of the wife–husband difference is contingent on color. The odds on *belong* is higher for black wives than for black husbands, a Wife:Husband odds ratio of 3.4; the corresponding ratio for whites is .29. We believe that these sex–color interactions trace to differences among sex–color groups in their occupational and industrial attachments.

Color influences membership in only three other kinds of organizations and does so in the same way for husbands as for wives. The odds on *belong* for Sports Teams are lower for black respondents, with the Black:White ratio of odds estimated as .41 for wives and husbands in each year. The color effect on participation changed between the 1950s and 1971 for the Neighborhood Improvement Association (odds ratio, Black:White, from .45 to 2.2) and the Neighborhood Club/Community Center (.75 to 5.5).

The influence of proxy reporting on participation and the strength of the wife–husband association in participation could not be shown to differ by color in any of the five voluntary associations in which the number of black members seemed sufficient to sustain analysis. We did find that black members more often are *active,* that is, attend meetings at least once a month, in the PTA, Church Groups, and Fraternal Organizations, the only voluntary associations for which there were sufficient numbers of active and inactive members to sustain analysis. But the apparently greater activity of black members may reflect nothing more than a denser schedule of meetings in the organizational units to which they belong.

In sum, where formal participation is a matter of volition, black husbands and wives differ in precisely the same ways as do white husbands and wives. Only where participation is constrained by job-status qualifications do black couples have a distinctive pattern of participation.

Systematic checks of the 1971 and 1959 data sets indicate that the wife–husband difference in participation nearly always reappears when the participation of women in some other marital-status category is contrasted with the participation of men in the same category. In other words, we cannot show that the sex effect for, say, the never married or the widowed differs reliably from the sex effect among the currently married. An exception is the Labor Union. The Wife: Husband odds ratio of .13 does not differ from the Female:Male ratio among the single, the separated, or the widowed; but the Female:Male ratio among the divorced is .49.

There is one other instance in which we detect marginally significant interactions between sex and marital status in relation to formal participation. This departure is somewhat instructive in that it suggests a factor other than job status that may facilitate or limit participation. We reported earlier that husbands and wives do not differ in their propensity to *belong* to a Neighborhood Club/Community Center; neither is there a sex effect among the separated or divorced. But the odds on *belong* for widows are only .33 times as great as the corresponding odds for widowers, and the odds on *belong* for never-married women are 4.4 times as great as the corresponding odds for single men. We suspect that differences in living arrangements and alternative opportunities to "get together" with other people underlie these interactions.

When we turn to a consideration of informal participation, we find that the sex effect on frequency of "getting together" with relatives is contingent on marital status, even after allowance has been made for any effects of color or labor-force status or tenure. We suspect that the availability of relatives with whom one can get together provides at least a partial explanation of the interaction. Only with respect to neighboring is there any suggestion of a sex–color interaction, and, as reported subsequently, the relevant contingency may be labor-force status rather than color as such.

HUSBAND–WIFE DIFFERENCES IN
INFORMAL PARTICIPATION

Although dicussion will focus on more compact summaries of the data, the full percentage distributions by frequency of visiting relatives, neighbors, and other friends for husbands and wives are displayed in Table 7-6. Shown in Table 7-7 are the corresponding distributions by frequency of getting together with co-workers outside work, as well as separate distributions for the wives who report that they are in the work

TABLE 7-6
Percentage Distributions by Frequency of Getting Together with Relatives, Neighbors, and Other Friends, for Husbands and Wives, 1959 and 1971

Frequency	Relatives 1959		Relatives 1971		Neighbors 1959		Neighbors 1971		Other friends 1959		Other friends 1971	
	H	W	H	W	H	W	H	W	H	W	H	W
Every day	<1	3	2	3	6	9	4	6	1	1	2	<1
Almost every day	3	5	2	4	3	6	5	6	2	1	2	2
1–2 times per week	37	41	32	28	21	20	16	18	20	23	22	22
Few times a month	21	21	21	22	14	11	13	10	16	21	20	21
Once a month	11	12	14	15	12	11	11	8	17	22	16	16
Few times a year	16	11	22	20	16	13	20	17	25	20	25	24
Less often	5	2	4	5	8	9	8	8	9	7	7	7
Never	5	3	3	3	20	20	23	28	10	6	5	6
Total	100	100	100	100	100	100	100	100	100	100	100	100

TABLE 7-7

Percentage Distribution by Frequency of Getting Together with Co-workers, for
Husbands and for Wives by Work Status, 1959 and 1971

| | 1959 | | | | 1971 | | | |
| | | W | | | | | W | |
Frequency	H	All	Work	Other	H	All	Work	Other
Every day	1	1	1	1	2	< 1	< 1	< 1
Almost every day	2	1	1	1	2	< 1	< 1	0
1–2 times per week	12	11	16	9	13	7	9	6
Few times a month	12	9	15	7	13	10	11	10
Once a month	14	11	10	11	13	13	15	11
Few times a year	29	22	31	19	26	29	29	29
Less often	11	13	7	15	10	12	11	12
Never	19	33	18	37	22	28	23	31
Total	100	100	100	100	100	100	100	100

force and other wives. The pattern of participation for working wives
clearly is distinct, whether compared with the participation of husbands or that of other wives, but we are in something of a quandary as
to interpretation. Recall the question wording, "with any people you
(or your husband) work with." Interviewers and working-wife respondents may have interpreted this to mean "people you or your husband
work with," hence increasing the pool of co-workers. Indeed, the usual
interpretation may have changed between 1959 (when the odds on *work*
for wives stood at .3) and 1971 (when the odds stood at .6).

For a compact summary of the sex differential in participation and
changes therein, we rely on graphic displays of variation in the sex ratio
by frequency of participation. Analytically, frequency of visiting was
treated as a variable taking on the values 0 (Never) to 7 (Every day) and
survey year was treated as a dichotomous variable; the log of the ratio of
married women to married men was regressed on frequency of visiting
and year. The possibility that the sex effect on participation is contingent on color or on tenure or on labor-force status was checked systematically via contingency analysis, and only with respect to visiting
neighbors was an interaction effect detected.

The sex differential in getting together with relatives can be seen in
the upper panel of Figure 7-4. If there were no sex effect on this kind of
participation, the log of the wife/husband ratio would be approximately
zero whatever the frequency of visiting; for married female respondents
are about the same in number as married male respondents in each

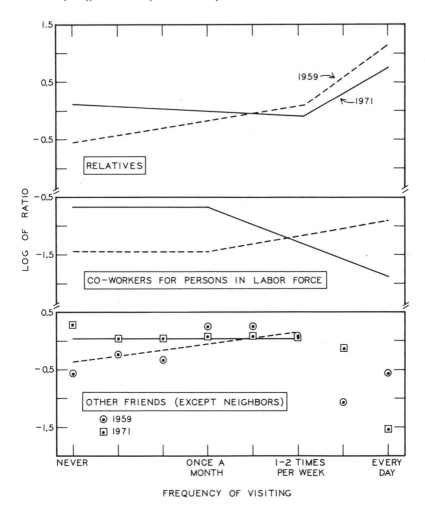

FIGURE 7-4. Fitted sex ratio (female:male) by frequency of getting together with relatives, getting together with co-workers for persons in the labor force, and getting together with other friends, for married respondents, 1959 and 1971.

survey. The log of the ratio is substantially greater than zero for the respondents who say they visit kin daily or nearly so, meaning that wives engage in intense interaction with kin more often than do husbands. In 1971 this is the only respect in which wives and husbands differ markedly with respect to informal participation with relatives. In contrast, the wife/husband ratio increased steadily as participation became more frequent in 1959. (The year-by-frequency term in the regres-

sion model is unambiguously significant. The model displayed incorporates this term along with a year effect, frequency effect, and a third
variable to capture intense interaction with scores of 2 for Every Day, 1
for Almost Every Day, and 0 for any other frequency. $Y^2 = 5.41, df = 11$.)
Aside from the very small minority of wives who continue to engage in
daily or near daily visiting with relatives, there remain no grounds for
labeling getting together with kin a "woman's kind of thing."

Labor-force status makes a difference in how often one gets together
with co-workers outside work, probably by way of the availability of
co-workers. The few husbands not in the work force must rely on
former co-workers for such interaction. Although wives not in the labor
force are to report interaction with their husbands' co-workers, contact
with them, at least initially, could be established only through the
husband. It is not clear that the relation between frequency of visiting
and sex is contingent on labor-force status, but we have chosen to
restrict analysis to persons in the labor force. If working wives and
working husbands did not differ in frequency of visiting, the log of the
wife/husband ratio would be approximately -1.4 at each frequency in
1959 and $-.82$ at each frequency in 1971. The display in the center panel
of Figure 7-4 shows, however, that as visiting becomes more frequent
than once a month, the wife/husband ratio increased steadily in 1959
and decreased steadily in 1971. (The model displayed incorporates a
year effect, a frequency effect, and a year-by-frequency effect, with the
frequency variable taking on values between 4 for Every Day and 0 for
Once a Month or less often. $Y^2 = 1.83, df = 12$.) A satisfactory explanation for this finding, taken in isolation, might be the growing share of
working wives who are mothers of young children and, hence, have
little leisure time in which to socialize with co-workers. Since wives,
nonworking as well as working, visit relatives less often in 1971 than in
1959—both absolutely and relative to husbands—this explanation may
be inadequate even if in accord with fact.

Wife–husband differences in frequency of getting together with
friends who are not relatives, co-workers, or neighbors are displayed in
the bottom panel of Figure 7-4. In both 1959 and 1971, some extremely
low wife/husband ratios are observed among the tiny minority who
visited with "other" friends on a daily or near daily basis. The low
ratios may be "flukes," but they are clearly counter to an argument that
this kind of intense informal participation is distinctively feminine.
Leaving aside the tiny minority who report intense participation, the
wife/husband ratio did rise as frequency of visiting increased in 1959;
but the wife–husband difference had disappeared by 1971.

Neighboring often is thought to fall in the domain of women, in part because it is they who are more often at home. Changes in the ratio of married women *not* in the labor force to married men in the labor force by frequency of neighboring generally conform to the stereotype, aside from the gentle decrease in the wife/husband ratio observed as frequency increases from Never to a Few Times a Year. This display in the upper panel of Figure 7-5 (based on a regression model with $Y^2 = 8.39$, $df = 13$) is misleading, however, in the sense that the sex effect is contingent on labor-force status. If we compare wives and husbands neither of whom are in the labor force, we find the ratio depressed at the extremes—Never and Every Day—and otherwise invariant; see the center panel of Figure 7-5 (based on a regression model with $Y^2 = 6.52$, $df = 14$). In contrast, among persons in the labor force, the wife/husband ratio decreases over the range Never to a Few Times a Month and then rises gently as frequency increases to Every Day; see the bottom panel of Figure 7-5 (based on regression model with $Y^2 = 6.34$, $df = 12$). The sex effect also is contingent on color. Furthermore, for blacks, the sex effect on neighboring changed between 1959 and 1971; whereas in the former year the wife/husband ratio was invariant, in 1971 it decreases steadily as frequency changes from Never to Every Day. For whites, in contrast,

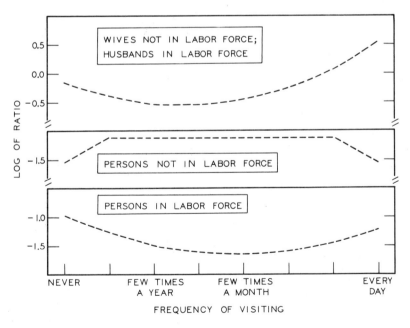

FIGURE 7-5. Fitted sex ratio (female:male) by frequency of getting together with neighbors, for married respondents by labor-force status, 1959 and 1971.

the wife/husband ratio falls gently as frequency increases from Never to Once a Month and then rises as neighboring becomes more frequent. See Figure 7-6 (regression model for blacks with $Y^2 = 9.78$, $df = 13$, and for whites with $Y^2 = 9.16$, $df = 13$). Our data base is simply too thin to sustain analysis of possible sex effects contingent on color and labor-force status.

Since the respondent was not asked about the informal participation of her or his spouse, the extent to which one marriage partner is informed about the visiting patterns of the other partner cannot be estimated. Neither do we know how much of the informal participation takes the form of the couple getting together with others. We do know, however, that men and women agree in their assessment of how much their neighbors interact. A question from the 1957 survey (restricted to Wayne County residents) that was replicated in 1971 asks, "In general, would you say that the people in your neighborhood keep pretty much to themselves, or do they get together quite a bit?" There is neither a sex nor year effect on response; and, in 1971, the responses of Wayne County residents do not differ from the answers of other respondents.

Working with tables in which respondents in each sex–year group are classified by educational attainment and frequency of visiting, we

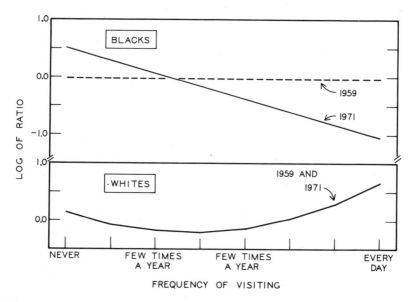

FIGURE 7-6. **Fitted sex ratio (female : male) by frequency of getting together with neighbors, for married respondents by color, 1959 and 1971.**

detect relatively few associations. In the case of getting together with relatives, independence cannot be rejected nor can a linear education effect be established for any sex–year group. We cannot reject independence between educational attainment and getting together with neighbors for married women in 1959 or 1971, nor can we establish a linear education effect for any sex–year group. Visiting with co-workers is excluded since the data base is too thin to control education and work status simultaneously. Linear education effects can be established for three sex–year groups, but formal tests fail to establish an education effect contingent on sex for visiting with other friends.

FORMAL AND INFORMAL PARTICIPATION

As a matter more of curiosity than an investment in an a priori hypothesis, we examined the association between formal participation (number of kinds of organization respondent belongs to) and informal participation (frequency of various kinds of visits). The most interesting and intelligible results were obtained for visiting with friends (other than relatives, neighbors, or co-workers). We confine our report to these results, which are succinctly summarized by the regression equation,

$$Y = 2.947 + .305\ X_1 - .316\ X_1X_2 - .121\ X_3 + .145\ X_2X_3 + .04125\ X_3^2$$
$$(.114)(.146)(.098)(.047)(.020)$$

where Y is the visiting score, ranging from 0 for Never to 7 for Every Day; $X_1 = 0$ in 1959 and 1 in 1971; $X_2 = 0$ for husbands and 1 for wives; and $X_3 = $ number of kinds of organization to which the respondent belongs, scoring 5 or more kinds as exactly 5. Standard errors of coefficients are in parentheses; $R^2 = .027$. Figure 7-7 provides a graphic interpretation of the regression equation as well as the observed mean visiting score for each distinct value of X_3. For both sexes, a high rate of formal participation goes with more visiting than does a low rate. However, the relationship over the whole range of formal participation is stronger for wives than for husbands. The equation implies virtually no change in the pattern for married women between 1959 and 1971 but an increase in visiting friends on the part of married men that does not vary by level of formal participation.

Before the fact one might have entertained either of two contrary notions about the relationship studied here. On the one hand, the two kinds of participation are competitive in the sense that time spent in one reduces the time available for the other. On the other hand, organi-

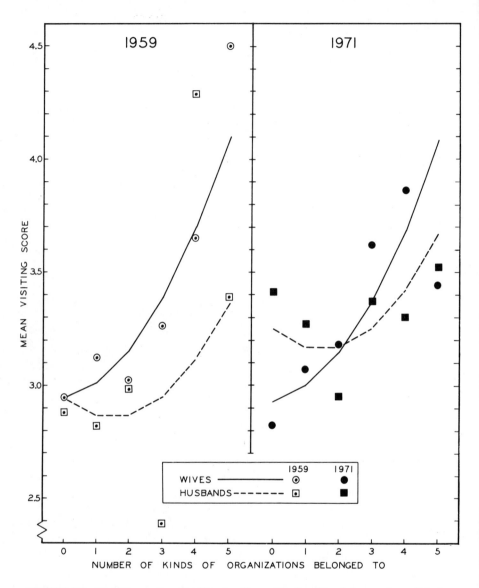

FIGURE 7-7. Mean frequency of getting together with other friends by number of kinds of organizations in which membership is held, for married respondents by sex, 1959 and 1971.

zations provide opportunities for making friends with persons who are not relatives, neighbors, or co-workers and occasions for encounters with them that may lead to extraorganizational contacts. Or one may be attracted to an organization if one's friends are members. Perhaps both the competition and the complementation principles operate but with varying relative strengths for different people. We might conjecture that the complementation effect is stronger, relative to the competition effect, for wives than for husbands.

To take the conjecture one step further, a partial explanation of the different patterns for husbands and wives may lie in the sex typing of formal participation—the most distinctively female organizations (Card/Social Clubs) are ones that emphasize conviviality, so that a spillover into visiting with fellow members is natural. We do not know, of course, that the friends visited are, in any definite proportion, fellow members. That, too, is a conjecture. As for the competition effect, we might imagine that husbands are more sensitive to the trade-off. Wives, we surmise, had an extra "leisure hour" per day and were able to devote more time to both "visiting" and "clubs" at least as late as the mid-1960s. Perhaps they had their fill of each kind of participation. (See Ennis, 1968, p. 555, Table 5, for information about time budgets by sex and work status.)

8

Wives and Husbands as Marriage Partners

"Whereas moderate feminists describe marriage as an unequal partnership, radicals define it as oppressive. In consequence, the moderates want to restructure the institution, the radicals to abandon it." So write Hole and Levine (1971, p. 213) in summarizing the feminists' critique of woman's social role and function.

Change in the extent to which a husband shares domestic chores with his wife and she participates in decisions affecting the couple's life style is a topic we can investigate. The baseline is the 1955 Detroit Area Study, results of which were reported by Blood and Wolfe in their widely cited monograph *Husbands and Wives* (1960). Their assessment of decision-making and chore-allocation patterns is a useful reference point. They report that "doing and deciding,"

> Both are equalitarian in the sense that both husbands and wives participate. But whereas the division of labor is highly specialized, the process of decision-making is considerably less unilateral. . . . decision-making is also less stereotyped than task performance, there being substantially more variation from family to family in who decides than in who does things at home.

> These differences are great enough to produce a general impression of flexible sharing in decision-making in contrast with stereotyped specialization in the division of labor [for household tasks] [p. 53].

Blood and Wolfe had no baseline from which to measure change in a precise way, but they surmised that for decision making "the emerging norm may not be a particular pattern of male dominance or equalitarianism but, rather, the idea of appropriateness," that is, "a mutual recognition of individual skills in particular areas of competence and the partners' dual stake in areas of joint concern [p. 45]." They envisioned less change in the pattern of chore allocation, for "the same biosocial reasons which shaped the traditional family still supply differential resources which men and women bring to marriage [pp. 73–74]." To study the division of labor between spouses, we have available reports of wives in 1955 and 1971 and husbands in 1971 on the allocation of six tasks that most families perform and the assignment of responsibility for six relatively important decisions that most couples face.

Another topic for which we can measure change from 1955 to 1971 is the value that wives attach to different aspects of marriage, such as the bearing and rearing of children or companionship with the husband. Each wife also reported on her satisfaction with these several aspects of her own marriage. Using data from the 1958 Detroit Area Study as a baseline, we can obtain an alternative perspective on the institution of marriage. This survey asked each respondent her or his views on the acceptability of divorce, couching the issue in abstract and moralistic terms; Chapter 9 is devoted to the topic of divorce.

The information available is by no means sufficient to determine how widespread the feminist view of marriage was in 1971. But we can at least say whether the "wife" role within the family had been redefined since the mid-1950s.

THE DIVISION OF LABOR: RESPONSE PATTERNS

In this section, we describe in some detail the changes that have occurred in the division of labor between wives and husbands, relying on the reports of wives in 1955 and 1971. We also address the question of whether wives and husbands perceive the division of labor differently, relying on the reports of wives (married women) and husbands (married men) in 1971. The term "division of labor" should be understood to include both the allocation of dometic chores between the spouses and the couple's way of resolving decisions. Blood and Wolfe restricted the term to task allocation although they observed that at least one task, Keeping track of the money and the bills, was administrative in character and linked with financial decision making (p. 52).

The interviewer introduced the domestic-chore items by saying, "We would like to know how you and your husband divide up some of the family jobs. Here is a list of different ways of dividing up jobs." and, then, presenting the respondent with the response options: *husband always, husband more than wife, husband and wife exactly the same, wife more than husband, wife always.* The specific items, introduced with the phrase, "Now, who . . .," are listed here.

1. does the grocery shopping?
2. gets your husband's breakfast on work days (your breakfast if a husband was the respondent)?
3. does the evening dishes?
4. straightens up the living room when company is coming?
5. repairs things around the house?
6. keeps track of the money and the bills?

(In the 1955 survey, two additional items—mows the lawn and shovels the sidewalk—intervened between 4 and 5 in the preceding list.) The topic of decision making was introduced with "In every family somebody has to decide such things as where the family will live and so on. Many couples talk such things over first, but the *final* decision often has to be made by the husband or the wife. For example, in your family who usually makes the final decision about . . .?"

1. what car to get?
2. whether or not to buy some life insurance?
3. what house or apartment to take?
4. what job your husband should take (you should take, if a husband was the respondent)?
5. whether or not you should go to work or quit work (your wife should, if a husband was the respondent)?
6. how much money your family can afford to spend per week on food?

(Two additional items followed the six items in the list in the 1955 survey.)

Shown in the top panel of Table 8-1 for each item is the distribution of couples by categories of the division of labor as reported by wives in 1971. Appearing first in the stub are the six domestic chores. Repairs is stereotypically a masculine task; Husband's Breakfast, Grocery Shopping, Living Room, and Evening Dishes are "feminine" tasks; and, continuing to follow Blood and Wolfe's classification, Money and Bills is an "administrative" task. The six kinds of decisions follow. Husband's Job and What Car are seen as "primarily the husband's prov-

TABLE 8-1

Division of Labor in Household Chores and Decisions, as Reported by Wives in 1971 and 1955 and by Husbands in 1971 (Percentage Distributions)

Chore or decision	Note	H only	H > W	H = W	W > H	W only
				Wives, 1971		
Repairs	—	64.1	16.0	8.2	4.5	7.1
Husband's breakfast	—	29.0	3.2	4.4	7.6	55.9
Grocery shopping	—	6.8	4.7	22.4	19.5	46.7
Living room	—	1.9	0.2	17.9	14.9	65.2
Evening dishes	—	1.2	0.9	11.1	12.3	74.5
Money and bills	—	23.1	6.9	24.4	9.6	36.1
Husband's job	—	86.9	7.5	4.1	0.3	1.2
What car	—	58.3	10.2	25.3	1.5	4.7
Wife's working	—	25.8	4.9	23.9	10.8	34.6
Food money	—	13.6	2.9	34.9	7.2	41.4
Life insurance	—	43.4	9.4	36.7	3.3	7.2
What house	—	16.6	5.7	63.0	5.4	9.2
				Wives, 1955		
Repairs	(a)	75.4	11.7	6.5	3.4	3.1
Husband's breakfast	(a)	16.2	4.5	4.4	7.2	67.8
Grocery shopping	(a)	7.5	6.9	28.9	19.7	37.0
Living room	(a)	1.1	1.4	16.6	15.4	65.5
Evening dishes	(c)	1.4	1.8	13.6	12.4	70.8
Money and bills	(a)	19.2	6.6	33.9	10.8	29.5
Husband's job	(a)	91.5	4.6	3.3	0.0	0.0
What car	(c)	56.7	12.7	25.3	2.2	3.1
Wife's working	(b)	27.2	5.1	18.5	9.0	40.2
Food money	(a)	9.9	2.8	33.3	11.6	42.4
Life insurance	(a)	32.2	11.4	41.9	4.6	9.9
What house	(a)	12.6	6.0	57.9	10.0	13.6
				Husbands, 1971		
Repairs	(d)	74.7	15.5	4.7	2.4	2.7
Husband's breakfast	(e)	31.0	4.4	5.5	8.8	50.4
Grocery shopping	(d)	5.0	6.0	20.7	27.6	40.7
Living room	(d)	0.9	1.6	16.8	20.9	59.7
Evening dishes	(f)	2.2	0.9	8.7	16.1	72.1
Money and bills	(d)	29.7	9.2	21.9	9.7	29.4
Husband's job	(e)	90.0	6.1	3.6	0.2	0.2
What car	(e)	59.3	14.6	20.8	1.6	3.8
Wife's working	(e)	29.1	6.1	21.2	8.9	34.7
Food money	(d)	14.6	4.0	31.0	12.5	37.9
Life insurance	(e)	47.3	11.0	32.8	3.3	5.5
What house	(f)	16.3	5.9	59.8	7.7	10.3

ince," by Blood and Wolfe (1960, p. 20), Wife's Working and Food Money as primarily the wife's province, and Life Insurance and What House as "joint decisions in the sense of having more 'same' responses than anything else." That *husband and wife exactly the same* (H = W) is not the modal category in the division of labor reported by wives in 1971 for Life Insurance is a first indication of change over time. Shown in the center panel of Table 8-1 are the corresponding distributions based on the reports of wives in 1955. A note accompanying each distribution indicates whether it differs reliably from the 1971 distribution for that item. As reported earlier by Duncan *et al.* (1973, p. 13 and Tables 4 and 5), the division of labor between husband and wife did change between 1955 and 1971 for all but two items—Evening Dishes and What Car.

We report here a more precise analysis of the data underlying these distributions. A primary purpose of the analysis is to ascertain how well the changes can be described by a simple shift of the distribution with respect to the five categories of the division of labor, that is, H, $H > W$, $H = W$, $W > H$, W. We understand the idea of a "simple shift of the distribution" in the following way. Let f_{0i} be the number responding with the ith category ($i = 1, ..., 5$) in 1955 and f_{1i} be the corresponding number in 1971. We consider the ratios $R_i = f_{1i}/f_{0i}$ as observations describing change and inquire whether the changes are adequately summarized by the regression of $\log_e (R_i)$ on i. The level (or intercept) of the regression is, of course, a mere reflection of the relative sizes of the two samples and has no substantive interpretation. The procedure is the one presented by Simon (1974) as his "Formulation A." If this regression contributes significantly to the fit of the model and if the chi-square statistic for the model is not significant, we conclude that the change is adequately described by a shift toward the wife (if the regression is positive) or the husband (if the regression is negative). Consider, for example, the item Repairs. The test of the hypothesis that the

TABLE 8-1 (Footnotes)

(a) Significant change between 1955 and 1971 for wives when tested for the whole distribution.

(b) Significant change between 1955 and 1971 for wives when tested for an appropriate partitioning of the distribution.

(c) Difference between 1955 and 1971 distributions for wives not significant.

(d) Significant difference between wives and husbands in 1971 when tested for the whole distribution.

(e) Significant difference between wives and husbands in 1971 when tested for an appropriate partitioning of the distribution.

(f) Difference between distributions for wives and husbands in 1971 not significant.

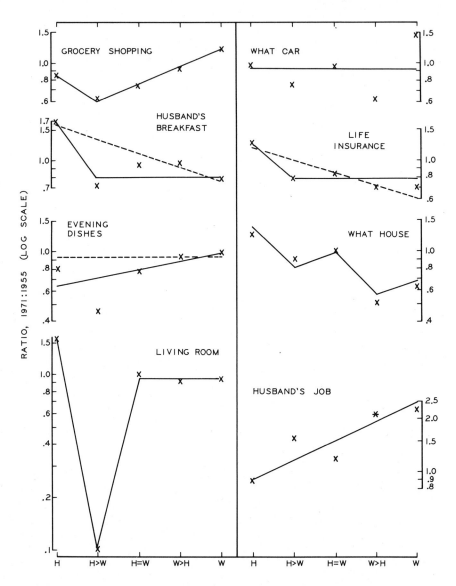

FIGURE 6-1. Change in division of labor as reported by wives, 1955 and 1971, observed and fitted. (Asterisk denotes an undefined odds, based on zero frequency in 1955.)

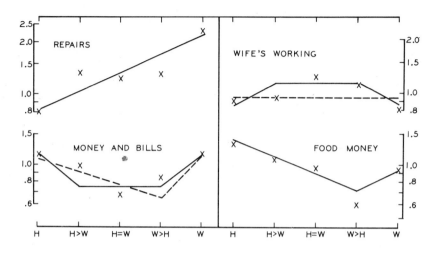

response distribution is independent of year yields $X^2 = 28.3$, $df = 4$, $p < .001$, so that the hypothesis of no change is rejected. The fit of the regression model is deemed acceptable, since $X^2 = 3.9$, $df = 3$, $p > .25$. The difference, $X^2 = 24.4$, $df = 1$, $p < .001$, is highly significant, so that the linear regression is clearly significant. As plotted in Figure 8-1, the slope is positive, so that we describe the change by stating that there has been a significant shift of Repairs away from the husband and toward the wife.

The possibility of describing changes in this fashion merits careful study, since the original investigators thought of the five categories as providing an interval scale of scores that might be averaged over items to provide composite indices of task performance and power in decision making. But if the changes are not well described by a model that incorporates the scoring convention, we obtain equivocal descriptions of change when we resort to such indices. It is of interest that fewer than half of the dozen items exhibit patterns of change that can be fairly summarized by the simple shift model.

Where that model is not satisfactory, we consider the alternatives (a) that it holds over four of the five categories but not the fifth and (b) that the change is best described by partitioning the response categories. For five items, Figure 8-1 depicts alternative models, since the tests of significance do not really provide a clear-cut choice. The model represented by the solid line is, however, judged to be slightly preferable to the one represented by the broken line.

Not only the limited applicability of the simple shift model, but also the diversity of models required for the remaining items is worth emphasizing. There simply is no general statement that one can make about shifts in the division of labor with respect to tasks or decisions. Different items change in different ways. These results might be taken to be consistent with the original investigators' surmise that "appropriateness" was gaining popularity as a criterion for the division of labor although they put in question the appropriateness of the investigators' technique for summarizing the data.

Three items, Evening Dishes (for which the change between years is marginally significant), Repairs, and Husband's Job, do seem to be best described by a simple shift; and all of these, as it happens, shift toward the wife. Since Repairs and Husband's Job are stereotypically masculine, the direction of shift might be interpreted as away from sexual stereotyping. But Evening Dishes is a "feminine" task; possibly the enhanced stereotyping is an artifact produced by the replacement of husbands by dishwashers of a mechanical kind. Two other items, Husband's Breakfast and Life Insurance, might also be described by a simple shift, in these cases toward the husband; but a slightly preferable description is that H gains at the expense of the other four categories, while the latter do not show a significant shift among themselves. In the case of Grocery Shopping, there is a shift toward the wife if we ignore the H category, the change for which is very similar to the change for the aggregate of the other categories.

For five more items, nonmonotonic patterns are required to describe the changes. For Money and Bills both H and W gain at the expense of intermediate categories, while just the opposite change occurs for Wife's Working. Changes for Food Money are toward the husband, except that W gains much more than would be expected from looking at the other four categories. To get an adequate fit for What House, we must put two "wiggles" in the curve, although the overall trend might be roughly described as a shift toward the husband. Finally, Living Room presents an anomalous pattern. Over three of the categories there is no significant change, but there appears to be a significant gain for H at the expense of $H > W$. But since very few couples are reported in either of these categories, it might be best to ignore these changes, despite the fact that they are statistically significant.

The twelfth item, What Car, seems to have no significant shift of any kind, that is, the 1971 division of labor with respect to this decision can be regarded as identical with the 1955 division of labor.

If the division of labor between spouses is an objective "fact" and if respondents report that fact precisely and veridically, then the distribution of couples by categories of the division of labor as reported by husbands should be the same as the distribution reported by wives, apart from sampling error. Indeed, a finding of this kind would help to assure us that the changes between 1955 and 1971 were real and not simply reflections of change in what wives consider, say, equal sharing. That this is not strictly the case is evident from the results reported in the bottom panel of Table 8-1. For five of the dozen items listed the distribution over categories of the division of labor based on husbands' reports differs from that based on wives' reports in a way that leaves little doubt about the significance of the difference. For an additional five items there appear to be significant differences between parts of the husbands' and wives' distributions although not for the entirety of the two distributions. Only for Evening Dishes and What House is the agreement so close that there are no grounds for rejecting the hypothesis that the spouses are reporting in a consistent manner.

There is, in sum, a real basis for affirming sex biases in reporting the division of labor in marriage. We need not jump to the conclusion that such differences represent distortions due to sexist ideologies, however. A perfectly simple explanation of the difference in regard to Repairs could be that the wives actually do a number of repairs in their husbands' absence without mentioning that fact to them. In that event, the husband might be wholly accurate in reporting that he alone does those repairs the need for which comes to his attention. On a similar line of argument, the wife may be unaware of some financial transactions, Money and Bills, handled directly by the husband. Quite a few of the discrepancies would be explained if we supposed that a small proportion of both husbands and wives make errors of one step on the scale used to measure the division of labor, but the errors tend to be in different directions. Whether the wife always does the Grocery Shopping or whether the wife does more than the husband might be a case in point.

Since we have no means of testing these or any other explanations of the discrepancies, perhaps it is enough to emphasize that the discrepancies are, from one point of view, minor. It seems clear that the spouses are reporting on the same state of affairs, even if their reports are filtered by mildly biasing perceptions. Certainly one would never confuse the husbands' reports on who decides about Life Insurance with the wives' reports on who takes care of the Money and Bills; that is, the differences between items look large compared to the differences between husbands' and wives' reports on the same item.

WORKING WIVES AND THE DIVISION OF LABOR

The employment status of the wife was seen by Blood and Wolfe as influencing the division of labor between spouses through both the working wife's contribution to the family income and the lesser amount of time available to her for housekeeping. In describing the impact of wife's employment on the division of labor, they wrote (1960), "The net result is greater equality in decision-making between husband and wife, and more participation by the husband in the total task of running the household—but not more collective participation in all task areas. Rather, the wife drops out of the husband's task areas as he moves into hers [p. 65]."

Three sets of reports on wife's work status and the couple's division of labor are available for analysis; the reports by wives in 1955; wives' reports in 1971; and reports by husbands in 1971, based on the husband's answers to questions about his wife's labor-force status and the division of labor between him and his wife. In a multiway contingency analysis, we treat the division of labor for each item as a five-category variable (save for Husband's Job where the uncommon answers of $W > H$ and W are eliminated) and wife's work status (currently employed versus other), sex of respondent, and survey year as dichotomies. Wife's work status influences the allocation of each household chore except Money and Bills as well as how decisions are made about What Car, Wife's Working, Food Money, and possibly Life Insurance, net of any effects of sex of respondent and survey year. Changes in the division of labor between 1955 and 1971, however, are not simply outcomes of the growing proportion of wives who work outside the home and the influence of wife's work status on chore allocation and decision making; for year effects on the division of labor remain significant.

We detect an unambiguously significant, but curious interaction effect with respect to decision making about What Car. Our model must incorporate either an interaction of work status, division of labor, and respondent's sex or an interaction of work status, division of labor, and survey year; and we cannot choose between alternatives on statistical grounds. The reports of husbands in 1971 and the reports of wives in 1955 imply quite different relations between wife's work status and the division of labor; the relation implied by the reports of wives in 1971 shares some features of each.

It seems worthwhile to try to capture the relation between wife's work status and the division of labor more succinctly than by describing variation in the odds on *work* over the five categories of the division of labor. First, with respect to chore allocation, Blood and Wolfe have offered an imagery that suggests that the odds on *work* would decline linearly as one moves from the *H* to the *W* category, or at least be lowest for the *W* category if the task is feminine and highest for the *H* category if the task is masculine. How the "greater equality" associated with working wives in the decision-making sphere should manifest itself is less clear although the lowest odds on *work* seemingly would be found for the *H* category. Second, we are interested in whether the relation between work status and the division of labor changed between 1955 and 1971. Results of the multiway contingency analysis indicate the possibility of detecting such interactions if the variation in the odds on *work* can be captured by a single contrast between categories or a set of ordered categories. Logit regression analysis, with the odds on *work* to be predicted from scored categories of the division of labor, sex of respondent, and survey year, offers the flexibility called for.

Using only the reports of wives, we find that the odds on *work* are highest for the *H* category and/or lowest for the *W* category for each household chore except the administrative task of Money and Bills. When the wife works, the husband more often assumes full responsibility for "his" chore of Repairs and shares "her" chores of Evening Dishes, Living Room, Grocery Shopping, and Husband's Breakfast. As is shown in Figure 8-2, the relation between wife's work status and who gets the Husband's Breakfast on work days takes the same general form in 1971 as in 1955, but has been modified in detail. One way of describing the change is to say that the negative association between taking full responsibility for getting the husband's breakfast on work days and holding a job outside the home became weaker. Whether change in breakfast habits, work schedules, or ideology is involved, we cannot say. The relation between work status and the division of labor also changes, dramatically so, with respect to who takes care of the Money and Bills. In 1955 the odds on *work* are invariant over categories of the division of labor, but in 1971 the couple more often opts for the flexible sharing represented by the categories $H > W$ and $W > H$ when the wife works.

When we turn to family decisions, the direction of the relation reverses: The odds on *work* typically are lowest for the *H* category. Although who decides about What House is unrelated to wife's work status, holding a job outside the home is positively associated with having the "final" say, at least some of the time, in each other kind of decision. The form of relation for Food Money conforms to the general rule, but is somewhat unusual. As is shown in Figure 8-3, Food–Money decisions are less often made by one spouse, either husband or wife, when the wife works; possibly this can be seen as an outcome of her

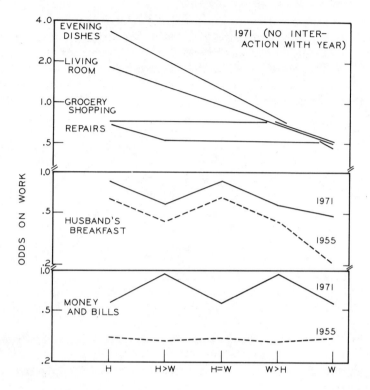

FIGURE 8-2. Relation between wife's work status and the division of labor for six family chores, 1955 and 1971 (wife's report).

enhanced power in making decisions and his greater role in the Grocery Shopping as such. Minor modification in the form of relation for Wife's Working is detected, but the most noteworthy feature remains the same: the wife who doesn't work outside the home attributes this decision to her husband.

We have by-passed the difficulty of distinguishing interactions involving wife's work status, division of labor, and survey year from interactions involving wife's work status, division of labor, and sex of respondent by restricting analysis to the reports of wives. When the data set based on reports of husbands in 1971 is included in the logit regression analyses, the difficulty with respect to What Car is not resolved; in fact, we encounter a similar problem with respect to a few other items. A cursory examination of the reports of husbands and wives, respectively, in 1971 about wife's work status and who makes decisions leaves open the possibility of subtle perceptual differences

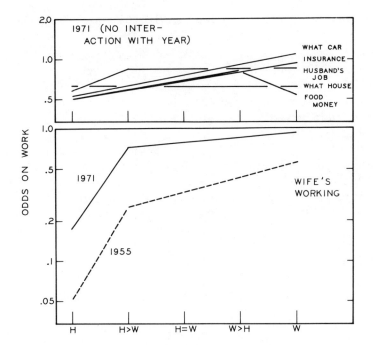

FIGURE 8-3. Relation between wife's work status and the division of labor for six family decisions, 1955 and 1971 (wife's report).

between spouses that are contingent on the wife's work status. By the account of husbands, the odds on *work* are .60 for the H category and .43 for the *"share"* and W categories of the division of labor with respect to decisions about the Husband's Job; by the account of wives, the corresponding odds are .56 and 1.0. A somewhat similar, marginally significant interaction is detected in the reports about Life Insurance: by his account, the odds on *work* are .59 for the H category, .58 for the other categories; by her account, the odds on *work* are .50 for the H category, .70 for the other categories. (Results based on multiway contingency analysis with formal variables for the H, *"share"* and W categories of the divison of labor.) Does working strengthen the wife's voice in decisions, or only influence her perception that she has a voice?

With the caution that the influence of wife's work status on the division of labor may be, in part, illusory, we conclude that Blood and Wolfe offered a sound assessment: the husband of a working wife assumes a greater role in the doing of household chores, and the two-worker couple more often shares in making the final decision about family matters.

DIVISION OF LABOR AND WIFE'S EDUCATION

There is much talk about effects of "social class" on family structure and sex roles. One authority (Yorburg, 1974) writes, "Class exists . . . and it cannot be defined away. . . . Occupation is the most accurate indicator of class. . . . Occupation is very closely related to educational level and income, and these factors are, in turn, very closely related to the values, attitudes, role conceptions, childrearing practices, and typical sexual identities of . . . people [pp. 177–178]." Yorburg argues that in all classes people learn cultural definitions of masculinity and femininity but that well educated persons do not feel so rigidly bound by the traditional definitions. She further claims—although it is not clear that she intends this as a consequence of the foregoing proposition—that there is "more sharing and mutuality in the relationship between middle class men and women."

We make no effort here to contrive an operational definition for "social class" but explore the association of wife's education with the division of labor. The reader who cares to match our results with Yorburg's proposition will have to decide for herself where to draw the line between "middle" and "working-class" wives on the education scale. We might note that in the DAS data, as in other general population samples, there is quite high assortative mating with respect to the educational attainment of spouses, $r = .6$. Hence, wife's education is virtually a proxy for husband's education; or, to put the same point differently, we could not hope to distinguish statistically between the effects of these two closely correlated variables.

Our analysis pertains to the 12 three-way tables (one for each item in the division of labor) of the form, year by wife's education (six classes) by division of labor (normally, five classes). The statistical results are quite voluminous, so that we do not attempt to record the complete details here, but rely on some illustrative analyses and a final schematic summary.

In studying Grocery Shopping we find evidence of a three-way interaction; that is, the association of division of labor with education is different in the 2 years. Formal partitioning of the division of labor discloses that the three-way interaction is confined to one category of that variable; and only one other category needs to be singled out in order to capture the education effect in either year. We take $H = W$ as the base for calculating odds and plot the odds on H, $H > W$, $W > H$, and W against education in each year (Figure 8-4). The odds on H and $H > W$ do not change with education. (This is, of course, a property of the model adopted here; but that feature of the model is acceptable in view

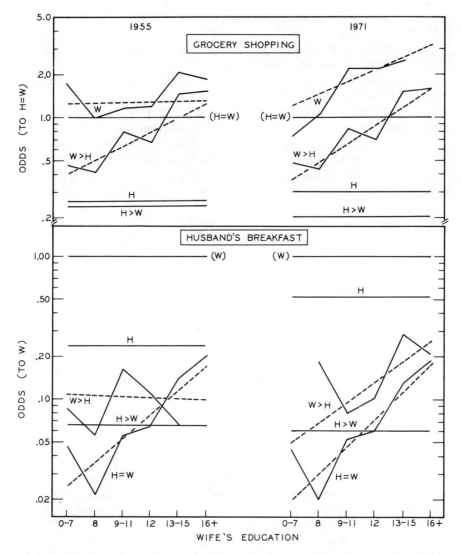

FIGURE 8-4. Odds on specified category in the division of labor between spouses, for two family chores, by wife's education, 1955 and 1971 (computed from expected frequencies under preferred model).

of the results of the tests of goodness of fit.) In both years, odds on $W >$ H generally increase with increasing education (the slope is positive). It would not be difficult to accept a straight line as a summary of the trend of the odds, so we have sketched in the dashed line to represent a judgment as to that trend—a judgment supported by some informal calculations but not by a formal statistical test. In the case of W, our statistical analysis indicates that the odds do not vary by education in the same way in the 2 years. There is a strong suggestion of a positive slope in 1971, but no such slope in 1955. Even so, the latter result could conceivably be dismissed as an unlucky result pertaining to the lowest education category. But for what it is worth, our evidence of differential change is to the effect that W was positively related to wife's education in 1971 but not in 1955.

A similar kind of interaction is noted for Husband's Breakfast. We observe a common positive slope for $H = W$ (relative to W) in the 2 years. But there is practically no slope for $W > H$ in 1955, although the slope for that category apparently is positive in 1971.

Attention is drawn to these two items, since they are the only 2 in the entire set of 12 for which we are obliged to acknowledge a possible differential change that takes the form of altering the nature of the relationship between education and the division of labor, that is, a change from zero to positive slope.

A different way of presenting the results is to use the expected frequencies under the preferred model to compute percentage distributions over the five division-of-labor categories for each level of wife's education. Figure 8-5, for example, shows that as education increases, the proportion of couples where wife always (W) makes the decision decreases, and the proportion in which it is made by husband more than wife ($H > W$) increases. Though it is not obvious from the diagram, changes in the other three categories with respect to each other are nil. (At least, that is true with respect to the relevant odds in terms of which the model is defined; it is only approximately true when those odds are transformed to percentages.)

Figure 8-6 gives an example of a different pattern. As education increases, the proportion of couples where either husband or wife always (H or W) makes the decision as to whether wife works decreases; compensating increases in the other three categories do not result in any change in their relative popularity with respect to each other.

The entire set of results for the whole dozen items is summarized in Table 8-2. In this table, "0" denotes a category chosen as base for computation of odds, *or* a category the odds on which do not change as education increases. A "+" denotes a category the odds on which

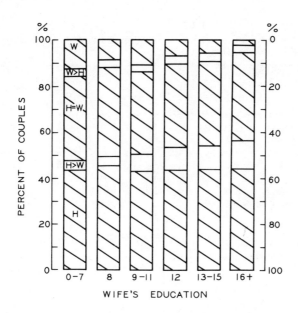

FIGURE 8-5. Division of labor with respect to life insurance, by wife's education, 1971 (computed from expected frequencies under preferred model).

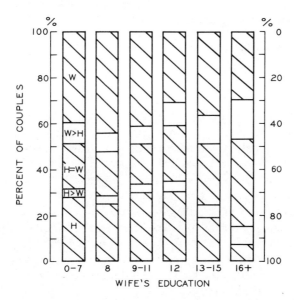

FIGURE 8-6. Division of labor with respect to wife's working, by wife's education, 1971 (computed from expected frequencies under preferred model).

TABLE 8-2
Categories in the Division of Labor between Spouses that Show a Relationship with
Wife's Education, 1955 and 1971

Chore or decision	Division of labor				
	H	$H > W$	$H = W$	$W > H$	W
Grocery shopping	0	0	0	+	+[a]
Husband's breakfast	0	+[a]	+	0	0
Evening dishes	+	+	+	+	0
Living room	—	—	+	+	0
Repairs	0	0	0	0	0
Money and bills	0	+	0	+	0
What car	0	+	0	0	0
Life insurance	0	+	0	0	—
What house	0	+	0	0	—
Husband's job	0	+	+	—	—
Wife's working	0	+	+	+	0
Food money	0	+	0	+	0

[a] 0 in 1955.

increase with education, and a "−" denotes one whose odds decrease.
The coding displayed in the table should be consistent with the four
illustrations already shown and the discussion of them.

VALUES IN MARRIAGE

In *Social Change in a Metropolitan Community* (p. 7) we noted pronounced shifts in the relative salience of some different values that
marriage has for wives. The trends recorded for 1955–1971 in the earlier
publication accelerated in the 5 subsequent years, as we can see from
Figure 8-7. We chart there a summary of the distributions of responses
to the question, "Thinking of marriage in general, which one of these
five things would you say is the most valuable part of marriage? [A] The
chance to have children, [B] The standard of living—the kind of house,
clothes, car, and so forth, [C] The husband's understanding of the
wife's problems and feelings, [D] The husband's expression of love and
affection for the wife, [E] Companionship in doing things together with
the husband." If odds are calculated with *children* as the base, we see
that the other four alternatives gained in the same measure, all at the
expense of children, between 1955 and 1971. Between 1971 and 1976 the
same sort of change occurred, but at a faster pace. While *standard of*

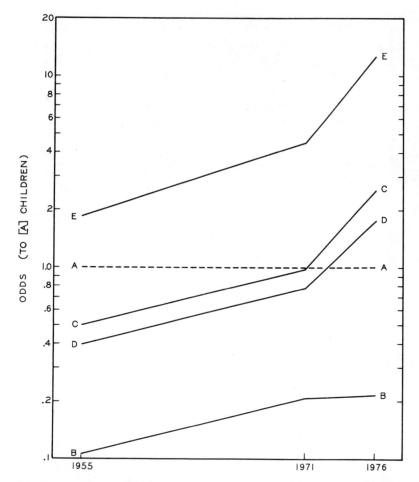

FIGURE 8-7. Observed odds on most valuable part of marriage, 1955, 1971, and 1976: [A] Children; [B] Standard of Living; [C] Understanding; [D] Love; [E] Companionship.

living appeared to gain more slowly than *companionship, understanding,* and *love*, the difference is significant only at the .1, not the .05 level. Among the five values, *chance to have children* was in a solid second place in 1955, was almost tied for second with *understanding* in 1971, but had dropped to fourth place by 1976.

Since we have used only the marginal response distribution from the 1976 Detroit Area Study, the remaining analyses of correlates of response are limited to the period 1955–1971.

Figure 8-8, where the data are cross-classified first by color and then

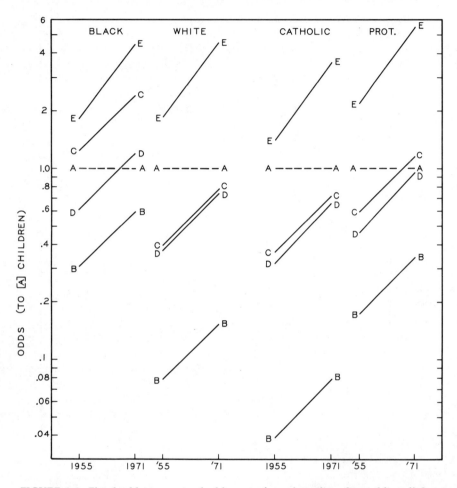

FIGURE 8-8. **Fitted odds on most valuable part of marriage, by color and by religion, 1955 and 1971: [A] Children; [B] Standard of Living; [C] Understanding; [D] Love; [E] Companionship.**

by religion, shows interesting differences between black and white and between Catholic and Protestant wives in their hierarchy of values; but the pattern of change is the same for all groups. (Each three-way analysis showed no significant differential change, either for the set of five response alternatives or under partitioning of those alternatives.) Each alternative value gains vis-à-vis the *chance to have children* between 1955 and 1971 for both black and white wives, for both Catholic and Protestant wives.

Although in each year blacks and whites agree as to the positions of *companionship* and *children,* they disagree in regard to *standard of living, understanding,* and *love,* each of which is chosen more frequently (relative to *children*) by blacks than by whites. Moreover, although these three values receive the same rank order in the aggregate choices of blacks as in those of whites, the "distances" between them are not the same in the two sets of data. In particular, *standard of living* is much more salient for blacks, although it is the least frequently chosen value for each group. The gist of the Catholic–Protestant differences is that Protestants designate each of the alternatives to *children* more frequently than do Catholics, and this tendency is especially pronounced for *standard of living.* That is, the relative positions of *understanding, love,* and *companionship* with respect to each other are the same for Protestants and Catholics, as determined by a partitioning of the response categories.

Results of the third analysis, with tenure as the factor affecting response, are readily summarized. There are no significant differences between home owners and renters in regard to changes in the response distribution. But, in both 1955 and 1971, renters are about twice as frequent among those choosing *standard of living* as among those choosing any other alternative as the most valuable part of marriage. No other significant differences in the choice patterns are detected.

When wives are classified by husband's occupation into broad socioeconomic levels, the data for both years suggest that emphasis on *understanding* (relative to *children*) is inversely related to occupational status. Since there are no differential changes, we cite only the fitted odds for 1971. For *understanding*:*children* these odds are 1.3 when the husband is a professional or salaried managerial worker, 1.1 when he is a self-employed proprietor or in a sales or clerical job, .87 when he is a craftsman or foreman, and .61 when he is an operative, service worker, or laborer. Corresponding odds, *standard of living*:*children*, are .24, .29, .096, and .084. The remaining odds (*companionship* and *love* to *children*) do not vary significantly by occupational status.

The association of wife's educational attainment and her first choice among the five alternatives is depicted in Figure 8-9. Again, we find no evidence of differential change. As far as we can tell with these data, the shift away from *chance to have children* was the same at all education levels. In the data for both years, the odds on *companionship* (relative to *chance to have children*) shows a weakly positive relationship to education; the entirety of the association is attributable to the two extreme education categories, less than 8 years of schooling and college graduate or more. The values *standard of living, understanding,* and *love,* relative to

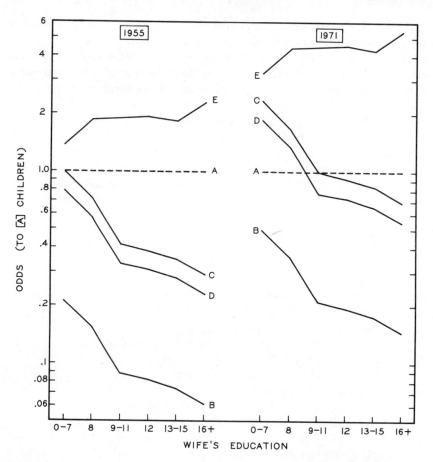

FIGURE 8-9. Fitted odds on most valuable part of marriage, by education of wife, 1955 and 1971: [A] Children; [B] Standard of Living; [C] Understanding; [D] Love; [E] Companionship.

chance to have children, manifest a negative relationship to education, especially pronounced at the lower end of the education scale. The figure shows the same regression (apart from the intercept) for all three values, since we were unable to detect any significant difference among them with respect to education effects in a partitioning of response categories. In view of the absence of differential change, the 1971 graph is the same as the 1955 graph, except for the relative downward shift of *chance to have children.* That shift, however, does result in a change in the way the value "profile" relates to education. In 1955 one could have correctly described the profile by noting that at all education levels, *companionship* was the most popular first choice, followed by *chance to have children, understanding, love,* and *standard of living,* in that order. College women and wives with only elementary schooling agreed in this respect, although the former vouchsafed a more highly differentiated pattern of first choices. By 1971 this consensus had partially broken down. Whereas *chance to have children* was the second most popular choice for high-school graduates and college women, it was fourth for wives with elementary schooling.

To conclude the report on factors related to the value selected as the most valuable part of marriage, we note that in neither 1955 nor 1971 was there a significant association between age of wife and value chosen. This is a surprising result, and we shall see shortly that a different way of looking at the data gives quite a different impression.

We have considered thus far responses to the query about "most valuable part of marriage." But this question was followed by "Which would you say is the next most valuable?" and then by ". . . third most valuable?" Our first impression was that these follow-up questions yielded information that was more or less redundant with the first question. If we look at the cross-tabulation of first choice by second choice by year, we find that second choice gives very much the same picture of year effects (that is, changes in relative popularity of the values) as first choice. There is no significant association of second choice with year, once we have taken into account changes in first choice and the association of second with first choices. But when we cross-tabulate first by second by third choice by year, we find that changes for third choice are significant even after we have taken account of changes in first and second choice and their association with third choice. The statistical details of these analyses, which involve models for so-called incomplete multiway contingency tables, are not given here, since our purpose is largely to justify the subsequent attention to part of the information contained in the second and third choices. (See, however, Appendix A, Example 5, for an exposition of the technique and some interesting national data on differences between men and women in the value of children.)

For wives in each birth cohort, we have calculated the mean of the ranks (1, 2, 3, or 4.5) assigned to the value *chance to have children;* the results are displayed in the lower panel of Figure 8-10. A downward shift in the mean rank assigned *children* is observed between 1955 and 1971 for each overlapping cohort. (Use of the dashed lines to summarize the variation between cohorts is justified by formal tests of goodness of fit.) In one sense, there is no mystery about this intracohort change. In 1955 the nation was still in the midst of the prolonged post-World War II

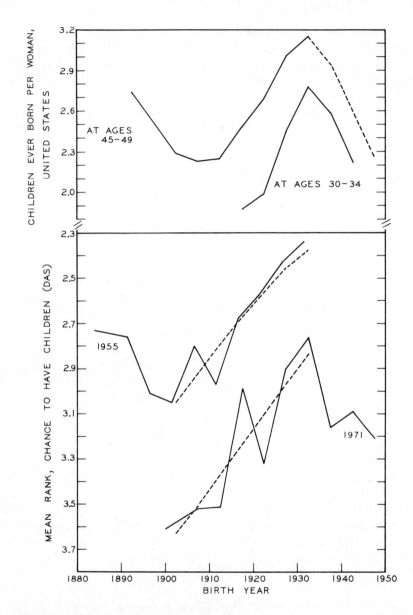

FIGURE 8-10. Mean rank of "Chance to Have Children" for Detroit area wives, by birth cohort, 1955 and 1971 (lower panel), and cumulative fertility of U. S. women at ages 45–49 and 30–34 (upper panel). For younger cohorts completed fertility is an extrapolation based on women's birth expectations. (*Source:* U. S. Bureau of the Census, *Current Population Reports, Series P-20,* Nos. 277 and 288.)

baby boom, and the birth rate was very near to the peak level recorded for that period. By 1971 the birth rate had plummeted to a level comparable with the trough of the 1930s. (It has since undergone some further decline.) In both years, one could argue, our respondents were merely reporting what they saw going on around them in regard to the relative numbers of women taking advantage of "the chance to have children."

Looking at the phenomenon from the standpoint of the wives, however, rather than as a fluctuation in demographic statistics, suggests that in both years the rate of childbearing was a consequence, among other things, of what women actually wanted. Women born before 1900 seemingly attached greater value to *children* than did women born around 1900. Thereafter, each successively younger cohort born through 1934 valued the *chance to have children* more highly than had the preceding cohort. Women born since 1934 attach lesser value to *children*. These differences among cohorts parallel the intercohort differences in children ever born (or expected at completion of childbearing in the case of the more recent cohorts); compare the configuration in the lower panel of Figure 8-10 with that in the upper panel. In 1955 the prime childbearing ages were occupied by the cohorts who attached greatest importance to the *chance to have children;* by 1971 they had been replaced by cohorts who valued this aspect of marriage much less highly.

Our evidence that wives found satisfaction in their marriages insofar as the chance to have children is concerned is indirect: Changes in completed family size are synchronized with changes in how valuable a part of marriage childrearing is for cohorts. But despite coincident changes at the aggregate level, some wives surely would have been disappointed on this score. We have direct evidence on the satisfaction of wives with respect to the other parts of marriage—standard of living, understanding, love, and companionship. In 1955 and again in 1971 the interviewer said to each wife, "Here is a card that lists some feelings you might have about certain aspects of marriage."

1. Pretty disappointed—I'm really missing out on that.
2. It would be nice to have more.
3. It's all right, I guess—I can't complain.
4. Quite satisfied—I'm lucky the way it is.
5. Enthusiastic—It couldn't be better.

The wife then was asked, "Could you tell me the statement that best describes how you feel about each of the following? For example, how do you feel about your standard of living, the kind of house, clothes,

car, and so forth? . . . about the understanding you get of your problems and feelings? . . . about the love and affection you receive? . . .
about the companionship in doing things together?" As was reported
in *Social Change in a Metropolitan Community* (p. 11), the response
pattern for Standard of Living and Understanding showed no change
between 1955 and 1971. With respect to Love, there is a shift of responses away from *all right—can't complain* to *nice to have more* and
really missing out on that, which may say that by 1971 complaint in the
face of unmet expectations had become more acceptable. A decrease in
satisfaction with Companionship also is registered, which takes the
form of an overall shift toward lower levels of satisfaction. The growing
dissatisfaction with this part of marriage may be worth a close look, for
companionship most often was said to be the most valuable part of
marriage and gained in popularity relative to *children* between 1955 and
1971.

Are wives who attach higher value to *companionship* than to *children*
more satisfied with the Companionship received in their marriages
than the wives who assign the higher value to *children*? We know that
the former have become more numerous; indeed, the ratio of wives
assigning the higher value to *companionship* to wives assigning the
higher value to *children* increased from 1.7 in 1955 to 3.7 in 1971. The
answer with respect to satisfaction depends upon survey year. If we
simply compute a mean satisfaction score for each group of wives,
using the code numbers of the responses as scores, we find that the
wives assigning the higher value to *companionship* were a bit more
satisfied with the Companionship received in 1955. Their mean satisfaction score is 3.88, in contrast to a mean score of 3.74 for the wives
assigning the higher value to *children*. Although they are overrepresented in the *nice to have more* category, they also are overrepresented in
the *couldn't be better* category and underrepresented in the *really missing
out on that* category. In 1971, however, the wives assigning the higher
value to *companionship* are no more satisfied. Their mean satisfaction
score is 3.69, as compared with a mean score of 3.75 for the wives
assigning the higher value to *children*. Study of the response distributions suggests that the prudent conclusion is no difference in satisfaction between these groups of wives. What is thought to be important in
marriage surely changes as a wife finds satisfaction with some parts of
her married life, dissatisfaction with other parts; and what constitutes
satisfaction with a particular part presumably depends upon how important that part is thought to be. Thus, it may be that we witness a
change in values with which change in satisfaction has not "caught
up."

The decrease in satisfaction with Companionship is not confined to a few strata; no evidence of differential change can be established when wives are classified by the kinds of social, economic, and demographic characteristics that we have been considering in earlier analyses. There are, however, clear-cut age and education effects on level of satisfaction.

Figure 8-11 shows the variation of satisfaction with age. Apart from the upturn at ages 65 and over in 1971, we find that a linear regression affords an excellent fit. There is no significant variation among the means other than a constant difference between years and the linear decline with age (up to 65). The slope of the regression is $-.0092$ per year of age and the 1971 line is .133 lower than the 1955 line, dropping by $.133/16 = .0083$ per year. For any annual birth cohort, therefore, the estimated change in satisfaction is $(16)(-.0092) - .133 = -.28$ over the period between surveys, about half of which could be attributed to "aging" and half to "social change," if one were to press that distinction. In these calculations, we disregard the extraordinarily high reading for 36 wives aged 65 and over in 1971. Their mean is statistically a significant outlier. It is tempting to conclude that older women have found the secret of happiness, but we should be loath to press any substantive interpretation of this result, pending its replication.

As the educational attainment of the wife increases, she reports greater satisfaction with the Companionship she receives in her marriage. From a linear regression model that provides an adequate fit to

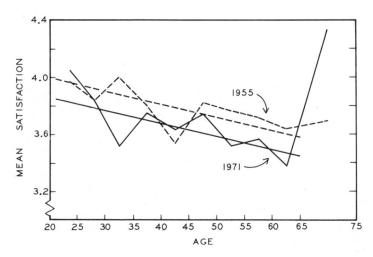

FIGURE 8-11. Regression of satisfaction with companionship on age, for wives in 1955 and 1971.

the observations, we estimate that in both 1955 and 1971 the mean satisfaction score for wives who completed college was .51 greater than the score for wives who failed to complete elementary school. The latter group of wives are, on the average, older; this means that we are somewhat overstating the effects of both aging and educational attainment. Of greater interest here, however, is the fact that at each education level, the mean satisfaction score fell by .189 during the 16-year period between surveys. Rising educational levels worked in the direction of masking the deterioration in wives' satisfaction with Companionship.

We have no way of knowing whether younger or better educated women actually receive more companionship or, indeed, whether wives' notions of what is companionable differ according to their age and education. We do find satisfaction with Companionship associated with the division of labor for all tasks and decisions save Money and Bills and Husband's Job. Shown in Table 8-3 is the variation in satisfaction scores by category of the division of labor. But why one style of doing or deciding should be more companionable than another is often far from obvious. It is true that the mean satisfaction score typically is at or near its maximum for the category $H = W$, which may represent

TABLE 8-3

Mean Score on Satisfaction with Companionship, by Division of Labor on Chores and Decisions, Pooled Sample of Wives in 1955 and 1971

Chore or decision	Note	Division of labor				
		H only	*H > W*	*H = W*	*W > H*	*W* only
Repairs	—	3.86	3.75	3.95	3.11	3.05
Husband's breakfast	—	3.69	3.47	3.93	3.56	3.83
Grocery shopping	—	3.84	3.71	4.01	3.67	3.65
Living room	—	3.90	4.27	4.03	3.83	3.67
Evening dishes	—	4.12	3.74	4.09	4.00	3.66
Money and bills	(a)	3.82	3.60	3.87	3.66	3.70
Husband's job	(a)	3.75	3.83	4.10	4.00	3.36
What car	(b)					
1955		3.73	3.67	4.09	3.93	3.86
1971		3.68	3.97	3.75	3.20	3.40
Wife's working	—	3.92	3.58	3.96	3.60	3.62
Food money	—	3.57	3.26	3.94	3.63	3.73
Life insurance	—	3.76	3.74	3.84	3.75	3.52
What house	—	3.51	3.64	3.87	3.67	3.64

(a) Association between task or decision and satisfaction not significant at .05 level.
(b) Association changed significantly between 1955 and 1971.

sharing in the sense of doing or deciding together. But are wives especially satisfied with Companionship when they always get the Husband's Breakfast (category *W*) because they have breakfast with their husbands? Are wives especially satisfied with Companionship when their husbands always do the Evening Dishes (category *H*) because their husbands are home for the evening meal? Speculation is idle. Answers to these questions must await the availability of data of another kind.

In sum, the obvious difficulty in interpreting the changed distribution of satisfaction with Companionship is that we have no adequate measure of the actual amount of companionship (defining the latter in whatever terms may be relevant to the respondent). It may be instructive, however, to consider a problem where this limitation is circumvented. In analyzing satisfaction with the Standard of Living (Duncan, 1975c), we were able to show a substantial regression of satisfaction on family income. Curiously, though, there was no change between 1955 and 1971 in the distribution of satisfaction even though real income (that is, dollar income adjusted for inflation) increased by about 40%. The two results are reconciled on the supposition that satisfaction with income depends, not on absolute amount of (real) income, but on relative income, that is, position in the income distribution. A detailed regression analysis showed that at any given *percentile* of the 1971 income distribution the average satisfaction was the same as at the corresponding percentile in the 1955 distribution. Thus, the Detroit results are seen as confirming the observation of Easterlin (1973), who reported, on the basis of studies of happiness in some 19 countries, "In all societies, more money for the individual typically means more individual happiness. However, raising the incomes of all does not increase the happiness of all [p. 4]." It appears that, within the United States, the evolution of the norm of a minimum standard of living has almost exactly paralleled the increase in real income (Rainwater, 1974). Thus, the higher the median income of all families, the greater is the amount that any one family would concede is an adequate minimum needed to get along.

Suppose, then, that in 1971 there was actually more companionship than in 1955. The Easterlin–Rainwater kind of argument would suggest that satisfaction need not have changed, since expectations would have risen as well. But what if there are factors other than actual amount of companionship that affect expectations concerning companionship? For example, if women want fewer children, actually have fewer, and put less value on having them, then they may by way of compensation escalate their subjective requirement for companionship. In that event, the exogenous increase in the expectations for companionship could

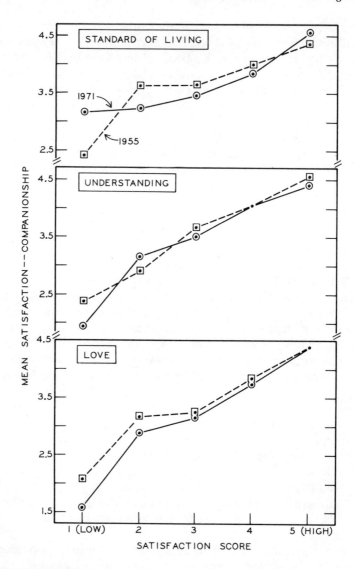

FIGURE 8-12. Mean satisfaction with companionship as a function of mean satisfaction with three other aspects of marriage, for wives in 1955 and 1971.

lead to a decrease in satisfaction with Companionship, if only the actual companionship enjoyed failed to increase, or to increase as fast as the expectations. The main element of plausibility in this suggestion is that, indeed, the emphasis on having children did decline. Whether the desire for companionship actually increased in an absolute sense—or only increased relative to the interest in children—we cannot tell.

Some wives do report considerable satisfaction with Companionship while admitting to dissatisfaction with some other facet of married life. That is, although the four kinds of satisfaction are substantially inter-correlated, they are not perfectly so. Displayed in Figure 8-12 are the mean scores on satisfaction with Companionship for wives expressing different levels of satisfaction with their Standard of Living or the Understanding or Love that they receive. Although satisfaction with Companionship increases as satisfaction with the other part of marriage rises, the relation is by no means one-to-one. Moreover, the relationship with Companionship is stronger for Understanding than for Standard of Living, and stronger still for Love. The evidence, then, suggests that women see married life as multifaceted, differentially evaluate its parts, and, presumably by some system of weighting, decide whether the marriage is good or bad, should be continued or dissolved. If so, the downward shifts in satisfaction with Companionship and Love are somewhat disquieting. But more disturbing is the fact that the relation between satisfaction with Companionship and satisfaction with Love became tighter between 1955 and 1971. (Multi-way contingency analysis detects no change in the relation of Companionship to Standard of Living or Understanding between 1955 and 1971.) To be sure, only a tiny minority of wives said that they were *really missing out* on Love in either 1955 or 1971; but only in 1971 did an overwhelming majority of these wives report that they were *really missing out* on Companionship as well.

9

The Secularization of Divorce[1]

In 1970, the divorce rate in the United States was 14.9 per 1000 married women, the highest level since 1945 when the rate peaked at 17.9. The 1945 high was an isolated occurrence; the rate increased by 24% between 1944 and 1945 and then decreased by 24% between 1945 and 1946. Gradual decreases, which reduced the rate to 8.9 in 1958, were followed by a sustained and accelerating rise to the 1970 high.

While a direct correspondence between attitudes about the morality of divorce and the actual incidence of divorce is not asserted, a belief that divorce is morally wrong should be an inhibitory factor in getting a divorce. To the extent that individuals perceive that moral barriers to an action are removed, the action will become more prevalent given the proper stimuli. It would be difficult to deny that there are strains in marriage which provide the stimuli. One might suppose, therefore, that Americans became more lenient in their attitudes toward divorce between 1958 and 1971.

Samples of residents of the metropolitan Detroit area were questioned on their attitudes about the morality of divorce in the 1958 and 1971 surveys. The 1958 question is especially well timed in that the divorce rate was lower in 1958 than in any other year in the postwar

[1] This chapter was prepared by James A. McRae, Jr. The helpful comments of Lawrence Santi are gratefully acknowledged.

period. In that year, 656 adults in the Detroit area were asked, "From the moral standpoint, how do you feel about divorce?" and allowed to answer: *always wrong, usually wrong, sometimes wrong,* or *never wrong.* This question was also asked of 1881 respondents in 1971 with identical response categories. The distribution of responses, given in Table 9-1, shows percentage decreases in the *always* and *usually* wrong categories and increases in the *sometimes* and *never* wrong categories between 1958 and 1971. The *sometimes wrong* response, which absorbed most of the increase, is interpreted by Duncan *et al.* (1973, p. 71) as implying that divorce is sometimes right. Likewise, the *usually wrong* response implies that divorce must be right on occasion.

Population movement from the position that divorce is *always* morally wrong to the position that it is only *usually* or *sometimes* wrong can be viewed as a shift from moral absolutism to situational ethics. The latter two responses seem to indicate that situations need to be considered individually; contingencies such as the degree of dependence of the parties involved become more crucial than insistence upon a moral rule.

The *never wrong* response was probably chosen for one of two reasons: The respondent either believed that divorce is simply not a moral issue or wanted to indicate more tolerance for divorce than is implied in calling it *sometimes wrong.* While different respondents undoubtedly had different reasons for choosing this response, findings about the nature of change lend greater support to the former interpretation.

Whatever the interpretation given the *never wrong* response, divorce

TABLE 9-1

Percentage Distribution of Responses to Question on Morality of Divorce, 1958 and 1971, and Ratio, 1971:1958

Response category	Percentage distribution		Ratio 1971:1958[a]
	1958	1971	
Always wrong	22.7	8.1	1.0
Usually wrong	20.4	10.0	1.4
Sometimes wrong	48.4	70.3	4.2
Never wrong	8.6	11.6	3.9
Total	100.0	100.0	2.9

[a] 643 of the 656 respondents in 1958 and 1859 of the 1881 respondents in 1971 answered the Morality of Divorce question. The 1971:1958 ratio results from dividing the number of 1971 respondents giving the specified answer by the number of 1958 respondents giving the same answer.

was being removed from the realm of the morally absolute for the population as a whole during the period of rising divorce rates. Since the national statistics on divorce provide little information on which subgroups of the population experienced greater changes in divorce rates, it is impossible to determine whether differential change in behavior parallels differential change in attitude between 1958 and 1971. The latter topic can be explored in some depth, however, with our data.

DIFFERENTIAL CHANGE

Although the response options appear to provide a scale of tolerance for divorce, utilization of a method developed by Simon (1974) reveals significant departures from a (logarithmic) linear relationship of response to year; and controlling for sex, color, and religion does not modify this result. The ratio, 1971:1958, given in Table 9-1 increases monotonically from *always* to *sometimes* wrong but is lower for *never* than for *sometimes* wrong, supporting the interpretation that the *never wrong* response is not the endpoint of a scale of moral tolerance but rather that the respondents who choose it do not believe divorce to be a moral question.

The changes in attitude toward divorce are further explored by cross-classifying Morality of Divorce by year by a demographic or social characteristic. The technique of partitioning polytomous variables in multiway analysis is used to pinpoint the significant contrasts among categories of Morality of Divorce. This results in the choice of a model that cannot be significantly improved upon but that cannot be simplified without a significant increase in X^2.

Utilizing this procedure, we find no evidence of differential change by sex, tenure, subjective class identification, political preference, or occupation. The absence of a differential change by sex is not only interesting from the standpoint of our general inquiry. It also supports our conclusion that respondents being asked about the morality of divorce actually responded in those terms. For if some question of women's rights were involved, rather than a question of morality equally applicable to both sexes, we would expect women to lead the way. In point of fact, there was no sex difference in response in either year.

Differential change by farm experience, education, and birth cohort is restricted to the contrast *always wrong* versus any other response. Differential change by color is captured by the contrast *never wrong* versus any other response. Dichotomizing the response categories fails to capture the entirety of the differential change by family income and religion. For the former, significant contrasts between *always, usually,* and (*sometimes + never*) are detected; for the latter, *always, sometimes,* and (*usually + never*) must be distinguished.

Another possible partitioning involves dichotomization between pairs of response categories, but no such dichotomy proves satisfactory in capturing the significant contrasts.

While a counsel of perfection would be to maintain formal variables for the four categories of Morality of Divorce throughout the analysis, this would be exceedingly tedious and presents many possibilities for error. Although any dichotomization loses some of the contrasts in the data, greater conceptual support can be marshalled for dichotomizing between *always wrong* and the other responses. It is the contrast of these categories over time that represents movement from the morally absolutist position, the change that is of primary interest. Fortunately, it is also this contrast that best captures the differential changes by social or demographic stratum reported previously. In the remainder of the analysis, Morality of Divorce will be treated as a dichotomy taking the values *always wrong* and any *other* response, unless otherwise noted.

Farm Experience

Farm experience has four categories—southern, northern, foreign, or none—for the area, if any, in which the respondent lived and worked on a farm. The preferred model ($X^2 = .90$, $df = 3$, $p > .50$) resulting from the analysis of the six-way table, Morality of Divorce by year by formal variables for farm experience indicates virtually no change for the southern category and equal change for the other categories. In 1958, the odds on *always wrong* are highest for those with foreign farm experience (.91), intermediate and identical for those with northern or no farm experience (.28), and lowest for the southern group (.15). By 1971, the foreign group still exhibits the highest odds (.24), but the groups with northern or no farm experience are lowest (.07) and the southern group is intermediate (.16).

The hypothesis that those with southern farm experience exhibit no change because of their more recent arrival in Detroit is supported in that this category has the highest odds on migrating to Detroit since 1958, but including residence in 1958, Detroit versus other, in the analysis does not alter the initial conclusion. A speculative interpretation is that a stronger normative system exists in the rural South; those who leave the area do not leave the values and norms learned there but rather resist the pressures to change in a northern metropolis.

Family Income and Education

Family income is a five-category variable with a control for inflation. In 1958, the categories are (0) less than \$2000, (1) \$2000–\$3999, (2) \$4000–\$6999, (3) \$7000–\$9999, and (4) \$10,000 and above. In 1971, the categories are (0) less than \$3000, (1) \$3000–\$5999, (2) \$6000–\$9999, (3) \$10,000 to \$14,999, and (4) \$15,000 and above. Using the technique of logit regression, the natural log of the odds on *always wrong* relative to *other* is regressed on year, income, and the interaction between year and income. The preferred model specifies a year by income effect but does not provide an acceptable fit ($p < .05$). However, there is no clear pattern of deviation from the regression lines. Including religion, Protestant versus Catholic, in the model, an acceptable fit is obtained ($Y^2 = 21.77$, $df = 14$, $.10 > p > .05$), although there is no significant joint effect of religion and family income. Again there is no discernible pattern of deviations. The preferred model is,

$$\hat{A} = -1.9146 + .0747Y + 1.4072R + .0476I - 1.0563YR - .3133YI,$$

where $\hat{A}$ is the expected logit, Y takes the values 0 in 1958 and 1 in 1971, R takes the values 0 when Protestant and 1 when Catholic, and I takes the values 0 through 4 with increasing income. Thus, the regression of *always* on income is almost flat in 1958 and is negative in 1971, indicating greater change with increasing income. The effect of religion will be discussed later, and an interpretation of the effect of income on change will be offered after examining the effect of education.

Education is measured by completed years of schooling and takes the values (0) elementary 0–7, (1) elementary 8, (2) high school 1–3, (3) high school 4, (4) college 1–3, (5) college 4, (6) college 5 and above. In examining the removal of an attitude from the realm of the morally absolute, we should expect this removal to be greatest among those most exposed to the secularizing effect of education. This is indeed the situation. The preferred model resulting from a logit regression of *always wrong* relative to *other* (A) on year (Y), education (E), and the interaction term is

$$\hat{A} = -1.1790 - .3098Y - .3532YE,$$

with $Y^2 = 12.88$, $df = 11$, $.50 > p > .25$. (The coefficient for E is zero.) A possible injustice to the data done by this model is for those with 5 years or more of college. In both years, the observed odds for this category produce the largest deviation from the regression line; the 1971:1958 ratio of the observed odds is 1.05. Perhaps the issue had already been secularized for those with graduate training in 1958.

Since education and family income are highly correlated and affect change similarly, the log of the odds on *always wrong* was regressed on year, family income, education (which is reduced to six categories to avoid exceedingly small cell sizes), and the two-way interaction terms involving year. When year is allowed to interact with education, it is not necessary to include a year by family income effect; doing so reduces Y^2 by 1.0, a nonsignificant decrease. However, after allowing year to interact with family income, it is still necessary to include a year by education effect. The preferred model ($Y^2 = 45.07$, $df = 54$, $p > .50$) does include an independent effect of family income. Thus, although increasing family income decreases the odds on *always wrong*, the greater change among the wealthier is a function of education.

The separate effect of income can be attributed to the individual's objective situation of facing fewer problems in a divorce because of greater financial security. The wealthier the family, the less difficulty it would face in absorbing the financial burdens of divorce and continuing to provide for the children.

The effect of education on change is interpreted as reflecting greater skepticism among the better educated about whether traditional moral rules fit present circumstances. In the 1960s, this skepticism was fueled by the message appearing in the media, reflecting in part the views of social scientists, that marital unhappiness is a problem that, like other personal problems, can be solved; the solution is divorce. Thus, the better educated were increasingly unwilling to insist that divorce is always morally wrong.

Birth Cohort

Two mechanisms of change that merit inspection whenever the period of interest is more than a few years are the replacement of old cohorts with new cohorts and changes within individual cohorts. In this analysis, there are 10 cohorts, defined by year of birth, that were sampled in both years, (0) before 1893, (1) 1893–1898, (2) 1898–1903, (3) 1903–1908, (4) 1908–1913, (5) 1913–1918, (6) 1918–1923, (7) 1923–1928, (8) 1928–1933, and (9) 1933–1937, as well as three cohorts sampled only in 1971, (10) 1937–1941, (11) 1941–1946, and (12) 1946–1950.

The regression of the log of the odds on *always* results in the preferred model, $\hat{A} = -1.1934 - .1724YC$, where YC is the year by cohort interaction ($Y^2 = 22.04$, $df = 21$, $p > .25$). Including terms in the model that allow the three "new" cohorts to have a different slope from that for the older cohorts or to have the same slope but to lie off the trend reduces Y^2 by less than 1.0.

The model shows younger cohorts changing more than older ones and all cohorts moving away from the morally absolutist position. In 1958, there are no reliable cohort differences; the coefficient describing the effect of cohort is not significantly different from zero. By 1971, however, the odds on *always wrong,* lowest for "new" cohorts, increase monotonically with age. Members of the older cohorts have had more time to solidify their moral beliefs and are less open to change than members of younger cohorts (Carlsson and Karlsson, 1970; Ryder, 1965). At least in regard to the secularization of divorce, the younger the individual, the greater is the odds that she or he will be a carrier of change in the normative structure.

Religion

As reported earlier, religious groups exhibit differential change on both the *always* and *sometimes wrong* responses. Religion comprises the three categories, Catholic, Jew, and Protestant. Analysis of the table, religion by year by formal variables representing Morality of Divorce results in the interesting but complicated model presented in Figure 9-1 ($X^2 =$ 6.23, $df = 4$, $p > .10$). The odds, *always:never,* decreases for both Protestants and Catholics but remains unchanged for Jews between 1958 and 1971. For Catholics, the odds in 1971 is only .16 of its 1958 value; the corresponding figure for Protestants is .46. Thus, it is among Catholics, a group whose church does not condone divorce, that the change was greatest. At least with regard to the morally absolutist position on divorce, members of the three major religious groups looked more alike in 1971 than in 1958.

Inspection of the graphs depicting change in the odds *usually:never* and *sometimes:never* is instructive. The odds on *usually wrong* decrease by the same ratio for the three groups; the odds ratio, 1971:1958, is .35. The odds, *sometimes:never,* increase for Catholics and Jews but remain about the same for Protestants. The ratios, 1971:1958, describing these changes are 1.4 for Catholics, 1.6 for Jews, and 1.0 for Protestants. While it appears from the first panel of Figure 9-1 that divorce is increasingly being removed from the moral realm, the increases in the odds, *sometimes:never,* indicate that the bulk of the increased tolerance is absorbed by the *sometimes wrong* response; divorce remains a moral issue but not one resolved by fiat.

In 1958, religious groups could be ordered by tolerance for divorce with Jews most tolerant and Catholics least tolerant. In the 1960s, the gaps between religions lessened. The drastic reduction in the propor-

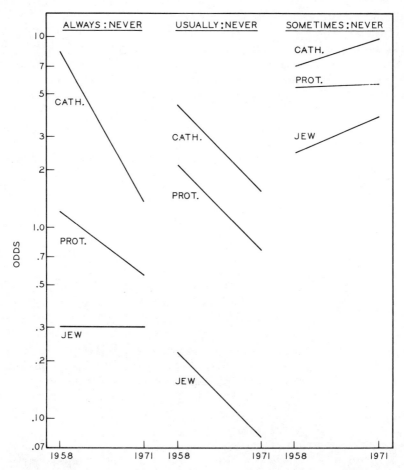

FIGURE 9-1. Fitted odds on specified responses to question on morality of divorce, relative to *never wrong,* for Catholics, Jews, and Protestants in 1958 and 1971.

tion of Catholics reporting that divorce is *always wrong* is quite surprising, since it occurred at a time when the Church hierarchy maintained its traditional stance that if the marriage is real, it is indissoluble. However, the 1960s were a period of rapid change and dissension in the Church as evidenced by Vatican II, which ended in 1965, and books such as James Kavanaugh's *A Modern Priest Looks at His Outdated Church* (1967). Further investigation of the relationship between religion and the movement from the absolutist moral realm on the issue of divorce should prove useful, especially in light of the recent softening of the Church's position on divorce.

ANALYSIS OF CHANGE WITHIN RELIGIONS

For this more detailed analysis of change within religious groups, Jews are omitted because their small numbers prohibit extensive cross-tabulations. This is probably not a serious omission because, among Jews, the odds on *always wrong* are not significantly different in the 2 years.

The effects of education and birth cohort on the log of the odds, *always wrong :other*, do not depend on religion. For example, there is no effect of being a young Catholic other than the separate effects of being young and being Catholic.

Although it is not feasible to study individually the many Protestant denominations, it seemed desirable to include a control on color. The "mix" of denominations to which blacks belong is different from that of whites. Color, however, turns out to be an unimportant factor. A four-category variable representing color by religion was constructed with the categories, black Catholic (Cb), black Protestant (Pb), white Catholic (Cw), and white Protestant (Pw). The preferred model, {YCbPbCwPw} {DYCw}, resulting from analysis of the table, Morality of Divorce (D) by year (Y) by formal variables representing the color–religion categories, indicates differential change for white Catholics only. The fit of the model is good; $X^2 = 2.89$, $df = 4$, $p > .50$. For purposes of studying change in the odds on *always wrong*, then, black and white Protestants need not be distinguished. The placement of black Catholics with Protestants results from their small numbers, and the difference between black and white Catholics should not be taken seriously.

Ask What God Wants

Respondents were asked, "When you have decisions to make in your everyday life, do you ask yourself what God would want you to do?" and allowed to answer *often, sometimes,* or *never*. Analysis of the table, Morality of Divorce (D) by Ask What God Wants (A) by year (Y) by religion (R) results in the preferred model, {AYR}, {DYR}, {DA}, specifying differential change in Morality of Divorce and a relationship between Morality of Divorce and Ask What God Wants that is independent of religious affiliation ($X^2 = 3.71$, $df = 6$, $p > .50$). (In this and subsequent analyses, the relationship between religion, year, and the selected religious characteristic is not of substantive concern, and the corresponding three-way marginal is routinely fitted.) Responding that one *often* asks what God wants relative to responding *never* raises the odds on responding that divorce is *always* wrong by a factor of 2.5; the *sometimes* : *never* ratio of the odds on *always wrong* is 1.4. Thus, the odds on *always wrong* increase with a greater frequency of asking what God wants, not a surprising result.

However, that the relationship between Ask What God Wants and Morality of Divorce is not significantly stronger for Catholics than for Protestants is surprising. One of the issues in the Protestant Reformation was the interpretation of the Divine Word imposed on members by the Church hierarchy. In asking what God wants, Catholics receive unambiguous advice from that hierarchy: Divorce is always wrong. Protestants, despite the lack of such clear guidance, exhibit an equally strong relation between these two variables.

This argument can be extended to suggest that those Catholics who often ask what God wants should show no change in Morality of Divorce. The Church has bent its position on deviations from doctrine but certainly not overturned it, the ruling on birth control in Humanae Vitae being a case in point. The reaction to Humanae Vitae among many Catholic theologians has been that Catholics need not agree with those teachings of the hierarchy not deemed infallible (Roche, 1968, pp. 317–318). One such fallible teaching concerns birth control; another, divorce. Apparently Catholics are less often using the Church hierarchy as a means of discovering the Divine Word if the movement from the morally absolute position on divorce is equally great among those who often, sometimes and never ask themselves what God wants them to do in their daily lives.

Prayer Before Meals

In 1958, women and men who had been married and had children were asked whether they ever pray before meals with response options, *yes* and *no*. In 1971, all respondents were asked this question, but information on children ever born was obtained only for women. The 1971 sample, then, consists of all men who had been married and women who had been married and had children. Although the results must be viewed with somewhat less than the usual confidence, controlling for sex does not alter the choice of a preferred model; sex affects neither Morality of Divorce nor the relationships between Morality of Divorce and the other variables. This indicates that the failure to obtain exactly comparable samples is probably not critical.

Analysis of the table, Morality of Divorce (D) by Prayer Before Meals (P) by year (Y) by religion (R) indicates a quite complicated preferred model, $\{PYR\}$, $\{DYR\}$, $\{DPR\}$, $\{DPY\}$ ($X^2 = 2.22$, $df = 1$, $p = .14$). Religion affects the change in Morality of Divorce, whether the respondent

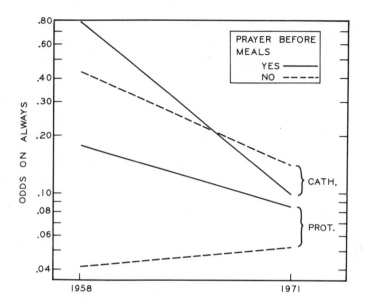

FIGURE 9-2. Fitted odds on responding *always wrong* relative to all *other* responses to question on morality of divorce, by prayer before meals, for Catholics and Protestants in 1958 and 1971.

prays before meals affects the change in Morality of Divorce, and the relationship between Prayer Before Meals and Morality of Divorce is different for Protestants and Catholics. The odds based on this model are presented in Figure 9-2.

As in every analysis involving religion, the decrease in the odds on *always wrong* is greater for Catholics than for Protestants. In both years, the relationship between Prayer Before Meals and Morality of Divorce is stronger for Protestants than for Catholics. Being Protestant rather than Catholic raises the Pray:Not Pray ratio of the odds on *always wrong* by a factor of 2.7. Presumably, Catholics rely more on official doctrine than do Protestants in forming opinions and behavior patterns, and non-prescribed behaviors such as praying before meals would have less meaning for them. Thus, one would expect greater association between Prayer Before Meals and Morality of Divorce among Protestants than among Catholics.

For both religions, the relationship between Prayer Before Meals and Morality of Divorce is weaker in the later year. The Pray:Not Pray ratio of the odds on *always wrong* in 1971 is only .38 of its 1958 value. Assuming that praying before meals is indicative of religious commitment, this analysis supports the hypothesis that attitudes on divorce are becoming secularized.

Right to Question the Church

Traditionally, Catholics have not had the right to question their Church's teaching on important matters, while this right has been a cornerstone of Protestantism. Respondents of both religions were asked, "Do you feel you have the right to question what your Church teaches, or not?" with response options, *yes, unsure,* and *no.* Analysis of the table, Morality of Divorce by year by religion by formal variables representing Right to Question the Church indicates a three-way interaction between Right to Question the Church, Morality of Divorce, and religion, and, again, a three-way interaction between Morality of Divorce, year, and religion. The significant contrast on Right to Question the Church is between *no* and (*unsure + yes*).

In order to simplify this result, a four-category variable was constructed by cross-classifying religion and Right to Question the Church. Partitioning this variable in relation to Morality of Divorce and year indicates that Catholics who believe they have the right to question the Church and Protestants who don't claim this right are indistinguishable on Morality of Divorce in both years; the odds on *always wrong* in 1958 and the rate of change are the same for both categories. The expected odds generated by the preferred model ($X^2 = 4.79$, $df = 3$, $p > .10$), presented in Table 9-2, indicate less change in Morality of Divorce among Protestants claiming the right to question the Church and equal change for the other categories. This is a remarkable situation in that Catholics who don't claim the right to question the Church in general are questioning the Church's morally absolutist position on divorce.

Choice of Friends and Spouse

Respondents were asked whether they thought it wiser for people of their religion to choose their close friends and spouses from their religion with response options, *yes, no,* and *unsure.* For Protestants, neither Choice of Friends nor Choice of Spouse is related to Morality of Divorce, independently or in interaction with year.

Among Catholics, however, these variables are interrelated. Analysis of the table, Morality of Divorce by year by formal variables representing Choice of Friends, reveals significantly different odds on *always wrong* for all categories of Choice of Friends and no change in this

TABLE 9-2
Fitted Odds on Responding Always Wrong to Question on Morality of Divorce, by Year
and Religious Attitude, and Odds Ratio, 1971:1958

Religion and attitude item	Odds on *always wrong*		Odds ratio 1971:1958
	1958	1971	
Protestant and			
Catholic respondents			
Right to Question Church			
Protestant, Yes/Unsure	.13	.07	.53
Protestant, No	.36	.09	.25
Catholic, Yes/Unsure	.36	.09	.25
Catholic, No	1.16	.30	.25
Catholic respondents only			
Choice of Friends			
Wiser own religion	1.12	.22	.20
Unsure	6.35	1.27	.20
Not wiser own religion	.50	.10	.20
Choice of Spouse			
Wiser own religion	.88	.10	.12
Unsure/Not wiser	.18	.13	.71
The True Church			
Yes	.97	.11	.11
Unsure/No	.31	.11	.36

relationship over time. The odds generated by this model ($X^2 = .82$, $df = 2$, $p > .50$) are presented in Table 9-2.

The odds on *always wrong* are highest among Catholics who are *unsure* about Choice of Friends, intermediate among those responding *yes*, and lowest among those responding *no*. While there is sentiment in the Church favoring Catholic friends, the ideal of bringing non-Catholics into the Church requires extensive contact with non-Catholics, perhaps even forming friendships. There is no clear guidance, then, on the issue of non-Catholic friends. There is, however, very pointed guidance on the matter of divorce: death is the only legitimate end of a marriage recognized by the Church. If those who respond that divorce is *always wrong* are forming this opinion on the basis of Church teachings, they might be unsure as to whether Catholics should choose others of their religion as close friends because the Church offers no clear teaching on this issue.

The preferred model ($X^2 = .67$, $df = 2$, $p > .50$) describing the table,

Morality of Divorce by year by formal variables representing Choice of Spouse, indicates that the greatest decrease in the odds on *always wrong* is among those who believe it is wiser for Catholics to marry other Catholics. The odds presented in Table 9-2 show virtually no association between Morality of Divorce and Choice of Spouse in 1971, whereas in 1958 there is a rather strong association. The Church's position on intermarriage is not firm, but there is a clear preference for endogamy. Among those holding to the official position on endogamy, support for the morally absolutist position on divorce has dwindled the most.

The True Church

Catholic respondents were asked whether their church is the only true church, and partitioning the responses in relation to year and Morality of Divorce indicates that the significant contrast is *yes* versus (*unsure* + *no*). The odds generated by the preferred model ($X^2 = .07$, $df = 2$, $p > .50$) are presented in Table 9-2. In 1958, Catholics who responded that theirs is the only true church exhibited significantly higher odds on *always wrong* than did other Catholics. However, in 1971, there is no relationship between Morality of Divorce and The True Church; the odds on *always wrong* are identical although the model does not constrain them to be so.

CHANGES IN THE CHURCH

In the entire analysis, not one major group exhibits a significant increase in the odds on *always wrong* from 1958 to 1971; there has been a general movement away from the morally absolutist position on divorce and, although the issue remains in part a moral one, its association with religious beliefs has generally decreased. Certain groups have been more involved in this change than others. Those with greater amounts of education show more change than others; the young have changed more than the old; those without southern farm experience change more than those with southern farm experience; and Catholics have changed more than Protestants.

The last mentioned finding was especially provocative. It led to a more detailed analysis of change among Catholics, which indicates that those Catholics who could be expected to uphold the morally absolutist position on divorce are affected by the secularization of this issue as much as, and sometimes more than, Catholics who would appear less committed to the teachings of the Church. The secular movement has created a dilemma for Catholics; the general response has been an increased removal of divorce from the moral authority of the Church.

McGready and Greeley (1972) indicate that the movement from the teachings of the Church is occurring on other issues as well. The Catholic Church maintains that missing mass on Sundays without good reason is a mortal sin, punishable by eternal damnation. Using National Opinion Research Center data for 1963 and 1972, the authors report a decline in the percentage of Catholics reporting weekly mass attendance from 71 to 55. The Catholic Church makes strong injunctions against premarital sex, but, in 1972, Catholics are indistinguishable from Protestants in their attitudes on this issue, although McGready and Greeley do not show that this situation is different from that in 1963. The Catholic Church also takes a strong stand against abortion, yet Catholics and Protestants became less restrictive on this issue by about the same amount. The authors state, "One possible interpretation is that Catholics are becoming more like the rest of the population in terms of their opinion on critical and controversial issues. They are less readily identifiable as a separate block . . . [p. 337]." The issue of divorce must be added to these critical and controversial issues.

Even those Catholics holding many traditional beliefs have become less willing to accept the teachings of the Church on divorce. One of the statements found in the documents of Vatican II (Roche, 1968) is, "An individual layman, by reason of the knowledge, competence, or outstanding ability which he may enjoy, is permitted and even sometimes obliged to express his opinion on things which concern the good of the Church [p. 148]." It is doubtful that the Church expected the groundswell of support for this statement.

On 4 May 1977, the National Council of Catholic Bishops repealed the law that required excommunication of Catholics who divorced and remarried. Such Catholics are still not eligible to partake of the sacraments without having their marriages annulled by the Church, but Bishop Cletus F. O'Donnell is paraphrased as saying that the Church would extend a "genuine invitation" to divorced, remarried Catholics to consult with priests and church tribunals to see if there are means for them to return to full sharing of Holy Communion (*Arizona Daily Star,* 5 May 1977).

The repeal of this law was initiated by the national Catholic Assembly, described as a "grassroots" organization comprising both lay and clergy (*Arizona Daily Star,* 3 May 1977). The movement from the morally absolute position on divorce among the laity has been documented in this chapter. Greeley (1972) reports that a survey of a national sample of Catholic priests undertaken in 1970 by NORC revealed that, "Only one third of the priests (but 58 percent of the bishops) think that divorce in a marriage *ratum et consummatum* is forbidden by divine law and never can be permitted by the Church [p. 66]." One can only conjecture that more than one-third of the priests would have been in accord with this somewhat different phrasing of the morally absolutist position on divorce in 1958.

The tension between the attitudes of the hierarchy and those of the clergy and the laity, especially the young and well educated who are vital to the future of the Church, forced the hierarchy to modify the canon law. Bishop O'Donnell's "genuine invitation" to divorced and remarried Catholics augurs further changes in the official position or, at least, the granting of annulments to many who divorce and remarry. Among other lessons, we learn from the material in this chapter that a student of social change is well advised to choose his or her survey dates shrewdly.

10
Socialization of Girls and Boys

This is the first of three chapters in which we investigate aspects of the rearing of children and expectations that parents and other adults have of them. The importance of socialization has been emphasized regularly in the literature on sex roles and Women's Liberation, although this emphasis is really just an extension of long-standing themes in academic social psychology (see, e.g., Sewell, 1963). A capsule formulation is that of Whitehurst (1977): "Socialization theory suggests why there are such great differences in the eventual achievements of women and men, because parents and others in the infant's social environment tend to foster different attitudes, behaviors, skills and orientations in girls and boys [p. 104]." Yet we are cautioned not to adopt a fatalistic orientation to the process of socialization, inexorable as its outcome has seemed to many analysts and critics. Keller (1972) inquires: "How do women manage successfully to escape the conventional trappings despite the cultural stereotypes, the chief emphases of girls' socialization, the biases of children's books, and the strictures of parents, teachers, and husbands or boyfriends? One is always astonished how many women do not conform to type, although this is not usually publicized [p. 284]." Maccoby and Jacklin's (1974) exhaustive review of psychological literature on sex typing in socialization leads them to question both the existence of some purported sex differences and the conventional explanations of those sex differences that are confirmed by respectable bodies of research. (An interesting study that supports Maccoby and Jacklin's position on the complexity of the processes giving rise to sex differences is Jenni and Jenni's [1976] investigation of how female and male students carry their schoolbooks.) Here, as is true throughout this volume, we make no attempt to resolve general issues in the domain of our investigation, but aspire only to contribute empirical findings that have some chance of being found critical to one line of argument or another.

CHILDREARING TECHNIQUE AND SEX OF CHILD

Our small contribution to this large topic is motivated by the substantial importance that has been attributed to early experience in the production of adolescent and adult sex-role patterns. We are here concerned not with specific cultural norms about what women and men should do or be, or at any rate not with norms of the kind that are overt and readily articulated in words by most normal adults. Instead, the focus is on the possibility that rather subtle differences in the way that boy and girl infants and young children are treated by their parents may produce substantial and pervasive differences in the ways that mature women and men behave.

An example of the sort of hypotheses put forward in this domain is found in a discussion by Lewis (1972):

> . . . very early in the child's life the parents behave in a sex-differentiated fashion; boy children are responded to in one way and girl children in another [p. 230].

> . . . in many aspects of the child's behavior—personality, social and cognitive development—there are early and profound differences as a function of its sex [p. 232].

> Parental behavior in the service of attachment varies as a function of the sex of the infant. . . . It has been found repeatedly that from the earliest age mothers look at and talk to their girl infants more than they do their boy infants. . . . this kind of parental behavior . . . reflects an important socialization process which is being taught differentially as a function of the child's sex [pp. 233–234].

The quoted author's discussion is appropriately cautious. As he notes, "The studies from which these data were obtained are too recent for me to be able to clearly state their consequences in terms of adult social patterns [p. 237]." We are in no better position on this score. Nor do we, in fact, have access to detailed observational data of the kind cited by Lewis to support his hypotheses. Our material comes from interviews with mothers on a diversity of topics relating to parenthood, and much of it is either retrospective or hypothetical. The major strengths of our data are that they pertain to a well-defined general population and, of course, that they afford the possibility of detecting major changes, over an extended time period, in patterns of childrearing reported by the mothers. It may actually be an advantage of our data that they were not collected with hypotheses of the kind adumbrated by Lewis foremost in mind, so that the possibility of observation biased toward or away from the hypotheses is lessened. But by the same token the pertinence of our variables to such hypotheses may in some cases be marginal.

The baseline survey for our analysis of change was carried out in 1953; results were reported by Miller and Swanson (1958). Their target population comprised mothers with one or more children under the age of 19 living in the home. If there was more than one such child, one of them, the "selected child," was designated at random to be the one referred to in several of the questions. Other questions did not refer specifically to a particular child, but we might suppose that the mothers sometimes thought of this child even when not directly asked to do so.

Several of the questions analyzed here were administered in open-end form. The responses had to be classified or coded, which step presupposes the construction and definition of the code categories themselves. We did not have access to the full rationale of the codes and detailed instructions for administering them, which were presumably available to the original investigators. The report on the 1953 study (Miller and Swanson, 1958) is not very informative in this regard. Hence, we had to work solely from short verbal descriptions, such as those in Table 10-1 (see p. 249). It seemed probable that coders' interpretations of these descriptions would differ according to whether their indoctrination in the theory of the investigation was relatively comprehensive (as we assume was the case in 1953) or minimal (as was certainly the case in 1971). Hence, it was important to find out whether our 1971 coders were giving the same *operational* meaning to the codes as the 1953 coders. This required us to have the 1953 data recoded by the same coders who worked on the 1971 survey. For this purpose, we had to work from the original interview schedules of the 1953 survey. Unfortunately, we found that about 100 of those schedules had been removed from the DAS files at some time and were never returned. Specifically, of the 258 Form B interviews that included questions on rewards and punishments, we located 221 and recoded them. For this selection of interviews there were a number of statistically significant and substantively nontrivial differences in the frequencies of various code categories assigned in 1953 and in 1971. We could only infer that the codes did not convey quite the same meanings to the 1971 coders as they did to the 1953 coders. Hence, in the analysis here we will use only the 1971 coding of the 1953 data. Some of the original 1953 data are given in *Social Change in a Metropolitan Community* (pp. 35–40); but the figures given here are thought to be preferable for the purpose of inferring changes.

For that purpose, it is important to know whether the located schedules comprise a fair sample of the original interviews. We compared the located with the missing interviews on a considerable number of demographic characteristics and childrearing items without finding any statistically significant differences. In particular, no association was found between answers to the question on rewards, as coded in 1953, and the status of the interview as located or missing in 1971 (10 response categories by located versus not located, $X^2 = 5.9$, $df = 9$, $p > .5$). Similarly there was no reliable association between the 1953 coding of punishments and whether the schedule was found in 1971 ($X^2 = 14.5$, $df = 9$, $p > .1$). We conclude that the schedules removed from the file were in effect designated at random. Thus, there should be no bias in our estimates of change, 1953–1971, if we use only the located interviews, even though in working with a small number of cases we are able to detect reliably only rather substantial changes.

In the case of one question our coders simply found it impossible to work with the original code, in the absence of detailed instructions; hence we revised the code categories themselves. (The editorial "we" is used loosely here. Actually, the complex enterprise of designing and managing the whole recoding project was in the capable hands of Elizabeth Martin.) Thus, the topics related to childrearing in which mothers were "interested" are defined differently here than in the original study.

A number of students of socialization have been interested in the possible impact of the literature concerning child care and child training on character and personality. Miller and Swanson (1958, Chap. 1) reviewed the major themes in the writings of Dr. Spock and his predecessors among popular advisers to parents. In the 1953 survey they asked mothers a question to ascertain which of them relied on such sources of information: "Have there been times in the last month when you've wanted to find out about what behavior to expect from children at a particular age, or about how to get children to do something?" In both 1953 and 1971 just 54% of mothers replied affirmatively. Although

Miller and Swanson's analysis of themes in the child training literature gave no particular reason to think that this behavior on the mother's part would vary with the sex of the child, it seemed prudent to check on this. We also included age in the analysis. The four-way table, response to the want-information question by year, sex of child, and age of child, can be adequately described if we include only the age effect and disregard any year or sex effects. The odds on a *yes* answer are 1.5 if the child is under 2 years of age, 1.3 at ages 2–5, 1.2 at ages 6–11, and .90 at ages 12–18. But these odds apply equally well to male and female children and equally well in both years.

If the mother responded affirmatively, she was asked, "What were the things you wanted to find out about?" Some of the distinctions in our code for this question were suggested by the way in which Miller and Swanson had categorized the responses, but we found that a new code was needed to reduce ambiguity for the coders. The categories noted in the list were used for both the 1971 and the 1953 data. Statements in quotation marks are examples of responses taken from actual interviews. Coders had these examples before them as well as the titles of the code categories.

1. Knowledge of child's dynamics (how he develops or grows psychologically or physically). "What responsibility they can take at a certain age, how they will react to junior high." "When a child should learn to talk." "If other children act like mine at that age."
2. Knowledge about child's non-home environment. "I wanted to know about drugs and the money crisis with the schools." "I wonder if her problems are related to changes in the method of teaching in the schools."

Knowledge of how to behave in relation to child's behavior or development:

3. When or how to control child's behavior. "How to get her to do a job or chore." "Potty training her." "How to get him to do his homework."
4. Other questions about mother's own behavior toward child (excluding explicit control behavior). "When to encourage a child to be independent and take a stand against others." "How to tell my children the facts of life. When to talk to my daughter about menstruation." "When to give in to a display of temper. Wondering was I being fair."

As many as two kinds of information were coded if the mother mentioned more than one. Actually, multiple codes were infrequent. The number of mentions per respondent was only 1.2 in 1953 and 1.1 in

1971. The reduction in the relative frequency of double responses to the question is, nonetheless, found to be statistically significant when a formal analysis of the data set is carried out. The explanation for the fact that the 1953 interviews were somewhat richer in content on this matter than the 1971 interviews is perhaps that the former were almost wholly concerned with parenthood and childrearing, whereas this was but one topic, treated rather cursorily, among many diverse questions in the 1971 survey.

The formal analysis takes account of the contraints on the response distribution imposed by the coding procedure, which allows for a maximum of two kinds of mention (see Duncan, 1975b). We find that there are no reliable sex differences in these data, nor is there evidence of significant differential change by sex in the relative popularity of the different kinds of information. There is, however, a reduction between 1953 and 1971 in the relative emphasis on information about how to *control the child's behavior*. This result could, with little difficulty, be linked speculatively to the theme of "permissiveness" in childrearing so much discussed in the mass media. We do not pursue that interpretation here, since our focus is on sex differences, and we find none in the data produced by this question.

Mothers also were asked how they would reward the child for "very good" behavior and punish the child for "very wrong" behavior. The complete wording of these questions is given in Tables 10-1 and 10-2. As in the case of some other questions, the answers must have been partly retrospective and partly hypothetical. Reference is made to a specific child (the "selected child" designated as the subject of many questions throughout the interview). But the qualification that the child is 10 years old means that some mothers were thinking ahead to imagine a situation that might arise some years hence while others were ostensibly describing the kind of thing that would have happened several years ago. The questions seem to be projective ones in considerable measure, rather than matters of fact in any strict sense. It will be noted that no reference to sex is made in the question phrasings, except that in giving the child's name and in referring to the child by the third-person pronoun the gender is made explicit. We have no way of knowing whether mothers would have acknowledged that their response would be different if the child were of the opposite sex.

Answers to the question on rewards (Table 10-1) show that most mothers make use of *verbal* praise. Substantial minorities use also (or instead) some kind of *material* reward or confer some kind of *privilege* as a response to especially good behavior on the child's part. Very few mothers report rewards of the kind that could be clearly coded as

TABLE 10-1
Rewards for Good Behavior, by Sex of Child, 1953 and 1971

	Percentage distribution					
Think about a time when [name of child] (will be/was) 10-years-old. (He/She) has just done something that you feel is very good, or (he/she) has been particularly good. What would you do at those times?	1953		1971		1971	
					fitted[a]	
	observed					
	Boy	Girl	Boy	Girl	Boy	Girl
Only one kind of reward mentioned						
1. *Psychic* reward: satisfactions expected to come from within the child for a job well-done (e.g., mother tells him he should feel good about it).	1	0	0	<1	0.4	0.1
2. Other *verbal* praise	39	51	44	47	42.9	44.1
3. Special *privileges* or freedoms	6	3	4	4	3.8	3.9
4. *Material* reward: money or gifts— concrete rewards	13	13	11	7	9.3	9.6
5. *Love* him, kiss him, overt affection	1	2	4	4	4.0	4.1
Two kinds of reward mentioned						
Psychic and —*Verbal*	5	0	2	1	2.6	0.7
—*Privileges*	0	0	0	0	0.0	0.0
—*Material*	1	0	0	0	0.2	0.1
—*Love*	0	1	0	0	0.3	0.1
Verbal and —*Privileges*	9	7	4	6	5.4	5.6
—*Material*	16	17	15	15	14.5	14.9
—*Love*	5	2	13	13	12.7	13.1
Privileges and —*Material*	4	4	2	2	2.4	2.4
—*Love*	1	0	1	<1	0.6	0.6
Material and —*Love*	1	0	1	1	0.9	0.9
(Number of mothers answering[b])	(109)	(100)	(254)	(341)	—	—

[a] Calculated from model which provides an adequate fit to the data and incorporates year effect on *love* and sex effect on *psychic*.

[b] Excludes mothers not doing anything and unclassified responses. Data for 1953 were recoded by 1971 coders and are limited to schedules located in 1971.

TABLE 10-2
Punishments for Wrong Behavior, by Sex of Child, 1953 and 1971

Now, please think about that same time when [name of child] (will be/was) 10-years-old. (He/She) has just done something that you feel is very wrong, something that you have warned (him/her) against ever doing. What would you do at such times?

	Percentage distribution					
	observed				fitted[a]	
	1953		1971		1971	
	Boy	Girl	Boy	Girl	Boy	Girl
Only one kind of punishment mentioned						
2. *Verbal admonitions:* scoldings, warnings, or threats (excluding shame, guilt)	3	3	5	6	4.6	5.5
3. *Physical punishment*	10	13	18	12	17.1	12.3
4. *Restriction* of behavior and withdrawal of privileges (kept home, no T.V., etc.)	37	44	28	32	27.1	32.6
5. Would *not punish,* do something positive (reassure, etc.)	7	7	7	9	7.7	9.2
Other (combined)	3	1	1	2	1.5	1.9
1. Psychic punishment: mentions specifically that guilt or shame feelings engendered in child						
6. Punish, not further specified						
7. Do something, what not stated						

250

Two kinds of punishment mentioned						
Verbal and —Physical	5	3	5	4	4.7	3.4
—Restriction	4	6	5	8	6.0	7.2
—Not punish	1	3	1	1	1.1	1.3
—Other	0	1	<1	1	0.4	0.5
Physical and —Restriction	17	9	15	11	15.9	11.4
—Not punish	5	3	4	3	4.0	2.9
—Other	0	0	1	1	0.6	0.4
Restriction and —Not punish	8	6	8	11	8.4	10.1
—Other	1	1	<1	<1	0.5	0.6
Not punish and —Other	0	0	1	<1	0.4	0.5
(Number of mothers answering[b])	(113)	(100)	(256)	(342)	—	—

[a] Calculated from model which provides an adequate fit to the data and incorporates year effect on *restriction* for single mentions only and sex effect on *physical*.

[b] Excludes mothers not doing anything and unclassified responses. Data for 1953 were recoded by 1971 coders and are limited to schedules located in 1971.

psychic. We note that our 1971 coders found even fewer cases of this kind in the 1953 data than the original coders did. This raises the possibility that our understanding of the category is not as well developed as it should be. Nevertheless, the possibility of detecting change reliably rests on the use of coding procedures for which there is a strong presumption of comparability. Hence we adopt our coding of the 1953 responses as the baseline.

Shown also in Table 10-1 are the distributions by kind of reward for boys and girls in 1971 obtained from the particular model that provides an adequate fit to the data and that includes all effects of either year or sex of child that were found to be significant. There are, in fact, only two such effects. The relative frequency of *psychic* rewards is found to vary by sex of child in both years, and the relative frequency of *love* and overt affection changed between 1953 and 1971 for both sexes. Differential changes by sex were not large enough to be significant. The sex effect on *psychic* relative to any other kind of mention (e.g., *verbal*) is reflected in a Boy:Girl odds ratio of 4.0. The odds on the *love* reward were 3.5 times larger in 1971 than in 1953. (If one had suspected that the masculine preponderance of *psychic* rewards was a function of the appearance of the masculine pronoun "him" in the code description, the evidence for *love* should be reassuring, for there is no reliable sex difference here even though "him" occurs twice.)

The question on punishments parallels the rewards question in form. Again, the matter of gender is explicit in the statement of the question; but there should have been no distractions to the coders arising from this source, since no explicitly masculine or feminine terms appear in the code descriptions (see Table 10-2).

The modal punishment, used by up to two-thirds of mothers, is *restriction* of the child or withdrawal of some privilege the child previously enjoyed. Rather less frequent, but second in popularity, is the use of *physical* punishment. Strictly *verbal* punishments occur still less frequently, almost as frequently as the statement on the mother's part that she would *not actually punish* the child but would do something else. (Such a statement did not prevent several mothers from mentioning some form of punishment in the remainder of their replies to the question.)

Reflected in the expected distributions shown in Table 10-2 is the one sex effect found to be significant. There is a substantial increase in the odds on use of *physical* punishment if the child is male. The odds ratio measuring the effect of sex of child on the odds on *physical* relative to another kind of punishment, Boy:Girl, is 1.7. There also is one significant year effect. For both male and female children, there was, among mothers reporting only one punishment, a decrease in the use of *restrictions* and withdrawal of privileges. The odds ratio, 1971:1953, reflecting change in the odds on this punishment is .56. For mothers giving double responses, however, there was no such change; indeed, the computed odds ratio for the year effect in this group of respondents is 1.2. This is the only instance in the data on rewards and punishments in which our estimate of an effect differs according to whether two responses or only one response was coded for the mother. Again, we find no differential change by sex.

It is a point of some interest that the sex difference in regard to punishment pertains to a practice employed by a very substantial minority of mothers, whereas the only sex difference in rewards turned up for a kind of reward (*psychic*) that is reported by only a tiny minority of mothers. Perhaps its frequency would be enhanced by more detailed probing in the interview. In any event, in summarizing our results in terms of the greater exposure of male children to *psychic* reward and *physical* punishment, we should bear in mind that the comparison has to do with odds ratios. It is not the case that many boys or girls get *psychic* rewards, while a great many girls, as well as boys, do receive *physical* punishment. For neither rewards nor punishments do we find evidence for a change in the sex effects.

The next question to be examined was even more clearly hypothetical. The complete wording was as follows:

> Mothers have different ways of handling a crying child of five months. Suppose that you were busy preparing the family dinner and the baby was cranky and crying—if you thought nothing was wrong with (him/her), and (he/she) only wanted attention, what would you do?

Mothers' responses were coded into the following categories:

1. Immediate or unconditional action. (Checking on child is not considered action.)
2. Delayed, or conditional action. (Takes action after a while, after checking, let him cry first, etc.)
3. Check if child alright [*sic*], no other action.
4. Sometimes let him cry or do nothing, and sometimes do something.
5. Do nothing, let child cry.
6. Some one other than mother would do something.
7. No answer.

The observed distributions of responses over these categories, by year and sex of the child, are shown in the first four columns of Table 10-3.

TABLE 10-3
Ways of Handling a Crying Child, by Sex of Child, 1953 and 1971 (Percentage Distribution)

| | Observed | | | | Fitted[b] | | | |
| | 1953 | | 1971 | | 1953 | | 1971 | |
Action taken[a]	Boy	Girl	Boy	Girl	Boy	Girl	Boy	Girl
1. Immediate action	35	38	47	41	41	40	43	42
2. Delayed action	5	5	7	4	5	5	5	5
3. Check on child	11	9	4	6	10	10	5	5
4. Maybe nothing	4	3	2	2	2	2	2	2
5. Nothing	44	40	39	43	40	39	43	41
6. Someone else would do something	1	4	1	4	1	4	1	4
Total	100	100	100	100	100	100	100	100
(N)	(108)	(129)	(257)	(343)	—	—	—	—

[a] See text for full description of categories. Excludes unclassified answers. 1953 data were recoded by 1971 coders and are restricted to schedules located in 1971.

[b] Model fits the full one-way marginal response distribution; year by sex; response 6 versus all other responses by sex; and response 3 versus all other responses by year. $X^2 = 8.8$, $df = 13$, $p > .75$.

254

What one "sees" in these distributions, however, may be in some measure a function of preconceptions, since there are so many comparisons that can be made and most of the differences "look" rather small. In a formal analysis we do find that response depends upon both year and sex, although there is no significant three-way interaction (that is, the changes may be regarded as being the same for the two sexes). In the second set of four columns in Table 10-3 we display the results of fitting the effects of both sex and year, as estimated upon partitioning the distribution of the six categories of action within the context of a three-way analysis. A more detailed description of the method is given by Duncan (1975b). We find that the year and sex effects can be adequately described by the contrast of one action versus all the others. This allows us to describe the relationships in a much more compact way than would be apparent at first glance. The year effect in the data is captured in the contrast between *check on child* and all other categories, the former decreasing between 1953 and 1971 and the remainder showing a relative increase. The sex effect relates entirely to the contrast between the last category, *someone else would do something,* and all other responses. The odds on this particular response are raised if the child is female.

Interpretations of these effects would have to be speculative. Certainly the time change is of modest proportions in that the net shift (index of dissimilarity between the 1953 and 1971 fitted distributions) amounts to only five percentage points. The sex effect is tantalizing in that we do not know who "someone else" might be. Since the action occurs while the mother is in the midst of preparing dinner, we might suppose that the father would be at home in many households. Perhaps it is he who does something about the daughter's, though not about the son's crying.

One other generalized theme in the socialization literature—that of child-training practices associated with what Miller and Swanson called "internalization"—remains to be analyzed. These authors report that they devised one question in particular in attempting to capture David Riesman's distinction between inner-directedness and other-directedness. According to Miller and Swanson's summary (1958), "Riesman thinks he observes that parents in the new middle classes place more emphasis on the child's learning to accommodate to the shifting desires of his peers and show an accompanying intolerance for the introspective and introverted individual [p. 111]." As they might well have mentioned, Riesman also claimed to discern a time trend in the balance of the two contrasting emphases, with the expectation being that the proportions other-directed (sensitive and responsive to peers) would increase.

The question proposed as bearing directly on Riesman's thesis reads as follows:

> Suppose a 14-year-old child were interested in some worthwhile activities that gave (him/her) little time to spend with other children. The things the other children are doing are just as worthwhile, but they don't interest this particular child. Would you encourage (him/her) in going on with (his/her) own interests, or would you rather see (him/her) change to something (he/she) can do with other children?

As we reported in *Social Change in a Metropolitan Community* (p. 40), the actual trend between 1953 and 1971 was in the opposite direction to that expected on Riesman's hypothesis. The possibility that differentials by sex of the child might be observed within the general trend concerns us here. It was convenient to include age as well as sex in the analysis, so that we are simultaneously looking for effects of age and sex and for changes between years. In this four-way analysis, only the time effect is significant. The odds on encouraging the child's *own interests* relative to urging him to *do things with others* were 1.1 in 1953 and 2.8 in 1971. This estimate fits the data for children of both sexes and of all ages.

We now turn to the mothers' answers to questions about age norms, that is, the age at which the child is expected by her or his mother to perform certain commonplace tasks. If we should find that boys are expected to master a task at an earlier age than girls, we might infer that boys receive earlier or more consistent training for independence and autonomy than girls. The tasks considered are picking up his/her own toys, putting away own clothes, dressing himself/herself completely, and running errands to a nearby store. The mother was asked, "Here are some tasks that some parents require of their children. Which of these did you or would you require of [selected child's name] and by what age?"

Inasmuch as the selected child could be of any age up to 19 years, some mothers were providing retrospective information (with varying periods of recall) while the answers for others must have been hypothetical. (We have no easy way to determine from our data how many of these hypothetical answers may have reflected actual experience with another child in the family.) For three tasks—Pick Up Toys, Put Away Clothes, and Dress Self—present age of the selected child is, in fact, associated with the age at which that child was or will be expected to perform the task. Such results could reflect time trends in age norms, but we doubt that such an interpretation in terms of actual shifts in

norms is warranted. The results seem to suggest, on the contrary, that
as the child approaches the age at which it is realistic to expect the task
to be learned, the mother's expectations become more realistic. For
example, quite a few mothers of children under 2 years of age expect the
child to pick up his or her own toys before reaching age 2. But many
fewer mothers of children aged 2 or older report that the task was
performed that precociously. Since we find that the expected age distributions are sensitive to the child's present age in what could be an
artifactual way, we substitute another analytical technique for our usual
multiway contingency table approach.

Our first step is to tabulate present age of child by age at which task
performance is required, classifying each by single years of age. If
present age is greater than required age, we can presume that the child
has already learned to perform the task. If present age is below required
age, we presume that the child has yet to do so. If the two ages are the
same, the situation is ambiguous, but we treat these cases as ones in
which the child has not yet learned the task. We can now examine, by
single years of age, the odds that the child already performs the task in
question. Restricting the analysis to the range of ages for which the odds
are neither zero nor infinite, we calculate the linear regression of the
logarithm of the odds on age, using the weighted logit procedure (Theil,
1972, Chap. 4). Finally, we interpolate along the regression line to
estimate the median age at which the task is learned, that is, the age at
which the odds is exactly unity. (Here we equate "age" to age at last
birthday, disregarding the fact that the actual age is approximately a
half year larger on the average; this tends to compensate for our earlier
decision to treat all ambiguous cases as ones in which the task is not yet
mastered.) Other terms are included in the regression where there are
significant effects of sex, year, the combination of the two, or interactions of either with age. (The determination of significance was made in
terms of a multiway contingency analysis; these results dictated the
specification of the logit regressions.) We think that the estimates obtained in this manner are perhaps closer to the actual facts of the
behavior of mother and child than are the expected age distributions
that ignore present age of the child or those that pertain to mothers
whose children are not near the age at which the task is actually learned.

For the task of Picking Up Toys, the estimated median age (3.3 years)
does not vary by sex or year.

For the task of Putting Away Clothes we have evidence of a sex-by-
year interaction that is not quite significant at the .05 level. Ignoring the
interaction, we estimate median ages of 4.3 and 5.2 for boys and girls
respectively in 1953 and 4.8 and 5.7 in 1971. With the interaction

included, we find medians of 3.9 and 5.5 for the two sexes in 1953, 5.0 and 5.5 in 1971. There is some indication, therefore, that requirements for boys and girls in regard to this task have converged, although boys are still expected to learn how to put away their clothes at an earlier age than girls.

Although there is some suggestion of a sex-by-age interaction in regard to Dressing Oneself, it does not particularly affect the medians. We estimate 5.0 and 5.3 years in 1953, 5.1 and 5.3 years in 1971, for boys and girls, respectively. The data can actually be fitted quite adequately if we ignore both year and sex effects entirely.

Finally, the data for Running Errands exhibit a sex-by-year interaction that is significant at the .1 level though not at the .05 level. Without the interaction, the estimates suggest large effects for both sex and year: 5.9 and 7.0 for boys and girls in 1953, 7.8 and 8.9 in 1971. Including the interaction we obtain, for the corresponding medians, 6.4 and 6.5 in 1953, 7.6 and 9.0 in 1971. Thus, there is an indication that the increase was substantially greater for girls than for boys. The changes for the two sexes are divergent.

What does one make of the heterogeneous findings about sex-specific childrearing techniques? Much depends on prior expectations as to how pervasive sex differentiation in regard to childrearing practices is and to what extent these practices are subject to change. In the quoted material from Lewis (1972) which opened the section it is asserted that "in many aspects of the child's behavior . . . there are early and profound differences as a function of its sex." But, of course, "many" is not the same as "all," nor is it equivalent to "most." Upon reflection, it does seem reasonable that some (if not "many") aspects of the socialization process should be more or less invariant with respect to sex. There are other things a child must learn besides how to behave like a boy or a girl. The indicators of the mother's strategy of socialization studied here were selected without reference to the possibility that they would manifest sex differences; the analysis of such differences was an afterthought. Hence, one should not draw any very strong conclusion from the fact that we fail to detect sex differences in several of the items. Only if the initial hypothesis had been that all facets of childrearing technique are differentiated by sex of the child should our results come as a big surprise.

We do find the following differences: Boys are more likely to receive *psychic* rewards and *physical* punishments than girls; *someone else* besides the mother is more likely to respond if a crying child is female; boys are expected to Put Away their Clothes at an earlier age than girls (but the sex difference diminished between 1953 and 1971); and in 1971 (though perhaps not in 1953) boys were expected to be able to Run Errands to a nearby store at a considerably younger age than girls.

Only the two items last mentioned manifest differential change by sex of the child over the 18-year period, 1953–1971. Other items do show change: The increase in use of *love* and affection for rewarding the child; minor shifts in the relative popularity of certain ways of responding to a crying baby; a decrease in relative importance of how to *control child's behavior*, among items about which mothers would like information; and the very substantial shift away from the "other-directed" emphasis in childrearing. Thus, the situation in regard to childrearing practices is somewhat fluid. Although in very broad outline mothers' responses in 1971 were like those given in 1953, there were enough changes in the details to suggest that mothers can adapt to new situations and do respond to new ideas about how to raise their children. If there were important external factors tending to induce different kinds of change for boys and girls, there is no obvious reason why our data would not reveal their effects.

From this perspective we may suggest one general inference from the two items that do exhibit differential change by sex of child. One of these items, the age at which the child is required to put away his or her clothes, appears to show a relaxation of mothers' expectations for both boys and girls. The change was greater for boys, though not great enough to wipe out the sex difference entirely. We find it difficult to think of a general environmental or situational factor that would tend to force mothers to make this change. That is, it is difficult to surmise what force external to the family would cause mothers in 1971 to handle this matter differently from their predecessors, the mothers of 1953. The other item showing differential change is age at which the child is expected to run errands. Here it is all too easy to conjecture what the environmental factors may have been. We suspect that over the 18-year period there was an actual decrease in the number of neighborhood stores located close enough to home that a 6- or 8-year-old child could reasonably be sent there alone. In part such a change would have come about through urban renewal, highway construction, and development of automobile-oriented supermarkets. In part it would follow from the dispersion of the resident population toward the suburbs. In addition, there is little difficulty in imagining that the realistic concern of mothers for the safety of their children when on the streets was greater in 1971 than in 1953.

The suggestion, then, is that the convergence in regard to the task of putting away clothes does reflect a general tendency to diminish the role of sex differentiation in socialization, given the absence of countervailing tendencies. But the divergence in regard to running errands points to the persistence of the assumption that boys can more easily take care of themselves, with this assumption becoming increasingly relevant to a particular task under changing environmental circumstances. We conclude that in this domain—as well as others considered in the remaining chapters—the explanation of sex-specific social changes will usually involve some combination of the general and the particular. We may suppose that there is a general trend toward reduction of sex differentiation but that particular cultural or situational factors may override that general trend. The selection of indicators of changing sex-role definitions is thereby considerably complicated, as we have ample opportunity to observe elsewhere in this volume.

PARENTAL VALUES

There are at least two questions to be distinguished in studying the socialization of children in relation to sex roles. The first question is whether or how the definitions, goals, or values of parents differ according to sex of the child. As Maccoby and Jacklin (1974) observe, "It is widely assumed that . . . parental attitudes and feelings must translate themselves into differential behavior on the part of parents toward sons and daughters [p. 303]." The preceding section contains most of what we have to offer on this subject. We are able to demonstrate some "differential behavior." Like Maccoby and Jacklin (1974), though, we mostly find "a remarkable degree of uniformity in the socialization of the two sexes [p. 348]." Our evidence does not speak to the issue of whether such differentials as we do observe in childrearing practices make any differences in the development of boys and girls.

The second question is whether mothers and fathers—or, for that matter, women and men in general—have different functions in the socialization process. Up to a point, the answer here is obvious. Mothers, of course, spend more time with infants and preschool children than do fathers and, therefore, hold the greater responsibility for early training (exceptions notwithstanding). It does not follow, however, that the division of labor in regard to childrearing tasks produces a specialization of the sexes with respect to the *goals* of childrearing. Mothers and fathers may agree that the child must learn to tie her or his shoes, even if it is the mother who ends up providing most of the tuition on this subject. But if some of the broader allegations about sex differences in our society are true, it would not be surprising to find that female and male definitions of the goals of socialization also were different. One would, for example, expect fathers to think first of such matters as the development of cognitive skills and acquisition of instrumental, vocationally useful techniques, while mothers would have the greater preoccupation with teaching the child to be effective and acceptable in social relations with others.

Our Detroit material pertaining to the possible differentiation by sex in parental values or goals in childrearing pertains to but two questions with overlapping content. Fortunately, we can supplement the Detroit data with an informative national series.

One of the most interesting questions in the 1971 survey (at least to one of the authors) reads as follows: "Which statement do you agree more with: 1. The younger generation should be taught by their elders to do what is right. 2. The younger generation should be taught to think for themselves even though they may do something their elders disapprove of." Among other reasons why this question is interesting are these. We have noted that some sophisticated respondents find it a difficult question to answer, perceiving, we surmise, that the choice is a somewhat artificial one and that there is something to be said for both alternatives. The general population is split about 50–50 on the question, or at least that was true in both 1956 and 1971, between which dates no significant change is detected if only the aggregate of all respondents is considered. On the other hand, as we shall observe shortly, there are pronounced cohort differences, intracohort changes, and differential changes by cohort when the data are properly disaggregated. The response to this question has an exceedingly strong regression on educational attainment, in the direction one would expect if one truly believed that the function of education is to teach people to think for themselves (see Duncan, 1975a).

Various hypotheses about sex differences in response to the question or about differential changes by sex come to mind. If one supposed that the role of inculcating moral precepts falls largely to the mother and the role of developing initiative to the father—that is, if one assumed a sex typing of socialization functions—then we should expect to find the Female: Male odds ratio for the odds on *think* to be less than unity. Yorburg (1974) asserts that the "need to be independent and autonomous is still a trait that is sex-typed for males rather than females [pp. 173–174]." If each sex were to prescribe for the younger generation a continuation of the extant sex bias, then the same outcome would be predicted. The basis of the prediction is qualified, however, by the circumstance that "younger generation" is not specified by sex, and we have no way of telling how male or female respondents may have taken account of sex differentiation in the younger generation.

If the cross-sectional prediction is ambiguous, the prediction of differential change is less so. On the assumption that ideas about liberation have been gaining ground among females, we should find them more disposed to assert their autonomy in recent surveys than they were in the 1950s.

The last prediction is verified, to the extent that it agrees with the sex differences observed in the samples for 1956, 1971, and 1976 (see Table 10-4). In the 2 earlier years the odds on *think* were slightly higher for men, but in the 1976 survey the direction of the difference was reversed, while both men and women endorsed this alternative more frequently than they had previously. Unfortunately, the only statistically reliable difference in the table is that between 1976 and the other 2 years. With 4 *df* we get $X^2 = 4.07$ for a model that incorporates that contrast with no sex difference. If the sex effect is entered into the model and allowed to change between 1956–1971 and 1976, the corresponding statistics are 2 *df*, $X^2 = 2.95$, not a significant improvement in fit. We simply cannot infer with any confidence that there was a sex difference in 1976 or that there was any change in this regard after 1956 or 1971.

Before we conclude that sex has nothing to do with response to Younger Generation, we should investigate the possibility that sex effects occur in population subgroups but in such a pattern that they cancel out when the data are aggregated to totals by sex. This possibility gains plausibility when we note that this very kind of interaction occurs with respect to both age and color differences. (Investigation of these factors pertains only to 1956 and 1971, since we have not analyzed the 1976 data in any detail.) Figure 10-1 records the main results of our analysis. In both 1956 and 1971 the odds on *think* were a positive function of birth year; that is, the younger cohorts voted for autonomy of the younger generation in greater proportions than did the older cohorts. Between the two surveys, however, there were counterbalancing changes. On the one hand, in 1971, the "new" cohorts (those under

TABLE 10-4
Odds on Responding Think to Younger Generation Question, by Sex, 1956, 1971, and 1976

Sex	1956	1971	1976
Men	.91	1.02	1.13
Women	.82	.98	1.26
Total	.86	1.00	1.20
(Sample size)	(756)	(1814)	(681)

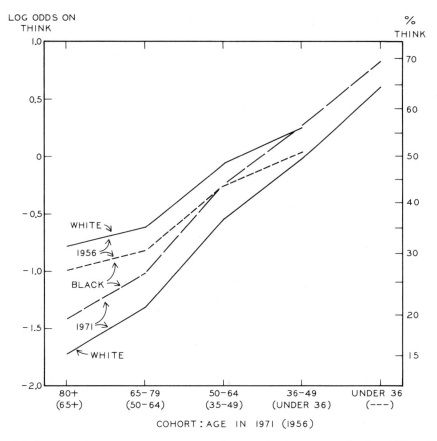

FIGURE 10-1. Response to younger generation question by cohort and color, 1956 and 1971.

21 years of age in 1956) who recently entered the adult population were considerably more in favor of *think* than their predecessors. On the other hand, among the older cohorts, especially those having attained age 50 or more by 1956, there was a distinct drifting away from *think*. The model used to calculate the odds shown in the graph represents the degree of intracohort change as a linear function of birth year, so that the greatest drop in endorsement of *think* occurred for the oldest cohorts. This pattern of differential change was not adequately described—indeed, it was glossed over—in our previous reports on these data (Duncan, 1975a, p. 124; Duncan *et al.*, 1973, pp. 41–42). Our present conjecture is that the two kinds of change were related in a positive feedback loop. It was precisely the demand of younger cohorts

for greater autonomy that led the older cohorts to become more authoritarian than even the "normal" process of aging would have led them to be by the end of the 1960s. And, as the aged became increasing critical of youthful impiety, youth reacted by escalating the demand for autonomy.

A similar mechanism could explain the differential changes by color depicted in the same graph. Whereas in 1956 whites were more sympathetic to the idea of a younger generation thinking for itself, by 1971 the color difference was in the opposite direction. Somehow, it would appear, blacks in disproportionate numbers came to identify with the cause of youth; and whites may well have perceived a threat on the part of blacks as one of the consequences of too much thinking going on in the younger generation.

The Younger Generation question, then, provides us with a very "active" social indicator, once we disaggregate the response distributions by the appropriate factors and use analytical methods well suited to detect the statistical interactions. But these results concerning differential changes by color and cohort only make it the more remarkable that no sign of a sex difference, or interaction of sex with time period or any other factor, emerges. The analysis underlying Figure 10-1 included a cross-classification by sex and the very same models that disclosed differential change by the other two factors revealed no such change for sex. Moreover, we have pursued the search for interactions involving sex most assiduously. There is no significant difference in education effects on Younger Generation by sex. Nor do we find sex interacting significantly with either tenure (home owners vs. renters) or subjective class identification as far as response to this question is concerned. We looked at the relationship of some religious indicators to Younger Generation and—while there are some interesting results concerning these indicators that we shall not report here—found no reliable evidence that this relationship varies by sex.

It even appears that the "generation gap" with respect to the Younger Generation question is unaffected by sex. In the 1971 survey, a randomly chosen half of the sample were asked, "How do you think your (father/mother) [parent of the same sex as respondent] would have answered this question when you were growing up? Which one would (he/she) have agreed with more?" As reported elsewhere (Duncan, 1975a), the parental generation is seen by offspring of all ages as being much more authoritarian than the offspring generation. But there is no difference between male and female perceptions of this gap. When we cross-classify Younger Generation by imputed parental response to the same question by sex, the data may be arranged as a 4 × 2 table, the 4 possible responses versus the 2 sex categories. The test of the hypothesis of independence in this table yields $X^2 = 1.7$, $df = 3$, $p > .5$. There is no sex effect on either response or the two responses considered jointly.

Have we, perchance, erected something of a strawperson to knock down with this array of negative evidence on the relationship between a taste for autonomy and one's own classification as female or male? If there are no sex effects on Younger Generation were we mistaken in thinking that a general approval of autonomy would logically be accompanied by a rejection of explicit sexual limitations on activities and interests? Yorburg (1974) emphasizes that "modern values—individualism, tolerance and cosmopolitanism, secularism, rationalism, achievement and equalitarianism—become incorporated into the roles that men and women play . . . and they transform typical expectations in the relationships between the sexes in modern societies [p. 88]." Surely the *think* response to Younger Generation should be construed as endorsement of a "modern" (as opposed to traditional) orientation.

In fact, we do find that endorsement of autonomy via the Younger Generation question is associated with the propensity to reject sex typed assignments of household tasks to children. The evidence is summarized in Table 10-5, where we show odds ratios measuring the association of Younger Generation with each of the items, Walks, Car, Dust, and Beds. (These items were introduced in Chapter 1 and are studied further in Chapter 12.) An odds ratio in excess of unity implies that the *think* response to Younger Generation goes with the *both* response to the indicator of sex typing. For three of these indicators, the excess over unity is statistically significant. Moreover, holding constant sex, color, and educational attainment of the respondent does not alter this result; and the net associations are just a little smaller than the gross

TABLE 10-5
Odds Ratios Estimating Gross and Net Association of Response to Younger Generation Question with Indicators of Sex Typing, 1971

	Walks	Car	Dust	Beds
Gross association	1.17[a]	1.97	1.60	1.89
Association, net of				
Age	1.18[a]	1.70	1.60	1.53
Sex, color, and education (3 classes)	1.12[a]	1.85	1.51	1.66

[a] Not significantly different from 1.0.

associations. We do not find, however, that the association of Younger Generation with Car, Dust, or Beds is stronger (or, for that matter, weaker) for female than for male respondents. There is, however, a significant association between Younger Generation and Walks for women (odds ratio = 1.4) but not for men (.92). But this association disappears in the multiway analysis when color and education are controlled.

We conclude that approval of autonomy and rejection of sex typing are ideologically linked for some fraction of our respondents, but that this fraction is no higher among women than among men. The conclusion, however, holds good only for 1971, since we have no earlier data to test it with and we have not examined the detailed data for 1976. It is quite conceivable that the situation reported here could have changed since 1971. We note, however, that the magnitude of the association of Younger Generation with objecting versus approving of women's work—studied in Chapter 3—was the same for women and men in both 1956 and 1971, even though there is a sex effect on response to the women's work question and a time trend in that response for both sexes.

Our second question on parental values inquires, "If you had to choose, which thing on this list would you pick as the most important for a child to learn to prepare him (*sic*) for life? [A] To obey; [B] To be well liked or popular; [C] To think for himself; [D] To work hard; [E] To help others when they need help?" The hierarchy of these five values in the whole population remains the same over the period 1958–1976, as may be seen in Figure 10-2. *Think* is the most often chosen, *be popular* the least in each of the three survey years. There are, however, some shifts in relative attractiveness of the alternatives; *think, help others,* and *work hard* all gained at the expense of *obey* between 1958 and 1971; but *work hard* lost its momentum between 1971 and 1976, declining relative to *obey* along with *be popular*.

We find no significant sex effect on response to this question, nor are there significant differential changes by sex from 1958 to 1971 or 1971 to 1976. In this regard, the findings are the same as those for Younger Generation. There is an obvious overlap between the two questions, since a version of *think* is included as an alternative in both. We note a significant association between the two responses in 1971, such that the (fitted) odds, *think : do right*, for Younger Generation is .42 when the response to Most Important Thing is *obey, be popular,* or *work hard*; .71 when it is *help others*; and 1.8 when it is *think*. It is not surprising, then, that Most Important Thing relates to the sex-typing indicators in somewhat the same way as was noted for Younger Generation. We find no

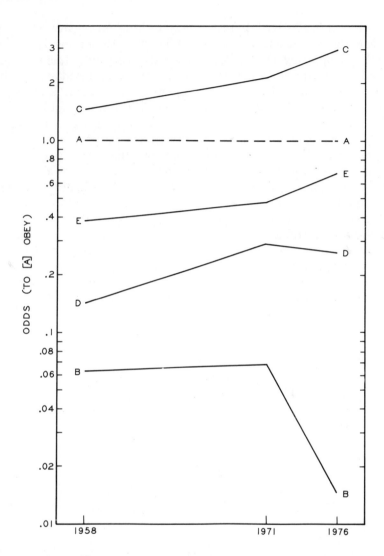

FIGURE 10-2. Odds on most important thing for a child to learn, 1958, 1971, and 1976: [A] Obey; [B] Be well liked or popular; [C] Think for himself; [D] Work hard; [E] Help others when they need help.

association of Walks with Most Important Thing. In regard to Car, the odds *both*:*boy* is raised by a factor of 1.59 when Most Important Thing is *think* (as opposed to any other alternative except *be popular*) and lowered by a factor of .44 when it is *be popular* (as opposed to any other alternative but *think*). The odds on responding *both* to Dust are raised if the Most Important Thing is *think*, but the effect is appreciable only for blacks, with an odds ratio of 1.90. The corresponding figure for whites is 1.14. Finally, *both* on Beds has an odds higher by a factor of 1.7 when Most Important Thing is *think* rather than any other alternative. In none of these analyses do we detect a sex differential such that the association between Younger Generation and Most Important Thing differs for men and women.

Although we find no reliable evidence that sex affects response to Most Important Thing, such evidence does emerge when we take account of the rankings of the five goals in childrearing that were obtained when that question was followed up by queries as to second, third, and fourth choices. Figure 10-3 shows mean rank for each of the goals, with a classification by color as well as sex. The data are limited to

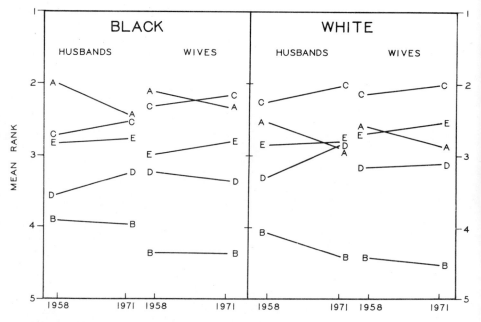

FIGURE 10-3. Mean ranks of values in childrearing, for parents by color and sex, 1958 and 1971: [A] Obey; [B] Be well liked or popular; [C] Think for himself; [D] Work hard; [E] Help others when they need help.

married persons with a child present in the home. (There is no significant interaction of sex or color with presence of child, but the latter factor
does have its own additive effects, which we shall not describe here.)
The means shown in the figure are calculated from regression equations. The equation includes every term that is significant for any one
of the goals, so that some of the small differences in the figure are not
necessarily significant. We comment only on those that are.

White men and women rank *think* higher than blacks; and we do not
find any differential change in this regard, contrary to the finding for
Younger Generation on this score. The sex effect depends on color.
White husbands and wives agree closely, but black wives put this goal
rather higher than black husbands. All four groups agree in regard to
the gain in rank for this goal between 1958 and 1971.

There is a rather strong color effect on *obey*; blacks rank it higher than
whites. There is no significant sex effect; black men agree with black
women, white men with white women. All four groups agree that this
goal became less important over the 13-year period.

Help others is seen as slightly more desirable by black men than by
black women; the sex effect for whites, if any, is in the opposite
direction. All the groups show only a very slight, though significant,
rise in the ranking of this goal.

Contrary trends by sex are noted for *work hard*. Men, black or white,
increased their endorsement of this goal between 1958 and 1971, but
there was little or no change for either group of women.

Finally, there is consensus across the four groups that *be popular* is the
least salient goal (among these five) of childrearing. In 1958, black and
white men put it somewhat higher than women in the same groups. But
white men (though not black men) allowed its rating to decline, bringing their view into line with that of white women.

An overall impression is that agreement between men and women as
to the hierarchy of goals was somewhat clearer in 1958 than in 1971. But
even in the latter year, sex differences amount to fairly small variations
on a consensual theme.

We also investigated the effects of education on the ranking of these
goals, limiting the analysis to white men and women (with or without
children in the home). The education effects are pronounced. A strong
positive effect is noted for *think* (consistent with the finding for
Younger Generation) and a moderately strong positive effect for *work
hard*. Quite a strong negative effect appears for *obey* and a moderately
strong one for *be popular*. Education effects on *help others* are not
significant. Inasmuch as none of these effects differs significantly by
sex, we do not report the details here. It appears that variation by

education is far more conspicuous than variation by sex, although we are keenly aware of the pitfalls in statistics that purportedly disclose the "relative importance" of two such incommensurable variables. Let us just say, then, that the hierarchies of men and women at any educational level are quite similar while the hierarchies at the two extremes of the educational distribution are quite different.

NATIONAL DATA ON PARENTAL VALUES

The items analyzed in this section were devised by Melvin Kohn (1969) for a study one main purpose of which was to "trace the effects of social class position on values." His study employed a national sample of about 1500 fathers of children 3–15 years old; they were interviewed by NORC in 1964. The question of interest here was phrased to pertain to a specific child, selected at random from the roster of children in the home: "Which three qualities listed on this card would you say are the most desirable for a (boy, girl) of (child's) age?" Further questions served to classify the 13 qualities studied into five levels of desirability; these are described subsequently.

Kohn's list of qualities (see Table 10-6) is replicated in the 1973 and 1975 NORC General Social Surveys. In these surveys, however, data were collected from all adults. The beginning of the question was slightly different, in that there is no reference to a particular child: "Which three qualities listed on this card would you say are the most desirable for a child to have?" We cannot identify exactly those men who would have been eligible as fathers under the 1964 study procedures. We classify respondents as "parents" if they have ever had a child and if there was at least one person under age 18 in the household. There is no specification of the question by either age or sex of the child; and the age range, 0–17, is slightly wider than that used by Kohn. There is also a change in wording that could affect comparisons of data from the two studies. In the 1964 survey, the fathers were given a card listing the qualities; item 7 read, "that he acts like a boy should (she acts like a girl should)." In the 1973 and 1975 surveys *should* was omitted (apparently because it did not appear on the 1964 questionnaire though it did appear on the card shown to respondents).

The effects of these changes in study design on the comparisons we shall offer is imponderable. For our particular purposes perhaps the most serious defect in comparability is that the sex of the child under consideration is not specified in the 1973 and 1975 surveys. It is also unfortunate that the child's age is not specified, although, in this

TABLE 10-6

Mean Scores of Parental Values Concerning Desirable Qualities of a Child, by Sex of Child in 1964 and by Sex of Parent in 1973 and 1975 (National Samples)

Parental values	1964, Fathers		1973		1975	
	Male child	Female child	Fathers	Mothers	Fathers	Mothers
	(1)	(2)	(3)	(4)	(5)	(6)
1. Has good manners	3.16	3.21	3.02	2.91	3.06	3.01
2. Tries hard to succeed	2.84[a]	2.66	2.87	2.75	2.82	2.87
3. Is honest	3.84[a]	3.72	3.98	3.99	4.06	4.08
4. Is neat and clean	2.54[a]	2.92	2.62	2.52	2.60[a]	2.47
5. Has good sense and sound judgment	3.04	3.09	3.37[a]	3.64	3.46	3.47
6. Has self-control	2.86	2.85	2.97	3.06	3.03	3.13
7. Acts like a boy (girl) [should]	2.84[a]	2.71	2.24[a]	2.06	2.14[a]	1.73
8. Gets along well with other children	3.17	3.23	2.98	2.96	2.92	3.01
9. Obeys his parents well	3.64	3.66	3.36	3.25	3.44	3.35
10. Is responsible	2.81	2.81	3.31	3.35	3.24[a]	3.44
11. Is considerate of others	3.12	3.19	3.25	3.32	3.29	3.34
12. Is interested in how and why things happen	2.75[a]	2.56	2.74	2.78	2.59	2.67
13. Is a good student	2.67	2.61	2.59	2.49	2.60	2.52
(Sample size)	(770)	(729)	(292)	(399)	(275)	(375)

[a] Difference between means (adjusted for social class and age of child) for male and female child in 1964 is significant ($p < .05$); or difference between means for fathers and mothers in 1973 or 1975 is significant ($p < .05$).

instance, we are somewhat reassured that our definition of "parents" implies that children both younger and older than those considered in the 1964 study may be relevant to the respondents in the later years. Since no resolution of these matters is possible, we simply warn the reader that Dr. Kohn, in correspondence, has taken a somewhat less sanguine view of the evidence for social change between 1964 and 1973–1975 than is suggested by our exposition.

The 1964 data, subdivided by sex of child, are reproduced in Table 10-6, taken from Kohn's Table 4-2 that shows "mean scores for sex of child, adjusted for social class and age of child." Inasmuch as there is no reason to assume any correlation between sex and age of child or sex of child and class, we have assumed that these adjusted means are equivalent to unadjusted means. (This conjecture is confirmed by inspection of the unadjusted means, kindly supplied by Dr. Kohn after our analysis was completed.) Kohn's scoring procedure, employed with the 1973/1975 data as well, is as follows:

> 5—the one most desirable quality
> 4—one of the three most desirable qualities, but not the most
> 3—not mentioned as most or least desirable
> 2—one of the three least desirable qualities, but not the least
> 1—the least desirable quality

Kohn treated these scores as an interval scale and used a conventional *t*-test of the difference between means to ascertain whether ratings by fathers for their male children differ from those by fathers for their female children.

For our purposes, it is interesting that Sex Role is 1 of 5 (out of 13) qualities for which Kohn found a significant difference by sex of child. It was more important to these fathers that a boy act like a boy should than that a girl act like a girl should. We do not know, of course, whether mothers shared the view that learning behavior appropriate to one's gender was more important for boys than for girls. Neither do we know what qualities fathers, or mothers, defined as appropriate to the respective roles. Among the qualities considered here, "tries hard to succeed," "honesty," and "interest in how and why things happen" are more highly valued as qualities of boys than of girls; "is neat and clean" is less highly valued as a quality of boys.

It is also of great interest that the effect of child's sex on father's response to the Sex Role item is dependent on the child's age. From unpublished tabulations of the 1964 data (supplied by Dr. Kohn) we can compute the regression of response to the Sex Role item on age and sex of child referred to (Figure 10-4). A standard series of *F*-tests on alternative regression models indicates that (1) the difference between slopes for boys and girls is significant; (2) the slope for girls, tested separately, is not significant; (3) the variation of means for individual years of age around the linear regressions is not significant (although we did not investigate specific curvilinear alternatives to the linear regression specification); and (4) the difference in the residual variances for boys and girls is not significant. Substantively, we conclude that "acts like a boy should" is much more important to fathers of very young boys than is "acts like a girl should" to fathers of very young girls, but the difference washes out—and apparently reverses—by the time the child is about 12 years old.

As just noted, it is not possible to control this age effect in the over-time comparisons. If fathers in the 1973–1975 studies were think-

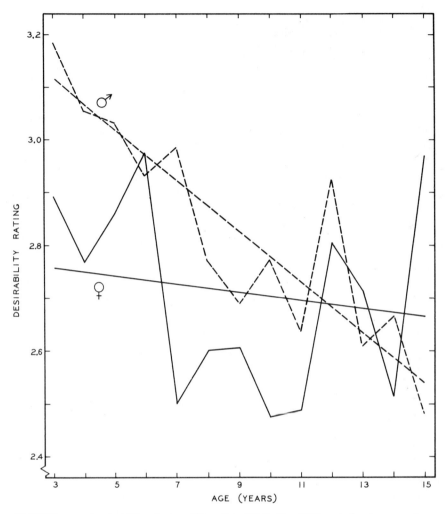

FIGURE 10-4. Desirability of "Acts Like a Boy (Girl) Should" in relation to sex and age of designated child, for fathers in 1964, national sample.

ing primarily of older children, then their rating of the importance of Sex Role (for example) would be downwardly biased relative to the 1964 data and we would be in danger of inferring change when no change may have occurred. To estimate the long-run changes, for fathers only (of necessity), we average the 1973 and 1975 scores for fathers (cols. 3 and 5, Table 10-6) and the scores for fathers of boys and fathers of girls in 1964 (cols. 1 and 2, Table 10-6). A cursory study of the differences

Kohn found significant and the differences found significant in the 1973 and 1975 data suggests that any change of more than .15 in an average rating should be regarded as significant. On this criterion, we find increases in the mean ratings of Honest, Good Sense, and Responsible, decreases for Obeys Parents, Gets Along Well, and Sex Role. There is no significant change for any of the remaining seven qualities. The changes for Obeys Parents and Gets Along Well are reminiscent of our finding that "to obey" and "to be well liked or popular" declined in importance in Detroit (see, for example, Figures 10-2 and 10-3). Of the qualities differentially valued in boys and girls in 1964, only Sex Role decreases in importance over time; we cannot say, of course, whether devaluation of this quality by fathers occurred at the same rate for their male and female children. In regard to the comparability problem we note that the 1973–1975 mean desirability of "acts like a boy (girl) [should]" for fathers was 2.2, well below any segment of either regression line in Figure 10-4.

The tests of significance, within years, for the differences between ratings by fathers and mothers in 1973 and 1975 were based on Simon's (1974) procedure for $2 \times k$ contingency tables with ordering of the columns. This gives much the same results as a t-test of the difference between means. When the data for the 2 years are pooled, several additional differences between ratings of mothers and those of fathers emerge as significant, though not necessarily in terms of the mean differences. In multiway contingency analyses, sex by year by five categories of the rating, we find significant sex-of-parent effects for Good Manners, Neat and Clean, Good Sense, Sex Role, Obeys Parents, Responsible, and Good Student. The only unequivocally significant three-way interaction pertains to Responsible, while the differential changes for Good Sense and Sex Role are significant at the .1 level. Significant year effects are noted for Good Manners, Honest, Sex Role, and Interested in Things. Despite the several significant sex differences, we note that the correlation between ratings of mothers and fathers, over the 13 qualities, is quite high (see Figure 10-5).

The evidence on short-run change in the desirability of "Acts like a boy (girl)" is intriguing. In an attempt to understand the sources of change, we subjected this item to a detailed regression analysis. At this stage of the work, the 1976 General Social Survey data became available, so that it was possible to consider the data from three surveys. In these analyses, nonparents as well as parents were included in the sample. However, the contrast of parents with nonparents was not significant, so that this contrast is ignored in reporting the results. (This finding, incidentally, is perhaps reassuring in regard to the problematical com-

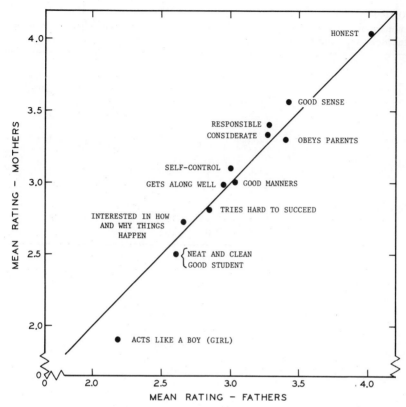

FIGURE 10-5. Mean ratings of desirability of qualities of a child, for fathers and mothers, national samples, average of 1973 and 1975.

parisons of 1964 with 1973–1975 discussed earlier.) Table 10-7 reports the regressions of desirability on education estimated after determining that neither of the product terms, sex by year and sex by education, was significant, and that the education coefficient could be regarded as the same in 1973 and 1975. We see that desirability of conforming to sex role expectations is inversely related to educational attainment for both sexes but that the effect was somewhat smaller in 1976 than in 1973 or 1975. The 1976 "backlash"—to exaggerate a bit—was therefore most pronounced among the college educated.

Also shown in Table 10-7 are regressions with cohort as the independent variable. The regressor is actually a coding of birth year, so that the negative coefficient for cohort implies that the more recent cohorts do not find "Acts like a boy (girl)" as desirable a quality as do the earlier cohorts. This effect is more pronounced for women

TABLE 10-7
Summary of Regression Analysis: Desirability of "Acts like a boy (girl)" on Year and Education, Year and Cohort

		Year					
Statistics	Sex	1973		1975		1976	
Mean desirability		$\bar{Y}$		$\bar{Y}$		$\bar{Y}$	
	Men	2.29		2.11		2.14	
	Women	2.12		1.86		1.92	
Regression on education[1]		*a*	*b*	*a*	*b*	*a*	*b*
	Men	2.53	−.079	2.31	−.079	2.31	−.057
	Women	2.32	−.079	2.09	−.079	2.09	−.057
Regression on cohort[2]		*a*	*b*	*a*	*b*	*a*	*b*
	Men	2.50	−.026	2.28	−.026	2.28	−.018
	Women	2.44	−.041	2.22	−.041	2.22	−.033

[1] Education scored 0 for less than 8 years of schooling, 1 for 8, 2 for 9–11 years, 3 for 12 years (high school graduate), 4 for 1 to 3 years of college, 5 for college graduate, 6 for 1 or more years post graduate. Regression equation is

$$\hat{Y} = 2.307 + .224X_1 - .216X_4 - .0788X_6 + .0221X_3X_6,$$

where

$$X_1 = 1 \text{ if } 1973, X_3 = 1 \text{ if } 1976, X_4 = 1 \text{ if female}, X_6 = \text{education}.$$

[2] Cohort (X_5) is in quinquennial units, scored 0 for cohort aged 85–89 in 1975,...,13 for cohort 20–24 in 1975. Regression equation is

$$\hat{Y} = 2.280 + .217X_1 - .061X_4 - .0257X_5 + .0074X_3X_5 - .0149X_4X_5.$$

than for men, so that it is plausible to see the young well-educated women as the vanguard of change in this value. Again, we find that the effect is less pronounced in 1976 than in 1975, so that the vanguard appears to be losing heart. The indicator, Sex Role, evidently will bear watching, for one reading of this evidence would be that an apparent incipient disappearance of education and cohort differentials is a sign that the deemphasis of sex role expectations has about run its course. Like the fragmentary evidence on recent changes reported in Chapter 12, this analysis raises questions it cannot answer. The answers lie in the future rather than in any data that could be examined at this time.

The 1975 GSS data allow us to explore further the meaning of the Sex Role item by relating to it some indicators of sex typing of adult roles. These are:

Home: "Women should take care of running their homes and leave running the country up to men." (Agree or disagree)

Work: "Do you approve or disapprove of a married woman earning money in business or industry if she has a husband capable of supporting her?"

President: "If your party nominated a woman for President, would you vote for her if she were qualified for the job?"

Politics: "Most men are better suited emotionally for politics than are most women." (Agree or disagree)

Each of these items, scored in the "liberated" direction, is directly related to *un*desirability of Sex Role. The associations are not significant for men, however, in the case of Work and Politics. For each of the four adult indicators, the regression is stronger for women than for men (see Figure 10-6). The sex difference in the regression coefficient is substantial and unmistakably significant for Work, President, and Politics. We conclude that women find more salient or more transparent the connection between an emphasis on sex-role socialization of children and the allocation of economic and political responsibilities in terms of sex. Or, to be more precise, the proportion of women who make this connection is apparently greater than the proportion of men who do so.

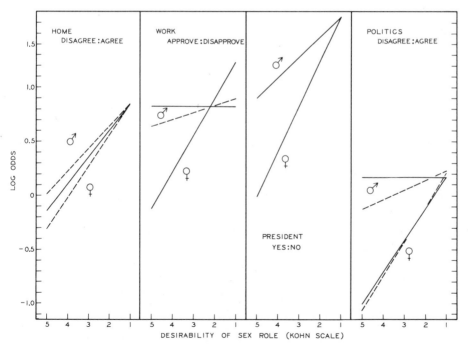

FIGURE 10-6. Regressions of four indicators of adult sex typing on desirability of sex role as a goal in childrearing, national sample, 1975 (desirability scale reversed).

11
Intergenerational Aspects of Sex Typing

Our initial concern is whether the characteristics of marriage partners and the style of interaction that evolves in the course of their marriage influence the importance that the husband or wife attaches to boys acting like boys and girls like girls. There is no need to posit that each couple espouses a particular ideology of relations between marriage partners. How they divide up the household chores or define what is important in a marriage may be fortuitous. But having fallen into a style of interaction that involves greater or lesser emphasis on the differentiation of wife's role from husband's role, they may view a similar degree of differentiation between a girl's role and a boy's role as natural or desirable. We consider finally the evidence on consistency of attitudes about sex typing across the adult–child boundary. It is, of course, not logically necessary to reject sex typing of children's tasks if one holds that adult women should be able to work if they choose. But if people make such a connection in their own thinking—or if some significant proportion do so—then we shall observe an association between the two kinds of indicator.

SHARING OF HOUSEHOLD CHORES

Not long ago the renowned Dr. Spock, author of the fabulously popular *Baby and Child Care*, confessed that he had formerly just assumed that a father would naturally reinforce the masculine identity of his son by selecting appropriate toys, topics of conversation, and household chores ("assigning him jobs in the yard and garage") while emphasizing dolls, cooking skills, and choice of feminine attire in guiding his daughter to an appropriate sexual identity. Now, he said (Spock, 1975), "I'm convinced that though sexual identity is psychologically important, . . . emphasizing differences in such matters as clothes, toys and chores is not necessary [p. 22]." He went on to argue that parents should not be apprehensive if the boy manifests some stereotypically feminine interests or the girl wants to be a tomboy some of the time, and to offer advice to those, particularly fathers, "who believe generally in the liberation of both sexes." One of his themes was that participation of both sexes of both generations is essential if the aim is to bring up a generation of children free of unconscious sex prejudice: "A son, and therefore his father, should share in all the various domestic activities, I feel. I'm thinking of the whole list: food shopping, preparation and serving; dishwashing; care of bedrooms (neatening, vacuuming, bedmaking); care of family rooms; laundering." The important criterion is not that everyone have an equal share of all duties but that the share depend on age and capability, not on sex, lest the home jobs come to be defined as "women's work and, by implication, less important than what men do."

Our concern here is not normative but descriptive. In families where the husband and wife seem to have recognized in some measure the principle of sharing, we inquire, is the same principle brought into play in assigning chores to the children? Evidence of such an intergenerational correlation in our data would suggest that some proportion of families were following Dr. Spock's advice, whether self-consciously or not, before he communicated it.

In the 1971 survey both husbands and wives were asked to describe the division of labor between the spouses in regard to half a dozen common household tasks and also to respond to the following question:

> Here are some things that might be done by a boy or girl. Suppose the person were about 13-years-old. As I read each of these to you, I would like you to tell me if it should be done as a regular task by a boy, by a girl, or by both.
>
> a. Shoveling walks.
> b. Washing the car.
> c. Dusting furniture.
> d. Making beds.

Since the responses of *girl* to Walks or Car and *boy* to Dust or Beds were very infrequent, we ignore them here and subsequently. Hence, our data format is a 2 × 5 table for wives and one for husbands responding in 1971, that is, a 2 × 5 × 2 multiway contingency table, child task by adult division of labor by sex of spouse reporting. Since only the husband or the wife in any sample household reported on the adult division of labor and responded to the somewhat hypothetical query about the child tasks, we cannot determine how well spouses agree in regard to the latter. (Some disagreement is implicit in the sex differences in response noted subsequently, and we showed in Figure 10-5 that fathers attach more importance to children learning the proper sex role than do mothers.) What we can do, however, is ascertain whether the association between adult division of labor and assignment of tasks to children (if any) is the same for husbands and wives.

The strategy of the analysis is best described in connection with an illustrative set of results, Figure 11-1. In analyzing response to Walks by division of labor, we partitioned the latter variable to ascertain whether the odds on a *both* response to Walks varies in such a way that any one of the five categories has a reliably higher or lower odds than the remainder. The finding for Walks is that for wives the odds on *both* is elevated when keeping track of Money and Bills is done by the husband more than the wife ($H > W$) but that effect is not observed for husbands. There is, then, a three-way interaction with respect to the one category of division of labor. Once that is taken into account, we find no reliable difference among the remaining four categories for either husbands or wives. For Car and Dust, we can fit the data satisfactorily suppressing all three-way interactions and allowing the two categories, husband more than wife ($H > W$) and wife more than husband ($W > H$) to have the same odds on *both*, elevated by comparison with the odds observed for the remaining three categories, husband always (H), husband and wife exactly the same ($H = W$), and wife always (W). There are no significant differences among these three categories. In the analysis for Beds, much the same pattern emerges, except that in order to get an acceptable fit, we must allow the husband more than wife ($H > W$) category to have a higher odds on *both* for wives than for husbands. In general, our idea was to minimize the number of contrasts among categories and the number of differences between effects for wives and husbands that had to be recognized in order to achieve a statistically acceptable fit to the data.

The results portrayed in Figure 11-1 are summarized in the last panel of Table 11-1, which also reports results for the other five items in the

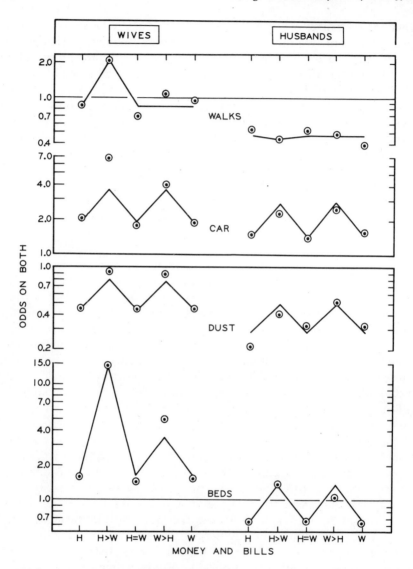

FIGURE 11-1. Assignment of child tasks by wives and husbands in relation to division of labor between spouses in regard to who keeps track of the money and bills, 1971.

TABLE 11-1
Association of Response on Child Task with Division of Labor between Spouses with Respect to Each of Six Chores, 1971

Adult chore	Child task	Wives					Husbands				
		H	H > W	H = W	W > H	W	H	H > W	H = W	W > H	W
Grocery	W	—	—	0	0	0	—	—	+	0	0
shopping	C	—	—	0	0	0	—	—	0	0	0
	D	—	—	0	+	0	—	—	0	+	0
	B	—	—	0	+	0	—	—	0	+	0
Husband's	W	+	+	+	+	0	0	0	0	0	0
break-	C	0	0	0	0	0	0	0	0	0	0
fast	D	+	+	+	+	0	+	+	+	+	0
	B	+	+	+	+	0	+	+	+	+	0
Evening	W	—	—	0	0	0	—	—	0	0	0
dishes	C	—	—	0	0	0	—	—	0	0	0
	D	—	—	+	+	0	—	—	0	0	0
	B	—	—	+	+	0	—	—	+	+	0
Living	W	—	—	0	0	0	—	—	0	0	0
room	C	—	—	+	+	0	—	—	+	+	0
	D	—	—	+	+	0	—	—	+	+	0
	B	—	—	+	+	0	—	—	+	+	0
Repairs	W	0	0	—	—	—	0	0	—	—	—
things	C	0	+	—	—	—	0	+	—	—	—
	D	0	+	—	—	—	0	+	—	—	—
	B	0	+	—	—	—	0	+	—	—	—
Money	W	0	+	0	0	0	0	0	0	0	0
and	C	0	+	0	+	0	0	+	0	+	0
bills	D	0	+	0	+	0	0	+	0	+	0
	B	0	+	0	+	0	0	+	0	+	0

Note: Plus (+) means odds on *both* response to child task is elevated by comparison with a zero (0); see text.

adult division of labor. In this table, we are considering only the pattern of the results in terms of locating the categories of the division of labor that have odds on *both* that are elevated by comparison with the remaining categories. Thus, the summary suppresses the finding of a three-way interaction in the analysis of Beds by division of labor by sex of respondent (since wives and husbands have the same "pattern"); but it takes note of the three-way interaction in the analysis for Walks, inasmuch as the three-way interaction there takes the form of an effect appearing for wives which does not occur for husbands. One other principle was followed in constructing Table 11-1, in the interest of simplicity. We ignored data on the tails of the division-of-labor distribution where that distribution was a unimodal one with mode at W or H and when the category falling in the tail accounted for less than 10% of the couples. The reason for this, of course, is to suppress some largely uninformative noise in the estimates of odds on *both*.

We note first that Walks and Car are somewhat less consistently associated with the adult division of labor items than are Dust and Beds. In the case of the first two items, a *both* response means essentially a willingness to allow or require girls to do a job that is traditionally masculine; while a *both* response to Dust or Beds implies that a boy will be assigned a chore that a substantial fraction of the population believes is best reserved for girls. It is suggestive, then, that the impact of the adult division of labor on the sex typing of children's tasks (if that be the direction of causation) is more readily detected when the alternative to sex typing is to put boys into "women's work."

One generalization will serve for all the first four adult tasks (Grocery Shopping, getting the Husband's Breakfast, doing the Evening Dishes, and straightening up the Living Room): the categories for which the odds on *both* are elevated are always ones other than W, that is, ones that involve some degree of participation in the task by the husband. Not all such categories produce a higher odds on *both*. Thus, in the case of Grocery Shopping, it is the wife more than husband ($W > H$) category, rather than the husband and wife exactly the same ($H = W$), that produces the higher odds on *both* for Dust and Beds.

The same summary applies to Repairs things around the house, except that here it is the husband always (H) category that is the mode. Location away from that mode, with the wife participating in even a small degree, results in a heightened probability of responding *both* to each of the child tasks, Car, Dust, and Beds.

Coming back to who keeps track of the Money and Bills, the pattern is the quite distinctive one of a sawtooth. The distribution of this task is trimodal: Large fractions of couples assign the task solely to one member, either husband or wife, while a third segment join in the work on a perfectly equal basis. It is the two intermediate categories where one spouse does most of the work, but not all ($H > W$ or $W > H$), that produces the elevated odds on *both* to all of the child tasks except Walks. Even in that case, the pattern appears in an attenuated form in the responses of wives. The generalization, therefore, is that it is having a deviant or atypical division of labor in regard to this oddly distributed adult task which leads to a deemphasis on sex typing in allocating chores to children.

One important feature of Figure 11-1 has received no comment thus far. All the curves—indeed, all the observed odds—for wives lie higher on the graph than those for husbands. Wives are more likely to respond *both* to any of the child tasks. Ignoring the adult division of labor, we may cite the sex effect on response to the child items in terms of the factors by which the odds on *both* are multiplied if the respondent is a wife rather than a husband: 1.9 for Walks, 1.3 for Car, 1.6 for Dust, and 2.5 for Beds. Since these sex effects will reappear frequently in subsequent discussions, there is no need to dwell upon them here.

In view of the fact that there have been a number of changes, albeit mostly modest ones, in the distribution of couples by division of labor, it would be of great interest to know whether the association between the adult division of labor and sex typing of children's chores has changed as well. Unfortunately, the 1955 survey, which provides our baseline for measuring change in the division of labor between spouses, contained no question on allocation of tasks to children. The 1953 study, where these questions appeared, did have a few questions on the division of labor between spouses, but not in a form strictly comparable with the questions used in 1955 and 1971. The preamble to the 1953 questions read: "Here are some things that might be done by a husband or wife. As I read each one of these to you, I would like you to tell me if, in your home, it is usually done by you, by your husband, or by both of you." Only two of the "things that might be done" are household tasks of the sort we have been considering, that is, Painting Rooms in the house and washing Dishes. The last-named is the more promising in terms of a close comparison with the 1971 data. Unfortunately, the scope of the 1971 question is restricted to the *evening* dishes, and the proffered answer categories number five in 1971 as compared with the coarser three in 1953. We treat wife always (W) in 1971 as equivalent to *wife* in 1953 and lump the remaining four categories in 1971 and the remaining two in 1953 into a single category, husband or both, for the sake of maximizing comparability. The 1971 sample is reduced, by comparison with the data earlier presented, to include only mothers with one or more children under age 19 in the household, since that was the target population of the 1953 survey.

Table 11-2 provides examples of both stability and change. In regard to Walks and Car, who does the Dishes does not relate to the wife's view of whether only boys or both girls and boys should shovel walks or wash the car. The result here for 1953 is like that already reported for 1971. In both years, the odds on a *both* response to Dust were raised if the husband participated to any extent in dishwashing. The difference in the odds for the two years is not significant. Finally, for Beds, there is

TABLE 11-2

Association of Response on Child Task with Division of Labor between Spouses with Respect to Washing Dishes, 1953 and 1971

Year and adult division of labor	Child task			
	Walks	Car	Dust	Beds
Observed odds on both				
1953				
Both or husband	.62	.49	.90	1.05
Wife	.46	.43	.39	.83
1971				
Both or husband	1.2	3.2	1.3	8.6
Wife	1.0	2.5	.44	2.1
Ratio, B/H : W				
1953	1.4	1.1	2.3^a	1.3
1971	1.2	1.2	3.0^a	4.0^a
1971 : 1953	.87	1.1	1.3	3.2^a

[a] Significantly different from 1.0 ($p < .05$).

a strong effect in 1971—if the husband does any dishwashing, the wife is keen on having boys as well as girls make beds—but no significant effect of this kind in 1953. The one detectable change in the intergenerational relationship, therefore, is in the direction of a heightening of the association between adult division of labor and sex typing of children's chores.

The other task for which we have 1953 data, Painting Rooms, is somewhat similar to the 1971 item, Repairs things. In 1953, this task was monopolized by the husband in the case of 45% of the couples, was done jointly in 42% and by the wife alone in only 13% of the cases. (The reader who is either too old or too young to remember what things were like in 1953 should perhaps be reminded that the technology of painting rooms in a house had not been streamlined then to quite the extent it is today.) We find that Painting Rooms is indeed like Repairs things, inasmuch as any participation by the wife increases the probability that she will reject a sexual basis for assigning children to chores. The odds on a *both* response are raised by factors of 1.8, 2.0, 2.2, and 1.6 for Walks, Car, Dust, and Beds, respectively, if the wife or both spouses paint the rooms by comparison with husband only serving as painter. The result is fairly similar to, but perhaps even more decisive than the one we obtain for Repairs things. It would stretch the interpretation to infer change from the comparison, in view of possible differences between the two items. We must rest content to note the general continuity in the pattern.

SPOUSES' EDUCATIONAL ATTAINMENTS

In discussing sex roles in the family, Epstein chooses to describe the "relationship of husbands and wives" in terms of the variation in that relationship by class or educational stratum. She writes (1976), "In the middle class, sex-role assignments more often overlap or are blurred, with husband and wife doing tasks together or substituting for one another [p. 446]." She contrasts this pattern with that of working-class husbands and wives who "rarely accept tasks associated with the opposite sex and generally consider it inappropriate for a man to do woman's work or for a woman to do man's work." The actual division of labor between husbands and wives described in Chapter 8 presumably is influenced by situational factors which may be class linked as well as by the education-linked preferences of wife and husband. In the case of the child-task items, however, the responses should be less contaminated by situational factors for the question pertains to a hypothetical 13-year-old person.

The data used in this analysis pertain to married persons in the 1971 survey responding to each of the sex-typing items in turn. Each respondent reported both her or his own education and the number of years of school completed by the spouse. We have reason to believe that these proxy reports are of high quality. For the six class intervals of school years completed (see note, Table 11-3) we find $X^2 = 2.6, df = 5, p = .75$ in testing the hypothesis that the reports of wives on their own education and the reports of wives' education by husbands come from the same population. The corresponding calculation for husband's education is likewise not significant ($X^2 = 8.6, p > .1$). Furthermore, there is no evidence that the association of husband's with wife's education differs by sex of respondent. Aggregating the two sets of responses, we find the Pearsonian correlation between wife's and husband's education to be .57, a figure in good agreement with other evidence to the effect that there is strong assortative mating by education.

It must be understood that we do not have paired data for the responses to the child task questions, since either the husband or the wife, but never both, were interviewed in each husband–wife household. There would be some advantage, from the standpoint of efficient statistical estimation, in having paired data. However, the correlation of husbands' with wives' responses would give no substantive informa-

TABLE 11-3
Regressions of Responses to Child-Task Items on Educational Attainment of Husband and Wife, 1971

Dependent variable[a]	Respondent	Intercept	Coefficient of	
			Husband's education[b]	Wife's education[b]
Walks	Husband	−1.033	.107	−.019
	Wife	−1.064	.187	.067
Car	Husband	− .742	.308	.006
	Wife	− .684	.273	.106
Dust	Husband	−2.058	.076	.180
	Wife	−1.766	.205	.073
Beds	Husband	−2.159	.270	.211
	Wife	−1.430	.288	.246

[a] Y = log of odds on *both*.

[b] Scaled 1 for less than 8 years of school completed, 2 for 8 years, 3 for 9–11 years, 4 for 12 years (high school graduate), 5 for 13–15 years, and 6 for 16 or more years (college graduate or more).

tion on the questions investigated here, which are (*a*) whether educational attainment of oneself and one's spouse both affect response and, if so, (*b*) whether the two effects are different. Our vehicle is regression analysis, making use of the equation forms,

$$Y_H = c_1 + c_2 X_H + c_3 X_W + U_H$$

$$Y_W = c_4 + c_5 X_H + c_6 X_W + U_W$$

(11-1)

where Y is the logarithm of the odds on *both*, X is educational attainment, scored in the fashion described in the note to Table 11-3, U is the error term, and the subscripts H and W are used to distinguish between the variables that pertain to husband and wife respectively. Minimum logit chi-square regression (Berkson, 1953) estimates of the coefficients for Eqs. (11-1) appear in Table 11-3. With one exception, all the coefficients are positive. For both husbands and wives, odds on responding *both* increase with own education and also with spouse's education.

What one makes of this result depends partly on comparisons with plausible alternative specifications of the relationship of response to education. In Table 11-4 we report chi-square statistics (Y^2) that may be used to evaluate goodness of fit of selected regression models. The

TABLE 11-4

Logit Chi-Square Values for Alternative Specifications of the Regression of Responses to Child-Task Items on Educational Attainment of Spouses

Equation	Independent variables in equation	df	Walks	Car	Dust	Beds
				Dependent variable		
				Chi-square value (Y^2)		
	Husbands					
—	(none)	24	26.14	41.57	34.93	53.77
(i)	X_H	23	23.34	13.28	28.69	19.14
(ii)	X_W	23	25.41	30.68	26.96	28.24
(iii)[a]	X_H, X_W	22	23.30	13.27	26.12	14.72
(iv)	$X_H, X_W, X_H X_W$	21	22.77	13.07	23.99	14.54
(v)	$(X_H + X_W)$	23	24.00	17.22	26.47	14.87
	Wives					
—	(none)	24	28.19	40.83	34.30	63.45
(i)	X_H	23	13.37	14.64	18.54	24.98
(ii)	X_W	23	19.23	25.78	24.95	32.29
(iii)[a]	X_H, X_W	22	12.84	13.35	17.94	19.31
(iv)	$X_H, X_W, X_H X_W$	21	12.56	13.02	17.54	16.75
(v)	$(X_H + X_W)$	23	13.48	14.57	18.68	19.38

[a] Values in this row pertain to the regression estimates in Table 11-3.

coefficient estimates in Table 11-3 pertain to the model designated as (iii) in Table 11-4. For both husbands and wives, specification (iii) yields an acceptable fit no matter which child task is examined. To this extent, the goodness-of-fit statistics support the use of Eq. (11-1) without modification. However, comparisons among the alternatives do not indicate that (iii) is the unequivocally preferred model in any of the eight sets of results.

The data for husbands fail to show a statistically significant effect of education, whether of husband or of wife, on response to Walks; that is, none of models (i) to (v) improves significantly on a model that ignores education effects entirely. Responses to Car, Dust, and Beds by husbands do show a significant association with husband's own education or wife's education, when these variables are studied one at a time in models (i) and (ii). Only for Beds, however, can we show that both spouses' educational attainments are needed in the equation, that is, that model (iii) improves significantly over both models (i) and (ii). For Car and Dust we find that if husband's education is in the model, no significant improvement in fit results from including wife's education. Comparing equation forms (iii) and (v), we test the hypothesis that the coefficient for husband's education is the same as the coefficient for wife's education. For Car we find that the difference in Y^2 for the two models is 3.95, $df = 1$, $p < .05$, so that (iii), which allows X_W and X_H to have different coefficients, does produce a significantly better fit than (v), which constrains the two coefficients to be equal. But this result is not replicated for Walks, Dust, or Beds.

Parallel comparisons for wives produce somewhat different results. For every child task, both husband's education and wife's education have a significant association with response. Only for Beds, however, can we show that both education variables are needed in the equation. For the other three items it turns out that once husband's education is taken into account, as in model (i), no significant improvement is obtained by including wife's education along with it, as in model (iii). For none of the four child tasks can we show that the coefficients for X_H and X_W are different since (iii) does not provide a significant improvement over (v).

Model (iv) was included to test for the possibility of a joint effect of husband's and wife's education. If the product term, $X_H X_W$, is included in the equation, we are allowing for the possibility that similarity of the educational attainments of husbands and wives has an influence on response, apart from the levels of education as such. While it would be interesting to speculate about the meaning of such an influence, there is no need to do so here, inasmuch as model (iv) fails to improve significantly on model (iii) in any of the eight comparisons.

There is a common theme in all these results: The difficulty in showing that husband's and wife's education have distinct effects on response. The statistical problem here is the well known one of collinearity of the two independent variables; as already noted, $r_{X_H X_W} = .57$ in the combined samples of husbands and wives. While it seems very reasonable to suppose that the two variables do not have identical effects on response, it would take a much larger sample than we have to distinguish their effects reliably.

Our firm conclusion, then, is that education affects the responses of both husbands and wives. It is possible, but not proven, that response depends not only on the respondent's own educational attainment but also on that of the spouse, and that these two effects are unequal in magnitude. The coefficient estimates in Table 11-3 show an interesting pattern of asymmetry in the husband and wife equations for Walks, Car, and Beds. Not only in the husband equation but also in the wife equation the coefficient for husband's education is greater than the coefficient for wife's education. For Dust, however, the coefficient for spouse's education is greater than the coefficient for own education in both the husband and the wife equation. We find it difficult to rationalize the finding for Dust—if, indeed, it is not a mere accident of sampling variability. It seems desirable, however, to attempt some interpretation of results that fall into the pattern observed for Car and Beds (taking the negative coefficient for X_W in the husband equation for Walks to be a sampling fluke). We offer an interpretation, to the effect that the pattern of coefficients for Car and Beds means that the husband has more influence on the formation of the wife's opinion than she has on his, or at least that this pattern of relative influence is more frequent in the population of married couples than its opposite. To formalize this interpretation requires some fairly extensive mathematical exposition. The reader whose appetite for this kind of material is easily satiated may prefer to skip the remainder of this section. Our empirical findings have already been reported, as has the gist of our highly tentative interpretation of part of them.

We postulate that the views of husband and wife on the suitability of a sex-based division of labor for children depend not only on the respective backgrounds and experiences of the two spouses prior to marriage, but also upon their more or less continuous social interaction throughout the period since they were married. From time to time they give each other cues as to their thinking on this and related matters; they may even have discussions or arguments about particular events or decisions that lead to an exchange of ideas on the subject. It would not be either practical or ethical to attempt direct observation of this interaction. We suppose it to be unobservable and hence enclose it in a black box. Of what goes on in this black box we can only say that wife's attitude may influence husband's attitude and husband's attitude may influence wife's; at any rate, the two are jointly determined. Our conceptual scheme is represented by the causal diagram, Figure 11-2. We have only two exogenous (input) variables, husband's and wife's educational attainments, although in principle there may be others that should be recognized. The exogenous variables may be correlated;

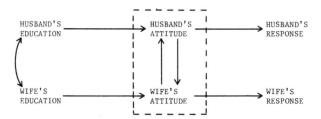

FIGURE 11-2. Interaction of spouses with respect to an unobserved attitude.

indeed, they are substantially so in our data, as already noted. But no causal interpretation is placed on this correlation—hence the arrows pointing in both directions from the single curve connecting the two exogenous variables. The two endogenous variables are husband's attitude and wife's attitude or, respectively, their underlying propensities to accept or reject sex typing as a principle in the rearing of children. These variables, like the mutual influence of each of them upon the other, we take to be unobservable. We can only make fallible inferences about them from the evidence of responses to such questions as Car and Beds. The response is supposed to depend on the underlying attitude, but only in a probabilistic manner, so that knowing the response one cannot be entirely sure of where the respondent basically stands.

To restate the notions depicted by the diagram in the language of algebra, let R be the dichotomous response ($R = 0, 1$) to one of the items, say Car. We assume that R depends on an unobserved variable Z (call it "propensity to reject sex typing," if any name is needed); that is

$$P = Pr\ \{R = 1|Z\} = f(Z). \tag{11-2}$$

We postulate, following Rasch (1968), that $f(\cdot)$ is the logistic function, so that

$$P = (1 + e^{-Z})^{-1}. \tag{11-3}$$

Linearizing the function, we have

$$\log \frac{P}{1-P} = Z. \tag{11-4}$$

Replacing P with the sample proportion p that estimates it and subjecting p to the logit transformation (Ashton, 1972; Cox, 1970) we have

$$\log (p/q) = Z + U, \tag{11-5}$$

where $q = 1 - p$ and U is a stochastic disturbance. In the sequel, Z and U will carry the subscript H or W, to distinguish the husband's from the wife's propensity. But the same function (11-3), relating response to propensity, holds for the two sexes.

We now specify a model to explain Z_H and Z_W:

$$\begin{aligned} Z_H &= a_0 + a_1 Z_W + a_2 X_H + V_H' \\[6pt] Z_W &= b_0 + b_1 Z_H + b_2 X_W + V_W', \end{aligned} \tag{11-6}$$

where X_H is an exogenous variable that appears only in the husband's equation (here, husband's education), and X_W is an exogenous variable that appears only in the wife's equation (here, wife's education). V_H' and V_W' are disturbances uncorrelated with the Xs but not, of course, with the Zs.

The reduced form of (11-6) is

$$Z_H = c_1 + c_2 X_H + c_3 X_W + V_H$$

$$Z_W = c_4 + c_5 X_H + c_6 X_W + V_W$$

$$(11\text{-}7)$$

where
$$
\begin{aligned}
c_1 &= (a_0 + a_1 b_0)/\Delta \\
c_2 &= a_2/\Delta \\
c_3 &= a_1 b_2/\Delta \\
c_4 &= (a_0 b_1 + b_0)/\Delta \\
c_5 &= a_2 b_1/\Delta \\
c_6 &= b_2/\Delta \\
\Delta &= 1 - a_1 b_1 \\
V_H &= (V_H' + a_1 V_W')/\Delta \\
V_W &= (b_1 V_H' + V_W')/\Delta
\end{aligned}
$$

Let Y_H and Y_W be the empirical logistic transform of husband's and wife's response respectively, so that (11-5) becomes

$$Y_H = Z_H + U_H$$

$$Y_W = Z_W + U_W$$

$$(11\text{-}8)$$

Substituting (11-7) into (11-8),

$$Y_H = c_1 + c_2 X_H + c_3 X_W + U_H + V_H$$

$$Y_W = c_4 + c_5 X_H + c_6 X_W + U_W + V_W.$$

$$(11\text{-}9)$$

Each equation in (11-9) takes the form of a model studied by Amemiya and Nold (1973). The unusual feature is the presence of two disturbances. The first, U_H or U_W, arises in consequence of sampling variation of p around P. The second, V_H or V_W, reflects the omission of determinants of Z_H and Z_W in model (11-6). Amemiya and Nold observe that maximum likelihood estimation of an equation like one of those in (11-9) is "generally infeasible." They propose an efficient method of estimation which involves a first round of calculation to obtain weights and a second round to secure the final weighted regression estimates. They also remark, however, that if the second disturbance (V) is ignored, estimates of coefficients "will still be consistent but less efficient." In this case the procedure then becomes equivalent to Berkson's minimum logit chi-square regression, which we have already used to estimate the reduced-form Eqs. (11-1), which are the same as (11-9) if the terms V_H and V_W are dropped from the latter.

Given the estimated reduced-form coefficients, $\hat{c}_1, \ldots, \hat{c}_6$, that is, the estimates of the c's in (11-9) or (11-1), we may compute the implied or indirect estimates of structural coefficients in (11-6). Thus, in view of definitions following (11-7), we have

$$\hat{a}_1 = \hat{c}_3/\hat{c}_6$$
$$\hat{b}_1 = \hat{c}_5/\hat{c}_2$$
$$\hat{\Delta} = 1 - \hat{a}_1\hat{b}_1$$
$$\hat{a}_2 = \hat{c}_2\hat{\Delta}$$
$$\hat{b}_2 = \hat{c}_6\hat{\Delta}$$
$$\hat{a}_0 = \hat{c}_1 - \hat{a}_1\hat{c}_4$$
$$\hat{b}_0 = \hat{c}_4 - \hat{b}_1\hat{c}_1$$

Taking the numbers in Table 11-3 as estimates of the c's and substituting in the foregoing formulas, we obtain as our estimates of structural coefficients

	Car	Beds
$\hat{a}_1$	.057	.86
$\hat{b}_1$	.89	1.1
$\hat{a}_2$	.29	.023
$\hat{b}_2$	.10	.021

Comparing $\hat{a}_1$ with $\hat{b}_1$ we see that in both sets of estimates the effect of husband's attitude on wife's attitude is greater than the effect in the opposite direction. The data for Car imply a very large disparity in the magnitudes of the two effects, whereas the data for Beds suggest that the disparity is moderate. In both sets of estimates the direct effect of own education (i.e., husband's education on husband's attitude, wife's education on wife's attitude) is positive, but the coefficients seem very small in the Beds set, although it is perhaps reasonable that a_2 and b_2 should be estimated to have similar values. In the Car set, it hardly seems reasonable that $\hat{b}_2$ should be so much smaller than $\hat{a}_2$, although there is nothing suspicious about the latter per se. Apart from their agreement on the proposition that husbands influence wives more than vice versa, the two sets of estimates do not show the good agreement one would have expected if Car and Beds were more or less interchangeable indicators of propensity to favor sex typing. If we believe both sets of estimates, we can hardly hold that Car and Beds are indicators of the same general attitude.

It is instructive to note why we cannot offer parallel estimates from the data on Walks and Dust. Such estimates can indeed be computed from the same formulas used for Car and Beds, but in each case the values obtained for $\hat{a}_1$ and $\hat{b}_1$ are such as to violate the condition $|a_1 b_1| < 1.0$, which is a requirement for equilibrium (Dempster, 1960). The problem with the Walks data is the negative value for $\hat{c}_3$. We could remedy this by estimating the reduced-form coefficients in a different manner, to impose the constraint $\hat{c}_2 = \hat{c}_6$, that is, the assumption that the net regression of response on own education is the same for husbands and wives. In that event, we obtain, instead of the values shown in Table 11-3, the reduced-form equations

$$\hat{Y}_H = -1.078 + .078\ X_H + .018\ X_W$$

$$\hat{Y}_W = -1.127 + .191\ X_H + .078\ X_W,$$

and solving for estimates of structural coefficients,

$$\hat{Z}_H = -.825 + .225\ Z_W + .035\ X_H$$

$$\hat{Z}_W = 1.511 + 2.446\ Z_H + .035\ X_W.$$

These estimates are hardly more plausible than those for Car and Beds, although they share the feature that $\hat{b}_1 > \hat{a}_1$, so that husband's influence outweighs wife's. This finding itself could be rationalized as conforming to the unpublished result of the 1955 Detroit Area Study obtained when Blood and Wolfe (1960) asked wives, "When you and your husband differ about something, do you usually give in and do it your husband's way or does he usually come around to your point of view?" According to the reports of 24% of the wives, husband usually or always gives in, while 34% report that wife usually or always gives in; the remaining answers fail to reveal any tendency one way or another.

We have no way, however, to use data on the Dust responses to support this proposition or, for that matter, its contrary. Perhaps we should conclude that the violation of the equilibrium condition is a meaningful clue—that as of 1971 the attitude tapped by this indicator was indeed in some kind of flux. In view of other findings in which

Dust seems to behave idiosyncratically, that would not be a hard conclusion to accept. But we really are asking too much of our little model
in requiring it to yield conclusions of that kind.

SEX TYPING IN RELATION TO VALUES
IN MARRIAGE AND SATISFACTION
WITH MARRIAGE

In this analysis, the population consists of wives in 1971. Most Valuable Part of Marriage (see Chapter 8) was run against each of Walks,
Car, Dust, and Beds, with a control on color. Table 11-5 shows the fitted
odds computed after partitioning Most Valuable Part of Marriage to
isolate all significant contrasts. Only for Car is the association between
response and Most Valuable Part of Marriage significant prior to partitioning. Hence, we may only have isolated the larger chance fluctuations in the other items. Perhaps this is why we find no consistency in
the pattern of effects across items for either black or white wives. The
statistical results call for rejection of the null hypothesis that values in

TABLE 11-5
Sex Typing of Children's Tasks by Wife's Values in Marriage, by Color, 1971

Color and Most Valuable Part of Marriage	Fitted odds on *both*			
	Walks	Car[a]	Dust	Beds[a]
Black				
[A] The chance to have children	.25	1.2	.50	.75
[B] The standard of living—the kind of house, clothes, car, and so forth	.84	2.0	.50	1.9
[C] The husband's understanding of the wife's problems and feelings	.53	1.2	.50	1.9
[D] The husband's expression of love and affection for the wife	.84	2.6	.50	1.9
[E] Companionship in doing things together with the husband	.84	1.2	.50	1.9
White				
[A] Children	1.3	2.4	.50	3.0
[B] Standard of living	.98	.62	.50	1.8
[C] Understanding	.61	2.4	.50	1.8
[D] Love and affection	.98	5.2	.50	1.8
[E] Companionship	.98	2.4	.50	1.8

[a] Three-way interaction significant at .1 but not at .05 level.

marriage and propensity to reject sex typing of children's tasks are unrelated. But the nature of the appropriate alternative hypothesis is not apparent from these results.

Satisfaction with marriage was rated by wives on a five-point scale for each of the aspects covered in the Values series, except *chance to have children*. Satisfaction and child task were analyzed in three-way tables with color as the third variable. No relationship of satisfaction with the Standard of Living to response was found significant for any of the four tasks. Nor were there significant associations of Walks, Car, or Dust with either satisfaction with Understanding or satisfaction with Companionship. That leaves for consideration the associations described in Figure 11-3. There is a strong positive linear relationship of response to Car and satisfaction with Love. Dust has a similar relationship which may, however, be stronger for black than for white wives inasmuch as the three-way interaction is significant at the .1 level. Walks also shows such a positive relationship, but it does not approach significance. Response to Beds is clearly associated with satisfaction with Love and affection; but the association is not linear. Very dissatisfied and highly satisfied wives have the greatest propensity to respond *both* to Beds. A similar U-shaped regression of Beds on satisfaction is found when either Companionship or Understanding is the aspect of marriage being rated.

None of these results has been studied with controls for education or other factors that may affect satisfaction and sex typing alike. Nevertheless it seems plausible that the associations represented in Figure 11-3 are in considerable measure produced by common causes. Marriages characterized by adequate amounts of love and affection happen to be the kinds that do not stress sex segregation of children's chores. Only for the one item, Beds, do we get some suggestion that a "liberated" attitude on that issue is the outcome of grave disappointment with the marriage. But we have not really tried to grapple with the issue of causal priority raised by that hypothesis.

ATTITUDE CONSISTENCY

We take up now the question whether rejection or acceptance of sex typing for children's chores goes with a similar orientation toward the issue of women working. We consider first the question, "Are there some kinds of work that you feel women should not have?" that was studied extensively in Chapter 3. We treat the response to this question as though it were an influence on response to Walks, Car, Dust, or Beds;

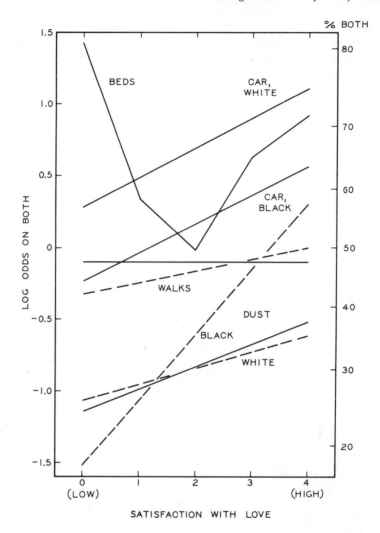

FIGURE 11-3. Sex typing of child tasks by satisfaction with love, for wives in 1971.

but this is only a convenience in presentation, since the statistical model being used does not depend on the assumption of causal priority of either response with respect to the other. Sex and color of respondent are included as controls. Table 11-6 reports net effects of sex, color, and attitude toward women's work on the odds on *both* for each child task. We find that there is indeed a tendency toward consistency. Respon-

TABLE 11-6
Odds Ratios for Association of Sex Typing of Children's Tasks with Sex, Color, and
Opinion on Women's Work in Three-Way Analysis, 1971

Odds ratio	Child task			
	Walks	Car	Dust	Beds
Female : Male	1.86	1.24	1.50	2.19
White : Black	1.61	2.26	1.0	1.31
Work not have? *no : yes*	1.36	1.45	1.57	1.66

dents who refuse to limit the work opportunities of women are more
likely, by a significant though certainly not overwhelming margin, to
reject sex as a consideration in assigning household chores to children.
The effect is somewhat greater for Beds and Dust than for Walks or Car,
although we have not carried out a formal test of this difference.

In Table 11-7 we introduce a second question about women's work,
"Do you feel that women have special problems working?" In the 1971
data there is a very modest association (odds ratio = 1.3) between the
two questions, in that respondents who think women have special
problems are a little bit more likely to feel that some kinds of work
should be closed to women. Table 11-7 is based on a five-way analysis,

TABLE 11-7
Odds on Both Response to Walks, Car, Dust, and Beds for White Females in Alternative
Models, in Relation to Responses to Questions on Women's Work, 1971

Problems working?	Work not have?	Child task			
		Walks	Car	Dust	Beds
		Set (i)			
Yes	Yes	.898	2.34	.461	1.70
Yes	No	1.22	4.55	.724	2.86
No	Yes	.898	2.15	.461	1.38
No	No	1.22	2.12	.724	2.32
		Set (ii)			
Yes	Yes	.938	2.24	.482	1.67
Yes	No	1.32	4.54	.842	3.18
No	Yes	.938	2.24	.482	1.67
No	No	.938	2.24	.482	1.67

adolescent chore item, by each of the women's work items, by sex and color. There are no significant three-way interactions involving sex and color, and the effects of these factors already cited need not be recapitulated. (The odds given in Table 11-7 for white females may be adjusted up or down if the corresponding odds for white males or blacks of either sex are desired, making use of the ratios in Table 11-6.)

Table 11-7 shows two sets of odds, pertaining to two different ways of analyzing the joint association of the women's work items with the adolescent chore item. In Set (i) the preferred model, selected after systematic screening of plausible competitors, allows both women's work responses to be separately associated with the response to Beds; only the Work Not Have item is associated with Dust and Walks; and the model for Car involves the response to that item in a three-way interaction with the two women's work questions. Although the models selected for Car and Beds are different, they agree in regard to the location of the highest odds on a *both* response; this occurs for respondents who say, *yes,* women do have special problems working, but *no,* there are not any kinds of work that women should not have.

In the lower half of Table 11-7, identified as Set (ii), the four categories of the joint variable created by the cross-classification of the two women's work questions are handled separately and a model is sought which includes any significant contrast of one of these categories with all the others. In all four problems the outcome is the same; only the *yes–no* sequence in the women's work questions produces a significant contrast with the other answer combinations. In the case of Car, the models in Sets (i) and (ii) are hierarchical, so that a formal comparison of the two models in terms of goodness of fit is warranted. In Set (i) we have $X^2 = 5.89$, $df = 10$, in Set (ii), $X^2 = 6.51$, $df = 12$. Clearly, the three-way interaction found significant in Set (i) is adequately captured by the Set (ii) model that specifies that this interaction pertains to a single contrast. As far as the other items are concerned, the chi-square statistics do not provide a basis for choice. There are two attractive features of Set (ii), however. First, in Set (ii) there is but one pattern of association of the adolescent items with the joint women's work variable, whereas there are three different patterns in Set (i). Secondly, the result for Beds in Set (i) is particularly awkward, since it implies that the association between Problems Working and Beds is in the opposite direction to what one would expect from the association of Problems Working with Work Not Have and the association of the latter with Beds. In Set (ii), on the other hand, we do not entertain the notion that the two women's work items have distinct associations with Beds or any of the other adolescent items. Rather, there is a synergistic pattern. When respondents feel that, despite acknowledged problems in working, women should not be barred from certain kinds of work, then they are more likely to answer *both* to any of the adolescent task items, particularly Car and Beds.

To conclude the analysis, we relate the joint variable describing attitude toward women's working to the four adolescent chore items simultaneously, taking account of color and sex as well. For convenience, the odds on a *yes–no* response concerning women's work (see lower panel of Table 11-7) is regarded as the dependent variable with sex, color, and responses to Walks, Car, Dust, and Beds as the independent variables. Taking as given the associations among the six independent variables, we find that the model which captures all significant effects on the response relating to women's work is a very simple one: it includes a sex effect but no color effect; and it specifies effects of Beds and Car, but no effects of Walks and Dust. The relevant odds ratios, estimating the factor by which the odds on a "favorable," that is, *yes–no*, answer to the women's work questions are raised, are 1.4 for sex, 1.6 for a *both* response to Beds, and 1.7 for a *both* response to Car. If the absence of a significant color effect, in particular, is surprising, we note that the fit of the model just described is given by $X^2 = 51.4$, $df = 53$, $p > .5$; with a color effect included in the model X^2 drops only to 49.4, a nonsignificant decrease of 2.0, $df = 1$, $p = .16$. It appears, therefore, that if we know the color differentials concerning the adolescent chore items and the relationship of those items to the women's work question, we can infer the color differential with regard to the latter without positing any association of color with attitude toward women's work arising from any other source.

In summary, attitude toward women's working (as measured by the two items in Table 11-7, taken jointly in the fashion of the lower half of that table) and the sex typing of adolescent chores are linked in two ways. First, the two sets of views are associated in the manner one would expect if they were measuring somewhat the same thing. Second, they respond to the factors of sex and color in roughly the same manner, although the color effect is not as consistently in evidence as the sex effect. It is, moreover, of interest that the two adolescent chore items that most explicitly relate to the women's-work variable—that is, Cars and Beds—are the ones showing the most pronounced changes between 1953 and 1971 and the strongest regressions on cohort in the latter year, as we observe in the following chapter.

THE ALUMNAE

"See? Girls DO enjoy trains and boys CAN have fun playing with dolls."

12

Changes in Sex Typing of Child Tasks

To study change in response patterns to the child-task items, we take the 1953 survey as the source of baseline data. This survey, in which these questions were first asked, was limited to mothers of children under the age of 19 years. We can identify the same population within the broader population surveyed in 1971. Thus, most of the analyses of change in sex typing reported in this chapter are based on the responses of some 250 mothers in 1953 and 600 mothers in 1971. The small numbers of respondents severely limit the analytical possibilities.

CHANGING RESPONSE DISTRIBUTIONS

The response distributions with which we will be working appear in Table 12-1 as a cross-classification of the four child-task items for mothers who answered either *boy* or *both* to the questions about Walks and Car and either *girl* or *both* to the questions about Dust and Beds. Very few mothers offered a clearly deviant response, that is, that only girls should shovel walks or wash the car or that only boys should dust the furniture or make beds. Four of the nine mothers excluded from the 1971 data set and 16 of the 26 mothers excluded from the 1953 data set volunteered that neither boys nor girls should wash cars. (A possible flaw in comparability of the 1953 and 1971 responses is mentioned for

TABLE 12-1

Four-Way Tabulation of Responses to Question on Task Assignment, for Mothers of Children under 19 Years Old, 1953 and 1971

Year	Walks	Car	Dust: Girl Beds: Girl	Girl Both	Both Girl	Both Both	Total
1953							
	Boy	Boy	86	24	7	21	138
	Boy	Both	12	8	4	8	32
	Both	Boy	20	12	2	7	41
	Both	Both	8	1	2	35	46
		Total	126	45	15	71	257
		(Other answers[a])					(26)
							(283)
1971	Boy	Boy	82	49	1	18	150
	Boy	Both	40	67	2	38	147
	Both	Boy	10	12	0	6	28
	Both	Both	32	80	4	153	269
		Total	164	208	7	215	594
		(Other answers[a])					(9)
							(603)

[a] Includes *girl* for Walks or Car, *boy* for Dust or Beds, "neither" for any item or no answer for one or more items.

sake of completeness, although we have no definite indication that it is serious. An additional item, fixing light cords, appeared between dusting furniture and making beds in the earlier study, but was dropped from the 1971 inquiry inasmuch as almost one-third of the mothers in 1953 volunteered that neither boys nor girls should fix light cords.)

We begin by looking at the marginal distributions of the child-task items taken one at a time. The odds on an answer of *both* by mothers in 1953 are contrasted with the corresponding odds in 1971 in Figure 12-1. For three items—Walks, Car, and Beds—we observe a substantial increase in the odds on *both*. That the increase is not readily attributable to sampling fluctuations is suggested by carrying out a test of independence in the 2×2 table, year by response, for each item. The chi-square statistic is statistically significant at the .001 level for Walks, Car, and Beds; but for Dust X^2 is only 1.2 ($p = .27$) so that we cannot be confident that any real change occurred, although the observed odds on *both* are slightly higher in 1971 than in 1953. A general conclusion, then, is that mothers were, by all available measures, less likely to endorse the

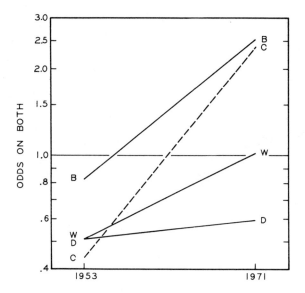

FIGURE 12-1. Responses to four child-task items, by eligible mothers in 1953 and 1971: Walks (W), Car (C), Dust (D), and Beds (B).

principle of sex differentiation in regard to children's chores in 1971 than in 1953, although the change recorded by one item was not large enough to rule out sampling error as an explanation.

Equally apparent in Figure 12-1 is the change in the item profile of responses. In 1953, as noted by Miller and Swanson (1958, p. 227), the four items had somewhat similar marginal distributions; by 1971 this was no longer so. Hence, the changes in response were apparently at varying rates for the four items. This conclusion is supported by formal tests, the details of which are omitted here. We find that in 1953 we cannot show that any two of Walks, Car, and Dust have reliably different marginal distributions although each of these does differ significantly from Beds. In 1971, while Car and Beds cannot be shown to have different marginal distributions, each of them differs significantly from Walks and Dust, and the latter two from each other. Moreover, a test of the significance of the difference in rate of change of the marginals for each of the six pairs of items produces a significant result. No two of the items, therefore, gives the same estimate of rate of reduction in extent of sex typing.

Although the four items give quantitatively different signals about the pace of change in prevalence of sex typing, they exhibit something close to invariance over time in regard to their mutual association. Let us focus on the pairwise relationships among the items; relevant summary statistics are given in Table 12-2. We find, for example, that the odds on a *both* response to Car are raised by a factor of 4.9 if Walks was answered *both* in 1953; the corresponding ratio in 1971 was 9.5. This example was chosen because we do detect a marginally significant ($X^2 =$ 3.6, 1 df, $p = .057$) three-way interaction in analyzing the table Walks by Car by Year. However, none of the other apparent changes in odds ratio (compare corresponding positions on opposite sides of the diagonal in Table 12-2) turns out to be significant by the same kind of test (p-values range from .24 to .67). Furthermore, in analyses of four-way tables (e.g., Walks by Car by Dust by Year) and the five-way table shown previously as Table 12-1, we find no significant higher order interactions. Of course, our chance of detecting such interactions is compromised by the small size of the samples. Nevertheless, the evidence we have points to a general stability in the pattern of association among the four items.

Readers accustomed to having the pattern depicted by correlation-like statistics may prefer the lower panel of Table 12-2, which shows the transformation of the odds ratio into Yule's Q, a widely cited coefficient of association which, in the case of the 2 × 2 table, is the same as Goodman and Kruskal's *gamma*. Conclusions already stated about the lack of significant change for five of the coefficients apply to the Q's as well, of course.

In view of the strong association for each pair of items and the approximate invariance of the pattern of association over an 18-year period, some investigators would conclude that the four questions are

TABLE 12-2
Odds Ratio and Yule's Q (Coefficient of Association) for Each Pair of Child-Task Items, Based on Data for Mothers, 1953 (Above Diagonal) and 1971 (Below Diagonal)

Item	Walks	Car	Dust	Beds
Odds ratio				
Walks	—	4.9	3.7	3.1
Car	9.5	—	6.4	3.5
Dust	4.9	5.5	—	13.3
Beds	4.0	4.7	24.0	—
Yule's Q				
Walks	—	.66	.57	.51
Car	.81	—	.73	.56
Dust	.66	.69	—	.86
Beds	.60	.65	.92	—

merely different measures of the same thing, although possibly not equally reliable measures of it. In that event, one might consider it justified to replace the detailed response distributions of Table 12-1 with some kind of index of propensity to give a sex-typed answer. The simplest technique for constructing such an index would be merely to count the number of *both* responses; scores for this variable would then range from zero to four. The mean score for 1971 would be found significantly higher than that for 1953, by the usual *t* test. And analyses of the factors affecting response would be considerably simplified by the use of a scale score as the dependent variable.

Convenient though it may be, this procedure is one that we rejected after much exploratory analysis and prayerful deliberation (some of the former is summarized in Appendix B). Even if the four items do "go together" in some sense, it is not obvious that the arbitrary summation of responses provides an undistorted reduction of the data. We have already shown that the four items do not behave in the same way in that they do not change at even approximately the same rates over time (Figure 12-1). Moreover, as we have seen in Chapter 11, they do not show the same relationship to the sex or educational level of the respondent. In that event, the measure of change (or effect of causal factors) depends on which item one looks at, or which combinations of items, and how they are weighted in the combination. Thus, we can imagine a mildly skeptical critic arguing that dusting furniture is really the most typical task in terms of "pure" sex typing, whereas the others are "contaminated" by one or another kind of extraneous consideration. On this argument, in place of the "good news," based on the aggregation of four items, that sex typing has decreased, we should have to report the "bad news" that hardly any change occurred in sex typing as such over the 18-year period, although for various adventitious reasons the two sexes share certain tasks—like shoveling walks, washing cars, and making beds—somewhat more now than they did in 1953.

We have, moreover, entertained a number of formal models that have been suggested as ways of capturing the idea that a set of items is unidimensional: the Guttman scale, as modified by Goodman (1975); Rasch's (1968) measurement model; and, among the various possible latent structure models, the latent dichotomy, the latent trichotomy, the latent double dichotomy, and the latent distance model, using techniques of estimation and testing provided by Goodman (1974a, b, c). We did not obtain a satisfactory fit with any of these models. On the other hand, it has been reported (Kempf, Hampapa, and Mach, 1975) that a modification of Rasch's model leads to an acceptable fit for the

1971 data (lower panel of Table 12-1). The modification involves the assumption that the response to each item depends in part on the response to the preceding one, via what is termed a transfer or learning effect, while the four items, apart from this serial dependence, serve as indicators of the dimension being measured. Despite the interest of this result from the standpoint of measurement theory, it is reached by a very arduous exercise in computation; hence, it hardly provides support for the ordinary procedures of index construction.

In the remainder of our work, therefore, we shall examine factors related to sex typing via parallel analyses for Walks, Car, Dust, and Beds. No doubt this will involve some redundancy in view of the partial overlap in the content of these items. But, as we shall have further opportunity to observe, these items frequently do not respond in the same ways to factors affecting response. We shall even offer a few suggestions as to specific situational circumstances that may affect response to one of the items but not the others, although we reach no determinate conclusions as to just what each of them is measuring besides acceptance or rejection of the principle that sex should be an irrelevant consideration in making work assignments for children.

SOCIOECONOMIC CORRELATES AND DIFFERENTIAL CHANGE

We have found that the odds on a *both* response were higher in 1971 than in 1953 for each child-task item, although the changes were at different rates and the change for the Dust item failed to reach significance at the conventional level. One way of summarizing these results is to state that the variable Year is associated with response. The mothers living in Detroit in 1971 differed from their 1953 counterparts not only in terms of their answers to the child-task questions, but also in terms of their socioeconomic characteristics—educational attainment, work status, husband's union membership, tenure, and class identification. The issue here is whether a simple "demographic" explanation of the change in response between 1953 and 1971 is adequate—do differentials in response by socioeconomic status and the changing status composition explain the change in response over the 18-year period? Since the answer is unequivocal, we may as well anticipate the results at this point. None of the socioeconomic characteristics mentioned explains the change in response; neither does the introduction of color as an additional characteristic of the mother.

Despite these results for particular socioeconomic variables, there is still the possibility that the changes in response detected in comparing the two surveys are due to population turnover in metropolitan Detroit—as a consequence of in- or out-migration a "different kind of people" lived there in 1971 than in 1953. (We retain here the nomenclature that typically is used when this argument is presented to us informally.) There is no general and conclusive refutation to this hypothesis. In particular, we have no way of knowing if out-migration from Detroit over the 18-year intersurvey period was selective of people with particular views on sex typing. However, we can make a check on the possible impact of in-migration. Residence histories given by respondents in the 1971 survey allow us to classify them as persons who moved to Detroit after 1953 or as persons who already lived in Detroit as of 1953, being native to the area or having moved there in 1953 or earlier. For none of our four items, Walks, Car, Dust, or Beds, is there a significant association between migration status and response. Although there remains the possibility of selective out-migration, we suspect that the demographic factor of migration is not one about which we need to be urgently concerned.

A somewhat different question is perhaps more interesting: are there differential changes, in the sense that change in response is more rapid for one subgroup defined by a socioeconomic variable than for another? Formally, differential change is equivalent to a three-way interaction of response by socioeconomic variable by year; and another way to describe such an interaction would be to state that the association of response with the socioeconomic variable differed in the 2 years. The potential interest of a finding of differential change is that it may suggest hypotheses about the process of change. In any case, the finding would put somewhat different requirements on a structural model that purports to explain change than would the finding that all groups are changing at about the same rate.

Mother's educational attainment is a characteristic of somewhat special interest, for we have found that education has a substantial effect on sex typing of children's chores in 1971 and well-educated women often are said to be in the vanguard of the "liberation" movement. We find that response to each item is related to mother's education in both years: As years of schooling increase, the odds on responding *both* increases in a regular manner, sampling fluctuations aside. There is, however, no reliable evidence of differential change at different educational levels.

The foregoing summary is based on several different analyses. We first treated education merely as six categories of a polytomous variable, ignoring the order of the categories, and found that for each of the four items there was a significant association of education with response but that the response-by-education-by-year three-way interaction was not significant. In a four-way analysis of response, color, education (elementary, high school, college), and year, we find no significant indication of differential change by either color or education. Despite the significant education effects and the upgrading of levels of educational attainment in the Detroit population over the 18-year period, the increase in educational attainment, per se, was not a major source of change in odds on a *both* response. For three items, all but Dust, a substantial year effect was required in the model along with the education effect.

In an analysis via orthogonal polynomials, we found that the education effects could be adequately described by the linear contrast of the education categories, even though the observed odds by educational category appear to fluctuate a good deal. This finding motivated the final, and most compact, mode of summarizing the education effect: in terms of a straight-line regression of the logit (natural logarithm of the odds) of response on level of educational attainment. In making the calculations for the linear regression model it was convenient to reconsider the question of differential change, since the test for a year-by-education interaction here is more sensitive than in the case where education is treated as a polytomous variable. For all responses except Dust, we cannot accept a regression that ignores year; but for none of the responses does the inclusion of the education-by-year interaction improve significantly on the model that includes only the separate effects of the two variables.

Table 12-3 provides numerical values of the estimated regression

TABLE 12-3
Estimated Coefficients in Regression of Logit Response to Child-Task Items on Education and Year

		Coefficient of	
Child task	Intercept	Education[a]	Year[b]
Walks	−1.195	.223	.564
Car	−1.464	.268	1.538
Dust	−1.206	.231	—
Beds	−1.342	.502	.831

[a] Scale for Education: 0, Less than elementary 8 years; 1, Elementary, 8; 2, High school, 1–3; 3, High school, 4; 4, College, 1–3; 5, College 4 or more years.
[b] Scale for Year: 0, 1953; 1, 1971.

coefficients. It is striking that the education effect is much the same for Walks, Car, and Dust, but markedly greater for Beds. Although we attempt no formal test of the significance of this difference, it seems much too large to attribute merely to sampling fluctuations. As usual, when the four items relate differently to an independent variable, there is no obvious explanation at hand for this particular difference.

Another presentation of the results is in Figure 12-2, where the observed odds are juxtaposed with both the linear regressions and the estimates of education effects secured from the multiway contingency analysis. The irregularities in the latter, as well as the scatter of observed odds, call attention to the considerable amount of noise in the data from these relatively small samples. But we have reasonable confidence that the apparent noise is, indeed, mostly noise. ($Y^2 = 12.8, 11.9$, and 5.4 for Walks, Car, and Beds, each with 9 *df*, and 9.1 for Dust with 10 *df*.)

There are at least two reasons why one might expect the responses to our items to vary according to whether the mother works. Working mothers, one might suppose, have an incentive to maximize the efficiency of household management in view of the shortage of their own time for this function. Hence, they might well be impatient with sex typing insofar as it interferes with getting the domestic chores done. Secondly, it is presumed that women who work, having rejected, de

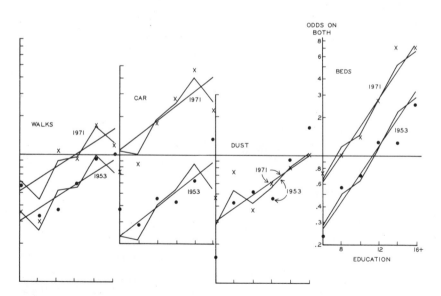

FIGURE 12-2. Regression of response to child-task items on educational attainment of eligible mothers, 1953 and 1971.

facto, one kind of sexual limitation on activity, would be more likely to have an ideological antipathy to such limitations than other women. Since we know that the rates of work-force participation vary by education and color, we classify mothers simultaneously by one of these characteristics and work status in studying the response pattern.

In Table 12-4 we report results for the effect of work status in an analysis that also includes color. The observed odds, of course, display a good deal of random variability. There is some suggestion that there was a convergence between 1953 and 1971 in the odds on *both* for several of the items, when comparing working and nonworking mothers. However, under our statistical tests none of the ostensible three-way interactions involving work status proved significant. Indeed, the pattern of results is quite a stark one, as inferred from the odds computed from fitted frequencies of the preferred models: Work status has a significant effect only on Dust, not on Walks, Car, or Beds. This effect is in the expected direction; the odds on a *both* response are 1.6 times as high for working mothers as for nonworking mothers. We also find that white mothers more often reject a sexual basis for assigning the task of shoveling walks, washing the car, or making beds, with the ratio of odds on *both*, White:Black, standing at 1.8, 2.7, and 1.6 for the respective chores. (The effect of color net of work status and year is

TABLE 12-4
Response to Child-Task Items, by Color and Work Status of Mother, 1953 and 1971

			Child task			
Year	Color	Work status	Walks	Car	Dust	Beds
			Observed odds on *both*			
1953	Black	Working	.40	.40	.75	2.5
		Not working	.40	.17	.24	.50
	White	Working	.82	.42	1.0	1.1
		Not working	.46	.48	.42	1.1
1971	Black	Working	.58	1.1	.89	2.1
		Not working	.66	1.2	.60	1.5
	White	Working	1.3	3.3	.66	3.1
		Not working	1.1	3.1	.52	2.7
			Fitted odds ratios			
Working:Not working			1.0	1.0	1.6	1.0
White:Black			1.8	2.7	1.0	1.6
1971:1953			2.1	6.5	1.0	2.4

substantially the same as the effect of color net of year only or net of year and education.) Year effects on Walks, Car, and Beds still are present.

In another four-way analysis, with education (three categories) replacing color as the fourth variable, we get the same result as far as work status is concerned. Its effect is significant only for Dust, and is estimated by the odds ratio of 1.5 for working relative to nonworking mothers. Education, as already reported, affects the odds on *both* for all the items. But there is no significant three-way interaction involving response, work status, and education.

The finding of a significant effect of work status on response to Dust puts a slightly different perspective on the finding reiterated in the preceding pages that there was no significant change in the odds on *both* for this item between 1953 and 1971. We note that there was a significant and substantial increase in the proportion of working mothers over this period. In our samples the odds that the mother reported herself as working rather than not working were .29 in 1953 and .56 in 1971, so that the odds ratio measuring the change is 1.9. Now, if year affects work status and work status in turn affects response, then year must affect response indirectly. Moreover, unless the direct effect of year on response is opposite to its indirect effect, there must be a nonzero total effect of year on response. Indeed, in our previous analyses we have noted such an effect, although it was not found large enough to be significant. The result mentioned here suggests that we should appraise the effect as real nonetheless, even though quite modest in magnitude.

By comparison with several of the other factors investigated, the results for husband's membership in a labor union (excluding mothers not currently living with their husbands) are extraordinarily uniform across the four items. There is a significant effect for each item, but no interaction of this effect with year. The odds ratios, Nonunion to Union, are 1.9 for Walks, 2.1 for Car, 1.8 for Dust, and 2.0 for Beds. Thus, the odds on a *both* response are approximately doubled for mothers married to a man who does not belong to a union, relative to those married to union members.

We have no doubt that husband's union membership is acting here as a proxy for some variable we have not identified, possibly one that was not even measured. Even if one supposes that sex typing is part of a hard-hat syndrome and that union membership is a good indicator of the latter, it would still have to be explained how that syndrome gets translated into the wife's (mother's) response. Or, if one supposes that the result for union membership of husband merely reflects the previously described result for education, there is the nagging question of why the education effect for Beds is dramatically different from the effects for Walks, Car, and Dust, while the union membership effect is uniform across items. Even without undertaking a multivariate analysis it is clear that we would not be able to dispose of such a conundrum. (Recall that belonging to a union decreased the odds on a *both* response, as reported in Chapter 1.)

Only one of the items, Walks, shows any significant association with whether the household occupies its own home or a rented dwelling. None of them shows differential change by tenure. For Walks, the odds on a *both* response are raised by a factor of 1.5 for home owners relative to renters.

There may be a very simple explanation of this effect, although we have no way to test the explanation. According to the 1950 U.S. Census of Housing, 83% of the owner-occupied dwelling units in the Detroit metropolitan area were in detached structures consisting of only the one dwelling unit, whereas only 18% of the renter-occupied units were in such structures. In 1970 the corresponding percentages were 90 and 20. Most often the rented unit is part of a structure comprising several such units. Hence, the child in a renter household who is sent to shovel walks may have a bigger job than the child from an owner household; he or she will be more removed from immediate parental supervision; and he or she is more likely to have to deal with others in the building in regard to this task, perhaps with actual strangers. For all these reasons, it is understandable that at least some mothers would be loath to assign this task to their girls.

All such explanations are, of course, ad hoc; and it is well to keep in mind the possibility that the finding itself, however intelligible it may seem, could be just a fluke. It is perhaps reassuring, if one thinks of flukes as being quite probable, that we find no effect whatever of the ownership of a television set on any of our four items. Even in 1953, to be sure, the vast majority of households did have a TV set; nonetheless, the marginal distribution for TV ownership would have permitted a significant effect to appear, had there been some genuine association or had this variable been minded to produce a fluke to discomfit investigators.

At this point the reader may find it helpful to have a "scorecard" of the detailed findings reported on socioeconomic correlates of sex typing. Table 12-5 reduces the numerical results to a simple indication of whether a significant association was found. The pattern, like the findings for some of the particular variables, is puzzling even if informative. But, at the least, it does tell us that responses to the four items do vary by socioeconomic characteristics. Moreover, the effects of those

TABLE 12-5
Schematic Summary of Significant (X) and Nonsignificant (0) Associations of
Independent Variables with Responses to Child-Task Items

Independent variable	Child task			
	Walks	Car	Dust	Beds
Year	X	X	0	X
Color	X	X	0	X
Education	X	X	X	X
Work status	0	0	X	0
Husband's union membership	X	X	X	X
Tenure	X	0	0	0

characteristics appear to be stable over time, in view of the dearth of significant differential changes. Should we say, then, that these items, which we are interpreting as indicators of sex typing, are perhaps nothing but crude manifestations of "class" perspectives or life styles?

No doubt the answer to this rhetorical question is in good part a matter of the sociologist's concept and definition of "class." But if we put that aside, we can at least investigate empirically whether the "class" identifications accepted by respondents are clearly correlated with their propensity to give sex-stereotyped answers to our items. The measure of class identification used here is the respondent's choice among four proffered labels, middle class, working class, lower class, and upper class. Since few mothers accepted the latter two, the class identification variable becomes a dichotomy in Table 12-6, which shows how the odds on responding *both* vary by class. It appears that "class," insofar as self-identification gets at that concept, has little to do with sex typing. The association of class identification with response is significant only for Walks, among the four items. While the observed odds suggest that this effect is confined to 1971, we cannot show that the apparent differential change, or three-way interaction, is significant. Hence, as Table 12-6 implies, the preferred model is one in which year and class identification have separate effects on response to Walks. It is curious, though possibly only a coincidence, that tenure is the only socioeconomic variable in Table 12-6 with the same profile of effects as class identification.

AGE, COHORTS, AND CHANGE

There are at least two reasons why we might expect to observe differences in sex typing by age of mother. First, as mothers get older

TABLE 12-6
Sex Typing of Children's Tasks by Class Identification of Mothers, 1953 and 1971

		Child task			
Year	Class identification	Walks	Car	Dust	Beds
		Observed odds on *both*			
1953	Middle	.53	.43	.58	.92
	Working	.51	.45	.46	.88
	Ratio, M:W	1.0	.95	1.3	1.0
1971	Middle	1.3	2.7	.69	3.0
	Working	.83	2.3	.58	2.2
	Ratio, M:W	1.5	1.2	1.2	1.4
		Fitted odds ratios			
	Middle:Working	1.4	1.0	1.0	1.0
	1971:1953	2.0	5.6	1.0	2.8

and gain experience in childrearing, their views on this matter may change in a systematic way. Second, at any given time, the younger mothers, whose own socialization has been more recent, may have been exposed to a different climate of opinion on sex typing from that which influenced the attitudes of older mothers. If, as seems likely, these and other factors producing age effects are operating simultaneously, it will not be easy to disentangle them. Nevertheless, it is still of interest to learn whether there are age differences in our survey years and, if so, whether the pattern of age differences has shifted.

In view of the small sample sizes subdivision by age leads to very small frequencies in some age groups, particularly the two groups above age 45. Hence, a great deal of the observed variation by age must be attributed to mere sampling error. At the same time, if there are strong age gradients, we should be able to detect them. A glance at Figure 12-3 discloses some examples of such gradients. But it also shows that no two of our four sex-typing items relate in just the same way to age. Hence, the description must be somewhat tedious.

Of the four items, Walks is the only one to show no significant age effect whatever. The horizontal regressions for 1971 and 1953 differ, therefore, only in regard to their intercept, that is, only in regard to the year effect, an effect that is presumably familiar to the reader at this point.

From a purely statistical standpoint, the neatest results are obtained for Car. The plot of observed odds on a *both* response shows an unmistakable negative relationship to age in 1971, a quite different pattern from that observed in 1953 when the relationship was, if anything, positive, but not very pronounced in any case. Thus, when we fit the regression of logit response on age and year we find that we must include in the equation the interaction of age and year with respect to response. Moreover, we find that the fit of the linear equation with this interaction term included is quite satisfactory: $Y^2 = 4.7, df = 10, p > .9$. It should be noted that the statistical tests associated with the regression procedure do not establish that the 1953 regression is other than zero, but merely that its slope is different from that of the 1971 regression of logit response on age. But this is all we need to pronounce the finding of differential change significant. Although the endorsement of the *both* alternative to Car rose between 1953 and 1971 at all ages, the increase was especially marked at the younger ages and comparatively small at the upper ages.

The results for Dust are rather ambiguous. On the one hand, there is no significant *linear* regression of logit response on age. On the other hand, if we allow the relationship to age to be unconstrained, treating age merely as seven unordered categories of a polytomous variable, the age effects turn out to be significant but not to differ significantly by year. Hence, only one curve is shown for Dust in Figure 12-3. The goodness of fit of the model corresponding to this curve is indicated by $X^2 = 7.7, df = 7, p = .36$. It seems likely that in entertaining a model which is so faithful to irregular fluctuations in the data we are in danger of fitting to noise rather than information. In any event, we are not prepared to "explain" the ostensible result that mothers in their early thirties and again after age 45 seem to "see the light" in regard to this task. Indeed, if the youngest age group is ignored, there really is not enough age variation to be interesting, by the standard we have been using implicitly for an "interesting" finding. For summary purposes, then, perhaps it is best to classify Dust along with Walks as an item that just does not have a pronounced relationship to age in either year.

The last item, Beds, shows the most dramatic reversal of the age pattern between 1953 and 1971. As suggested by the linear regressions, there was a strong positive relationship of the *both* response to mother's age in 1953, and an almost equally strong negative relationship in 1971. Hence, while for young mothers the increase in this response over the 18-year period was quite pronounced, for older mothers the increase was negligible. The reversal of slope here is reminiscent of that observed for Car, although the details are somewhat different. In particular, the model constraining the regression to be linear does not provide a satisfactory fit in the present case: for the regression on year, age, and

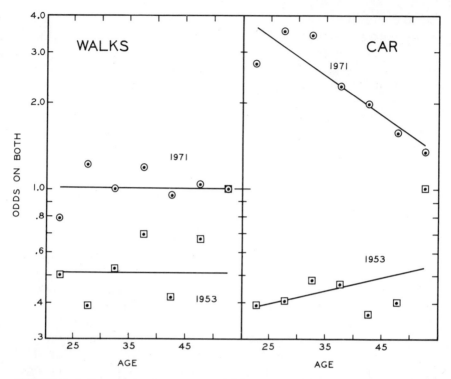

FIGURE 12-3. Regression of response to child-task items on age of eligible mothers, 1953 and 1971.

year-by-age, we find $Y^2 = 21.4$, $df = 10$, $p < .025$. Moreover, if we allow the regression to be nonlinear, treating age as a polytomous variable, the multiway contingency table model fitting all two-way marginals while assuming zero three-way interaction is likewise unsatisfactory: $X^2 = 17.2$, $df = 6$, $p = .009$. The essence of this interaction is captured in the fact that the two dashed lines representing the relationship of response to age in the 2 years are quite dissimilar.

Although it is not an adequate summary of the data for Beds to state that the *both* response increases with age in 1953 and decreases with age in 1971, still this summary is roughly true as far as it goes. It captures what seems most interesting about these data, especially since we have no plausible interpretation of the departures from linearity, other than sampling variation (which is surely present, even if there is some systematic nonlinearity as well).

A drastic but useful simplification of Figure 12-3, therefore, would be that age is not a factor in regard to Walks and Dust, but that the age

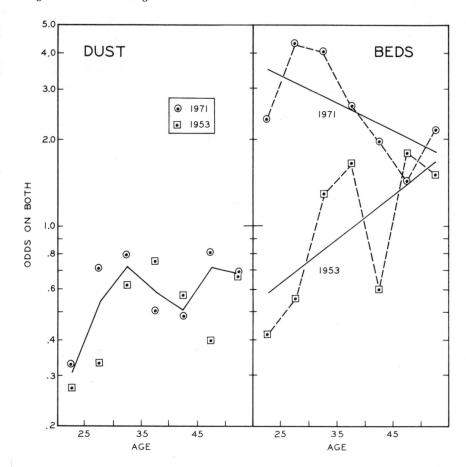

gradient was reversed between 1953 and 1971 for Car and Beds, shifting from a positive to a markedly negative regression. It is surely of interest to pick up such unequivocal evidence of differential change, even if it pertains to only two items. We found almost no examples of differential change when the factors under study were the socioeconomic characteristics of the mothers. There must be something special about the relationship of age to social change that sets it apart from those variables.

It might be useful to put ourselves in the position of an analyst having only the 1953 data available for study some time in the mid-1950s. She would have noted, for example, that sex typing is decreased by increments to schooling. Being aware of the long-term secular trend toward higher levels of educational attainment, she might have forecast, more or less correctly, that the future would bring about a decrease in sex typing. The term "more or less" is well advised, because the 1953 evidence on sex typing in relation to education would not have been helpful in anticipating which of the four items would register the greatest changes. If the analyst had been even bolder and suggested, for example, that the appeals of an emerging feminist movement would be stronger or more immediate for people with greater amounts of educational attainment, then she would have forecast, erroneously, that the regression of sex typing on schooling would be stronger in 1971 (or some such date) than it was in 1953. The attempt to forecast social change from a study of cross-sectional regressions of response on education would not have been a total failure, therefore, but neither would it have been an unqualified success.

By contrast, it is hard to see how anything that might have been learned from the study of the 1953 age data would have been other than misleading to the analyst trying to anticipate what was to come. The data for Walks might have suggested that age was not a factor in response; but by that same token, the age data would not have given any basis for expecting the substantial decrease in sex typing registered by the Walks item. If the 1953 age data for Beds had been read as suggesting that mothers become less eager to monopolize the function of making beds, or more willing to share it with their male children, as they get older, the analyst could have offered some interesting reflections about the process of aging, but these would not have been helpful as cues to forthcoming changes. If, on the contrary, she saw the young mothers of 1953 as harbingers of the future division of labor by sex, she would have been led into the most serious error possible. The trend in regard to sex typing would have been in the opposite direction to her forecast and the reversal of the age gradient would have been completely unanticipated.

There is no suggestion that a new data set and the advantage of hindsight permit us to specify how the hapless analyst in the parable could have done better. The meaning of the parable, on the contrary, is that the changes registered by at least two of our items really are unusual. These two items, Car and Beds, are, as the reader may have noted, the same two that showed the more rapid aggregate change, 1953–1971, in Figure 12-1. We now see that it is primarily among the younger mothers that this rapid change occurred. As a consequence of the rapid change at the younger ages, the character of the age gradient for these two items was quite different in 1971 from what it was in 1953. Perhaps this is what lay analysts mean in describing the ideological

changes of the 1960s in terms of the emergence of a "generation gap"—
although that term, of course, is fatally imprecise and misleading.

In the foregoing discussion, only one meaning of the term "change"
has been employed. We have recognized as change the difference observed in comparing similarly defined populations at two points in
time. The populations here are the "eligible mothers" of 1953 and 1971,
that is, women with one or more children under the age of 19 living in
the mother's household. We have not hitherto taken note of the fact
that, even though the time interval is fairly long, 18 years, some Detroit
women were actually in the category of eligible mothers on both dates.
By and large, these women would be found primarily among the
younger mothers at the earlier date and the older mothers at the later
date, of course. But the category of eligible mothers also underwent a
good deal of turnover in the 18 years. A substantial number of women
who were too young to have been mothers in 1953 were eligible in 1971,
while another substantial number who were eligible mothers in 1953
were still mothers (in that they had borne one or more children at some
time in the past) but were no longer eligible in 1971 because the child or
children were all above age 18 or no longer in the home.

These distinctions are formalized to permit the three interyear comparisons offered by Table 12-7. The "new" cohort of eligible mothers in
1971 comprises about 350 women in the 1971 sample who were 20–38
years old and thus too young to have been included in the 1953 survey.
The "overlapping" cohort of eligible mothers comprises about 250
women in the 1971 sample who were 39 years old and over at that time;
many of them would have been eligible in 1953 although some, of
course, had not begun their childbearing at that time. These two

TABLE 12-7
Odds on Responding Both to Child-Task Items, for Eligible Mothers in 1953 and Three
Groups of Mothers in 1971

		Child task			
Year	Population	Walks	Car	Dust	Beds
1971					
	"New" cohort of eligible mothers	1.1	3.0	.60	3.3
	"Overlapping" cohort of eligible mothers	.92	1.7	.59	1.8
	Older mothers no longer eligible	.78	1.5	.45	1.1
1953	Eligible mothers	.51	.44	.49	.87

categories together are the eligible mothers from the 1971 study for which we have presented data earlier in this chapter. The third category of mothers in 1971 comprises those who presumably were, for the most part, eligible in 1953 but were no longer so in 1971; that is, they reported having borne one or more children, but none of their children was living in the household at the time of the 1971 survey. Inclusion of these women enlarges the sample by about 275 respondents. No data concerning them have been shown previously.

Given this classification of the 1971 respondents, it would have made sense to distinguish between those 39 and over and those under age 39 in 1953, paralleling the distinction between "new" and "overlapping" in the later year. However, only about one-tenth of the 1953 sample were 39 and over, and no significant differences between their responses and those of the younger women emerged on any of the items.

The import of Table 12-7 is clear. It makes a difference, particularly for two of our items, Car and Beds, which set of mothers in 1971 is chosen for comparison with the 1953 mothers in assessing the amount of change. Indeed, for all four items we find an invariant ordering of the groups, with the highest odds on responding *both* found among "new" mothers in 1971, followed by the "overlapping" cohort of eligible mothers in the same year, and then by the older mothers at the later date. Except for Dust, the lowest odds occur for the 1953 mothers. Not all these differences are statistically significant, as earlier analyses have disclosed. Nevertheless, the pattern suggests that change in regard to sex typing came about in the 1950s and 1960s in two distinct ways. First, mothers in the earlier year were gradually replaced in the population by women born later who, at a comparable stage in the course of their own lives, were much more prone to reject sex typing in responding to the items Car and Beds, and somewhat so in responding to Walks, although the change for Dust was not significant. Second, the mothers of 1953, as they themselves grew older, changed their ideas measurably, though not drastically, in the same direction. From a quantitative standpoint, the former source—intercohort change—was the one of greater importance. We have not, of course, achieved a very precise estimate of intracohort change, because our broad categories are not completely closed with respect to eligibility, not to mention migration and mortality. Nevertheless, it seems reasonable to assume that comparisons of 1953 with older mothers and with the "overlapping" cohort in 1971 bracket the estimate one might generate if a tighter definition of intracohort change could be employed.

In considerable measure, of course, the data in Table 12-7 recapitulate the results of our analyses of age differentials in response. Our purpose here was to call attention to the cohort interpretation of the life-cycle classification of women. This in turn leads us, with the present data, to the conclusion that the demographic metabolism of the population was the prime source of change in sex typing between 1953 and 1971. We are closer at this point to a legitimate reference for the idea of "generation gap," although we continue to insist that this term be eschewed in the interest of clarity.

In our final variation on the theme of age and change, we return to a detailed age—or better, date-of-birth—classification, merging the 1971 samples without regard to eligibility. That is, the 1971 sample now consists of all women who had ever borne one or more children; the 1953 sample, as before, pertains only to mothers with one or more children under 19 living with them. To effect a cohort match, it was necessary to use non-standard dates of birth. In Figure 12-4, the numerals identify cohorts according to the following code for birth year:

1:	before 1888	8:	1918–1922
2:	1888–1892	9:	1923–1926
3:	1893–1897	10:	1927–1931
4:	1898–1902	11:	1932–1936
5:	1903–1907	12:	1937–1941
6:	1908–1912	13:	1942–1946
7:	1913–1917	14:	1947–1951

Although the birth-year interval varies slightly, the cohort numbers were taken as the regressor values, ignoring the minor error incurred in assuming equal intervals.

To emphasize the shift in point of view, Figure 12-4 is plotted with ascending cohort numbers on the abscissa, so that age groups are in the opposite order from that employed in Figure 12-3. The new convention, of course, is consistent with the idea that birth year rather than age is the significant factor. Reading from left to right, one can see the "wave of the future" emerging in the responses of the more recent cohorts. While our intention is to facilitate such a cohort interpretation of the data, no mere convention of presentation can ensure that this interpretation is correct. We noted earlier that both aging and cohort succession are likely to be involved in the changes here described; and no simple statistical trick will enable us to disentangle them.

Before commenting on the substance of Figure 12-4 we review the evidence supporting the regression summaries of the data. In Table 12-8 we find that the observations for Walks are adequately fitted by a model that includes only a year effect; including cohort or cohort-by-year in the equation does not produce a significant improvement in the fit. For

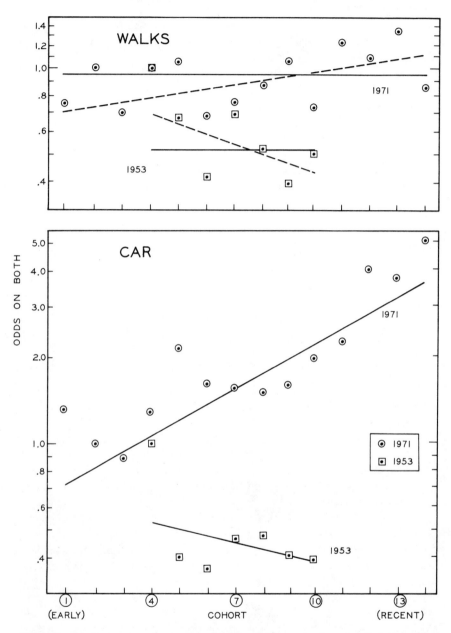

FIGURE 12-4. Regression of response to child-task items on cohort, for eligible mothers in 1953 and expanded sample of mothers in 1971.

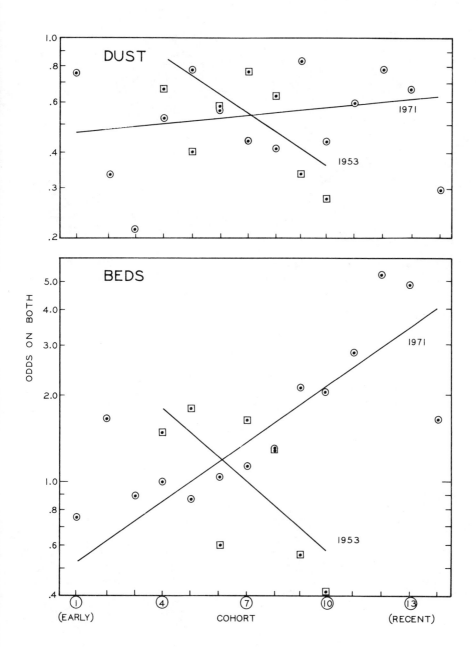

325

TABLE 12-8

Logit Chi-Square Values (Y^2) for Testing Fit of Various Regressions of Responses to Child-Task Items on Cohort and Year, for Eligible Mothers in 1953 and All Mothers in 1971

		Child task			
Independent variables	*df*	Walks	Car	Dust	Beds
(1) Year	19	13.6	—	—	—
(2) Cohort	19	30.8^a	129.3^a	25.4	91.6^a
(3) Year, cohort	18	12.0	14.3	25.1	47.4^a
(4) Year, cohort, year × cohort	17	10.1	10.7	21.5	30.4^a

^{a} $p < .05$ (all others, $p > .1$).

comparison with the other items, however, we show as broken lines the computed regression corresponding to Model (4). For Car, the equation must include both year and cohort; the chi-square value for Model (3) suggests that these variables could come into the equation in a simple additive fashion, in which case the 1953 and 1971 regressions would be parallel. But Model (4), which provides for the year-by-cohort interaction, yields an improvement over Model (3) that is almost significant at the .05 level, and that is the model we have chosen to display in the figure. Similarly, for Dust, Model (4) yields an almost significant improvement over Model (3). The analysis for Dust here comes out quite differently from that suggested by the earlier treatment (Figure 12-3) in terms of age groups. The 1953 and 1971 observations, having been realigned in terms of cohorts, no longer show the rough parallelism that is seen in Figure 12-3. On the cohort interpretation, the picture for Dust is no longer totally unlike that for Car or Beds. The chi-square values for Beds in Table 12-8 leave no doubt that not only year and cohort but also year-by-cohort effects are required in the regression equation. But even Model (4) does not provide a wholly satisfactory fit. It is evident in Figure 12-4 that the points scatter widely around the fitted regression. But since it is not evident that any simple nonlinear function would provide a better representation of the data, we adopt the linear model as a rough description.

To summarize, only by adopting flexible criteria for acceptability of fit can we compel all four items to obey the same regression model, one which forces the relationship of logit response to cohort to be rectilinear but allows the slope of the line to differ in the 2 years. But when this is done, it is interesting that the pattern is the same for all the items: a negative slope in 1953 contrasting with the positive slope in 1971.

Let us suppose that this statistical representation is a roughly veridical account of "how it really happened." A narrative description would then run as follows. New cohorts (cohorts 11–14) entering the population of mothers after 1953 were more likely to reject sex typing than their immediate predecessors (cohorts 7–10) had been in 1953. But the predecessors themselves modified their views over the 18-year period so that their responses in 1971 showed measurably less sex typing than had their earlier responses. Among still older women (cohorts 1–6) changes were inconsistent, depending upon which item is studied. For Car, all cohorts gave fewer sex-typed responses in 1971 than in 1953. For Dust and Beds, however, there was more sex typing among the older cohorts in 1971 than one would have predicted from the regression of response on cohort in 1953. Any inference as to change in these cohorts is exceedingly risky, however, inasmuch as the very earliest cohorts (1–3) are represented only in the 1971 data.

We see no method, other than sheer speculation, for linking the two aspects—intercohort and intracohort—of change. But if speculation be allowed, we would suggest that the intracohort shifts away from sex typing on the part of such cohorts as 7–10 may well have occurred under the influence of the new ideas championed by new cohorts 11–14. Whether or not this suggestion has merit, it is well to recognize that the most problematic aspect of the data may not be the positive regression of response on cohort in the later year, but the negative regression in 1953. Why were the younger women in that year more prone to give sex-typed responses than the older ones? Perhaps we should recall that 1953 was a year in which the national birth rate was near the crest of a long swing running from the low rates of the mid-1930s through the "baby boom" of 1946–1963 back down to the low rates of the early 1970s. The early 1950s, some feminist writers have averred, constituted a retrogression from the standpoint of the sexual liberation movement. Young women were—for whatever reason—preoccupied with childbearing and homemaking; and to them sex typing would have been a "natural" expression of their concept of the female role.

The methods used here—detailed comparative statistical analysis of cross-sectional survey data—are not likely to give us any definitive answer to the question of what the 1953 data really mean, for the simple reason that we have no such data for earlier years. Future repetitions of the questions on sex roles from the 1953 and 1971 studies could, however, tell us whether the 1953–1971 changes lie on a long-term historical trend line extending through the present and later decades.

While awaiting the accumulation of data from post-1971 studies, it may be slightly reassuring to know that the regressions of response on birth year for 1971 just reported for women are quite similar to the corresponding regressions for men. In an analysis employing the full 1971 sample, classified by sex, color, and level of schooling (elementary, high school, and college), we find that there is no significant difference in the slope of the regression of response on birth year between men and women, black and white, or college and high-school respondents, regardless of which of the four child tasks is studied. The one such interaction pertains to the two items, Car and Beds. The form of the interaction is such that for respondents with elementary schooling only the regression of odds on a *both* response on birth year is essentially nil, whereas the regressions for high-school and college educated respondents are much like the one already seen in Figure 12-4. In short, the cohort differences emerge only in that segment of the population with some minimal level of schooling. But since that level of schooling has become virtually universal in the more recent cohorts, the result is a very minor qualification of the one already reported.

POSTSCRIPT: CHANGES TO 1976

After the preceding material was prepared, we received tabulations of the marginal response frequencies, by sex, for the replication of the four items in the 1976 Detroit Area Study. (The tabulations supplied to us involved deletions from the 1976 sample of extra cases secured in over-sampling certain strata for purposes of the 1976 study. It appears that with these deletions the two surveys are quite comparable.)

Figure 12-5 reproduces the 1953–1971 changes for eligible mothers already discussed and adds to them the 1971–1976 changes for all women and all men. The most striking result is an acceleration of the velocity of change. This invites further speculation on the matter of timing. It seems credible that the pace of change was slow during the 1950s but perhaps accelerated slightly in the early 1960s. We suspect that the strong upward trend over the whole period, 1953–1971, especially notable for Car and Beds, actually reflects a more sharply defined acceleration beginning perhaps as late as 1969, with which the 1971–1976 trend is continuous.

A further important observation is that there is no differential change by sex; women and men changed their response distributions to just the same degree over the 5-year period. Thus, the sex differences observed in 1971 also are obtained in 1976. Odds ratios, Women:Men, are estimated at 1.8 for Walks, 1.2 for Car, 1.5 for Dust, and 2.1 for Beds in both years. Although we have not made a formal test of the signifi-

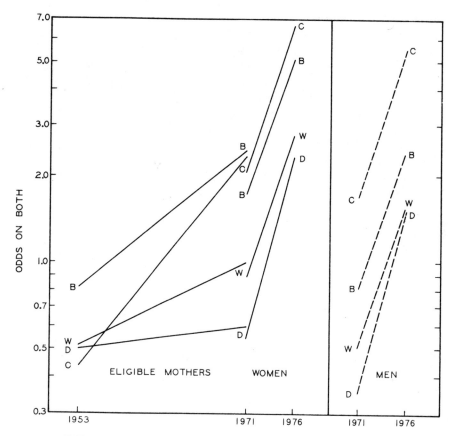

FIGURE 12-5. Changes in response to child-task items, 1953–1976.

cance of these differences among items, it seems unreasonable to attribute them to chance. We conclude that men are most willing to relinquish the male prerogative in regard to washing the car but least willing to accept coordinate responsibility for making the beds. This has not changed within recent years.

We note, finally, that the changes for all items are at about the same rate, with the possible exception of Dust. Odds ratios, 1976:1971, for both men and women are 3.1 for Walks, 3.2 for Car, 4.3 for Dust, and 2.9 for Beds. This approximation to homogeneity in rates of change is in contrast to the pronounced contrasts among the four items in their rapidity of change from 1953 to 1971. In the light of the observations for the most recent five years, we can suggest that Car was in the vanguard of change while Dust lagged. The 1971–1976 period, therefore, wit-

nessed some catching up by Dust; but otherwise the pattern of inter-
item differences held firm—a curious sort of permanence superimposed
on the otherwise fantastically rapid transition.

We have no way to determine whether these changes in the Detroit
area are representative of national changes. However, we can put the
Detroit materials in a national context, with the aid of the data in Figure
12-6. The 1974 Virginia Slims Poll (Roper Organization, n.d.) included
11 items registering "role expectations of children" that are similar to
our Walks, Car, Dust, and Beds. In the figure we graph the log odds on
the response *either* (that is, the designated chore should be performed
by children of either sex) from the sample of women against log odds

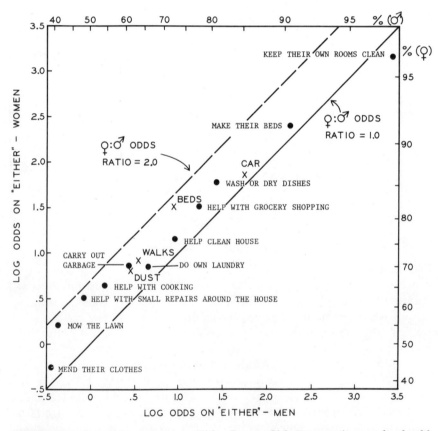

FIGURE 12-6. Log odds on response, "Either Boys or Girls," to question on who should
perform specified household chores, by sex of respondent, 1974 Virginia Slims Poll, and
log odds on *both* for Walks, Car, Dust, and Beds, by sex of respondent, 1976 Detroit Area
Study.

on *either* for the male respondents. For comparison, the graph also includes the 1976 points for Walks, Car, Dust, and Beds in the Detroit-area samples. None of our items is exactly replicated in the Roper list; and differences in results invite speculation about the effects of wording. For example, in the Roper data there is less sex typing for "make their beds" than we find in the Detroit data for "making beds." Our conjecture is that the qualification "their" is interpreted as limiting the chore to the child's own bed and, as some Detroit respondents told us, why not?—they do it in the Army and the Boy Scouts. In any case, the Roper data make it quite clear that prevalence of sex typing is quite item specific, as we had already concluded. Indeed, there is fantastically close agreement between the sexes just how sex typed the items are, in a relative sense: The rank correlation over the 11 items is .989. This does not gainsay the reality of the sex effect on sex typing, which looks much the same in the Roper data (apart from "keep their own rooms clean") as in the Detroit data.

At this point, it may be relevant to recall the trends in sex typing of adult roles suggested by the Woman-for-President item (studied in Chapter 1) and the question on approval of a married woman's gainful employment (Chapters 1 and 3). We detect no change, 1972–1975, in the Woman-for-President item. But it is relevant to note here a finding not reported earlier. There is a strong and approximately linear cohort effect on the response to this question in the General Social Survey data for 1972, 1974, and 1975, such that for each quinquennial increment to birth year the odds on *yes* (would vote for a woman) increase by a factor of $e^{.128} = 1.14$. There is no sex difference, nor does sex interact with cohort. Although there is no significant short-run increase in the odds on *yes* for the general population as a whole, a longer-run increase could be predicted if the currently observed cohort differences persist and if new cohorts come into the population at a level comparable to that of the youngest adults in 1975. As noted in Chapter 3, there has been an increase in approval of a married woman's working, and the change is differentiated by cohort. Although there is a sex effect on response, that effect does not depend on cohort or labor-force status.

It is of interest to see how the two items are related to each other. We compute the odds, *approve : disapprove*, for the Woman-Working item for each category, *yes* or *no*, of the Woman-for-President item, and then the odds ratio, *yes : no*. (A simple transformation of this odds ratio gives the well-known coefficient of association, Yule's Q, which is equivalent to the coefficient "gamma" for a 2 × 2 table.) The data from the 1972, 1974, and 1975 General Social Surveys yield the following estimates of the association between the two items, by sex of respondent.

Year	Men	Women
1972	1.4	1.8
1974	2.1	2.7
1975	8.2	10.8

The sex effect on the ratio is marginally significant. (Difference in X^2 between models without and with this interaction is 3.11, $df = 1$, $p = .08$.) If we accept the estimates as shown, the association between the two items is 1.3 times as large for women as for men in each year. Even more striking, and unmistakably significant, is the increase in the magnitude of the association over the short period of time. In another context, Mason, Czajka, and Arber (1976) present evidence that "women's attitudes toward their roles in the home have become increasingly related to their attitudes toward their rights in the labor market since the rise of the women's movement [p. 593]." The evidence just cited suggests that the trend toward greater consistency of responses to different sex-role questions is not confined to women. Indeed, it may not be peculiar to the area of sex-role attitudes. Nie, Verba, and Petrocik (1976, p. 123) have a chapter on "The Rise of Issue Consistency," in which they claim to demonstrate that "there has been a major increase in the level of attitude consistency within the mass public," with respect to a variety of issues taken to define aspects of liberal–conservative ideology. It would be of interest, though beyond the scope of inquiry, to determine whether sex roles provide just another instance of an issue that conforms to the trend of increasing "attitude constraint" noted by Nie and his collaborators.

Two other questions relating to adult sex roles were treated briefly at the end of Chapter 10. Each of them has been asked in the General Social Survey in only 2 years thus far, 1974 and 1975. It is not so surprising, then, that we detect no recent change. Both questions do, however, show quite strong cohort effects and, interestingly, a sex differential in regard to the cohort effects. Since the findings are parallel, we juxtapose them in Figure 12-7. The model used for both items in this figure allows cohort effects to vary freely, except that they are constrained to follow the same pattern for men and women. Moreover, the Female:Male odds ratio for the odds *disagree:agree* is constrained to vary linearly with cohort. In the case of Politics ("Most men are better suited emotionally for politics than are most women"), we estimate that this odds ratio increases by a factor of 1.055 for each quinquennium of birth year. The comparable figure for Home ("Women should take care of running their homes and leave running the

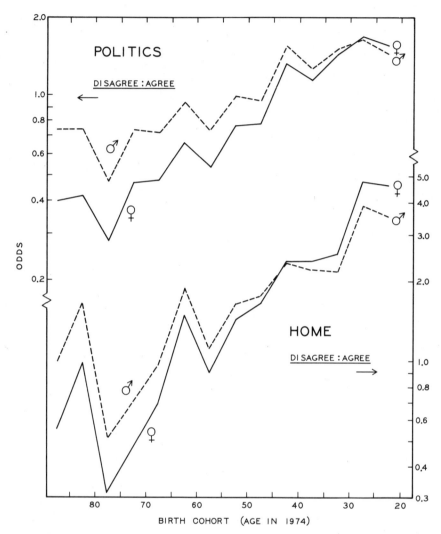

FIGURE 12-7. Odds on *disagree* for two questions on adult sex roles, by sex and cohort, under a model that contains a linear cohort effect on the female:male odds ratio, for national samples, 1974–75.

country up to men") is 1.07. Much the same results are obtained if we simply fit straight lines to the log odds, *disagree : agree*, for men and women separately. There is a pronounced slope for both sexes, but in each case it is greater for women. Once again, although we do not detect short-run change, our cohort differences are prognostic of longer-run changes in the future, barring a reversal of the intercohort trend, of which there is no evidence as yet.

Both the Detroit and the national data examined in this chapter concern symbolic or ideological or normative aspects of sex-role stereotyping, as distinct from actual or "real" or behavioral differences between the sexes. It is entirely possible that change comes more easily when the item has to do with an abstract prescription or norm. After all, despite the trend in proportion who would vote for a woman for president, the country has not yet had a female chief executive. (Somewhat to the opposite effect, however, is the timing of the gains in verbal approval of women working at some lag behind the actual increase in female labor-force participation.) We do not know if the proportion of Detroit teenage girls washing the car or boys dusting furniture has really changed greatly in the last quinquennium, but we doubt if these behaviors have changed as fast as the responses of adults to our questions. When Fairlie (1971) suggested that the cause of Women's Liberation had already been won, he may well have had in mind changes in verbal protestations already observable at that date. Although these changes have continued, we are not entitled to conclude that there has been any revolution in the role of sex in the American social structure.

Appendix A

The purpose of this appendix is to present examples of the kinds of statistical analysis used in this research in some detail so that the interested reader may follow the steps taken in reaching the kinds of conclusions stated in the text. While the examples will serve as an introduction to the statistical techniques, this appendix does not provide a comprehensive or rigorous exposition of the techniques. For that, it is necessary to refer to the cited literature.

EXAMPLE 1: A 2 × 2 TABLE

In Chapter 1 we considered the responses to a question on whether there are some kinds of work women should not have for a subsample of the 1971 sample comprising persons employed as clerical and kindred workers, craftsmen and foremen, and operatives. Table A-1 shows the frequencies (f_{ij}) of the two responses cross-classified by the sex of the respondent, where i stands for either the first or the second row and j for either the first or second column of the table. In the analysis of this table we are interested in two questions. First, do these sample data provide reliable evidence of an association between response and sex in the population from which the sample was drawn? Second, if so, what is our estimate of the magnitude of that association?

   The first question invites a test of the null hypothesis that sex and
response are independent. We must compute the frequencies expected
on the assumption that this hypothesis is true. To do so, we calculate
the marginal frequencies for Table A-1, obtaining $f_{1.} = 349$ men and $f_{2.}$
$= 178$ women (the one-way marginal totals by sex) and $f_{.1} = 368$ *yes* and
$f_{.2} = 159$ *no* responses (the one-way marginal totals by response). The
grand total for the sample is $349 + 178 = 368 + 159 = 527 = f_{..} = n$. We
obtain expected frequencies ($\hat{F}_{ij}$) from the formula $\hat{F}_{ij} = f_{i.}f_{.j}/n$, for example, $\hat{F}_{11} = (349)(368)/(527) = 243.70$, and so on. These are recorded in the
lower panel of Table A-1. Inasmuch as the expected frequencies are
calculated from the one-way marginals and the grand total of the sample, without regard to the observed frequencies in the cells of the table,
we may characterize the expected frequencies as *fitted* frequencies,
making it explicit that in the process of fitting the only information used
is the two sets of one-way marginals. (It is not actually necessary to
stipulate that the grand total is used, since a set of fitted frequencies
that add up to either set of one-way marginals will ipso facto add up to
the grand total.)

   When the expected frequencies are constrained to sum to both the
row and the column marginals, it is clear that only one degree of
freedom remains. As soon as any one cell frequency is assigned a value,
the frequencies in the remaining three cells can be obtained by subtrac-
tion from the given marginals. This analysis yields the same result as
the usual formula for *df* in a two-way contingency table under the
hypothesis of independence of the row and column classifications: $df =$
(rows $-$ 1)(columns $-$ 1).

   The test of the hypothesis may be accomplished with the familiar
chi-square statistic of Karl Pearson, computed as $\Sigma_i\Sigma_j[(f_{ij} - \hat{F}_{ij})^2/\hat{F}_{ij}]$.

TABLE A-1
Response by Sex, Worker Subsample, 1971

Sex	Response Yes	No	Odds, *yes:no*
	Observed frequency		
Men	264	85	3.11
Women	104	74	1.41
	Expected frequency		
Men	243.70	105.30	2.31
Women	124.30	53.70	2.31

We obtain from the data in Table A-1 the chi-square value 16.60 and refer to a table of percentiles of the chi-square distribution for one degree of freedom, which shows that a value this large would occur less than 1 time in 1000 ($p < .001$) in sampling from a population in which the null hypothesis is true. We conclude that the hypothesis should be rejected. Sex and response are not independent; they are associated.

Another way to describe the procedure followed here is to state that our objective is to test the acceptability of a *model* that is specified by mentioning the marginal totals fitted when computing expected frequencies under the model—in this case, the one-way marginals for sex and the one-way marginals for response. Pearson's statistic can then be regarded as a measure of the goodness of fit of the model, and the question being raised is whether the discrepancies between observed and expected frequencies are so great that we must call the model into question. The interpretation of a "significant" value of chi-square is that fluctuations of sampling cannot easily explain the departures of the sample frequencies from the expected frequencies, so that the model is rejected.

The foregoing exposition made use of Pearson's chi-square statistic, because it is presumably familiar. However, in our analyses of two-way and multiway contingency tables we have used instead the likelihood-ratio chi-square statistic, defined by the formula,

$$X^2 = 2\ \Sigma_i\Sigma_j f_{ij} \log \frac{f_{ij}}{\hat{F}_{ij}}$$

where log stands for natural logarithm. For the data in Table A-1 we find $X^2 = 16.20$. The interpretation of this value is just the same as the interpretation of the value of Pearson's statistic. With 1 df, $p < .001$, so that the model under study, or the hypothesis expressed by it, can be rejected with confidence. While Pearson's statistic and the likelihood-ratio statistic need not have the same value, their values are usually quite similar. (According to the statistical theory underlying both statistics, the two are asymptotically equivalent under the null hypothesis and both have, asymptotically, the chi-square distribution under that hypothesis.) While there is no particular reason to prefer the likelihood-ratio statistic for the present problem, in multiway problems it does have the advantage that it can be partitioned exactly whereas Pearson's statistic lacks this property. (A possible advantage of Pearson's statistic for the 2 × 2 case is that it is easily modified to accomplish a "correction for continuity." This correction is not available for X^2; but neither is it required for larger tables.)

Our answer to the first question, in summary, is that we infer an association between sex and response. Turning to the second question, we note that the ratio of the number of *yes* to the number of *no* responses among men is 264/85 = 3.11 and the corresponding ratio for women is 104/74 = 1.41. These are the *observed odds* on responding *yes* for the two sexes, respectively, and serve as estimates of their counterparts in the population that was sampled. Further, we note that the male observed odds is 3.11/1.41 = 2.2 times as large as the female observed odds. The ratio 2.2 is the observed *odds ratio*; it serves to estimate the odds ratio in the population. Its meaning is simply that the odds on *yes* are larger by a factor of 2.2 for men than for women.

It would be equally appropriate to calculate the odds on *no* (they are simply the reciprocals of the odds on *yes*) and/or to calculate the odds ratio as the quotient of the odds for women divided by the odds for men. If we make both these modifications, we get the same value of the odds ratio, 2.2; if we make either one but not the other, we get 1/2.2 = .45. The odds ratio and its reciprocal are regarded as equivalent, inasmuch as the same comparison of odds is effected by either. That is, to state that the male odds is 2.2 times as large as the female odds is the same thing as saying the latter is .45 as large as the former.

As the reader can easily verify, the same odds ratio can be computed in a different manner, that is, by dividing the ratio of men to women among respondents answering *yes* by the ratio of men to women among those responding *no*. Thus, the odds ratio expresses the association of the two variables, sex and response, in a symmetrical way; one need not specify which is the "independent" and which is the "dependent variable" in order to calculate the odds ratio. Readers acquainted with the idea of regression for quantitative variables may see this property of the odds ratio as an undesirable one in a situation, like the present one, where it seems natural to regard one variable (sex) as causal and the other as an effect. We would argue, on the contrary, that the regression model for quantitative variables, although it has a useful analogy here, does not carry over to the extent that the distinction between the regression of Y on X and the regression of X on Y is meaningful. Under close scrutiny the difference between the two regressions hinges on the possibility of defining a residual, $Y - \hat{Y}$, from the regression of Y on X (or $X - \hat{X}$ from the regression of X on Y) such that the residual is uncorrelated with the independent variable in the sample. There is no counterpart to this situation in the case of qualitative variables. (For further discussion of properties of the odds ratio, see Fleiss, 1973.)

To bring out the analogy with regression, let us transform the two observed odds by taking their natural logarithms; then let us estimate the log odds for men as $\hat{Y} = \log(3.11) = 1.135$ and for women as $\hat{Y} = \log(1.41) = .344$. What we have done can be described by the regression-like formula,

$$\hat{Y} = .344 + .791X,$$

where X is a formal variable that assumes the value zero if the respondent is a woman and the value unity if the respondent is a man. The coefficient of $X(.791)$ is the natural logarithm of the odds ratio, whose (rounded) value was just given as 2.2. Thus, there is a very strict sense in which the odds ratio performs the same descriptive function as the regression coefficient performs in the case of quantitative variables.

Let us suppose for the moment that we had found it possible to accept the hypothesis of independence, that is, to accept the model described by the procedure of fitting the two sets of one-way marginals. In that event, it would be appropriate to estimate the odds on *yes* from the fitted frequencies; and we see (lower panel, Table A-1) that the estimates for men and women would be identical. The odds ratio in that event would be 1.0. Since the logarithm of unity is zero, this case is exactly parallel to that of a zero regression coefficient, the meaning of which is that the dependent variable is unrelated to the independent variable.

EXAMPLE 2: A THREE-WAY TABLE

The upper panel of Table A-2 is the $2 \times 2 \times 2$ contingency table obtained when response is classified not only by sex but simultaneously by sex and color of respondent. We note that Table A-1 provides one set of two-way marginal totals for Table A-2, to wit, the response-by-sex marginals, abbreviated {RS}. There are two other sets of two-way marginals, {RC} (response by color) and {SC} (sex by color). There are also three sets of one-way marginals, {R}, {S}, and {C}. We shall consider alternative models for the data in Table A-2. Our aim is to ascertain whether and to what extent, sex, color, both factors separately, or the two jointly affect response. We would prefer to represent any such effects by a model that is as parsimonious as possible. Thus, the generic questions raised here are the same as in the previous example. But the situation is complicated by the presence of two potential factors affecting response in place of just one. Hence we must systematically examine a variety of possible patterns of effects.

Following Goodman (1972a, 1972b) we will specify models by listing the sets of marginals fitted. Table A-3 lists the four models to be

TABLE A-2
Response by Sex and Color, Worker Subsample, 1971

Color	Sex	Response		Odds, *yes:no*	Log odds	Percentage *yes*
		Yes	No			
		Observed frequency				
Black	Men	81	13	6.23	1.829	86.2
	Women	25	22	1.14	.131	53.2
White	Men	183	72	2.54	.932	71.8
	Women	79	52	1.52	.419	60.3
		Expected frequency, Model (2)				
Black	Men	71.11	22.89	3.11	1.135	75.6
	Women	27.46	19.54	1.41	.344	58.4
White	Men	192.89	62.11	3.11	1.135	75.6
	Women	76.54	54.46	1.41	.344	58.4
		Expected frequency, Model (3)				
Black	Men	70.67	23.33	3.03	1.109	75.2
	Women	35.33	11.67	3.03	1.109	75.2
White	Men	173.08	81.92	2.11	.747	67.9
	Women	88.92	42.08	2.11	.747	67.9
		Expected frequency, Model (4)				
Black	Men	75.52	18.48	4.09	1.409	80.3
	Women	30.48	16.52	1.85	.615	64.9
White	Men	188.48	66.52	2.83	1.040	73.9
	Women	73.52	57.48	1.28	.247	56.1

considered. Other models for the three-way table could be entertained, but they would not be relevant to our immediate purpose. We consider only models including the two-way marginals {SC}. That is, we take as given an association of sex and color. In point of fact, that association is virtually nil in the sample with which we are working. Since we are not interested in investigating it, however, we may as well take for granted whatever association there is. The models differ, therefore, only in regard to how the response variable enters.

In Model (1) we fit only the one-way marginals {R} in addition to {SC}. In effect, we are regarding the table not as a three-way contingency table but as a two-way table with four rows and two columns. The four

TABLE A-3
Likelihood-Ratio Chi-Square Values and Degrees of Freedom for Selected Models Fitted to Data in Top Panel of Table A-2

Model	Marginals fitted	*df*	X^2	*p*
(1)	$\{R\}, \{SC\}$	3	25.32	<.01
(2)	$\{RS\}, \{SC\}$	2	9.12	<.01
(3)	$\{RC\}, \{SC\}$	2	22.64	<.01
(4)	$\{RC\}, \{RS\}, \{SC\}$	1	6.44	<.025
Differences				
$X^2(H_1) - X^2(H_2)$		1	16.20	<.01
$X^2(H_1) - X^2(H_3)$		1	2.68	>.1
$X^2(H_2) - X^2(H_4)$		1	2.68	>.1
$X^2(H_3) - X^2(H_4)$		1	16.20	<.01

rows pertain to the joint variable, sex-by-color, which functions in Model (1) just like a single variable with four classes. Model (1), therefore, expresses the hypothesis that response is independent of the joint variable, sex-by-color. This hypothesis can be tested in the same fashion that we tested the hypothesis of independence in the two-way table of Example 1, with the modification that a two-way table with four rows and two columns has $(4 - 1)(2 - 1) = 3$ *df*. Actual frequencies are compared with frequencies expected under the hypothesis by means of the likelihood-ratio chi-square statistic, $X^2 = 2 \Sigma f \log (f/\hat{F})$, the formula given earlier. As Table A-3 shows, we decisively reject the hypothesis in this case. Model (1) does not provide a satisfactory fit.

Model (2) calls for fitting the two-way marginals $\{RS\}$ in addition to $\{SC\}$. We shall not provide the formula that describes how this fitting is accomplished (although it is not a complicated one), nor shall we explain how to carry out the arithmetic, since that step is taken care of by a computer program. But, since the second panel of Table A-2 shows the expected frequencies under Model (2), it is easy to verify that they do fit in the prescribed fashion. With reference to the fitting of $\{SC\}$ we note that the expected total of black men is $71.11 + 22.89 = 94.00$ in agreement with the observed total (= $81 + 13$); and the same is true of the totals for black women, white men, and white women. Moreover, with reference to the fitting of $\{RS\}$ we note that the expected total of men responding *yes* agrees with the observed total of men responding *yes*: $71.11 + 192.89 = 81 + 183 = 264$. Similarly, expected and observed totals of women responding *yes* are the same, $27.46 + 76.54 = 25 + 79 = 104$; and so on. Thus, the analyst need not be completely at the mercy of the computer. It is a matter of simple arithmetic to verify that the marginal totals that were supposed to have been fitted were actually fitted. Knowing this, one could even reconstruct from the fitted frequencies what model was specified, if this information were lost! We can determine, for example, that Model (2) does not fit {RC}, since the expected total of blacks saying *yes*, $71.11 + 27.46 = 98.57$, is not the same as the corresponding observed total, $81 + 25 = 106$.

Another way to describe Model (2) is to state the hypothesis that it expresses. This hypothesis is that response and color are *conditionally* independent, given sex. That is, among men, response and color are independent; *and*, among women, response and color are independent. The reader should verify that if the 2×2 table, color by response, for men only, is extracted from the top panel of Table A-2 and the expected frequencies on the hypothesis of independence are computed, they will agree with the expected frequencies for the corresponding cells in the second panel of Table A-2; and if the same is done for the 2×2 table, color by response, for women, the same sort of agreement will be seen.

Still a third way to describe Model (2) is to state the substantive relationship implied by the model. Response is taken to be related to sex but not, *directly*, to color, so that if sex is "held constant," or one "partials on" sex, any relationship of response to color that may have appeared when the factor of sex was ignored will vanish in the subtables obtained by "partialling."

We note that Model (2) does not provide a satisfactory fit, in view of the significant size of X^2. We cannot conclude that response and color are independent within classes of the variable, sex.

Our treatment of Model (3) can be quite brief, inasmuch as it takes the same form as Model (2), with the positions of sex and color being interchanged. That is, Model (3) asserts that response is related to color but not, directly, to sex. It represents the hypothesis of conditional independence of response and sex, given color. For the present data, this model, too, must be rejected (see X^2 in Table A-3).

The three models considered thus far can all be described by using either the concept of independence, as in the case of Model (1), or the concept of conditional independence, as in the case of Model (2) or Model (3). We now encounter, with Model (4), a model that cannot be described in terms of the concepts independence and conditional independence. Models (1), (2), and (3) are said to correspond to certain *elementary* hypotheses, whereas Model (4) corresponds to a certain *nonelementary* hypothesis, the hypothesis of no three-way interaction among the variables response, sex, and color. We will shortly make the meaning of this hypothesis more explicit.

Model (4) is characterized in Table A-3 by the fact that it requires the fitting of three sets of two-way marginal totals. It is not possible to give a closed-form formula for carrying out the computation required by this specification. Instead, it is necessary to resort to a procedure called iterative scaling or iterative proportional fitting (Fienberg, 1970). It is feasible, though very tedious, to carry out the computations by hand, but a computer can do them expeditiously. Again, even if the process by which the computer obtains the expected frequencies under a nonelementary hypothesis is mysterious, it is easy to verify that the fitted frequencies do agree with the observed frequencies in regard to the specified marginal totals. (Verification of this condition for the last panel of Table A-2 is suggested as an exercise for the reader.) Sometimes it is important to make this check. Since the calculation is iterative, there is the possibility that the computer did not go through enough cycles of computation to achieve satisfactory agreement (within errors of rounding in, say, the second decimal place) of expected and observed marginal totals. (The remedy is to instruct the computer to carry out more rounds of calculation.)

We have seen how expected frequencies under each of the four models are computed and have noted that the statistic X^2 is used to measure the discrepancy between the actual and the expected frequencies. To evaluate this discrepancy, we must refer to the appropriate chi-square distribution, which is a function of the number of degrees of freedom. In connection with each model, therefore, we must know how to calculate df, unless we are willing to leave that step to the computer. In fact, in this research we frequently encountered problems of a kind for which the computer program was not designed to calculate degrees of freedom. Hence, an understanding of the principle involved is not merely of theoretical interest.

The general method for calculating df is to note, first, the number of cells for which expected frequencies are to be computed and, second, to subtract from it the number of *independent* constraints imposed on the expected frequencies in fitting the specified marginals. With reference to Model (1), we note that fitting {R} amounts to the imposition of two constraints, since there are two response categories. Fitting {SC} involves four constraints, since there are four categories of sex-by-color. We must not, however, conclude that $4 + 2 = 6$ independent constraints have been imposed, inasmuch as both the one-way marginals {R} and the two-way marginals {SC} are themselves constrained to have the same sum, the sample total.

To avoid the error of double counting—that is, including in the count some constraints that are not independent—it is best to think of the fitting process as though it proceeded in a hierarchical manner. When we fit any set of marginals we thereby fit the sample total, since a set of marginal totals must always sum to n. Moreover, when we fit any set of two-way marginals (for example, {SC}) we thereby fit the one-way marginals for each of the two variables (in this example, {S} and {C}). Let us suppose, therefore, that we first fit the sample total, n, then each of the one-way marginals that will ultimately be fitted, then each of the two-way marginals, and so on. In the case of Model (1), we first fit n, then the one-way marginals {R}, {S}, and {C} in turn; and finally the two-way marginals {SC}. Fitting the sample total (n) imposes one constraint. Fitting {R}, while it imposes two constraints, one for each category of response, imposes only one *additional* constraint, since the one-way response marginals themselves must sum to n. Similarly, fitting {S} imposes only one *additional* constraint; and fitting {C} imposes just one more. Finally, although fitting {SC} imposes four constraints, only one of them is independent of those already fitted, since the marginals of sex-by-color are themselves constrained to sum to the sample total, to the one-way marginals for sex, and to the one-way marginals for color. Altogether, therefore, we count as independent constraints 1 (for sample total) + 1 (for response) + 1 (for sex) + 1 (for color) + 1 (for sex-by-color) = 5. Hence, recalling that we are computing expected frequencies for eight cells, $df = 8 - 5 = 3$. This agrees with the result obtained earlier, where we made use of the special formula for the two-way table, $df = $ (rows $-$ 1)(columns $-$ 1).

Going on to Model (2), we note that it is hierarchical to Model (1), in that in Model (2) we fit all the constraints of Model (1) and something more. The additional constraint in Model (2) is imposed when we fit {RS}. But this accounts for only one independent constraint, since we have already allowed for the constraints imposed in fitting {R} and {S}. Thus we compute for Model (2) $df = 3 - 1 = 2$, that is, df for Model (1) diminished by the one additional constraint imposed in fitting Model (2).

On the same reasoning, Model (3) is hierarchical to Model (1), and fitting {RC} involves the imposition of just 1 additional constraint; hence, $df = 3 - 1 = 2$.

Model (4) is hierarchical to both Models (2) and (3), as well as Model (1). If we begin with the 2 df for Model (2) we note that fitting {RC} for Model (4) imposes just 1 more constraint, so that $df = 2 - 1$. Or, beginning with Model (3) and its 2 df, we find that Model (4) fits in addition the marginals {RS} and that this involves just 1 additional constraint; again, $df = 2 - 1 = 1$.

The principle of hierarchy in regard to fitting and the calculation of df carries over in a useful way to the matter of comparing alternative models. When the models are hierarchical, in the sense that one fits everything that the other does and also something more, the former will have the larger number of *df* and its X^2 will also be larger (or, in any case, no smaller) than the X^2 for the latter. We may then compute the difference between the X^2s and the degrees of freedom; and that difference itself may be regarded as a chi-square statistic. For example, in Table A-3 $X^2(H_1) - X^2(H_2) = 16.20$ with $3 - 2 = 1$ *df*. This is, of course, a significant value. Its meaning is that, in including in Model (2) the requirement that we fit $\{RS\}$ in addition to the marginals fitted in Model (1), we secure a significant improvement in the goodness of fit of our model. The reason is that response and sex are not independent as Model (1) takes them to be. In fact, in Example 1 we tested that very hypothesis and obtained $X^2 = 16.20$, $df = 1$, exactly the same value as we have now obtained by making a hierarchical comparison in the three-way context. The equivalence is not coincidental, for exactly the same hypothesis is being tested in each case.

The second difference in Table A-3, $X^2(H_1) - X^2(H_3)$, is only 2.68 with 1 *df*, not a significant value. We do not significantly improve the fit of Model (1) by specifying the additional relationship of response to color. In the light of the preceding paragraph, we may also interpret $X^2 = 2.68$ as the appropriate statistic for testing the hypothesis that response and color are independent (sex being ignored). With 1 *df*, $p > .1$, so that the hypothesis of independence cannot be rejected on this evidence. (We shall shortly observe, nevertheless, that it would be wrong to ignore color in identifying the factors in response.)

· The last two hierarchical comparisons in Table A-3 answer the question of whether Model (4) has a significantly superior fit by comparison with Models (2) and (3) respectively. We find that including $\{RC\}$ in Model (4) does not result in a significant improvement over Model (2), but that including $\{RS\}$ does produce a significant improvement over Model (3). It will be noted that in this particular analysis apparently $X^2(H_2) - X^2(H_4) = X^2(H_1) - X^2(H_3)$ and $X^2(H_3) - X^2(H_4) = X^2(H_1) - X^2(H_2)$. These equalities are only approximate, however, and do not hold beyond the second decimal place. More important, *these equalities do not hold in general*. The reason why they seem to hold in this illustration is that sex and color, as noted previously, are virtually independent; but it is rare in survey data (though not in experimental data) for two factors to be independent.

What do we make of these results? We have not yet commented on the fact that none of Models (1), (2), (3), and (4) affords a satisfactory fit to the data, even though some fit significantly better than others. In particular, Model (4), which corresponds to the hypothesis of no three-way interaction, must be rejected. Since Model (4) is hierarchical to each of the other models, if H_4 (no three-way interaction) must be rejected, none of them can be accepted either. We conclude that these data describe a population in which there is a three-way interaction of response by sex by color. To clarify the substantive meaning of this conclusion, we review the several models one last time.

If Model (1) were accepted, or H_1 was held to be true, the odds on a *yes* response would be taken to be the same for each of the four combinations of sex by color; and we would estimate that odds from the marginal totals for response, 368 *yes* to 159 *no* or 2.31 (compare expected odds in Table A-1). The last three panels of Table A-2, third column, show odds on *yes* for Models (2), (3), and (4), respectively. We see that Model (2) incorporates a sex effect, estimated by the odds ratio 3.11/1.41 = 2.2 (compare Table A-1), but no color effect, since the same odds are obtained for white and black men and for white and black women. Model (3) includes a color effect, estimated by the black : white ratio of 3.03/2.11 = 1.4, but no sex effect, since white men and women have the same odds, and black men and women also have the same odds.

Model (4) includes both a sex effect and a color effect. Among blacks, the sex effect is estimated by the ratio 4.09/1.85 = 2.2; among whites it is estimated as 2.83/1.28= 2.2. The agreement of these two estimates (within errors of rounding) is *not* a coincidence; it is required by the nature of the model. The agreement of these estimates of the sex effect with the estimate obtained from Model (2) *is* a coincidence and will not ordinarily be observed. (The reason why it happens here has already been mentioned—that sex and color are hardly associated in our sample.) We also have two estimates of the color effect, 4.09/2.83 = 1.4 among men, and 1.85/1.28 = 1.4 among women. Again, this agreement (within errors of rounding) is imposed by the model. But the close similarity to the estimate of the color effect obtained from Model (3) is an accidental feature of this particular set of data.

The property of Model (4) that the sex effects for blacks and whites are the same and color effects are the same among men and women is the essence of the hypothesis of no three-way interaction. Another way to state this property of Model (4) is to remark that this model allows for *separate* effects of the two factors, sex and color. Hence, in describing the sex effect it is not necessary to mention which color category is under consideration; and in describing the color effect, it is understood to hold for the two sexes alike. But it is precisely this property of the model that leads to a poor fit with the particular data under study here. Let us examine the observed odds in the third column of the first panel of Table A-2. Among blacks the sex effect is estimated at 6.23/1.14 = 5.5

while among whites it is only 2.54/1.52 = 1.7. Such a discrepancy conceivably could be attributed to sampling error, but we have already assured ourselves that this is not the case here, since H_4 (which we have rejected) implies that these two ratios are estimates of the same ratio in the population. Alternatively, we may estimate the color effect either for men or for women; we find that for men it is 6.23/2.54 = 2.5 but for women it is 1.14/1.52 = .75. Again, rejection of H_4 is tantamount to rejecting the hypothesis that this discrepancy is attributable to sampling variation.

The odds under Model (4) and those computed from the observed frequencies so as to estimate the three-way interaction are shown graphically in Figure A-1. Plotting the odds is recommended, not only for the presentation of results but also as a major aid to the analyst in grasping the relationships implied by the models under consideration. Actually, the figure offers two alternative representations of the same results. In the left-hand panel the regression of log-odds on *yes* is

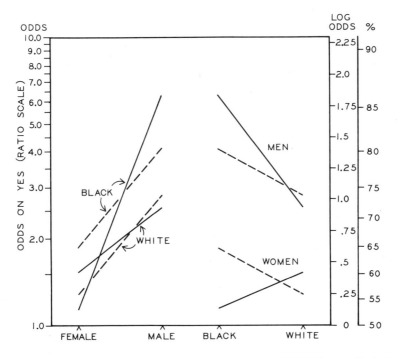

FIGURE A-1. Observed odds (solid line) and odds under model (4) (broken line), from Table A-2.

shown for blacks and whites. Under Model (4) the two regressions are constrained to be parallel and the vertical distance between them represents the separate color effect. In contrast, the three-way interaction shows that the regression is more pronounced for blacks than for whites, corresponding to the greater magnitude of the sex effect in the former subpopulation. From the point of view of the sex effect, however, we might term the three-way interaction a "benign" interaction in the sense that the *direction* of the sex effect is the same for blacks and whites. Indeed, if there were urgent need for a single odds ratio to represent the sex effect, we could resort to the one computed under Model (4), on the understanding that it averages (in a sense) the two distinct sex effects.

The right-hand panel shows the regression of response on color for men and women separately. We see that from this point of view we are dealing with a "vicious" rather than a "benign" interaction, inasmuch as the very direction of the color effect for men is the reverse of the direction among women. Model (4), of course, cannot cope with this reversal. It "averages" the two effects, yielding a result that resembles the color effect among men more than the color effect among women, since the former is the stronger effect and men outnumber women in the sample. But we really cannot accept the notion of a single color effect. The earlier analysis showed that if sex is ignored there is no significant color effect. The opposite effects for men and women almost cancel out. The essence of three-way interaction is that it is meaningless to discuss sex effect and color effect as though they can be described separately—the idea of separate sex and color effects is captured, rather, by Model (4). With three-way interaction, on the contrary, we have to deal with *joint* effects of sex and color.

Let us see how the joint effects may be expressed algebraically in a regression-like formula. Suppose we define formal variables X_1 and X_2 such that $X_1 = 0$ for black respondents and $X_1 = 1$ for white; similarly, $X_2 = 0$ if the respondent is female and 1 if male. There are four possible combinations of values of these two variables $(0, 0)$, $(0, 1)$, $(1, 0)$, and $(1, 1)$. For each of them we have a different odds on *yes*. Let $\hat{Y}$ be the value of the log-odds on *yes* expected for each combination of the independent variables. We may write,

$$\hat{Y} = a + b_1 X_1 + b_2 X_2 + b_3 X_1 X_2$$

The tabulation that follows shows how the combination of independent variables yields the appropriate $\hat{Y}$, applying this formula:

Color	Sex	X_1	X_2	$\hat{Y}$
Black	Men	0	1	$\log(6.23) = a + b_2$
Black	Women	0	0	$\log(1.14) = a$
White	Men	1	1	$\log(2.54) = a + b_1 + b_2 + b_3$
White	Women	1	0	$\log(1.52) = a + b_1$

The values of $\log(6.23)$ etc. are shown in Table A-2. It is an easy step to solve for $a = .131$; $b_1 = .419 - a = .288$; $b_2 = 1.829 - a = 1.698$; and $b_3 = .932 - a - b_1 - b_2 = -1.185$. A further derivation from the general regression formula is the set of equations corresponding to the lines as plotted in Figure A-1. For the right-hand panel we note that when $X_2 = 0$, $\hat{Y} = a + b_1X_1$ and when $X_2 = 1$, $\hat{Y} = (a + b_2) + (b_1 + b_3) X_1$. The reader may verify that these are the two solid lines in the figure. For the left-hand panel the same kind of algebra shows that when $X_1 = 0$, $\hat{Y} = a + b_2X_2$ and when $X_1 = 1$, $\hat{Y} = (a + b_1) + (b_2 + b_3)X_2$.

The reader should repeat the exercise carried out in the preceding paragraph, using the odds under Model (4) in place of the observed odds. It will be found that the value of b_3 is zero (within errors of rounding). In other words, the regression equation for Model (4) is simply $\hat{Y} = a + b_1X_1 + b_2X_2$. It is, therefore, the product term X_1X_2 that captures the three-way interaction or that conveys the nature of the *joint* effects of sex and color when such an interaction obtains.

Let us take the antilog of both sides of our regression equation. We find that we can write the expected odds on *yes* (that is, the antilog of $\hat{Y}$) as

$$\text{Odds on } yes = c_0c_1c_2c_3$$

where

$c_0 = e^a$ (that is, antilog of a)
$c_1 = $ antilog b_1X_1 (that is, $c_1 = 1$ when $X_1 = 0$ and e^{b_1} when $X_1 = 1$)
$c_2 = $ antilog b_2X_2 (that is, $c_2 = 1$ when $X_2 = 0$ and e^{b_2} when $X_2 = 1$)
$c_3 = $ antilog $b_3X_1X_2$ (that is, $c_3 = 1$ when either $X_1 = 0$ or $X_2 = 0$ and $c_3 = e^{b_3}$ when $X_1 = X_2 = 1$).

The cs, therefore, provide a formula stated in terms of multipliers that yield the expected odds when values of X_1 and X_2 (that is, categories of sex-by-color) are specified. Of course, the expected odds are already known. Hence, if we like we can calculate the multipliers. For example, the odds in the third column of the first panel of Table A-2 are given by the formulas

$$6.23 = c_0 c_2$$
$$1.14 = c_0$$
$$2.54 = c_0 c_1 c_2 c_3$$
$$1.52 = c_0 c_1$$

suppressing the c when it takes the value unity. From the foregoing, we obtain $c_0 = 1.14$, $c_1 = 1.52/1.14 = 1.33$, $c_2 = 6.23/1.14 = 5.46$, and $c_3 = 2.54/c_0 c_1 c_2 = .307$. A tabulation of our results follows:

	c_0	c_1	c_2	c_3	Product
Black men	1.14	1.0	5.46	1.0	6.23
Black women	1.14	1.0	1.0	1.0	1.14
White men	1.14	1.33	5.46	0.307	2.54
White women	1.14	1.33	1.0	1.0	1.52

These exercises with the different ways of conveying the results are presented in the hope that going through them will yield a deeper understanding of the models we are working with. Evidently, from a purely mathematical point of view there is no reason to prefer the logarithmic to the multiplicative version of the regression or vice versa. Indeed, there is usually no reason to make either version wholly explicit, since the gist of the results is captured in one or a few odds or odds ratios or by the configuration of points plotted on a graph.

A final comment concerns the choice of scale. It is a matter of indifference whether we plot odds on a ratio scale (left-hand scale, Figure A-1) or log-odds on an arithmetic scale (see "log-odds" scale, Figure A-1). Our algebraic exercises have shown that the meaning of the two plots is exactly the same. A more serious issue arises, however, if one considers the possibility of plotting the percentage making a given response instead of the odds or log-odds on that response. It is, of course, possible to convert odds to percentages or vice versa; thus, 80% corresponds to the odds $.8/.2 = 4.0$ and the odds 3.0 corresponds to $3/(3 + 1) = 3/4 = 75\%$. The transformation from log-odds to percentage or vice versa is not a linear one. However, it is *approximately* linear in the range 30–70% or even 25–75%. But if our percentages stray outside this range, this is no longer true (compare the two right-hand scales of Figure A-1). The consequence is that a model which has no three-way interaction when formulated in terms of odds or log-odds will appear to have such an interaction in terms of differences between percentages. Consider the expected odds, expected log-odds, and expected percentages under Model (4), in the three right-hand columns of Table A-2. The odds ratios, Men:Women, are the same for blacks and whites, 4.09/1.85

= 2.83/1.28 = 2.2; and the differences in the respective log-odds are the same, 1.409 − .615 = 1.040 − .247 = .793 (neglecting rounding error). But the percentage-point differences are not the same, 80.3 − 64.9 = 15.4 while 73.9 − 56.1 = 17.8.

It is, of course, possible to formulate models that show no three-way interaction in terms of percentages. Such models, however, run into "ceiling effects" or "floor effects" that make them substantively implausible when the response is one given by a very large majority or a very small minority. Statistical inference for such models, moreover, is not so straightforward as it is for the models discussed here.

EXAMPLE 3: A FOUR-WAY TABLE

Most of the principles involved in the analysis of four-way and higher dimensional tables (when only one variable is regarded as the response variable and the others are factors in response) have already been illustrated in the preceding example. Consequently, we can go into less detail here. Our example is obtained by introducing still another cross-classification of the data already scrutinized. Table A-4 shows response tabulated by sex, color, and union status simultaneously. The new variable, unlike those considered hitherto, is a polytomy; that is, it has

TABLE A-4
Response by Union Status, Sex, and Color, Worker Subsample, 1971

Union status	Color	Sex	Response frequency		Odds, *yes : no*			
			Yes	No	Observed	Model (12)	Model (14)	Model (16)
UAW	Black	Men	48	5	9.60	8.03	10.57	11.10
		Women	3	0	*a*	1.97	6.14	3.84
	White	Men	69	23	3.00	3.65	3.39	3.32
		Women	10	2	5.00	2.60	1.98	2.23
Other	Black	Men	23	3	7.67	5.03	3.89	4.82
		Women	6	6	1.00	1.23	2.26	1.65
	White	Men	59	27	2.19	2.28	2.33	2.25
		Women	15	9	1.67	1.63	1.36	1.51
None	Black	Men	10	5	2.00	4.32	1.80	2.61
		Women	16	16	1.00	1.05	1.05	.90
	White	Men	55	22	2.50	1.96	2.36	2.17
		Women	54	41	1.32	1.40	1.37	1.45

a Odds not defined (zero denominator).

more than two categories. We shall find that this extension is easily handled when the polytomy is a factor. Even when it is a response variable the extension is feasible, albeit somewhat messy. In either case, appropriate modifications in the calculation of degrees of freedom are necessary. The three categories of union status are UAW member, member of any other union, and not a union member.

To exhaust the possibilities, it is necessary to consider a much larger number of models for the four-way table than were entertained for the three-way table. Any one or any pair or all three of the factors may affect response; and the effects may be joint or separate. Altogether there are 18 models (those listed in Table A-5) that are available to represent all possible combinations of these possibilities.

Model (1) expresses the hypothesis that response is independent of the joint variable, sex-by-color-by-union status. In effect this hypothesis regards Table A-4 as a two-way table and states that the row and column classifications of this table are independent. This model, of course, is rejected in view of the large X^2. Models (2) through (8) allow some one, some pair, or all three factors to affect response (directly); but where two or all three factors are relevant, the effects are taken to be separate. In all the remaining models, (9) through (18), there are joint effects of one, two, or three pairs of factors. In the case of Models (12), (13), and (14), there is a joint effect of one pair of factors and a separate effect of the third factor.

Only a few of the models correspond to elementary hypotheses. Model (1) has already been characterized in terms of the hypothesis of independence. Model (2) hypothesizes that response and the joint variable, color-by-union status, are conditionally independent, given (partialling on, within categories of) sex. Models (3) and (4) are of that same form but with the variables permuted. Model (9) corresponds to the hypothesis that response is conditionally independent of union status, given the joint variable sex-by-color. Models (10) and (11) are of this same form with the variables permuted. All the remaining models listed in Table A-5 correspond to nonelementary hypotheses. Model (18), for example, since it calls for fitting all possible sets of three-way marginals, embodies the hypothesis of no four-way interaction. We note that there is no difficulty in accepting this hypothesis for the present data, since $X^2(H_{18}) = 2.64$, $df = 2$.

Calculation of degrees of freedom follows the principle already stated in connection with the three-way table. In the present example, it is expedient to begin with df for Model (1), obtained as $(12 - 1)(2 - 1) = 11$, in view of the correspondence of Model (1) to the hypothesis of independence for a certain two-way table. We then note the number of

TABLE A-5
Statistics for Various Models Fitted to the Data in Table A-4

Model	Marginals fitted	df	X^2	p
(1)	$\{SCU\}, \{R\}$	11	38.45	<.01
(2)	$\{SCU\}, \{RS\}$	10	22.25	.01
(3)	$\{SCU\}, \{RC\}$	10	35.77	<.01
(4)	$\{SCU\}, \{RU\}$	9	20.94	.01
(5)	$\{SCU\}, \{RS\}, \{RC\}$	9	19.56	.02
(6)	$\{SCU\}, \{RS\}, \{RU\}$	8	14.51	.07
(7)	$\{SCU\}, \{RC\}, \{RU\}$	8	19.64	.01
(8)	$\{SCU\}, \{RS\}, \{RC\}, \{RU\}$	7	12.80	.08
(9)	$\{SCU\}, \{RSC\}$	8	13.13	.11
(10)	$\{SCU\}, \{RSU\}$	6	12.32	.06
(11)	$\{SCU\}, \{RCU\}$	6	12.80	.046
(12)	$\{SCU\}, \{RSC\}, \{RU\}$	6	7.61	.27
(13)	$\{SCU\}, \{RSU\}, \{RC\}$	5	10.25	.07
(14)	$\{SCU\}, \{RCU\}, \{RS\}$	5	6.81	.24
(15)	$\{SCU\}, \{RSC\}, \{RSU\}$	4	4.96	.29
(16)	$\{SCU\}, \{RSC\}, \{RCU\}$	4	5.30	.26
(17)	$\{SCU\}, \{RSU\}, \{RCU\}$	3	3.85	.28
(18)	$\{SCU\}, \{RSC\}, \{RSU\}, \{RCU\}$	2	2.64	.27

Differences

	df	X^2	p
$X^2(H_8) - X^2(H_{12})$	1	5.19	<.05
$X^2(H_8) - X^2(H_{13})$	2	2.55	>.25
$X^2(H_8) - X^2(H_{14})$	2	5.99	.05
$X^2(H_9) - X^2(H_{12})$	2	5.52	<.1
$X^2(H_{11}) - X^2(H_{14})$	1	5.99	<.05
$X^2(H_{12}) - X^2(H_{15})$	2	2.65	>.25
$X^2(H_{12}) - X^2(H_{16})$	2	2.31	>.25
$X^2(H_{12}) - X^2(H_{18})$	4	4.97	>.25
$X^2(H_{14}) - X^2(H_{16})$	1	1.51	>.1
$X^2(H_{14}) - X^2(H_{17})$	2	2.96	>.1
$X^2(H_{14}) - X^2(H_{18})$	3	4.17	>.1

additional constraints involved in fitting the other models, all of which are hierarchical to Model (1). Fitting Model (2) requires imposition of only one more constraint when we fit $\{RS\}$ inasmuch as Model (1) already involved fitting $\{R\}$ and $\{S\}$. But Model (4) has two more constraints than Model (1) because there are three categories of union status. When fitting $\{RU\}$, having already fit $\{R\}$ and $\{U\}$, we are imposing two additional constraints.

Expected frequencies under each of the models are obtained with a computer program that uses the method of iterative scaling. The program also computes the likelihood-ratio chi-square statistic (X^2) that measures the extent to which the observed frequencies deviate from those expected under the model. A first step in deciding which models merit close scrutiny is to note the p-value; it tells us how frequently chi-square would equal or exceed the obtained X^2 if the null hypothesis were true. In this research we have ordinarily not regarded models with $p < .05$ as acceptable from the point of view of goodness of fit. Indeed, unless there is no plausible alternative model, we are loath to adopt a model that yields $p < .1$. These are, of course, only arbitrary rules. Researchers working with sample sizes quite different from ours might prefer different critical p-values from these. In any event, this criterion suggests that we might concentrate on Models (9), (12), and (14) through (18) as possible structures for these data. But our inspection of these models may be aided somewhat by hierarchical comparisons involving still other models.

Comparing Models (1) and (2) gives us the same information about the sex effect (ignoring color and union status) that we obtained from Table A-3; and the comparison of Models (1) and (3) recapitulates what we learned from that table about the effect of color (ignoring sex and union status). In the same fashion we may compare Models (1) and (4); the difference in X^2s is 17.51 with 2 df. Thus, union status (ignoring sex and color) has a highly significant effect on response. We do not tarry, however, with models that involve separate effects of our factors, since none of Models (2) through (8) provides a really satisfactory fit. We turn to the hierarchical comparisons summarized at the bottom of Table A-5, which pertain to various tests of models that provide acceptable fits.

Comparisons of Models (12), (13), and (14) with Model (8) serve to test the significance of specific joint effects on response. We find that {RSC} contributes significantly to the fit of Model (12), by comparison with Model (8); and {RCU} contributes significantly to the fit of Model (14) in the same sense. But inclusion of {RSU} in Model (13) does not result in a significant improvement over Model (8).

Model (9) has some plausibility, and we note that none of the models hierarchical to it—that is, models that fit {RSC} and something more—achieves a fit that is significantly better at the .05 level. In particular, the difference in X^2 for Models (9) and (12) is 5.52, with 2 df, significant at the .1 but not at the .05 level. Nevertheless, we do not give further consideration to Model (9), since an appropriate partitioning of union status results in a modification of Model (12) that does yield a significantly better fit than Model (9). (Results under models obtained by partitioning are described briefly later in this section.)

Model (14) is of the same form as Model (12), and it is interesting to note that in a hierarchical comparison of Model (14) with Model (11) we obtain clear evidence that the former is better suited to these data.

At this stage of our work, therefore, we have two models of the same form—one joint effect of a pair of factors and a separate effect of the third factor—that fit quite well. Each of these models is preferred to any model that is hierarchical to it and that is simpler (that is, has more degrees of freedom). But Models (12) and (14) are not hierarchical to each other. Hence, we cannot compare them directly with respect to goodness of fit (even though they do have different numbers of degrees of freedom). A kind of indirect comparison is obtained, however, by inquiring whether there is a model that is hierarchical to both Models (12) and (14) that provides a significantly superior fit to one of them but not the other. Most pertinent is the case of Model (16). It may be regarded as a model that replaces {RU} in Model (12) with {RCU}; or, alternatively, it replaces {RS} in Model (14) with {RSC}. It turns out that neither of these results in a significant improvement in fit. Indeed, there is no model hierarchical to either Model (12) or Model (14) that fits significantly better than it does. Yet each of them significantly improves on Model (8), and each achieves a satisfactory goodness of fit.

This kind of situation, in which there is not enough evidence from statistical tests to permit choice between two models, is not a terribly common one in our experience. But it does happen often enough to deserve a name. We call it the "cliffhanger." There appear to be two possibilities for rescue in this desperate situation. One is to invoke substantive or theoretical considerations (including analogies to other bodies of evidence) that indicate some basis of preferring one model to another. Here one could perhaps feel a little more comfortable with a joint sex-by-color effect on response than with a joint color-by-union effect. Sex and color are ascribed characteristics and have presumably been operative in the fashioning of the respondents' views of sex roles throughout the life cycle. Union membership, by contrast, is a contingent factor that is changeable in the course of the life cycle, and its impact on response (or on the attitude presumed to underlie response) may be transitory, at least for some persons. This may seem like a weak argument to invoke, but the situation is a desperate one. Unless a better argument can be found (to the same conclusion, or to the opposite one), we would tend to invoke this one as a criterion for choosing Model (12) over (14).

The other alternative is to avoid the choice, by selection of a compromise model. Although both Models (12) and (14) improve significantly upon Model (8), the latter does provide a barely acceptable fit at the conventional .05 level. It "averages out" the three-way interactions of the other two models and provides a very compact summary of the data. A less objectionable compromise, however, may be Model (16). It includes both the joint effects found to be significant in certain tests, although not significant in comparing Model (16) with Models (12) and (14), respectively. Acceptance of Model (16), of course, involves us in representing as significant some effect or effects not actually found significant; this choice enlarges the risk of a Type I error.

Neither decision should be taken, to be sure, in abstraction from the substance of the results. To make clear the implications of a choice among the alternatives considered, it is well to compute and graph the odds under each of the competing Models. This is done in Figure A-2 (top half of the chart). We see that according to Model (12) the effect of union status is the same for each sex-by-color category. The salient contrast is between UAW and the other two categories of union status. The joint sex-by-color effect is very much like that described in our earlier analysis, where union status was ignored. Model (14), by contrast, enforces the condition that the sex effect is the same for blacks and whites and the color effect is the same for men and women. What it does is to highlight the difference between blacks and whites in the effect of union status. This effect is much more pronounced for blacks, it appears. Moreover, whereas there is virtually no difference in response between other union and nonunion members for whites, this contrast is quite marked for blacks. Model (16) combines features of the other two models. It shows a more pronounced union status effect for blacks than for whites; and it allows the sex effect likewise to be greater for blacks than for whites. The models all agree, incidentally, that the union effect does not depend on sex. Indeed in no hierarchical comparison afforded by Table A-5 does the inclusion of {RSU} in a model result in significant improvement upon a model to which it is hierarchical. If the clarification of this matter were the chief goal of the analysis, then our cliffhanger would not seem so desperate after all.

Some further light—although in the present example, not a great deal—can sometimes be shed on a problem involving one or more polytomous variables by considering various ways to partition such a variable in the context of a multiway contingency analysis. The details of this procedure are quite messy, albeit straightforward. Hence, we shall not reproduce a numerical example here. Three detailed examples are given in Duncan (1975b). In the present example, the outcome of various tests is quite a simple one. We lose no information in replacing the trichotomous union-status variable with the dichotomy, UAW versus non-UAW, including in the latter category both members of unions

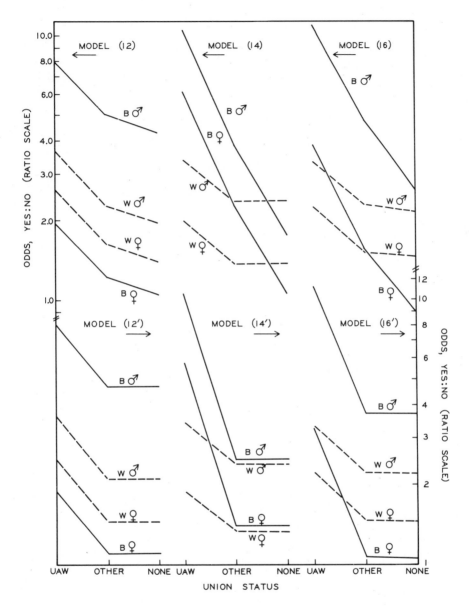

FIGURE A-2. Fitted odds on response, by sex, color, and union status, under alternative models.

other than the UAW and persons belonging to no union. It is important to note that this step was taken in the light of formal tests of significance, and the collapsing of union status would not be recommended if the contrast of other union and nonunion were found significant, either as a separate effect on response or in terms of a joint effect with sex or color. All these possibilities actually were examined and only when it was learned that none of them yielded reliable evidence of a response difference was it decided that the new dichotomy would suffice. It should further be noted that the dichotomy is not where some analysts might have tended to put it a priori, that is, between all union members and nonunion persons. It turns out that this decision would have led to a rather misleading summary of the present data.

Results obtained upon partitioning are depicted in the lower part of Figure A-2. One of the major implications of the comparison between the upper and lower halves of the figure is that the apparent contrast between other union and nonunion that seemed so large for blacks is just not significant. (This fact is not surprising in view of the numbers involved; see Table A-4.) Partitioning in this case, unfortunately, does not shed any light on the choice among the three models, since we are still in a cliffhanger situation with regard to Models (12'), (14'), and (16'). We may still conclude that either the sex effect or the UAW effect is stronger for blacks than for whites. Possibly both effects are stronger among blacks, but we simply do not have enough evidence to be sure of this. In analyzing any body of data, there are likely to be some questions on which the data bear but which cannot be decided in the light of that evidence. One of the merits of the approach to statistical inference taken here is that the analyst gets fair warning when this kind of a question is under consideration.

EXAMPLE 4: A TWO-WAY TABLE WITH ORDERED COLUMNS

Our first example concerned a special case of the two-way table: the one in which both the row and column classification are dichotomous. In general, however, we must be prepared to deal with tables in which either the row or the column variable has more than two categories. In elementary statistics courses the student learns to test the null hypothesis of independence for such a table, in the fashion already illustrated in Example 1 for the 2 × 2 table. But the student is also warned that she would do well not to allow the analysis to rest with a determination of whether there is an association in the table. Sometimes the advice is to calculate a coefficient to measure the "degree" of association. Despite the ubiquity of this advice and the frequent publication of such coefficients, we have not really found them useful in understanding the structure of our data and have eschewed them in this research. A second procedure—one that deserves to be more widely employed, although it must be used with circumspection—is that of partitioning the table on its rows and/or column variables. The utility of partitioning is demonstrated in an instructive example given by Snedecor and Cochran (1967, pp. 252–253). Goodman (1968, especially pp. 1102–1103, 1117, 1122–1123) gives a more comprehensive discussion of the technique. He indicates that the likelihood-ratio chi-square statistic is especially appropriate for this purpose. A simple example of the utility of partitioning a 4 × 2 table is given by Duncan (1975a). We shall include no further examples here.

A third possibility, in addition to the calculation of a coefficient of association and the partitioning of the table, is to inspect the table for trends. This possibility arises when the columns (or rows) of the contingency table pertain to a variable with ordered categories. The experienced analyst confronted with Table A-6 would probably calculate percentage distributions for the six columns and take note of the fact that the percentages in some rows tend to rise, reading from left to right, and in some other rows to fall. The discussion of the table would probably consist largely in the identification of these trends and the informal disposition of exceptions to them. In the present case, there are several such exceptions. They make the cautious analyst a little bit reluctant to diagnose the relationship between education and values in marriage in an unequivocal way. If the percentages are graphed in the usual manner, as a set of six 100% bar charts or as a set of five lines showing the regression of each response category on education, the job of smoothing the irregularities in the data is left to the reader's eye. Here, as in various other connections, a formal approach to the discernment of the relationship is a useful supplement and aid to the graphic or nongraphic inspection of the data.

Simon (1974) describes a method suited to the analysis of what he calls the singly ordered contingency table—one in which the columns are ordered but the rows are not. (Of course, if the rows are ordered, the table can be transposed. Moreover, if both variables are ordered, the analyst could choose to ignore the ordering of one of them.) The gist of the method is the fitting of a model whose expected frequencies agree with the observed frequencies with respect to (i) the row marginals, (ii) the column marginals, and (iii) the weighted sum of the column numbers. Let the frequencies in the table be designated by f_{ij} with the rows

TABLE A-6
Most Valuable Part of Marriage by Educational Attainment: Wives in 1971 DAS Survey

	School years completed					
	Elementary		High school		College	
Most valuable part of marriage	0–7	8	1–3	4	1–3	4+
	Observed frequencies					
[A] Chance to have children	2	4	26	39	14	6
[B] Standard of living	1	2	3	10	2	1
[C] Husband's understanding	11	5	18	38	13	4
[D] Husband's expression of love and affection	5	6	12	32	9	8
[E] Companionship	8	22	91	175	66	47
	Fitted frequencies					
[A]	3.84	5.53	20.87	39.50	13.31	7.95
[B]	1.12	1.43	4.78	8.02	2.39	1.27
[C]	6.72	7.81	23.74	36.19	9.82	4.73
[D]	3.31	4.63	16.94	31.08	10.16	5.88
[E]	12.01	19.60	83.68	179.21	68.32	46.18
	Fitted odds					
[B]:[A]	.292	.258	.229	.203	.179	.160
[C]:[A]	1.75	1.41	1.14	.916	.738	.595
[D]:[A]	.862	.837	.812	.787	.763	.740
[E]:[A]	3.13	3.54	4.01	4.54	5.13	5.81

numbered $i = 1, 2, \ldots, I$ and the columns $j = 1, 2, \ldots, J$. Then the row sums are $f_{i.} = \Sigma_j f_{ij}$; the column marginals are $f_{.j} = \Sigma_i f_{ij}$; and the weighted sum of the column numbers is $E_i = \Sigma_j j f_{ij}$. It may aid in becoming accustomed to the latter concept to note the possibility of computing a mean score for each row, taking the column numbers $1, 2, \ldots, J$ as values of a quantitative variable. This mean would simply be $\bar{j}_i = E_i / f_{i.}$.

The fitting of the model is accomplished by a generalization of the method of iterative scaling. Calculations are carried through as many cycles as necessary to produce convergence to a specified criterion of agreement between observed and fitted row and column marginals and weighted sums of column numbers. The expected frequencies obtained in this manner are maximum likelihood estimates of the frequencies expected under the model that underlies this procedure. (Here, as in previous discussion, we make no attempt to formulate the underlying mathematical structure of the model being described but only to bring out some of its important properties.) Hence, it is appropriate to measure the extent to which the observed frequencies depart from the expected frequencies by the likelihood-ratio chi-square statistic, computed by the formula given earlier in connection with our Example 1.

With the fitted frequencies as shown in the second panel of Table A-6, we find that X^2 for the fit of the model is 17.11. We calculate degrees of freedom as $(I - 1)(J - 2)$, that is, (rows $-$ 1)(columns $-$ 2) or $(5 - 1)(6 - 2) = 16$ in this example. Hence, the model fits rather well ($p > .25$). Interpretation of this result is aided by computing X^2 for the usual test of independence of row and column classifications. For the data in Table A-6, we obtain $X^2 = 29.71$, $df = (I - 1)(J - 1) = 20$, $.05 < p < .1$. We now have information concerning two models: H_0, the hypothesis of independence; and H_1, the hypothesis that the row and column classifications are related in the manner specified by the Simon model. These two models are hierarchical, since in calculating expected frequencies for testing H_1 we fit the row and column marginals just as we do in testing H_0, but also the weighted sum of column numbers. We may, therefore, inquire whether the Simon model improves on the model asserting complete independence. To test the significance of the improvement we compute $X^2(H_0) - X^2(H_1) = 12.60$ with $df = 20 - 16 = 4$ ($= I - 1$). With $p < .025$ the improvement is clearly significant.

The example is an instructive one in that H_0 was not decisively rejected, in view of the marginally significant value of $X^2(H_0)$. Yet it is possible to show that there is a model positing a certain relationship of the row and column classifications that unmistakably improves on the model of independence and is, therefore, preferred to it. We are thus reminded that failure to reject a hypothesis (such as H_0) is no guarantee of the truth of that hypothesis.

Although it is not intuitively obvious from the method of finding expected frequencies, the Simon model is one that does assert the existence of "trends" in the table, indeed, trends that are linear in a certain sense. This property of the model is brought out (among other ways) when we select one category of the row variable as base and compute odds on each other category relative to that base within each column, making use of the fitted frequencies. (See lower panel of Table A-6.) The fitted odds change monotonically upward or downward across columns. A little calculation will show that in each row the odds is increased by a constant (within errors of rounding) multiplier in going from the odds in column j to the odds in column $j + 1$. For example, the multiplier for the odds [B]:[A] is approximately .884, so that .258 = (.884)(.292), .229 = (.884)(.258), ..., .160 = (.884)(.179), within errors of rounding. Obviously, if we converted the odds to logarithms, the trend across columns would be linear, with the logarithm of the multiplier as the slope. One way of looking at the Simon model, therefore, is to describe it as the regression of a qualitative polytomous variable on the set of integers standing for the order of the columns. (We do not consider the generalization to the case of columns that, though ordered, are not assumed to be spaced at equal intervals, although Simon mentions the possibility of such a generalization.) For our illustrative data we find that the regression is positive in regard to the odds on *companionship* and negative in regard to the odds on *standard of living, understanding*, and *love*, when the odds in each case is calculated to *children*. The choice of *children* is, of course, arbitrary. No essential feature of the model or the results would be altered by making a different selection. Hence, the analyst is free to choose as the common base for the several odds the category that makes the description most convenient or intelligible.

EXAMPLE 5: AN INCOMPLETE THREE-WAY TABLE

Table A-7 reproduces data reported by Blake (1974) that were obtained in a national Gallup survey when men and women were asked,

A typical married couple usually goes through a number of stages in the family cycle from marriage to when the last child leaves home. Which of the following stages do you think is the happiest?

[A] Before the couple has children
[B] When the babies are being born and the children are very young
[C] When the children are all in school
[D] When the children have left home (for college, or work, or marriage)
[E] All equal, can't choose

Respondents were also asked to designate the second happiest stage of the family cycle. Response [E] is ignored here, as are the respondents with "no opinion," since the frequencies in these categories are quite small.

The special feature of this table—a cross-tabulation of second choice by first choice by sex—is that the four diagonal cells in the panels for men and women are constrained to have null frequencies, since the same stage cannot be chosen both first and second. When such constraints are imposed by the logic of the problem or by the investigator's decision to ignore certain cells in the table, the affected cells are said to contain structural zeros (Fienberg, 1972). (The latter are to be distin-

TABLE A-7
Happiest and Second Happiest Stages in a Couple's Life, as Reported by White Men and Women in a National Sample, September 1972

Sex	Happiest stage		Second happiest stage			
			[A]	[B]	[C]	[D]
Men	[A]	Before couple has children	[a]	46	21	13
	[B]	When babies being born and children very young	74	[a]	139	62
	[C]	Children all in school	29	73	[a]	49
	[D]	Children have left home	15	23	28	[a]
Women	[A]		[a]	33	20	14
	[B]		90	[a]	178	59
	[C]		28	86	[a]	30
	[D]		7	21	13	[a]
			Expected frequencies, Model (8)			
Men	[A]		[a]	40.62	22.67	16.71
	[B]		74.04	[a]	139.50	61.46
	[C]		29.87	75.30	[a]	45.83
	[D]		14.09	26.08	25.82	[a]
Women	[A]		[a]	38.38	18.33	10.29
	[B]		89.96	[a]	177.50	59.54
	[C]		27.13	83.70	[a]	33.17
	[D]		7.91	17.92	15.18	[a]
			Expected ratio, women:men			
	[A]		[a]	.94	.81	.62
	[B]		1.22	[a]	1.27	.97
	[C]		.91	1.11	[a]	.72
	[D]		.56	.69	.59	[a]

Source: Blake (1974, Table 7); data collected in a Gallup survey.
[a] Structural zero.

guished from so-called sampling zeros, which merely result from sampling variation.) With appropriate modifications in regard to degrees of freedom, the analysis of Table A-7 is carried out in much the same way as the analysis of a complete three-way table like Table A-2.

As before, models for the incomplete multiway table are specified by designating the sets of marginals fitted. The fitting proceeds by the iterative method used for a complete table. However, the computer program must have a special provision for constraining the expected frequencies in the relevant cells to take the value zero. The X^2 statistic enables us to assess the fit of the model in the light of its degrees of freedom. As to the latter, we first note that the table, sex (S) by Happiest stage (T) by Second happiest stage (U), comprises 32 cells, but only 24 cells may have nonzero frequencies. In fitting the sample total we use 1 df; in fitting $\{S\}$ we use another df; in fitting $\{T\}$ we use 3 more df; and in fitting $\{U\}$ we use still another 3 df. Hence, Model (1), wherein the three one-way marginals are fitted, has $df = 24 - 1 - 1 - 3 - 3 = 16$. To calculate df for the other models, we note that fitting $\{ST\}$ or $\{SU\}$ uses three additional degrees of freedom, after the respective one-way marginals are fitted. Moreover, fitting $\{TU\}$ uses five additional degrees of freedom, assuming $\{T\}$ and $\{U\}$ have already been fitted. (This may not be quite obvious. We note that the $\{TU\}$ two-way table has 12 nonzero cells. The fitting of the sample total and one-way marginals $\{T\}$ and $\{U\}$ uses up $1 + 3 + 3 = 7\ df$. Hence, when fitting $\{TU\}$ we impose only $12 - 7 = 5$ additional constraints.)

Statistics computed in seeking a suitable model for these data are shown in Table A-8. We note that sex is reliably associated with first choice, in view of the fact that $X^2(H_1) - X^2(H_4) = 11.67$ with 3 $df, p < .01$. This comparison is equivalent to the result we would obtain in testing the hypothesis of independence for the two-way table, $\{ST\}$, ignoring second choice. We also find that sex is not reliably associated with second choice, ignoring first choice, since $X^2(H_1) - X^2(H_3) = 3.45, df = 3, p > .25$. But this result is equivocal in view of the dependence of first choice and second choice, which is revealed by the comparison, $X^2(H_1) - X^2(H_2) = 16.84, df = 5, p < .01$. Whether second choices contain information not conveyed by first choices is more appropriately tested by $X^2(H_6) - X^2(H_8) = 5.20, df = 3, .1 < p < .25$. According to this result, we may ignore second choices in connection with the comparison of men's and women's values as elicited by Blake's question.

TABLE A-8
Statistics for Models Fitted to the Data in Table A-7

Model	Marginals fitted[a]	df	X^2	p
(1)	$\{S\}, \{T\}, \{U\}$	16	39.84	$<.01$
(2)	$\{S\}, \{TU\}$	11	23.00	$<.025$
(3)	$\{SU\}, \{T\}$	13	36.39	$<.01$
(4)	$\{ST\}, \{U\}$	13	28.17	$<.01$
(5)	$\{SU\}, \{TU\}$	8	19.55	$<.025$
(6)	$\{ST\}, \{TU\}$	8	11.33	$>.1$
(7)	$\{ST\}, \{SU\}$	10	22.09	$<.025$
(8)	$\{ST\}, \{SU\}, \{TU\}$	5	6.13	$>.25$

[a] Symbols for variables: S—sex of respondent, T—happiest stage, U—second happiest stage.

Considering first choices only, we find that the ratio of women to men is 1.19 among respondents selecting [B], .95 for those choosing [C], .84 for those choosing [A], and .62 for those choosing [D]. Odds ratios estimating the sex effect on response are, accordingly, 1.9 for [B]:[D], 1.5 for [C]:[D], and 1.3 for [A]:[D].

Since our own study of values in marriage (Chapter 8) was restricted to women, we may comment briefly on the substance of these results from Blake's research. Clearly the gratifications to be found in marriage are different for the two sexes. Women prize especially the period during which young children are present and babies are coming along; men are relatively overrepresented among respondents who like most the stages before the children come or after they have left home. The trend, noted in the DAS data, for women to put a lower value on the chance to have children may, therefore, represent a convergence of the values of the two partners to the marriage.

For sake of illustration, let us consider the possibility that second choices also are related to sex, once first choices are taken into account. In that event, Model (8) would be the appropriate model for these data. The expected frequencies under this model are shown in Table A-7, the bottom panel of which shows the ratios of women to men in the 12 cells of the cross-classification of first by second choice, computed from the expected frequencies. The pattern of these ratios is not quite obvious, but is nonetheless simple. From either the first or the third column we may compute the odds ratio [B]:[D]; that is, $1.22/.56 = 1.27/.59 = 2.2$ (rounding errors ignored). From the ratios in the first and second columns we find $.91/.56 = 1.11/.69 = 1.6$ for the odds ratio [C]:[D]. And from the ratios in the second and third columns we compute the [A]:[D] odds ratio as $.94/.69 = .81/.59 = 1.4$. These ratios measure the effect of sex on first choice, net of second choices. Similarly, working within rows we may compute odds ratios measuring the effect of sex on second choice, net of first. We find 1.5 for [B]:[D], 1.3 for [C]:[D], and 1.25 for [A]:[D]. Thus, the pattern of sex effects on second choices is the same as the pattern for first choices, but the effects are attenuated. They are not, of course, statistically significant and were computed only for illustrative purposes.

NOTE CONCERNING OTHER TECHNIQUES

The foregoing examples illustrate the statistical techniques used in most of the analyses of this study. However, we have also, on occasion, used statistics suited to the analysis of quantitative variables (comparison of means, regression, correlation). Moreover, several problems involved a dichotomous dependent variable and one or more quantitative independent variables. In this situation we resorted to minimum logit chi-square regression, as proposed in the classic paper of Berkson (1953) and treated more recently by (for example) Ashton (1972), Cox (1970), Gart and Zweifel (1967), and Plackett (1974). A reasonably detailed presentation of one of our analyses is in Chapter 10, where we consider the regression of response to questions on sex typing on the educational attainments of wife and husband. This presentation may serve in lieu of an example here.

Appendix B

This appendix presents some details of the multivariate analyses of the four child-task items, Walks, Car, Dust, and Beds (see Chapter 12).

In Table B-1 we show a rearrangement of Table 12-1. For each of the four items response is coded 0 for *boy* or *girl* and 1 for *both*. Each of the 16 possible ways to answer the four items is referred to as a response pattern. The variable, *score*, is just the sum of the four item codes, that is, the number of *both* responses to the four items. This score, as remarked in Chapter 12, is the sort of "index" that survey analysts commonly resort to in order to simplify the analysis of multiple responses. Our analysis here tends to indicate how such a simplification could be seriously misleading.

The last two columns show the frequencies of the response patterns in the 1953 and 1971 samples of eligible mothers. Before proceeding, we add the constant $\frac{1}{2}$ to each of these frequencies, taking note of the work of Gart and Zweifel (1967). The dependent variable in further analysis is the ratio of the 1971 to the 1953 frequency. We will treat that ratio as a logit, even though such a procedure is unorthodox. Table B-2 lists 19 models considered as possible ways to summarize the variation of the logit across the 16 response patterns. Model (2) is of special interest, since it assumes that the change in responses between 1953 and 1971 is adequately summarized by the score. Since, by definition, $S = W + C + D + B$, Model (2) amounts to a regression of logit on the four items,

TABLE B-1
Distribution of Eligible Mothers by Response to Child Task Items, 1953 and 1971

Response pattern	Response to item					Frequency in year	
	W	C	D	B	Score	1953	1971
1	0	0	0	0	0	86	82
2	0	0	0	1	1	24	49
3	0	0	1	0	1	7	1
4	0	0	1	1	2	21	18
5	0	1	0	0	1	12	40
6	0	1	0	1	2	8	67
7	0	1	1	0	2	4	2
8	0	1	1	1	3	8	38
9	1	0	0	0	1	20	10
10	1	0	0	1	2	12	12
11	1	0	1	0	2	2	0
12	1	0	1	1	3	7	6
13	1	1	0	0	2	8	32
14	1	1	0	1	3	1	80
15	1	1	1	0	3	2	4
16	1	1	1	1	4	35	153

TABLE B-2
Logit Chi-Square Values for Alternative Models Fitted to the Data in Table B-1

Model	Independent variables[a]	df	Y^2
(1)	—	15	116.33
(2)	S	14	71.85
(3)	S, W	13	65.35
(4)	S, C	13	36.81
(5)	S, D	13	44.72
(6)	S, B	13	71.10
(7)	S, W, C	12	34.87
(8)	S, W, D	12	19.17
(9)	S, W, B	12	65.22
(10)	S, C, D	12	25.77
(11)	S, C, B	12	17.13
(12)	S, D, B	12	44.42
(13)	S, W, C, D	11	12.69
(14)	S, W, C, D, (WC)	10	7.81
(15)	S, W, C, D, (WD)	10	11.49
(16)	S, W, C, D, (CD)	10	12.55
(17)	S, W, C, B, (WB)	10	12.17
(18)	S, W, C, B, (CB)	10	11.15
(19)	S, W, C, B, (DB)	10	10.79

[a] S, Score; W, Walks; C, Car; D, Dust; B, Beds.

where the four coefficients for the items are constrained to be equal. (It is doubtful that investigators constructing an "index" always understand that this strong constraint is imposed by the procedure.) Obviously, Model (2) is not acceptable. That is, we reject the hypothesis that the four items changed in the same measure between 1953 and 1971.

Models (3) through (6) consider the possibility that three items have the same coefficient, which differs from the fourth. None of these models is acceptable, nor is any of Models (7), (9), (10), and (12), each of which constrains some pair of coefficients to be equal. One might accept either of Models (8) and (11), which have this same feature, except for the fact that Model (13), which has no two coefficients the same, improves significantly on each of them. We conclude, then, that the four items all provide reliably different estimates of the rate of change in sex typing. Under the circumstances, the estimate of change we would obtain from any composite of these items would depend on which combination of items was selected and how the items were weighted.

Models (14) through (19) introduce, one at a time, the six possible product terms. Only one of these is significant, so that the final choice of a model is number (14). That model, of course, could equally well be described by the combination of independent variables, W, C, D, B, (WC). Inclusion of the product variable (WC) allows for the change in association of Walks and Car between 1953 and 1971 that was noted in Chapter 12.

For the reader disturbed by our high-handed definition of the "logit" in the foregoing exercise, we note that the outcome of that work, as represented in Model (14), is much the same as the outcome of a multiway contingency table analysis of Table B-1 viewed as a five-way table, {WCDBY}, where year (Y) is treated as a fifth dichotomous variable. By the usual kind of comparisons among hierarchical models, we find that the data are described quite well ($X^2 = 15.3$, $df = 14$, $p = .36$) by the model employing the marginals {WCD}, {WCY}, {WB}, {CB}, {DB}, {DY}, {BY}. Figure B-1 shows the fitted ratios of 1971 to 1953 frequencies under this model. The dashed line in this figure traces the ratio for the observed numbers of respondents at each score (i.e., number of *both* responses), aggregating over all response patterns contributing to that score. It is interesting to see how the three-way interaction involving year, {WCY}, is represented on the graph. If one imagines a line connecting points C and CB and another line connecting D and BD, these two lines are seen to be parallel. However, the lines C to CW and B to BW are not parallel, illustrating how the association of Walks with Year is conditional on the category of Car and vice versa.

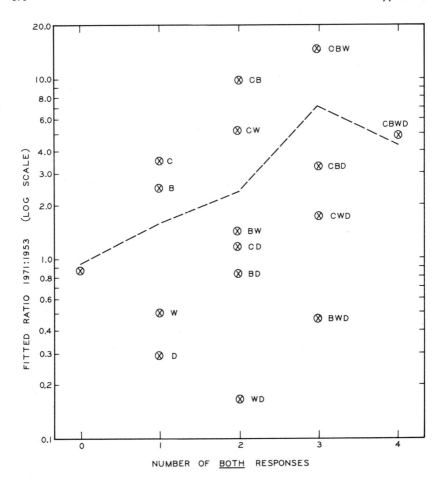

FIGURE B-1. Ratio, 1971:1953 frequencies, in relation to number of *both* responses, for eligible mothers (see Table B-1).

If all items were changing in the same way, all the points in a column would coincide (or nearly so) and these points would trace out a monotonic regression on score (number of *both* responses). The failure of such a regression to appear, or even a decent approximation to it, suggests that we should pay attention to the diversity of changes exhibited by the four items.

The appearance of the three-way interaction, {WCD}, in the preferred model for the data in Table B-1 is intriguing. We could describe this interaction by noting how the association of any two of the responses among Walks, Car, and Dust is conditional on the response to the third. Instead of presenting these results, however, we shall investigate another possible approach to the understanding of such three-way interactions among responses. The vehicle for our investigation is a different data set, the responses of all respondents (men and women, without regard to parenthood) in the 1971 survey. These data are shown in Table B-3.

In that table, we introduce two contrived variables: Response consistency with respect to Walks and Car, and Response consistency with respect to Dust and Beds. Responses to Walks and Car may be either the same (whether *boy* or *both*) or different (*boy* on one item, *both* on the other). Similarly, responses to Dust and Beds may be the same (whether *girl* or *both*) or different. Once the pattern of responses to the individual items is specified, the coding of the two response-consistency variables is, of course, determined. Hence, the cross-tabulation of item responses by response-consistency variables is highly constrained: Three-fourths of the cells in the table contain structural zeros. We may, nevertheless, analyze Table B-3 as an incomplete multiway contingency table (see Example 5 in Appendix A).

TABLE B-3
Distribution of All Respondents by Response to Child-Task Items, 1971

				Response consistency				
Response to item				WC-s		WC-d		Expected frequency,
W	C	D	B	DB-s	DB-d	DB-s	DB-d	Model (4)
0	0	0	0	419	*	*	*	422.97
0	0	0	1	*	106	*	*	105.51
0	0	1	0	*	7	*	*	4.62
0	0	1	1	28	*	*	*	26.90
0	1	0	0	*	*	201	*	199.25
0	1	0	1	*	*	*	193	191.26
0	1	1	0	*	*	*	12	12.16
0	1	1	1	*	*	121	*	124.32
1	0	0	0	*	*	44	*	40.68
1	0	0	1	*	*	*	26	25.84
1	0	1	0	*	*	*	0	1.74
1	0	1	1	*	*	10	*	11.75
1	1	0	0	132	*	*	*	133.10
1	1	0	1	*	146	*	*	148.38
1	1	1	0	*	14	*	*	14.48
1	1	1	1	381	*	*	*	377.03

* Structural zero.

Table B-4 summarizes the results obtained with various models applied to Table B-3. We note first that adding either of the response-consistency variables one at a time to Model (1) is redundant; that is, Models (1), (2), and (3) are equivalent. In Model (4), however, we consider the two-way marginals {KL} for the two response-consistency variables. Including these along with the other two-way marginals in Model (1) greatly improves the fit. Alternatively, we note that Model (7), which includes two three-way marginals, also improves the fit, as is shown by the calculation $X^2(H_1) - X^2(H_7) = 8.40, 2\,df, p < .025$. However, once the model includes {KL}, the cross-classification of the response-consistency variables, no further gain is achieved by considering three-way interactions. Thus, $X^2(H_4) - X^2(H_{10}) = 1.98, df = 2, p > .25$. It is also true that, once the model includes the two three-way interactions, there is no gain achieved by considering the {KL} marginal, since $X^2(H_7) - X^2(H_{10}) = 1.95, df = 1, p > .1$.

We may, therefore, take our choice as to whether we want to describe the response distribution as involving a couple of three-way interactions among items or as involving what has been called (for convenience) a response-consistency effect. The latter, if one likes, is just a way of capturing the former.

Better to understand the nature of the response-consistency effect, we may note that *exactly* the same results are obtained if the two response-consistency variables are defined in terms of the consistency of Walks with Dust and Car with Beds, or in terms of the consistency of Walks with Beds and Car with Dust. That is, what we have called a {KL}

TABLE B-4
Likelihood-Ratio Chi-Square Values for Alternative Models Fitted to the Data in Table B-3

Model	Marginals fitted[a]	df	X^2	p
(1)	{WC}, {WD}, {WB}, {CD}, {CB}, {DB}	5	13.95	<.025
(2)	(1) and {K}	5	13.95	
(3)	(1) and {L}	5	13.95	
(4)	(1) and {KL}	4	5.38	.25
(5)	(1) and {WCB}	4	12.52	<.025
(6)	(1) and {WCD}	4	10.28	<.05
(7)	(1) and {WCB}, {WCD}	3	5.55	>.1
(8)	(4) and {WCB}	3	5.09	>.1
(9)	(4) and {WCD}	3	3.54	>.25
(10)	(4) and {WCB}, {WCD}	2	3.40	>.1

[a] Symbols for variables: W, Walks; C, Car; D, Dust; B, Beds; K, Response consistency, W and C; L, Response consistency, D and B.

interaction in Table B-4 can be viewed mathematically as a property of the whole multiple response pattern rather than a property of particular pairs of variables.

The expected frequencies under Model (4), shown as the last column of Table B-3, further elucidate the nature of the response-consistency effect. Let us use the first four of these frequencies to calculate the odds ratio, $(422.97)(26.90)/(105.51)(4.62) = 23.34$ and the next four to compute the odds ratio $(191.25)(124.32)/(191.26)(12.16) = 10.65$. The ratio of these two odds ratio is $23.34/10.65 = 2.19$. That is, the association of Dust with Beds (in the sense of the odds ratio) is 2.19 times as great when Walks and Car are answered consistently as it is when the latter two items are answered inconsistently. The same result may also be obtained using the third and fourth sets of four expected frequencies. Even more important, we may obtain it by considering the association for *any two* of the items, conditional on the consistency or inconsistency of responses to the other two items.

The discovery of a response-consistency effect suggests, again, the inadvisability of constructing a composite score or index as a simple summation of item responses. It further implies that our entire analysis would, as a matter of principle, be best carried out with the response pattern as the dependent variable rather than with the responses to individual items as the four dependent variables in as many separate analyses. But this is a counsel of perfection, difficult to implement because of computational expense, statistical complexity, and small size of samples. Hence the route taken in Chapter 12.

References

Items with asterisk (*) are based on Detroit Area Study data and thus provide additional information about the variables treated in this book. Numbers in square brackets, e.g. [301], are pages where works are cited; the list of references, therefore, serves in lieu of an Author Index.

Amemiya, T., and F. Nold (1973) *A modified logit model.* Technical Report No. 113, The Economics Series, Institute for Mathematical Studies in the Social Sciences, Stanford, California: Stanford University. [293]

Ashton, W. D. (1972) *The logit transformation. Griffin's Statistical Monographs and Courses, No. 32.* New York: Hafner Pub. [40, 292, 366]

Berkson, J. (1953) A statistically precise and relatively simple method of estimating the bio-assay with quantal response, based on the logistic function. *Journal of the American Statistical Association 48:* 565–599. [40, 288, 294, 366]

Bishop, Y. M. M., S. E. Fienberg, and P. W. Holland (1975) *Discrete multivariate analysis: Theory and practice.* Cambridge, Mass.: M. I. T. Press. [7]

Blake, J. (1974) Can we believe recent data on birth expectations in the United States? *Demography 11:*25–44. [362, 363, 364, 365]

*Blood, R. O., Jr., and D. M. Wolfe (1960) *Husbands and wives.* New York: Free Press. [195, 196, 197, 199, 204, 207, 295]

Campbell, A. (1972) Aspiration, satisfaction, and fulfillment. In A. Campbell and P. E. Converse (Eds.), *The human meaning of social change.* New York: Russell Sage Foundation. [108, 111]

Cantril, H., and M. Strunk (1951) *Public opinion: 1935–1946.* Princeton, N. J.: Princeton University Press. [98, 101, 102, 126]

Carlsson, G., and K. Karlsson (1970) Age, cohorts and the generation of generations. *American Sociological Review 35:* 710–718. [233]

Chafe, W. H. (1972) *The American woman: Her changing social, economic, and political roles, 1920–1970.* New York: Oxford University Press. [2, 3, 6]

Converse, P. E. (1972) Change in the American electorate. In A. Campbell and P. E. Converse (Eds.), *The human meaning of social change.* New York: Russell Sage Foundation. [104–105]

Cox, D. R. (1970) *The analysis of binary data.* London: Methuen. [8, 292, 366]

Demerath, N. J., III (1968) Trends and anti-trends in religious change. In E. B. Sheldon and W. E. Moore (Eds.), *Indicators of social change.* New York: Russell Sage Foundation. [143]

Dempster, E. R. (1960) The question of stability with positive feedback, *Biometrics 16:* 481–483. [295]

*Duncan, B., and M. Evers (1975) Measuring change in attitudes toward women's work. In K. C. Land and S. Spilerman (Eds.), *Social indicator models.* New York: Russell Sage Foundation. [7, 27, 65, 70]

*Duncan, O. D. (1975a) Measuring social change via replication of surveys. In K. C. Land and S. Spilerman (Eds.), *Social indicator models.* New York: Russell Sage Foundation. [7, 261, 263, 264, 359]

*Duncan, O. D. (1975b) Partitioning polytomous variables in multiway contingency analysis. *Social Science Research 4:* 167–182. [9, 31, 119, 248, 255, 356]

*Duncan, O. D. (1975c) Does money buy satisfaction? *Social Indicators Research 2:* 267–274. [223]

*Duncan, O. D., H. Schuman, and B. Duncan (1973) *Social change in a metropolitan community.* New York: Russell Sage Foundation. [1, 85, 133, 144, 155, 156, 167, 199, 212, 220, 228, 246, 256, 263]

Easterlin, R. A. (1973) Does money buy happiness? *The Public Interest* (No. 30): 3–10. [223]

Ennis, P. H. (1968) The definition and measurement of leisure. In E. B. Sheldon and W. E. Moore (Eds.), *Indicators of social change.* New York: Russell Sage Foundation. [193]

Entwisle, D. R., and E. Greenberger (1972) Adolescents' views of women's work role. *American Journal of Orthopsychiatry 42:* 648–656. [62, 140]

Epstein, C. F. (1976) Sex roles. In R. K. Merton and R. Nisbet (Eds.), *Contemporary social problems.* New York: Harcourt Brace Jovanovich. [287]

Ernest, J. (1976). Mathematics and sex. *American Mathematical Monthly 83:* 595–614. [140]

Erskine, H. (1971) The polls: Women's role. *Public Opinion Quarterly 35:* 275–290. [3, 63]

Fairlie, H. (1971) On the humanity of women. *The Public Interest* (No. 23): 16–32. [1, 334]

Fienberg, S. E. (1970) An iterative procedure for estimation in contingency tables. *Annals of Mathematical Statistics 41:* 907–917; corrigenda, *42:* 1778. [343]

Fienberg, S. E. (1972) The analysis of incomplete multi-way contingency tables. *Biometrics 28:* 177–202; corrigenda, *29:* 829. [362]

*Fischer, E. M. (1972) *Sampling report for the 1971 Detroit Area Study.* Ann Arbor: Detroit Area Study, University of Michigan. [1]

*Fischer, E. M. (1974a) *Change in anomie in Detroit from the 1950s to 1971;* Ph. D. dissertation, Ann Arbor: University of Michigan. [103]

*Fischer, E. M. (1974b) Anomy and social participation. Unpublished manuscript. [114]

Fleiss, J. L. (1973) *Statistical methods for rates and proportions.* New York: Wiley. [338]

Francis, J. D., and L. Busch (1975) What we now know about "I don't knows." *Public Opinion Quarterly 39:* 207–218. [135]

Freeman, Jo (1973) The origins of the Women's Liberation Movement. *American Journal of Sociology 78:* 792–811. [2]

Gallup, G. H. (1972) *The Gallup Poll: Public opinion 1935–1971.* 3 volumes. New York: Random House. [97, 102, 106, 145, 154]

Gart, J. J., and J. R. Zweifel (1967) On the bias of various estimators of the logit and its variance with application to quantal bioassay. *Biometrika 54:* 181–187. [366, 367]

Goodman, L. A. (1968) The analysis of cross-classified data: Independence, quasi-independence, and interactions in contingency tables with or without missing entries. *Journal of the American Statistical Association 63:* 1091–1131. [359]

Goodman, L. A. (1970) The multivariate analysis of qualitative data: Interactions among multiple classifications. *Journal of the American Statistical Association 65:* 226–256. [7]

Goodman, L. A. (1972a) A modified multiple regression approach to the analysis of dichotomous variables. *American Sociological Review 37:* 28–46. [339]

Goodman, L. A. (1972b) A general model for the analysis of surveys. *American Journal of Sociology 77:* 1035–1086. [7, 339]

Goodman, L. A. (1974a) The analysis of systems of qualitative variables when some of the variables are unobservable. Part I—a modified latent structure approach. *American Journal of Sociology 79:* 1179–1259. [307]

Goodman, L. A. (1974b) Exploratory latent structure analysis using both identifiable and unidentifiable models. *Biometrika 61:* 215–230. [307]

Goodman, L. A. (1974c) The analysis of systems of qualitative variables when some of the variables are unobservable. Part II—the use of modified latent distance models. Unpublished manuscript. [307]

Goodman, L. A. (1975) A new model for scaling response patterns: An application of the quasi-independence concept. *Journal of the American Statistical Association 70:* 755–768. [307]

Goodman, L. A., and W. H. Kruskal (1954) Measures of association for cross classifications. *Journal of the American Statistical Association 49:* 732–764. [306]

Greeley, A. M. (1972) *Priests in the United States: Reflections on a survey.* Garden City, N. Y.: Doubleday. [241]

Harris, L., and Associates (n.d.) *The 1972 Virginia Slims American Women's Opinion Poll: A survey of the attitudes of women on their roles in politics and the economy.* [108]

Harris, L., and Associates (1976) *A second survey of public and leadership attitudes toward nuclear power development in the United States.* New York: Ebasco Services Inc. [99]

Hess, R. D., and J. V. Torney (1968) *The development of political attitudes in children.* Garden City, N. Y.: Anchor Books, Doubleday. [140, 141, 142]

Hole, J., and E. Levine (1971) *Rebirth of feminism.* New York: Quadrangle. [2, 6, 11, 89, 122, 195]

Janeway, E. (1975) *Between myth and morning.* New York: William Morrow. [93]

*Janowitz, M., and D. Wright (1956) The prestige of public employment: 1929 and 1954. *Public Administration Review 16:* 15–21. [132]

Jenni, D. A., and M. A. Jenni (1976) Carrying behavior in humans: Analysis of sex differences. *Science 194:* 859–860. [244]

Kasperson, R. *et al.* (1976) Nuclear energy, local conflict, and public opposition. Draft manuscript, cited by permission. [99]

Kavanaugh, J. (1967) *A modern priest looks at his outdated church.* New York: Trident. [234]

Keller, S. (1972) The future status of women in America, in Commission on Population Growth and the American Future. *Research Reports, Volume I, Demographic and Social Aspects of Population Growth.* Washington: Government Printing Office. [243]

*Kempf, W. F., P. Hampapa, and G. Mach (1975) *Conditional maximum likelihood estimation for a dynamic test model. IPN-Arbeitsberichte 13.* Kiel: Institut für die Pädagogik der Naturwissenschaften an der Christian-Albrechts-Universität. [307]

Kirkpatrick, J. J. (1974) *Political woman.* New York: Basic Books. [117]

Kohn, M. L. (1969) *Class and conformity: A study in values.* Homewood, Ill.: Dorsey Press. [270, 274]

*Lenski, G. (1963) *The religious factor.* Garden City, N. Y.: Anchor Books, Doubleday. [54]

Lewis, M. (1972) Parents and children: Sex-role development. *School Review, 80:* 229–240. [244, 245, 258]

Maccoby, E. E., and C. N. Jacklin (1974) *The psychology of sex differences.* Stanford, Calif.: Stanford University Press. [243, 260]

Mason, K. O., J. L. Czajka, and S. Arber (1976) Change in U. S. women's sex-role attitudes, 1964–1974. *American Sociological Review 41:* 573–596. [332]

McGready, W. C., and A. M. Greeley (1972) The end of American Catholicism? *America 127:* 334–338. [241]

Mencken, H. L. (1922) *In defense of women.* Rev. ed. New York: Alfred A. Knopf. [94]

*Miller, D. R., and G. E. Swanson (1958) *The changing American parent.* New York: Wiley. [245, 246, 255, 305]

Nie, N. H., S. Verba, and J. R. Petrocik (1976) *The changing American voter.* Cambridge, Mass.: Harvard University Press. [332]

North, C. C. (1926) *Social differentiation.* Chapel Hill: University of North Carolina Press. [143, 154, 166]

Plackett, R. L. (1974) *The analysis of categorical data.* New York: Hafner Press. [7, 366]

Quinn, R. P., G. L. Staines, and M. R. McCullough (1974) *Job satisfaction: Is there a trend? Manpower Research Monograph No. 30.* Washington: Government Printing Office. [46]

Rainwater, L. (1974) *What money buys.* New York: Basic Books. [223]

Rasch, G. (1968) An individualistic approach to item analysis. In P. F. Lazarsfeld and N. W. Henry (Eds.), *Readings in mathematical social science.* Cambridge, Mass.: M. I. T. Press. [292, 307]

Roche, Douglas J. (1968) *The Catholic revolution.* New York: D. McKay Co. [236, 241]

Roper Organization (n.d.) *The Virginia Slims American Women's Opinion Poll: A survey of the attitudes of women on marriage, divorce, the family and America's changing sexual morality. Volume III.* [110, 330, 331]

Rosenfeld, C., and V. C. Perrella (1965) *Why women start and stop working. Special Labor Force Report No. 59.* Bureau of Labor Statistics, U. S. Department of Labor. [29, 54]

Ryder, N. B. (1965) The cohort as a concept in the study of social change. *American Sociological Review 30:* 843–861. [233]

Seeman, M. (1972) Alienation and engagement. In A. Campbell and P. E. Converse (Eds.), *The human meaning of social change.* New York: Russell Sage Foundation. [114]

Sewell, W. H. (1963) Some recent developments in socialization theory and research. *Annals of the American Academy of Political and Social Science 349:* 163–181. [243]

Simon, G. (1974) Alternative analyses for the singly-ordered contingency table. *Journal of the American Statistical Association 69:* 971–976. [199, 229, 274, 359, 361]

Snedecor, G. W., and W. G. Cochran (1967) *Statistical methods.* Sixth ed. Ames: Iowa State University Press. [359]

Spock, B. (1975) How fathers can teach their children sexual equality. *Redbook Magazine 144:* 22–26. [279, 280]

Sweet, J. A. (1970) Family composition and the labor force activity of American wives. *Demography* 7: 195–209. [51]

Theil, H. (1972) *Statistical decomposition analysis*. Amsterdam: North-Holland Pub. [257]

U. S. Bureau of the Census (1943) *Sixteenth Census of the United States: 1940, The labor force: employment and family characteristics of women*. Washington: Government Printing Office. [6]

U. S. Bureau of the Census (1952) *U. S. Census of Population: 1950, Volume II, Part 22*. Washington: Government Printing Office. [6]

U. S. Bureau of the Census (1964) *U. S. Census of Population: 1960, Volume I, Part 1*. Washington: Government Printing Office. [3]

U. S. Bureau of the Census (1975) *Statistical Abstract of the United States, 1975*. Washington: Government Printing Office. [6]

Whitehurst, C. A. (1977) *Women in America: The oppressed majority*. Santa Monica, Calif.: Goodyear Pub. Co. [243]

Yorburg, B. (1974) *Sexual identity: Sex roles and social change*. New York: Wiley. [208, 261]

Index

(Entries in *italics* are pages where exact question wordings appear.)

QUANTITATIVE STUDIES IN SOCIAL RELATIONS

Consulting Editor: Peter H. Rossi

UNIVERSITY OF MASSACHUSETTS
AMHERST, MASSACHUSETTS